Ethical Theory in Global Perspective

Ethical Theory in Global Perspective

Edited by

Michael Hemmingsen

Published by State University of New York Press, Albany

© 2024 State University of New York

For information, contact State University of New York Press, Albany, NY
www.sunypress.edu

Library of Congress Cataloging-in-Publication Data

Name: Hemmingsen, Michael, editor.
Title: Ethical theory in global perspective / edited by Michael Hemmingsen.
Description: Albany : State University of New York Press, [2024] | Includes
    bibliographical references and index.
Identifiers: ISBN 9781438496856 (hardcover : alk. paper) | ISBN
    9781438496870 (ebook) | ISBN 9781438496863 (pbk. : alk. paper)
Further information is available at the Library of Congress.

10 9 8 7 6 5 4 3 2 1

Contents

Acknowledgments

First and foremost, I would like to thank the contributing authors to this volume, who generously offered their time and expertise to this project. I would also like to thank those friends and colleagues who provided their invaluable comments and feedback on my own chapters in this volume: Youngsun Back, Jeremy Burgess, Gordon Davis, Monique Deveaux, Nicholas Drake, Rika Dunlap, Allauren Forbes, and Elisabeth Gedge. This book also would not have been possible without the continuing support of my PhD advisory committee members from the Department of Philosophy at McMaster University—Violetta Igneski and Elisabeth Gedge— and my external examiner at the University of Guelph—Monique Deveaux—who have supported my work well after I completed my doctorate, far beyond what anyone could reasonably expect or ask for. Finally, as always, I am grateful to Mariko and Aki, who make it all worthwhile.

Introduction

Global Philosophy and Ethical Theory

Ethical Theory

While we touch on a range of different philosophical traditions in this book, our focus is squarely on what the philosophers from these traditions have to say about "ethical theory" specifically. It is therefore worth considering what is meant by the term "ethical theory."

Ethical theory is a branch of the broader category of ethical or moral philosophy. In the Western tradition, moral philosophy is traditionally divided into three main branches: applied ethics, normative ethics, and metaethics. Ethical theory is sometimes another name for the second of those branches: normative ethics (though aspects of metaethics can fall under it as well).

Normative ethics can be contrasted with the other two branches of ethics. We can think of these branches as being related to each other in a hierarchy, with metaethics as the most fundamental branch, normative ethics on top of that, and applied ethics at the highest level.

Metaethics deals with the most basic concerns of ethics. What does it mean to call something "moral" in the first place? Is morality something in the world (are there "moral facts"), or is it merely a matter of taste or cultural belief? If there *are* moral facts, what are they, and how do they relate to other things in the world, such as natural facts—facts about the world around us—or human psychology?

At the other end, applied ethics deals in specific moral issues. For instance, if we want to know whether euthanasia is morally permissible, whether it is okay to eat meat, what we owe fellow citizens, or the extent to which we are obliged to act to prevent climate change, we should engage in applied ethics.

Situated between the specific and the basic, we have normative ethics. Normative ethics is more general than applied ethics. It is not directly concerned with specific issues, but rather with how we *work out* what we should do. In this sense, we might think of normative ethics as standing behind applied ethics. For instance, if we want to know whether it is okay to steal when hungry, we can look to different normative ethical theories as a way of providing an answer. So applied ethics rests to some extent on normative ethics.

Normative ethics is concerned with the development of ethical theories. Ethical theories aim to provide guidance as to *what* is right and wrong, as well as provide an explanation as to *why* it is so. What's more, normative ethical theories work at a basic level; that is, they are not simply a collection of principles or ideas, but a systematized account of what makes something right or wrong *fundamentally*.

Normative ethics will often draw on applied ethics, or at least on the kinds of concrete cases discussed by applied ethicists. For instance, many of the chapters in this book criticize ethical theories using thought experiments. In these experiments, a particular theory is applied to a concrete scenario. Then the critic draws attention to the fact that the theory's recommendation is striking or absurd in some way. However, fundamentally this book is not about applied ethics (or metaethics, the main exceptions being in the last section of the book, where we look at ethical views that reject generalization and theorizing in ethics). The other two levels of moral philosophy only arise here in the context of developing, defending, or criticizing systematic accounts of morality.

So why discuss normative ethical theory? Will studying ethics help you to be a better person? One way of thinking about the study of ethics is to analogize it to the study of fungi or astrophysics: you don't study fungi or astrophysics in order to be a better mushroom or star: mushrooms and stars are the *subject* of your inquiry. Similarly, according to this view, the job of ethicists is to understand what ethics *is*, rather than how to *be* more ethical ourselves.

On the other hand, ethics is clearly a subject closely tied to our practices. It discusses issues such as what we ought to value, how we ought to live, and how we should treat those around us. In this sense, ethics is both highly personal and directly applicable to our lives. Perhaps, then, ethics is more like subjects such as music or literature. We might reasonably expect that studying music and literature allows us to appreciate music or literature more fully, and perhaps even to *make* better music or literature; similarly, studying ethics can give us the conceptual resources for thinking about what you ought to value in your own life and what kind of person you should be: to appreciate our moral natures more fully.

Thinking about normative ethics also helps us to move past the obvious. Most people already have a sense of right and wrong. But in coming to appreciate the underlying nature of morality, we can understand not just *that* certain things are right or wrong, but *why* they are. And in coming to understand the *why* of ethics, we might also come to *change* our views about what things are right and wrong; we might find that our previous beliefs about morality were not well justified. Insofar as we care that our moral judgments are accurate—rather than merely expressing what we have unreflectively learned from others—engaging in ethical theorizing is an important and valuable activity.

Evaluating Moral Theories

We can distinguish between philosophical ethics—which is normative—and what we might call "sociological" or "anthropological" ethics—which is descriptive. If we were to take a sociological interest in ethics, our job would be merely to describe what beliefs people in different societies happen to hold regarding moral matters. We would note what they take to be valuable, what actions they take to be right or wrong, what kind of people they find morally admirable.

But philosophical ethics is not just about *what* people believe; it is more centrally about what people *ought to* believe. So, whereas a sociologist would describe a group's beliefs, and then try to explain *how* those particular beliefs came about in the first place—perhaps in terms of social forces, environmental factors, and so on—a philosopher is interested in what *arguments* there are in favor of those beliefs. The central concern of philosophers is therefore not the factors that *caused* certain beliefs, but whether those beliefs are *well justified*.

The purpose of this book is therefore not merely to present a range of ethical theories side by side and leave things there. Instead, the aim is to put these different theories into dialogue, with the goal of thinking through what the *right* theory of ethics might be. This textbook is therefore intended to facilitate a *conversation* between different proposals for the right ethical theory. The reader's task is to adjudicate this conversation; to assess and critically evaluate the different theories presented, with the goal of working out what the reader takes to be the most plausible of these theories, and why.

To establish whether any of the theories in this book are well justified, we need to adopt a critical stance toward them. In everyday terms, the word "criticism" typically has a negative valence. But in philosophy, criticism is a constructive, rather than destructive, activity. Productive criticism first involves trying to "think along" with the theories, to understand why someone might find them persuasive, what plausible justifications they might have. Then the reader can begin to evaluate the justifications offered for the theories and assess their plausibility. Ultimately, my hope is that the reader will be able to form or clarify their own position regarding normative ethics through a critical engagement with the ethical theories found in this book.

But how do we go about assessing the plausibility of moral theories? Moral philosophy is not necessarily difficult, but it has been going on for a long time, and in a short introduction like this one we do not have room to cover every possible factor that may come into play when evaluating a moral theory. However, below are a range of criteria that can get us started.

First, we can ask whether an ethical theory is internally consistent. If the various principles of the theory cannot be cashed out in logically coherent way, or the theory tells us that a particular action is both morally right *and* morally wrong at the same time, then we have very good reason to reject it, or at least to expect that it be modified to remove the contradiction.

We can also "test" moral theories. This is analogous to how we test scientific theories: we work out what the theory tells us should happen in novel cases—our prediction—then we run an experiment to see if what *actually* happens is consistent with our prediction. If so, this is evidence in favor of the theory; if not, it counts against it. While moral theories do not make predictions in quite the same way, we can do something similar: we can work out what the theory says we should do in various concrete cases and see how these "predictions" accord with our considered moral judgments. For instance, if a "thought experiment" tells us that a particular theory entails that genocide, mass murder, slavery, and rape are morally acceptable, this would count against the theory.

Of course, we must be careful in approaching ethics in this way. After all, our moral judgments are not foolproof, and it would be very surprising—and rather suspicious—if normative ethics did nothing more than confirm our society's moral common sense. We therefore need to be open to the possibility that a moral theory might contradict what we take to be right or wrong, and that the mistake is with *us* rather than with the theory.

To apply this critical tool correctly, then, it helps to distinguish between levels of certainty and consensus and be aware of the ways in which our own beliefs may be parochial. For instance, our level of confidence about the wrongness of rape, genocide, or slavery is presumably much greater than our confidence about issues such as euthanasia, polyamory, or genetic engineering. If a moral theory disagrees with our beliefs about the latter, we should be far less sure that it is the theory that is wrong rather than us. We should also try to avoid drawing large conclusions from single cases. A moral theory that makes predictions at odds with our considered judgments across a *range* of cases is more likely to be wrong than one that gives us the "wrong" answer in just a few instances.

A good moral theory should also explain our wide-ranging practices of morality. Here this is not a matter of particular *judgments* of right and wrong, but rather the moral *concepts* we use. For instance, our everyday moral practices draw on ideas such as fairness, harm, loyalty, happiness, and so on. A good moral theory can make sense of the range of moral concepts we intuitively rely on, whereas a weak one has nothing to say about them or cannot account for their importance. As with singular judgments, moral theorizing might mean rethinking or modifying some of our everyday moral concepts. But all things being equal, the more moral concepts a theory can incorporate or explain, the better.

Relatedly, the theory should be able to provide a plausible explanation for *why* certain things are moral or immoral. Does the justification the theory offers for why murder is wrong, for instance, make sense? Or does it explain the wrongness of murder by citing features that do not seem to really connect to what we take to be morally significant about it? For instance, one theory might explain the wrongness of murder in terms of the valuable future that has been taken from the victim, whereas another might understand the issue in terms of "theft," that is, that the victim owns their own body, which the murderer then takes from them. Arguably, the "loss of a valuable future" explanation seems to capture the wrongness of murder more credibly than the "theft" account. If so, then the theory that gives rise to the "loss of a valuable future" view is the more plausible one.

It also counts in favor of a theory if it is compatible with a plausible moral psychology. That is, it can explain why we ought to be moral, why the fact that something is moral ought to motivate us.

Finally, a theory usually also gains support if it can *unify* our moral judgments. The more basic concepts a theory needs to rely on to account for our moral practices, the less plausible it seems. This is like the principle of parsimony in science: if more than one theory explains the data equally well, then we ought to prefer the simpler theory. Of course, there is always a balancing act to be had here with explanatory power, and the simpler theory may not always be better. But all other things being equal, we would usually say that a more parsimonious theory is more plausible than a less parsimonious one.

The Structure of the Book

This book differs from typical ethical theory textbooks in respect to the theories covered. Traditionally, the options presented are usually taken mostly—and often exclusively—from the Western philosophical canon. This book aims for a wider conversation and considers ethical theories from Western, East Asian, South Asian, and African philosophical traditions. When it comes to moral philosophy, this is no means exhaustive: to even attempt a truly comprehensive discussion of ethical theory from a truly "global" perspective would take up far more space than is available to us here. Given the huge diversity of fascinating and worthwhile ethical theories that could have been included, difficult choices had to be made.

On what basis, then, have I chosen the ethical theories in this book? My central aim with this book was to put the different theories we discuss into *conversation*. This means choosing theories that I am confident can speak to each other productively. But this leads to a familiarity bias, and the choice of theory therefore speaks at least partly to my own personal background and expertise. As such, a theory not being included in this book is in no way an indication that it is not worth taking seriously. So, while every theory we discuss in this book deserves its place in it, it's important to note at the start the partial—and at least somewhat arbitrary—nature of the selection process.

Nonetheless, every chapter of this book provides an important, unique perspective on ethics from a range of the most significant, impactful, and long-lasting schools of thought in world culture. The reader should therefore hopefully gain an understanding of, and appreciation for, many of the key ethical theories that have shaped society throughout human history.

Structurally, I have divided the different theories found in the book into four categories: character-based theories, consequence-based theories, principle-based (or deontological) theories, and anti-theoretical/particularist/other theories.

The categories of the book are the fundamental *kind* of theory in Western analytic philosophy. Each kind of theory can contain a range of different views that disagree with each other in important ways, but all are united in terms of what is of *fundamental importance* in ethics. Character-based theories, for instance, take the development of a certain character to be what ethics is about, whereas consequentialist theories hold that at the most basic level we ought to be concerned with the consequences of our actions.

However, in our everyday moral decision-making, all the different approaches often seem to be saying the same thing. After all, most commonsensically morally good actions reflect a virtuous character, lead to good consequences, *and* follow plausible moral principles all at the same time. For instance, robbing a bank is not the kind of thing a virtuous person would typically do; it leads to bad consequences (on the whole) and contravenes commonsense moral principles such as "do not steal" (as well as more fundamental ones such as "treat others with respect").

Nonetheless, there are times—in principle at least, though almost certainly in practice as well—when character, consequences, and principles come apart. Sometimes acting from a virtuous character will lead to less-than-optimal consequences (why spend time and energy developing our moral character when children are starving, after all) or will require us to contravene an important moral principle (it may be kind to tell our friend that their new shirt looks good even when this requires us break a prohibition against lying). Sometimes achieving the best consequences requires acting in unvirtuous ways (for instance, killing an infant Hitler in his crib may lead to the best consequences, but it may not be the action of a truly virtuous person and certainly contravenes a prohibition against killing). And following the right moral principles may sometimes require us to forgo the optimal consequences (for instance, it may be better overall to harvest the organs of strangers against their will, but this certainly contravenes the principle of autonomy) or act in an unvirtuous way (coldly following a moral rule even when it lacks kindness).

Hence, in principle different approaches to ethics come apart at a basic level. For all the times that they converge in what they require, there are nonetheless times when they demand different— and fundamentally incompatible—actions. So, while it is tempting to subscribe to all the different approaches—to say "it's a little bit of all of them"—this answer is just too easy. It certainly does seem that each approach offers something valuable. But if each approach is "grounded" in incompatible ways—if each approach sees a different thing as being that which *makes* something morally good or bad—then we need to be sensitive to these fundamental disagreements.

In saying this, any plausible moral theory almost certainly needs to incorporate character, consequences, and principles in *some* way. After all, these *all* seem central to our everyday moral thinking. And most theories *do* incorporate all in some way. For instance, consequentialists value both principles and character. After all, even if we are concerned with bringing about the best consequences, it often is not easy to know what actions will in fact lead to the best consequences. Hence, adopting moral principles—such as "do not kill" or "do not steal"—as "rules of thumb" is likely to help us to act in beneficial ways. Similarly, developing certain traits of character—kindness, courage, patience—is in practice likely to lead to good consequences.

But note what is going on here: what *truly* matters in this picture are the consequences. Principles and character *only* matter insofar as they enable us to bring about desirable consequences. They do not have any value in and of themselves: their value is derivative rather than intrinsic. If a virtue or principle leads to *un*desirable consequences, for the consequentialist it ceases to have value.

Similarly, deontologists will probably need a plausible moral psychology. After all, being the kind of person who always follows the right principles is not easy. Developing our character in certain ways can help with this. So providing an account of how we connect up our basic human psychology to the principles we are obliged to follow is important. Similarly, consequences usually matter in at least *some* way to deontologists. For instance, respecting others will often involve intentionally acting in ways that benefit them. It is questionable whether we can describe someone as respecting others if they have no regard for how their actions impact those others. In fact, some deontological theories—such as contractualism and discourse ethics—build a concern for consequences into the generation of their moral principles in the first place.

But again, we need to be clear about what is being said here: for deontologists, the *fundamental* thing is abiding by the right principles. Character and consequences only play a role insofar as they help us to apply (or generate) those principles. The difference between the different theories is therefore in which feature *grounds* ethics and which operate at a higher, less fundamental level. Part of our task in ethical theorizing is therefore to be clear about the relationship between these features of ethics.

In short, *at the most basic level*, each of these approaches differs: each grounds morality in a different way. In this respect, they are *rivals*, and we cannot agree with more than one. When it comes to higher-level matters—concrete questions of applied ethics—the different approaches may converge. Similarly, they may rest on (or be compatible with) the same metaethical views. But when it comes to the question of *what really matters* in ethics, these theories conflict with one another. Part of our task when reading this book is to be attentive to precisely how and why this is the case.

Global Philosophy

This book is divided into four sections, each containing a "kind" of ethical theory. Each of these sections contains ethical theories from different philosophical traditions. However, this system of categorization itself is one that developed within Western analytic philosophy and arguably reflects the interests and concerns of that tradition. It is questionable whether this way of dividing the theories truly captures the uniqueness of the different theories we discuss; in some ways it may distort them, forcing them to fit a shape for which they were not intended, or requiring them to speak to issues that matter to Western analytic philosophers but are not of central concern to the tradition they are from. Nonetheless, I have divided these theories in this way. Why?

There are two main reasons, both of which are about ensuring that this book achieves its aim of not merely *informing* the reader of different viewpoints, but rather enables a conversation between them: that it makes possible the activity of *global* philosophy.

The first is that conversations about grounding ethical theories in terms of character, consequences, and principles are already taking place in communities of philosophers who specialize in non-Western philosophical traditions. This division therefore may not be perfect, but it has been *useful enough* to provide a tool for thinking about ethics across a range of traditions. For instance, this book contains three different chapters on Buddhist ethics, each of which is found in a different section. While each chapter is nominally discussing a different branch of the extremely diverse Buddhist tradition, it also reflects an ongoing discussion among scholars of Buddhist philosophy about just what kind of moral theory Buddhism *really* advocates.

Similarly, there are two chapters on Confucianism (the first arguing that it is about character, the second that it is about principles). In fact, Confucian philosophers have discussed how Confucianism ought to be grounded at length, and there are advocates for placing it in each of the four sections of this book. The same kind of thing can be said about African philosophy: the chapter on Akan ethics outlines the extensive disagreements among Twi-speaking philosophers regarding how Akan ethics should be categorized according to the typology being used in this book.

In short, if the aim of this book is to enable conversation between ethical theories from different philosophical traditions, there are worse places to start than by using a system of categorization that—despite its shortcomings—has found widespread use among Western and non-Western philosophers alike.

Second, this categorization is a useful tool for us to begin to explore similarities and differences between different views. After all, without *some* common ground, conversation is impossible, and the various views discussed in this book will end up merely talking past one another. Whether the conversation will *remain* on the similarities and differences that this system of categorization helps us to identify—or whether the conversation will move on to different questions and concerns entirely—is very much an open question. But as a place to begin, dividing the theories in this way can be productive.

We therefore do not need to treat this system of classification as an immutable structure for the conversation to nevertheless find it useful as a tool to provoke discussion, debate, and disagreement by offering a starting point for engagement. And so long as the book's classificatory schema is taken in the provisional way that it is intended, it can be extremely useful.

Section 1

Character-Based Moral Theories

Character, Virtue, and Continence

This first kind of moral theory we will consider in this book focuses on *character* as the fundamental concern of ethics. This means that these theories approach ethics from a different direction than theories from other sections of the book. Whereas both consequentialist and deontological theories are concerned with determining which *actions* are right (and why), character-based approaches are more interesting in working out the kind of *person* we should be (Suikkanen 2015, 124).

Character-based approaches start with the idea of the morally worthy or morally unworthy person. What kind of character does the morally worthy person have, as opposed to the morally unworthy person? This is often thought of in terms of "virtue"; a morally worthy person is a person who possesses virtue, whereas the morally unworthy person is one who *lacks* virtue (or is "vicious," e.g., possesses vices rather than virtues).

We can think of a virtue such as courage, then, by contrasting the actions of a "continent" person with those of a virtuous one. A continent person may act correctly—they may behave *as* a courageous person would behave, in terms of their actions. But doing so involves overcoming their inclinations otherwise. For a virtuous person, by contrast, being courageous is easy, since it is the action that naturally flows from who they are. As Julia Annas puts it, the virtuous person "does the right thing, undividedly, for the right reason" (Annas 2006, 517), whereas the continent person has to force themselves to act as the virtuous person would. The term "undividedly" is important here: the virtuous person does not experience an internal conflict when doing the right thing; all aspects of her character naturally point in that direction in a unified way.

The distinction between virtuous and continent persons in many ways tracks our everyday attitudes. After all, if a person is morally admirable, they are not doing the right thing "by chance"; because they are afraid of the consequences, because the conditions of the situation aligned just right. The person who does the right thing wholeheartedly—not because they *have* to but because they *want* to—is someone we might look up to.

The distinction between virtue and continence is one we will find in all moral theories that focus on character. Whether we are talking about Akan humanism, Confucianism, a virtue-ethical reading of Buddhism, or Aristotle's virtue ethics, there is a difference between merely performing the right action "by chance" and that action flowing from the right kind of settled dispositions of character.

The Role of Character

Character-based theories are not the only theories that have an interest in character per se. As Jussi Suikkanen puts it, the issue that distinguishes character-based theories from others is not whether or not character matters, but rather the "order of explanation" (Suikkanen 2015, 124); that is, where character fits into the overall picture of morality. For instance, consequentialist theories are in principle happy to accord virtue a derivative value (Copp and Sobel 2004, 515). After all, it may well be the case that a virtuous person is more reliable at bringing about the good than a continent person. If so, then the consequentialist has reason to promote the development of virtuous character.

But for the consequentialist, virtue is only valuable *insofar* as it maximizes the good. Having a worthy character is not valuable in and of itself; it is only valuable instrumentally for the achievement of a separate good. Virtue may therefore be valuable, but only indirectly and conditionally. For consequentialists, then, the *good*—not *character*—is primary or basic.

Similarly, deontologists are concerned with *right action*; with respecting and acting in accordance with moral rules or principles (Kawall 2009, 1). It seems reasonable to think that certain characters are better than others at living by the right moral principles. Hence, deontologists have reason to value a person having that kind of character. But here again, character is not *basic*; it is valuable *because* it assists in bringing about right action, not because it has value in itself.

What is distinctive about the moral theories in this section of the book, then, is that character is the basic normative concept. Instead of starting with the good, or with right action, and understanding worthy character in terms of the ways it can achieve the good or ensure right action, we start with *virtue* and understand the good and right action in light of this (Driver 2007, 137).

But what does it mean to understand the good and right action in terms of character or virtue? Essentially, that the good is what a virtuous person values, and right actions are the actions that a virtuous person performs. It is important to be clear on precisely what is being said here. For instance, we might understand virtue as a *tool* for *working out* what the good or right action is. Understood in this way, the virtuous person is merely a reliable indicator of what is morally valuable, but what is morally valuable is still defined independently of virtue. In other words, observing the virtuous person is merely a way of *coming to know* what is morally valuable. For example, we might notice that a virtuous person always acts so as to bring about the most pleasure, or always affirms the doctrine of inclusive care, or consistently follows the categorical imperative, or lives by Habermas's universalization principle. If so, then that gives us good reason to think that these ideas are morally correct. But what *makes* them correct is not that the virtuous person follows them; rather, the virtuous person follows them *because* they are *correct already*. And if so, under such as view we cannot say that morality is *grounded* in character, and the theories in the character/virtue section of this book would not be offering a fundamentally competing vision of ethics.

Instead, then, when something is good or right because a virtuous person values it or acts that way, this is *not* merely an *indication* that the thing is good or the act is right, but rather is an *explanation* as to *why* that thing is good or that act is right. In other words, there is "no prior account of rightness that could be used in order to flesh out the notion of doing what a virtuous agent would characteristically do" (Svensson 2010, 258). *First* we work out what it means to have a worthy character—to be virtuous—*then* we can spell out what things are good or what actions are right. We *derive* the morally good and right from character (Cullity 1999, 277). As Jason Kawall puts it, then, in a truly character-focused theory, "rightness and goodness [are] explained in terms of the virtues or virtuous agents" (2009, 1), and not the other way around.

This takes us back to the distinction between virtue and continence. If we understood virtue as merely indicating the good or the right—if these ideas are independent and more basic than virtue—then *in isolation* an act by a continent person that brings about the right consequences or follows the right principles is *just as good as* that of a virtuous person. The fact that the act is performed by a virtuous person or a continent one makes no difference to our moral evaluation of it. One the other hand, if right character is primary, then even in isolation the actions of a continent person are not the same, morally speaking, as those of a virtuous person, *even if* they *appear* identical. What makes the act *right* is *that* it stems from the right character; since a continent person does not have that right character, their actions lack the essential feature that makes them morally good.

Teleology

So far, we have looked at the ways in which character-based moral theories are distinctive from the other kinds considered in this book. However, both character-based and consequentialist approaches are often seen as being *teleological* theories. To call a theory "teleological" is essentially to say that it aims at some good.

It is easy to understand how consequentialist moral theories can be considered to be aiming at some good. After all, such theories *start* with the good—for example, pleasure—and then understand "right" as those actions that bring about that good. What may be less clear, though, is how character-based theories can also be teleological. After all, we have already discussed the fact that such approaches take virtues—dispositions of character—as fundamental, rather than either a good (consequentialism) or the right (deontology).

Character-based approaches to ethics are typically seen as having two main concerns: they ask what kind of person we should be and what it means to live well. The settled dispositions that can be evaluated in specifically *moral* terms are those dispositions that are connected in some way to our flourishing as a human being; in other words, to living life *well*. And this is precisely where teleology comes in: the virtues are part of achieving the *goal* of living well as a human being. Character-based theories aim at human flourishing and are in this sense teleological.

But then, what is the difference between consequentialist and character-based theories? One possible difference is the focus on character. After all, consequentialism typically takes as its final good something like pleasure or desire satisfaction, or at a stretch goods such as friendship or beauty. However, while it may certainly be the case that the most well-known consequentialist theories do not have character as their goal, there is no reason why such an end is *incompatible* with consequentialism in principle. For example, we can easily imagine a consequentialist moral theory that takes virtue as of ultimate value: in answer to the question of what we ought to try to bring about the most of in the world, they would answer "virtue." If so, then is there really any *fundamental* difference between character-based theories and consequentialism?

The aim of human flourishing—or flourishing *as* a human being—plays a key role in distinguishing character-based approaches from other theories. For a consequentialist theory concerned with virtue, either virtue is the ultimate aim: in which case, we miss out on the *why* of virtue; that it enables us to flourish as human beings. Or flourishing is our end goal: in which case, virtue is only instrumentally valuable insofar as it helps us to reach that goal. But with character-based approaches, we cannot easily separate virtue and flourishing. Living virtuously is not merely a *means* to human flourishing; it's *constitutive* of it (Deigh 2010, 58). So, for instance, courage, or wisdom, or benevolence, are not just *paths* to flourishing, but are themselves essential parts of it. We simply cannot specify flourishing independently of the excellences of human character that are the virtues. Conversely, we cannot describe those excellences without reference to the highest good of human flourishing (Putnam 1988, 380).

In this sense, then, we can say that character-based approaches are teleological, but not consequentialist. While they have an ultimate aim—human flourishing—and so can be considered to be *goal* (*telos*) oriented, that aim cannot be achieved by just any means available. It is not that the virtues just happen to be an efficient means of achieving flourishing; rather, developing a virtuous character is itself a part of what it means to flourish. Hence, the achievement of flourishing is constrained by the fact that the goal is itself bound up inseparably with the means of achieving it. It is inconceivable, for instance, that benevolence could be abandoned in favor of some more efficient means of flourishing. And this is not true *contingently*, but *necessarily*; there is no possible world in which flourishing is achieved without benevolence, not because it just happens to always be a useful means, but because flourishing itself is partly constituted by benevolence. If we get rid of the means—benevolence—we abandon the goal at the same time.

Flourishing

Human flourishing is the ultimate aim of character-based approaches. But precisely what it means to flourish is a matter of disagreement between the various theories examined in this section of the book.

Our first chapter, on Aristotle's virtue ethics, discusses the goal of *eudaimonia*. The nature of this goal is determined by what makes us characteristically *human*. Whereas plants have only a nutritive soul (concerned with growth, nutrition, and reproduction) and animals have nutritive and sensitive souls (unlike plants, they can also move and perceive things), human beings have a rational soul as well. In other words, the capacity for rational thought is the unique capacity of human beings. Hence, for Aristotle, developing this rational capacity is what it means to live well *as a human being* and what will allow us to achieve a state of *eudaimonia*.

Though this gives Aristotle a somewhat intellectual account of virtues, it does not mean that virtue is a *purely* intellectual exercise. Virtues are concerned with *practical* reason—how we act—rather than merely theoretical reason, that is, our ability to be good philosophers, mathematicians, or scientists. He also has a notable role for emotion to play in his account of virtue, in that he is interested not just in having the right thoughts, but in having the right emotions as well. Nonetheless, Aristotle considers us to be fully achieving our nature as human beings only when the rational part of our soul governs the other parts. As for our emotions, Aristotle's main concern is that we gain the right emotions by learning to make the right *judgments* that underlie our moral responses. In these respects, then, Aristotle's pursuit of *eudaimonia* involves an emphasis on the excellences of our shared *rational* nature.

By contrast, the early Confucians, discussed in our second chapter, see our human nature as resting more in our moral emotions than in our rational natures. For instance, Mengzi held that human beings are born with four moral "sprouts" (*duan* 端). Every human being naturally has a feeling of commiseration, a feeling of shame, a feeling of modesty, and a feeling of approving and disapproving of things. If these sprouts are able to develop correctly, the virtues of humanity (*ren* 仁), righteousness (*yi* 義), propriety (*li* 禮), and wisdom (*zhi* 智) will result. While individual human beings may or may not develop these sprouts fully, possessing them in the first place is the defining mark of being human. A person who allowed these feelings to disappear entirely would cease to be a human being. For the early Confucians, the full development of these virtues results in the ultimate fulfilment of our nature: becoming a *junzi* (君子), or gentleman.

In the third chapter, we examine the highest good of Theravāda Buddhism: *nirvāṇa*. This chapter argues that we should understand Theravāda (not uncontroversially) as a character-based moral theory. According to this perspective, Buddhists see human nature as fundamentally one of suffering caused by desire (*taṇhā*). Desire here can be identified with three basic vices: greed, hatred, and ignorance. The aim of the Theravādan is to replace these three vices with unselfishness, benevolence, and understanding. The achievement of this, via the path of morality, meditation, and wisdom, is simultaneously the achievement of *nirvāṇa*.

While there are similarities between this reading of Theravāda and the Aristotelian and Confucian theories already discussed, one noteworthy difference is the role of meditation or contemplation. For many Buddhists, an important aspect of *nirvāṇa* is the realization of certain truths. For instance, "wisdom" consists in part of holding right views, such as the four noble truths (that there is suffering, the cause of that suffering, that the suffering can end, and the path to accomplish this), or a realization of the dependently originating, impermanent, and empty nature of the self. Hence, meditative activities that lead to the realization of the truth of these views—activities that might be considered "passive" in other character-based theories—are here understood as important, positive steps toward achieving the *telos* of Theravāda Buddhism.

The Akan view, discussed in the fourth chapter, is distinctive in several ways. For one thing, it holds that human beings are a moral tabula rasa—a blank slate—when they are born. According to Kwasi Wiredu, human beings are born with the capacity for conceptual mapping but need to have that capacity trained through moral instruction (1996, 21). The role of the community is therefore essential for the moral development of the individual.

But the community is also vital in another way for the Akan: being a member of a community is an essential part of human personhood. Hence, human flourishing is at the same time the flourishing of the community. Mutual interdependence and reciprocity are the natural modes of existence for human beings. Human personhood is an achievement, not a given: we become human by learning how to fulfill our obligations to others. To the extent that someone has a bad character (*suban bone*), then, they are not a person (*onnye onipa*). The virtues of Akan moral theory to which we aspire as human beings are therefore focused on those qualities that promote the social good, rather than the good of the individual.

Advantages and Disadvantages

There are several reasons we might look favorably on character-based accounts of morality. For one thing, such views have an easy time accounting for moral motivation: the question of why we should act morally in the first place. From a consequentialist or deontological perspective, it can sometimes be hard to see why we should do the right thing, especially when doing so involves sacrificing our own interests. But for the character-based theory, the answer is simple: ultimately it *is* in our interest to act morally, since doing so is part and parcel of living well and flourishing as a human being.

Such approaches to morality also capture the common intuition that moral action requires sensitivity, rather than just being a mechanical application of rules or principles to a situation. (This is something we will see returning in the final section of the book, when we consider particularist and anti-theoretical approaches.) We often think that moral judgement is a skill; it is not simply reading from a rule book or an "ethics manual" (McNaughton and Rawling 2006, 453). The real world is simply too complex and nuanced for such a thing to be possible. Ethics is therefore a matter of practical expertise, much like learning to cook, play cricket, or drive a motorcycle.

We might also note the important role for emotions in character-based approaches. Consequentialist and deontological theories tend to intellectualize ethics. But in character-based approaches, emotional intelligence is essential as well. As Russ Shafer-Landau puts it, "A person with . . . a blank emotional life, is bound to be morally blind. Virtue ethics perfectly explains why that is so" (2012, 256). Ethics involves not just *performing* the right action but also *understanding* and *feeling* the *why* of it. By contrast, to a deontologist—who is focused on right action—mechanically following the rules without understanding might be fine (so long as they are the correct rules); and to a consequentialist—who is focused on achieving good results—it does not really matter *why* you do something (so long as the outcomes are the correct ones).

However, there are some aspects of character-based ethics that seem less plausible to some. For instance, becoming virtuous involves a significant degree of luck. If we are not born into the right circumstances, then reaching *eudaimonia*, achieving *nirvāṇa*, or becoming a *junzi* or *suban pa* (someone with good character) is simply beyond us. The Confucian Mengzi's analogy between moral growth and the growth of a tree illustrates this point well: just as a tree will grow in a stunted way without the right nutrients, sunlight, water, and so on, a human being's moral sprouts will not grow properly without the right conditions. Similar concerns apply to the Aristotelian and Akan views and virtue-ethical readings of Buddhism. Yet whether those conditions obtain is usually not up to the person themselves: it is a matter of the situation they find themselves in.

Of course, this is only a *problem* for these views if we have good, independent reasons to think that the ends of moral growth *should* be open to everyone. It may simply be a fact of the matter that not everyone can achieve human flourishing; at least, not in the world we live in. While this may be lamentable, it is not necessarily a mark against the theories themselves.

A second possible concern with character-based theories is that they are ethically conservative (Annas 2006, 525). After all, they all start with a socially embedded individual who is trained in morality by others. The worry, then, is that character-based approaches may simply lead to the reproduction of society's already-existing morality, a morality that is likely to be deficient in at least some ways (imagine, for instance, being raised in a society that viewed slavery positively).

In response, a character-based moral theorist might point out that while we need to learn about our society's morality, the truly virtuous individual never merely reproduces what they are taught. This is where understanding the *why* of morality matters. Someone who does nothing but copy the behaviors of others will never reach a state of *eudaimonia*. A person who fails to consider on their own how best to support the good of their community will never be *suban pa*. Certainly, achieving *nirvāṇa* is impossible without an appreciation for unselfishness, benevolence, and wisdom that transcends the conventional. And Confucians are quite clear that a *junzi* can reinterpret and modify their inherited social rites from a state of advanced moral perception.

Finally, we might wonder whether it makes sense to think of character as basic. Consider as an example what we do when we identify someone as being benevolent. We first observe that the person performs benevolent actions and then conclude from that they are themselves benevolent (Kawall 2009, 3). But if we have already identified certain actions as "benevolent," does this not mean that actions are benevolent (or not) *independently*, and that the *virtue* of benevolence is therefore derivative of whatever makes those actions benevolent?

We might use the metaphor of symptoms and disease to push back against this objection (Kawall 2009, 3). When we identify a disease, we do so by observing its symptoms. So, for instance, we might note that a person has a cough and a runny nose and conclude from this that the person has a cold. But we would not then construe this as saying that having a cough and a runny nose in some way *causes* or *explains* the cold. The cold is something further, of which the symptoms are just an expression. The cold symptoms are *cold* symptoms only due to the fact that there really is a cold there *first*; and we might then use that knowledge to identify colds in others by observing the same symptoms. The cold is therefore primary, and the symptoms secondary.

We can perhaps say something similar about virtues. Just as we describe a cough and runny nose as cold symptoms—and use those symptoms to identify the presence of a cold—we might describe certain actions as evincing a benevolent character. We come to know what acts are benevolent first only because they are the kinds of acts a benevolent person would perform; with that knowledge, we can then watch for the same acts in others to determine whether or not *they* are benevolent. The benevolence (of character) is primary, and the acts of benevolence secondary (Kawall 2009, 5).

We might also wonder whether the primacy of the virtues is consistent with the way we go about picking out right and wrong actions. For instance, we are quite able to identify torturing an innocent as being wrong, and it does not seem as if we typically make any reference to virtues when doing so. That is, we do not ask whether a virtuous person would torture an innocent, then, upon concluding that they would not, decide that torturing an innocent is wrong. Rather, we jump straight to the judgment that torturing an innocent is wrong in an unmediated way. Why would this be the case, if it were not that the wrongness of torturing an innocent is independent of character (Kawall 2009, 8)?

Here the character-based theorist might draw attention to the fact that we do not do our thinking about morality as a blank slate. While most people may not be *paragons* of virtue, usually they do possess virtue already to *some* degree. Our ability to identify the wrongness of torture comes from the virtue of compassion that we have already developed. In which case, the judgment that torturing an innocent is wrong is from our character; it is not something that we just pluck out of the air or simply read off from features of the situation that explain its wrongness independently of character (Kawall 2009, 9). Hence, the fact that we are able to pick out right and wrong actions without *explicitly* referring to virtue is only possible because we are already *implicitly* drawing on the virtues that we *already possess* in doing so (Kawall 2009, 16).

Summary

In this chapter we have introduced character-based approaches to ethics. We have considered the ways in which they differ from both consequentialist and deontological theories, most notably in their focus on being a good person and living well as opposed to the good and right action. For character-based approaches, we ought to understand the good and right action as being derivative of virtue; we can only know what things are good, or which actions are right, by first knowing what goods a virtuous person would value and what actions a virtuous person would perform. What is more, this is not just a matter of using the virtuous person as a *means* of identifying the goods or actions that are *independently* justified. Rather, the fact that a virtuous person likes or performs them is what *make* those things morally valuable/right.

However, character-based moral theories are, like consequentialist ones, fundamentally teleological. This means that they are goal oriented. However, unlike consequentialist theories, the goals of character-based approaches—*eudaimonia, nirvāṇa*, or becoming a *junzi* or *suban pa*—are inherently tied up with the *means* of achieving those states. In other words, developing virtue is not just a useful means of *getting* to the *telos*: it is itself *part* of it.

Further Reading

Annas, Julia. 2006. "Virtue Ethics." In *The Oxford Handbook of Ethical Theory*, edited by David Copp, 515–36. New York: Oxford University Press. https://doi.org/10.1093/oxfordhb/9780195325911.003.0019.

Copp, David, and David Sobel. 2004 "Morality and Virtue: An Assessment of Some Recent Work in Virtue Ethics." *Ethics* 114, no. 3: 514–54. https://doi.org/10.1086/382058.

Cullity, Garrett. 1999. "Virtue Ethics, Theory, and Warrant." *Ethical Theory and Moral Practice* 2: 277–94. https://doi.org/10.1023/A:1009903128864.

Deigh, John. 2010. *An Introduction to Ethics*. Cambridge: Cambridge University Press.

Driver, Julia. 2007. *Ethics: The Fundamentals*. Malden: Blackwell.

Kawall, Jason. 2009. "In Defense of the Primacy of the Virtues." *Journal of Ethics & Social Philosophy* 3, no. 2: 1–21. https://doi.org/10.26556/jesp.v3i2.32.

McNaughton, David, and Piers Rawling. 2006. "Deontology." In *The Oxford Handbook of Ethical Theory*, edited by David Copp, 424–58. New York: Oxford University Press. https://doi.org/10.1093/oxfordhb/9780195325911.003.0016.

Putnam, Ruth Anna. 1988. "Reciprocity and Virtue Ethics." *Ethics* 98, no. 2: 379–89. https://doi.org/10.1086/292947.

Shafer-Landau, Russ. 2012. *The Fundamentals of Ethics*. 2nd ed. Oxford: Oxford University Press.

Suikkanen, Jussi. 2015. *This is Ethics: An Introduction*. Wiley Blackwell.

Svensson, Frans. 2010. "Virtue Ethics and the Search for an Account of Right Action." *Ethical Theory and Moral Practice* 13: 255–71. https://doi.org/10.1007/s10677-009-9201-7.

Timmons, Mark. 2013. *Moral Theory: An Introduction*. 2nd ed. Plymouth: Rowman and Littlefield.

1

Feelings, Virtues, and Happiness in Aristotle's *Nicomachean Ethics*

DIRK BALTZLY

Introduction

Virtue ethics in its modern revival distinguishes itself from two different kinds of normative ethical theories: consequentialist and deontological theories. Both kinds of normative ethical theory give some weight to reasons for action that concern consequences for everyone. A deontological theorist like John Rawls who supposes that persons have rights doesn't deny that *sometimes* considerations about consequences should be decisive in our moral reasoning. What deontologists deny is that they are *always* decisive and that *nothing* apart from that sort of consideration matters (as the consequentialist supposes). According to deontologists, rights may matter too (if there are rights at stake in that particular situation). And so may other duties that arise from different sources—for example, from the fact that I made a promise to someone to do something. Many find this response from deontologists to consequentialist theorists convincing. You might think, "Yes—in moral decision-making things are not always that simple. Sometimes rights matter even if respecting them doesn't produce good consequences, even in the long, long, long run." On this basis, you may conclude that consequentialism is too simple in its reasoning about right action, and some alternative theory should be preferred. Perhaps you might think that a deontological approach is truer to our experience of moral reasoning.

Even so, you might think that there are still more things than rights or rules that matter when it comes to moral reasoning. What about *feelings*? Isn't the fact that I feel sympathy for a person a good moral reason to comfort him? What about terms of moral evaluation apart from "morally right" or "morally wrong"? If I describe an action as cowardly or selfish, then certainly part of what I'm saying is that it was the wrong thing to do. But I'm also saying more than that. A cowardly action is a specific kind of wrong action—the kind that cowardly people regularly perform. It seems clear that I have good moral reasons not to be cowardly, but instead to be brave; not to be duplicitous, but instead to be forthright; not to be selfish, but instead to be generous; not to be mean, but instead to be kind. Deontological and consequentialist theories do not address themselves *directly* to these moral virtues or desirable character traits and the way in which they figure into our moral reasoning. A consequentialist might acknowledge that kindness, honesty, courage, and the like are valuable characteristics *insofar as they promote good consequences*. Some of us, however, think that there is more to it than that. Some philosophers suppose these character traits to be valuable even independently of their tendency to promote the greatest good for the greatest number.

Finally, you might well wonder about the relation of moral actions to our own *happiness*. Are moral reasons for action inevitably opposed to considerations about *my own* happiness? When can I act on the basis that it will make *me* happy rather than on the basis that it will, for instance, promote overall preference satisfaction? Some forms of deontological ethics raise this concern about the relationship between doing the right thing and happiness in a particularly acute manner. In a famous (and perhaps not entirely representative) passage in his *Groundwork for the Metaphysics of Morals*, the Enlightenment philosopher Immanuel Kant suggested that a person of "sunny disposition" who simply takes a natural enjoyment in helping people performs actions that have, in Kant's terminology, "no moral worth." Kant claims in order for an action to have moral worth, the person must act from the recognition that this is her moral duty—whether she likes it or not. Kant's remark fits naturally with a modern outlook that sees moral duty as inevitably opposed to self-interest.[1] But if good moral reasoning never leaves any room for me, then it doesn't seem likely that people are going to act very often on the basis of moral reasons. So a normative ethical theory ought to say something about moral reasons and my own happiness.

Ancient ethical theorizing is not like most contemporary philosophical writing on ethics in any of these respects. For philosophers writing in the tradition of consequentialist or deontological ethics, the central question for normative ethical theory is "What actions are morally right?" In ancient Greek and Roman philosophy, the questions for moral philosophy are "What is happiness?" and "What is the relation of the moral virtues to happiness?" Rather than focusing on morally right actions, these theories focus on *what the good person is like*. Hence this tradition in ethical theory is often called "virtue ethics." In addition to being focused on moral virtues like bravery, generosity and kindness, Aristotle's virtue ethics in particular has an important role for feelings. So let's focus on him in preference to other schools of thought in ancient Greco-Roman philosophy (such as Platonism, Stoicism, or Epicureanism). While these schools of thought also prioritize the concept of virtue, they have less—or less plausible—things to say about feelings.

Eudaimonia and Happiness

Aristotle's ethical theory, as well as those of the Stoics and Epicureans, is *eudaimonistic*. It takes *eudaimonia* as the goal of living—the thing we should all be striving for—and asks what *eudaimonia* is and what sort of people we need to become to achieve it. The ancient Greek word "*eudaimonia*" is frequently translated as "happiness." Given that this is so, many people find it perplexing that anyone might have thought that a philosophical answer with any generality could be had to the questions "What is happiness?" and "How can I become happy?" After all, different things make different people happy. And, moreover, isn't there more to life than just being happy? What this shows, however, is not that Aristotle was extremely naive, but rather that the English word "happiness" carries some connotations that the Greek word "*eudaimonia*" doesn't.

We often use "happy" for a specific pleasant and untroubled state of mind. This state of mind can be fairly fleeting. We say things like "I was really happy today until the boss called me in and told me that I was to be made redundant. But my friends bought me dinner and we talked and I was pretty happy about the whole thing afterward." This state of mind is *not* what *eudaimonia* is. To prevent this kind of confusion, some translators have tried "human flourishing" instead of "happiness" for "*eudaimonia*." But there need not be that much confusion if we remember that we sometimes also use the English word "happiness" for a long-term state of well-being. Imagine that your friends have their first baby and they are talking about what kind of life they want her to have. Will she grow up to be a doctor or a scientist or a concert pianist? You say (very sensibly, in my opinion), "I just hope she'll be happy." I take it that it is inconsistent with your wish for her that she be a drug addict or mass murderer who smiles a lot and has a pleasant and untroubled state of mind. What you wish for her is a *long-term state of proper functioning*—that she will develop whatever talents she possesses and successfully integrate the exercise of these natural gifts into a life that includes love, intellectual investigation, self-discovery, economic means sufficient to her needs, and so on. Happiness in this sense is "a good life," and not merely in the narrowly moral sense that she doesn't do morally wicked things. What you want for your friends' daughter is that she is able to "live well" (*eu zên*) or to "do well" (*eu prattein*). Aristotle says that this is what everyone means by "*eudaimonia*" or "happiness" (*Nicomachean Ethics* 1095a19).[2] What people disagree about is what happiness or living and doing well consist of. It will do no harm to continue to call *eudaimonia* "happiness," provided that we remember that it is this sort of thing that we are talking about.

The Objectivity of Happiness

But is happiness for *me* the same thing as happiness for *you*? The obvious answer seems to be "No." However, remember we are no longer talking about happiness in terms of that fleeting, pleasant state of mind. The question is whether "doing well" is the same for both of us. Aristotle's answer to this question was "Yes and No." It is Yes when happiness is described at the highest level of generality, but No if it is described in a more specific way. This should be unsurprising. Consider two football codes like rugby and Australian Rules Football. Is a successful season the same thing for the Newcastle Knights rugby team as it is for the St Kilda AFL team? Yes and No. Yes: if we describe success in terms of a winning record in the regular season and a finals campaign that ends in a premiership. But the teams that each will play in their competition are different, and so are the strategies and tactics that they'll try to use to get themselves to a Grand Final. Aristotle argues that *at a certain level of generality*, happiness—that is, success in life—is the same for all of us just because we are humans. At the same time, he also recognizes that our success as humans will be concretely implemented in importantly different ways. Let us follow his argument for this point of view.

Aristotle seeks to ground the common character of happiness in our shared common nature by means of the so-called "function (*ergon*) argument" in *Nicomachean Ethics* (1097b23–98a19). He thinks that there is a general connection between the function or work of a thing of a particular kind and being a good thing of that kind. His general principle is that if the function of an x is to do something, then the function of a *good* x is to do that thing *well*. So, if the flute player's function or job is to play the flute, the good flute player is one who plays it well. Now, he also argues that there must be a human function, for it would be absurd if all of the parts of our bodies each had its function and yet the whole person had none. By this he does not mean that humans were made by God for a purpose.[3] If you accept the idea of evolution by natural selection, you too don't think that your liver was literally designed for a function. Yet it has one. By "function" I mean only "the characteristic thing that it does so that it counts as a liver." Even an artificial liver would be—in the relevant sense—a liver. It does what livers do. All Aristotle means when he talks about the human function is *the pattern of activity that makes a creature count as human.*

What could this pattern of activity be? The human function cannot simply be the life of growth and reproduction, or even of sensation, for these are not unique to human beings but are shared with plants and animals. The only capacity unique to humans is the capacity for *rational thought*. So—by analogy with the flute player—the function of the *good* human being is to live the life of rational activity *well*. Furthermore, performing the function appropriate to the kind of thing that you are essentially and not merely accidentally is what well-being or happiness consists of. The good flute player is not automatically a happy person.[4] But if you perform the human function well, you are not merely doing well in your chosen profession, you are *doing well as a human being*, and this is just what happiness is.

This brings us to the topic of virtues. The word for virtue (*aretê*) is sometimes translated as "excellence" because it is perfectly sensible to talk about the *aretê* of a horse or a knife. *Aretai* (plural) are not exclusively what we call *moral* virtues. An excellence is simply a quality of a thing that allows it to perform its function well. So if the function or job of a knife is to cut things, then qualities like having a blade made from a metal that keeps a good edge will be a virtue or excellence of knives. You can probably list virtues for various jobs. So the disposition to apply tests methodically would seem to be a virtue in a pathologist. You don't want a pathologist who tests for diseases haphazardly, but rather one who systematically eliminates classes of possible causes until she arrives at the right explanation for the symptoms. Aristotle says that anything that is done "in accordance with" or that "expresses" (*kata*) the appropriate virtue is done well. So the pathologist who works methodically works well. Her activity embodies the virtues of a good pathologist. Generalizing from particular functions (like being a pathologist) to the human function, Aristotle concludes that the good life for human beings (i.e., happiness) is *the life lived in accordance with the virtues of the rational parts of the soul*. Or, as Aristotle puts it:

> It thus follows that the human good is the activity of the soul that expresses excellence or virtue. And if there are several human excellences or virtues, the activity that expresses the best and most complete among them. Moreover, this excellent activity must occur across a complete lifetime, for one swallow does not make spring,

nor does one fine day; and similarly one day or a brief period of flourishing (*eudaimonia*) does not make a person supremely blessed and happy. (*Nicomachean Ethics* 1098a15–21, my translation)

Reason and the Moral Virtues

We are still working at a very high level of generality in this preceding description of happiness. All we know so far is that the happy life is one in which you exercise those qualities (whatever they might be) that allow you to use your capacity for rationality *well*. But what is meant by rationality? And what are the virtues or excellences of the rational faculty?

Aristotle supposed that we manifest our rationality in two different ways: practically and theoretically. Theoretical reason aims at uncovering truths about the world, and it is this aspect of our rationality that we use when doing science or mathematics. In relation to theoretical reason, we can speak of various virtues or excellences. These will be character traits or ingrained dispositions that make a person good at getting to the truth. Being thorough or being insightful might be examples of intellectual virtues.

We can also be rational in deciding how to act. This is practical reason applied to the sphere of human action. Aristotle speaks of the part of the soul that, though it is not itself reason, *listens* to reason. The virtues of this aspect of the human psyche are often called "the virtues of character" or "the moral virtues" to distinguish them from intellectual virtues. Aristotle differentiates them by the sphere in which we apply them in our practical reasoning. He also thinks that each virtue—that is to say, each way of reasoning well in that sphere of activity—is flanked on either side by a different pattern of practical reasoning that regularly gets things wrong (see table 1.1 on the next page).

To better understand this, let's think about a simple example. Let's take the way in which you use your reason in deciding how to handle expenses with your circle of friends. Sometimes you buy dinner if you go out. Sometimes you divide the bill. Sometimes you keep a careful eye on who had what. Other times you just

Table 1.1. Table of Virtues/Vices

Sphere of activity	Virtue	Excess	Defect
Feelings			
Feelings of fear	courage	rashness	cowardice
Feelings of anger	even-tempered	hotheaded	being a doormat
Pleasures relating to food, drink, and sex	appropriate self-control	self-indulgence	repressed
External goods			
Give and take of money in small matters	liberality	prodigality	meanness
Large public benefits	magnificence	tastelessness	being a cheapskate
Honor and dishonor	pride	humility	vanity
Big achievements	nameless	overly ambitious	unambitious
Social interactions			
Telling the truth	truthfulness	boastful	mock modesty
Social pleasantries	witty	complete clown	boring

Source: Author's own material.

split it evenly. Consider not just one specific choice about sharing costs among friends, but the general pattern of your choices. One general pattern of choosing could be one that is a bit too tight-fisted. Think about that friend who always wants to figure out exactly who had what and never wants to order another bottle of wine even when everyone else does. Aristotle thinks this person exhibits a moral vice when it comes to the give and take of money: he's mean or cheap. Now think about the other friend who is always happy to buy drinks for the whole pub. Do you worry about how this friend, who seems a bit too free with his money, will finish up eventually? Even if he has and will continue to have plenty of money, what about his effect on other people? Does he sometimes make people uncomfortable because he always insists on paying? Aristotle thinks that this disposition is the opposite vice of being cheap. This person's pattern of behavior marks him as prodigal—he doesn't use good sense when it comes to money. The middle way here is liberality. But Aristotle is clear that this is a disposition to offer to pay and to accept the offer of others to pay that is complex and responsive to little differences that may matter a lot. So sometimes it's important to accept a contribution toward the bill from someone you know cannot afford it as easily as you can because otherwise the person feels bad—as if he's a freeloader or powerless and pathetic.

Aristotle's view is that liberality is a virtue of practical reasoning. It is—to put it in our terms—a way in which your capacity for using reason in practical decision-making can be *properly tuned*. It's not a single rule or a set of rules you follow. Rather, it is a *sensitivity* to a whole bunch of considerations in virtue of which you respond in the right way under a whole range of slightly different circumstances. In some ways, it approximates the modern idea of "social intelligence" since Aristotle thinks that manifesting the virtue of liberality is one way of being intelligent—that is, it is a right use of our rational capacity—but also involves "reading" people and social situations. Although the choice of the virtuous person can be justified by giving reasons, it doesn't appear that virtues are just rules. They are settled ways of responding to situations that are justifiable but are—at the time—experienced as natural and effortless ways of being in the world. According to Aristotle, a moral virtue like courage is

> *a state of character concerned with choice, lying in an intermediate position*, i.e., the intermediate relative to us, *this being determined by a something rational*—the thing by which the person of practical wisdom would determine it. Now it is intermediate between two vices, one of which expresses excess and the other of which expresses

> deficiency; and again it is intermediate because the vices respectively fall short of or exceed what is right in both feelings and actions, while virtue both finds and chooses that which is intermediate. (*Nicomachean Ethics* 1107a1–5)

It is important to the connection with happiness that virtues are settled states of character. Being courageous, like being methodical, is a matter of a *fixed* disposition or state of character. We don't call someone courageous when taking the courageous course of action is the exception with him and not the rule. But it is not automatic, like the knee-jerk response. The methodical person doesn't decide *whether or not to be methodical*; he decides about *what the methodical way to proceed is* in this particular instance. Similarly, the courageous person is the person for whom the cowardly action is just not a real option. What he decides about is what courage requires in this situation—a vain but glorious sacrifice or a firm tactical withdrawal. The cowardly rout just doesn't show up on his list of possibilities. So *to acquire a virtue is to make yourself into a kind of person who finds particular things worthwhile and others as simply incompatible with who you are as a person.* Virtues are lived from the inside rather than being constraints imposed on you from the outside that you feel limit your freedom. Virtuous actions express, rather than limit, the virtuous person's identity.

Aristotle thinks that virtues are acquired by practice and following examples. To become a person who manifests the value of liberality, you follow and observe someone who handles those kinds of interactions well and watch the interpersonal reactions. In the fullness of time, you will come to rank the options that are available to you as she does. Moreover, you will acquire the sensitivity to differences and circumstances that allow her to choose the liberal action in a new context. It would seem that there aren't hard and fast rules for this. Rather, what you take on through practice is an ability to spot the right course of action. This is why Aristotle does not spend much time discussing the rules or principles for being just or honest, courageous, and so forth. It is something that you acquire a knack for. While you could, retrospectively, give good reasons for what you've done, at the moment you are like the master mechanic who *just sees* what needs to be done to fix the motor.

Reason and Emotion

Note that some of Aristotle's virtues and vices involve emotions, like fear. The person who is courageous is the person who not only acts correctly in the context of situations, but who also fears just those things that are worth fearing. Bravery or courage thus is not simply a matter of overcoming fear, but also of experiencing fear *correctly*—that is, in relation to things that are worth fearing and to the right degree for the right circumstances. Similarly, Aristotle sees that there are right and wrong patterns in the way in which we get angry. The person who is even-tempered does get angry, but she gets angry to the right degree with the right people in the right circumstances.

You may wonder how this is possible. The virtues are supposed to be ways in which our capacity for practical *reason* can be correctly tuned in the various spheres in which it operates. But now Aristotle is identifying *emotions* as one of those spheres. Moreover, he seems to be saying that a virtue like bravery is not merely a matter of how we deal reasonably with the fear we feel, but in addition how we *fear reasonably*.

The solution to this puzzle is that Aristotle thought that emotions like fear were *partly made up of* judgments. As a result, they can be reasonable or unreasonable. So he took emotions in general to be complex packages of judgment, pleasure, and/or pain, plus desire. Anger, for example, is a kind of painful *distress* that arises from the *judgment* that you or those close to you have suffered a conspicuous harm, conjoined with a *desire* for revenge and even, in many cases, an anticipatory *pleasure* at the prospect of getting your own back.

What evidence can he provide for this view? First, he pointed out that we sometimes call anger "sweet" (*Rhetoric* 1378a31–b11). We positively *like* to get hot under the collar, and this, he supposed, was because the anticipatory pleasure we take in the thoughts of revenge is gratifying to us. Second, we reason with angry people as if they were angry because they'd formed a judgment. How many times have you said to someone who was angry with another person, "Calm down. He didn't really mean it that way. He just says stupid things sometimes." If there weren't a judgment implicit in the person's anger, then giving him more information to change the light in which he sees the episode would be pointless. But that's exactly what you do when you say things like that. And notice that sometimes it works! How to explain this? Aristotle would say the best explanation is that emotions involve judgment as at least a constituent part.

Nonetheless, the judgments involved in emotions are not ones that we simply decide to make as we do in other cases—like when I look at the records of the two teams, which players are out with injuries, who has the home field advantage, and then judge, "Probably the Saints will win." I do not similarly weigh up all the evidence and then decide whether to get angry or not. Instead, I see that person doing that stupid thing *yet again* and I just get angry. But that's not an overwhelming objection to the idea that emotions involve implicit judgments, because we make all kinds of judgments habitually, without any decision process we are aware of, and those judgments can be hard to shake. In most cases, sexism and racism work like this. Suppose I have one extra ticket to the Saints' football match on Saturday, and I offer it to my friend Rob without for a moment thinking that I should ask Helen instead. I wasn't aware of going through any explicit chain of reasoning like: Helen's a woman and no women like football, but Rob's a bloke and every real man likes football. I just made the automatic and thoughtless judgment that Rob would want to go and Helen wouldn't be interested. However, just as I can take classes on anger management that help me bring to consciousness the presuppositions of my angry outlook on the world, so too I can fight the cultural conditioning that disposes me to make sexist assumptions about who does and doesn't like football.

We can and do reprogram the kinds of implicit judgments we make in relation to all kinds of things, and often the first step is the simple awareness that we have, in fact, made a judgment and that's why we feel this way. On Aristotle's view of virtues and emotions, we are rather like (imperfect) self-tuning radios. We can, with some effort, notice that we aren't emotionally tuned in to our surroundings. We can then, with more effort, engage in self-conscious efforts to adjust the dial of our instantaneous judgment-making capacity so that we are better tuned in to the reality around us. Aristotle would concede that this can be hard, and he thought it was a lot harder if you'd had a particularly bad upbringing from childhood. You need to have some people around you who are emotionally tuned in. Otherwise, you're unlikely to notice that you aren't. You also need friends to help support you in the process of moving your emotional dial—breaking bad habits of judgment and removing yourself from the patterns of behavior that reinforced them. Aristotle's *Nicomachean Ethics* contains a long section on the nature of friendship, and it is clear that he thought that our success in becoming virtuous and happy people required the right kind of friends. This emphasis on the *moral* importance of friendship is largely lacking in deontological or utilitarian approaches to ethics.

Summary

Aristotle's ideas about ethics returned to prominence from the 1950s onward in large part because of the frustration of philosophers like Elizabeth Anscombe (1919–2001) with what she saw as the pointless deadlock between deontological and consequentialist approaches to reasoning about morality. From that time, virtue ethics has evolved to be a third major perspective alongside these more modern theories. Not all modern forms of virtue ethics preserve all of the features of Aristotle's own specific form of virtue ethics. In particular, not all versions of modern virtue ethics are eudaimonistic. Nor do all forms of modern virtue ethics adhere to Aristotle's idea that each virtue is a middle point or mean between two vices. Yet Aristotle has undoubtedly been the most influential ancient Greek thinker on modern virtue ethics—whether modern writers follow his general approach or define themselves in opposition to his form of virtue ethics.

Virtue ethics resonates in many ways with our ordinary thinking about morality. First, many of us tend to think about ethics as somehow tangled up with what we might loosely call "the meaning of life." Though "meaning of life" is not Aristotle's vocabulary, he would certainly recognize the idea that there is something that we *should be doing* with our lives. If you put it to him, he might even agree that the meaning of life is happiness. But he would also insist that happiness is not merely whatever makes you feel good. It is the objective condition of human flourishing or *eudaimonia*.

That certainly is connected to ethics, as he understood it, since it involves acquiring and exercising the excellences of our shared rational nature—the practical and theoretical virtues. Second, many of us also tend to think that ethics ought to involve both "the head and the heart." Aristotle's virtue ethics leaves room for that idea since many of his virtues are not simply about what we do, but about how we feel. We ought not merely help the unfortunate. They are also fit objects for the feelings of pity, and those who don't have the right feelings in relation to the right circumstances just aren't tuned in to moral reality. There's more to being a kind person than doing the kind thing.

Nonetheless, virtue ethics also leaves many students of philosophy a bit frustrated. If you think it is the job of moral philosophy to provide you a guide for action and for making the morally right decision in a complex situation, you may find that virtue ethics doesn't give the same kind of moral guidance that, say, utilitarianism at least *purports* to give. But you should ask yourself whether it is too much to ask of a normative ethical theory that it provide an easy-to-follow recipe for making correct moral choices. Given the complexity of the world we find ourselves in, is this asking too much of philosophy? Can moral philosophy do better than simply describing the kinds of character traits that would allow us to choose well, if only we were people who had such virtues? The disagreement between Aristotelian virtue ethics and more rule-driven ethical theories runs deep and includes the higher-order question of what one can reasonably hope for from the enterprise of moral philosophy.

Notes

1. "To be beneficent when we can is a duty; and besides this, there are many minds so sympathetically constituted that, without any other motive of vanity or self-interest, they find a pleasure in spreading joy around them and can take delight in the satisfaction of others so far as it is their own work. But I maintain that in such a case an action of this kind, however proper, however amiable it may be, has nevertheless no true moral worth, but is on a level with other inclinations, e.g., the inclination to honour, which, if it is happily directed to that which is in fact of public utility and accordant with duty and consequently honourable,

deserves praise and encouragement, but not esteem. For the maxim lacks the moral import, namely, that such actions be done from duty, not from inclination" (Kant 1785, 398).

2. References to the works of Aristotle typically use "Bekker page numbers." Most translations will print page and line numbers in the margins. These correspond to the pagination in the earliest standard edition of the Greek text prepared by August Immanuel Bekker (d. 1871). This allows teachers, students, and scholars to know what bit of Aristotle is under discussion—even if they happen to be using different modern-language translations of Aristotle's works.

3. While Aristotle's philosophy includes a role for a supreme god, this being is not much like God as most people understand Him/Her/It. First, Aristotle's god does not create the world. Rather, Aristotle supposed that the world has existed forever, just as it is now. Second, Aristotle's god doesn't bother thinking about any of you: that's a subject unworthy of divine attention! Rather, the Prime Mover or Aristotle's god is "thought thinking itself," and its cosmic function is to provide a paradigm of effortless, simple, and eternal activity that every sensible thing—the heavens, all living beings—emulate to the best of their ability. The heavens imitate the divine activity by going around ceaselessly in a circle, while plants and animals approximate the activity of thought thinking itself forever by reproducing more of their kind. So Aristotle's god is neither creator nor divine commander.

4. Though it will be true that if he is a good player and knows this, he can hardly have any complaints or misgivings about his professional life. He may not want to be a flute player, but if he does, he can't be (rationally) dissatisfied with his achievements.

Further Reading

PRIMARY SOURCES

Aristotle. 1984. *Rhetoric*, translated by W. Rhys Roberts in *The Complete Works of Aristotle: The Revised Oxford Translation*, edited by Jonathan Barnes. Princeton: Princeton University Press.

———. 1985. *Nicomachean Ethics*, translated by Terence Irwin. Indianapolis: Hackett Publishing.

There are of course many editions of Aristotle's most-read text on ethics, but Irwin's is particularly good for students. It includes a glossary on Aristotle's terminology, as well as helpful notes.

Kant, Immanuel. 1785. *Grounding for the Metaphysics of Morals*. Translated by Thomas Kingsmill Abbott via Project Gutenberg.

SECONDARY SOURCES

Curzer, Howard. 2013. *Aristotle and the Virtues*. Oxford: Oxford University Press, 2013.

This book goes through Aristotle's list of moral virtues one by one and defends the underlying insight behind each. Curzer is not afraid to modify Aristotle's ideas a little bit and to argue for what Aristotle should have said, but didn't quite.

Hutchinson, D. S. 1995 "Aristotle's Ethics." In *The Cambridge Companion to Aristotle*, edited by Jonathan Barnes, 195–232. Cambridge: Cambridge University Press.

Hutchinson presents a nicely organized explanation of Aristotle's view that is easily accessible to students. He solves the problem of translating *"eudaimonia"* by referring to Aristotle's "theory of success." "Success," of course, means *"real success"*—not conventional marks of being successful, like a flashy car or designer shoes.

2

Confucianism

YAT-HUNG LEUNG AND YONG HUANG

Introduction

This chapter introduces Confucianism, a philosophical tradition
in China founded by Confucius (the Latinized form of Kongfuzi
孔夫子, or commonly Kongzi 孔子, who lived from 551–479 BCE).
We first introduce Confucian ethics as a kind of virtue ethics and
discuss its relationship to principles and consequences (sections
2 and 3). Next, we illustrate the differences between Mencius (or
Mengzi 孟子) (371–289 BCE) and Xunzi 荀子 (298–238 BCE) as an
internal disagreement in Confucianism, their different emphases
on what human beings are and the cultivation methods thereof
(sections 4 and 5), and how Confucianism would respond to the
objection that it is self-centered (section 6).

Confucianism as a Virtue Ethics

Confucian ethics has a number of features that align it with virtue
ethics. First, like virtue ethics, it focuses on *agents* being good or
bad in contrast with *actions* being right and wrong. It is thus not
surprising to see that Kongzi makes repeated contrasts—almost

twenty times in the *Analects* (a collection of sayings attributed to Kongzi)—between superior persons (*junzi* 君子), whom we ought to become, and inferior persons (*xiaoren* 小人). For example, while superior persons seek virtues, inferior persons seek land (*Analects* 4.11); while superior persons are concerned about moral rightness, inferior persons are concerned about profit (*Analects* 4.16); while superior persons aim to cultivate admirable rather than deplorable qualities in others, inferior persons do the opposite (*Analects* 12.16); while superior persons seek harmony instead of uniformity, inferior persons seek uniformity instead of harmony (*Analects* 13.23).

Nevertheless, the focus on agents is not to say that Confucians are not concerned about actions at all (more in Section 3). But for Confucians, while morally right actions are what morally virtuous people characteristically do, it is not enough just to do what virtuous people do: one ought also to do things in the way virtuous people do them. In other words, one ought to become a virtuous person themselves, rather than merely perform the correct actions. Kongzi says, "Guide them by edicts, keep them in line with punishments, and the common people will stay out of trouble but will have no sense of shame (*chi* 恥). Guide them by virtue (*de* 德), keep them in line with ritual propriety (*li* 禮), and they will, besides having a sense of shame, reform (*ge* 格) themselves" (*Analects* 2.3, adapted from Lau 2000, 11). For Kongzi, people's actions under government with laws and punishments and government with virtues and rites are roughly the same. What is important is whether the agents have a sense of shame and whether they become good.

Mengzi—arguably the most foundational Confucian philosopher after Kongzi—expresses a similar view when he distinguishes between "practicing *from* humanity and rightness" (*you ren yi xing* 由仁義行) and "practicing humanity and rightness" (*xing ren yi* 行仁義) (*Mengzi* 4B19). While the actions of humanity (*ren* 仁) and rightness (*yi* 義) are apparently the same, in the former one takes humanity and rightness, which are one's virtues, as the source of one's actions (they come "from" humanity and rightness). But in the latter, one just performs the actions of humanity and rightness without their corresponding virtues. This emphasis on the source of motivation reveals the Confucian concern with the agent's own moral well-being.

Also, one should do the virtuous things naturally, effortlessly, and joyfully. This is best exemplified by Kongzi himself. When he reached seventy years of age, he claimed he could do whatever his heart-mind (*xin* 心)[1] desired without worrying about trespassing moral bounds, as his heart-mind desired nothing but what morality required. Thus, Kongzi complains that "I have yet to meet the man who is as fond of virtue as he is of beauty in women" (*Analects* 9.18, in Lau 2000, 81). This line suggests that it is not enough to do virtuous things. Instead, one should take delight in doing them so that one can do so joyfully and effortlessly. Kongzi also says, "To be fond of it is better than merely to know it, and to find joy in it is better than merely to be fond of it" (*Analects* 6.20, in Lau 2000, 51). This emphasis on joy is also seen when Mengzi stresses the importance of music and joy: "The most authentic expression of music is in taking joy in these two [i.e., humanity and right-ness]. When there is joy, they grow; when they grow, how can they be stopped? When they come to the point where they cannot be stopped, then, without realizing it, one's feet begin to step in time to them and one's hands begin to dance them out" (*Mengzi* 4A27, in Bloom 2009, 84).

Principles, Consequences, and Practical Decision-Making

To characterize Confucian ethics as a virtue ethics doesn't mean that there is no concern with principles of action (deontology) and consequences of action (consequentialism). It only means that virtue is primary in Confucian ethics, while the value of rules/principles and consequences is reducible to, derivable from, and defined by virtues. Concerning practical decision-making, the Confucians act from virtues.

VIRTUE AND MORAL PRINCIPLE

One way to approach the Confucian view of the relationship between virtue and moral principle is to show Kongzi's view on the virtue of humanity (*ren* 仁) and ritual principles as involved in ritual propriety. Humanity is the most important virtue, which takes love or concern of (*Analects* 12.22) or commiseration with people (*Mengzi* 2A6) as its essence. The ritual principles of the Zhou dynasty were used to govern people's behavior long before Kongzi's time. Hence, while Kongzi desired to restore these lost ritual principles, the principles themselves are not his invention. Rather, Kongzi's unique contribution is to emphasize the importance of the virtue of humanity as the essence of ritual principles. Although the ritual principles are usually reliable in guiding many of our actions (*Analects* 6.27, 15.18), they are sometimes in need of additions and abridgements to cope with changing circumstances (*Analects* 2.23), and Kongzi precisely highlights that the yardstick of adjustment—in fact, the essence—of ritual principles lies in humanity. In answering his student's question on the basis of ritual propriety, Kongzi says, "In mourning, it is better to express deep sorrow than be particular about tedious formalities" (*Analects* 3.4, in Ni 2017, 115). It is the moral emotion and the virtue of humanity that ground the ritual propriety. In fact, Kongzi says, "What does a man who is not humane have to do with ritual propriety?" (*Analects* 3.3).

Since humanity is the essence of ritual principles, we can understand Kongzi's saying that "to discipline oneself according to ritual principles is to practice the virtue of humanity" (*Analects* 12.1): though the person who needs ritual principles to discipline themselves has not yet cultivated the virtue of humanity, disciplining oneself with ritual can help a person acquire the virtue of humanity in the first place. However, ritual principles are useless once a person has become a virtuous person. Such a person—like Kongzi himself after turning seventy—can act according to their heart's desire without worrying about ritual principles (*Analects* 2.4).

VIRTUE AND CONSEQUENCES

Similarly, it's clear that Confucian ethics prioritizes virtues over consequences. For instance, Kongzi says that "superior persons are concerned about [the virtue of] rightness, while inferior persons are concerned about profit" (*Analects* 4.16). Mengzi, too, when responding to his advisee King Hui of Liang's question about what benefit he (Mengzi) can bring to the king, says, "what is the point of mentioning the benefit? All that matters is that there should be [the virtues of] humanity and rightness" (*Mengzi* 1A1). Here, both Kongzi and Mengzi emphasize that we ought to act from the virtue of rightness instead of being concerned about our actions bringing about good consequences, that is, benefit or profit for us.

However, this doesn't mean that Confucianism considers beneficial consequences to be irrelevant or insignificant. What Confucians emphasize is that virtue will naturally bring out beneficial consequences and vice harmful ones, both to their possessors and to others. Mengzi, for example, tells the king to be virtuous. If the king were to become virtuous, this would set an example for his people to follow. This in turn would lead to good consequences for the king, since "there have never been persons with [the virtue of] humanity who will abandon their parents, and there have never been persons with [the virtue of] rightness who will be negligent of the interest of the king" (*Mengzi* 1A1). In his famous commentary on this passage, the greatest Confucian of the Song dynasty, Zhu Xi 朱熹, quotes his Song Confucian predecessor, Cheng Yi 程頤, who says that "to be humane and morally right, superior people don't seek benefits and yet such benefits will result as a matter of fact" (Zhu 1994, 280).

PRACTICAL DECISION-MAKING

Confucianism, as a virtue ethics, doesn't ignore the question about the right and wrong of actions, but only says that it is not a primary question in comparison with the question of the good and bad of the human agent. Concerning practical decision-making, Confucianism can agree with some virtue ethicists that the right actions are actions that a virtuous person would characteristically do (cf. Hursthouse 1999, 28), and wrong actions are actions that a virtuous person would not characteristically do or a vicious agent would characteristically do (cf. Van Zyl 2011, 87). It can also accept the idea of "virtue-rule" suggested by Rosalind Hursthouse: "Not only does each virtue generate a prescription—do what is honest, charitable, generous—but each vice a prohibition—do not do what is dishonest, uncharitable, mean" (Hursthouse 1999, 36). While ritual principles usually provide reliable action guidance, they are sometimes in need of adjustment considering how they can best manifest our virtues. That is, they are not always perfect. Mengzi especially emphasizes the need of expedience (*quan* 權) in some cases. For example, it is according to ritual that "in giving and receiving things, men and women should not touch one another"; however, "if one's sister-in-law were drowning and one did not save her, one would be a wolf" (*Mengzi* 4A17, in Bloom 2009, 82). Here the rescue by using one's hands is a matter of expedience and weighing of the importance of different virtues. This weighing is carried out in accordance with and for the virtue of humanity, the core virtue. In this case, saving life is more important than following the ritual principle. It is in this sense that there is no detailed or rigid principle of action in Confucianism. Or, if we must say there is one, it is humanity that serves as the general yardstick: "There are just two ways: humanity and inhumanity (*bu ren* 不仁)" (*Mengzi* 4A2). The former is good and right, and the latter the opposite. The concrete actions that best manifest the virtues are contextual.

We can then explain virtuous persons having disagreements. In that case, most likely we are facing a moral dilemma, where one has to choose between two equally problematic alternatives. Consider the famous Trolley Problem: let the trolley move ahead to kill five people on the track or shift it to a different track and kill one person there. A virtuous person, just like anyone else, can only choose to do one of them, and two equally virtuous persons may make two different choices depending on how they weigh the way in which the virtue of humanity is best manifested. What's more is that both persons can be virtuous not because of the course of action they take but because of there being what Hursthouse calls "moral residue" when they act: their actions are accompanied by some feelings of regret, guilt, remorse, or some other negative feelings as well as desires to make some compensations afterward, if possible, for the party harmed or unhelped (see Hursthouse 1999, 75–77).

The Confucian Conception of Human Nature

As shown above, Confucian ethics, as a virtue ethics, is primarily concerned with how to be a human being with good character, that is, virtue. The question, therefore, is how to determine whether a human being is good or whether a human character is good or virtuous. Here, as Peter Geach has pointed out, the meaning of "good" as an attributive adjective (e.g., "good apple," "good orange," "good human being") cannot be understood without knowing what the thing regarded as good fundamentally is. This is because the meaning of the "good" in "a good apple" is different from the meaning of the "good" in "a good orange." We need to understand what an apple or an orange is before we can understand the meaning of the "good" that describes them (Geach 1956). To determine whether a human being is good or whether a human character trait is good or virtuous, we therefore need to understand what makes one a human being or what human nature is. A good human being is then one whose human nature is properly developed according to that understanding of what it is to be a human being.

Kongzi doesn't have anything explicit to say about human nature; the only thing we can find him saying about it in the *Analects* is that "humans are alike by their nature (*xing* 性) and become different only by what they do" (*Analects* 17.2). Here he doesn't say in what sense humans are alike in their nature. Yet Kongzi does have a clear conception of human nature. Before Kongzi, not only were ritual principles regarded as of utmost importance, but ritual propriety was even considered to be a distinguishing mark of being human (see *Liji* 1.9). As we have seen above, however, for Kongzi, the virtue of humanity (*ren*) is more important than ritual propriety (*li*). Thus, for Kongzi it is *ren* that is constitutive of a human being, not *li*.

The Confucian view of human nature is more fully developed by Mengzi and Xunzi, who are usually taken to be holding contradictory views: human nature is good (*xing shan* 性善) and human nature is bad (*xing e* 性惡), respectively. As we will see, this apparent disagreement is resolved when we understand their different usages of the character for human nature—*xing* 性.

Mengzi argues that human nature consists of four unique qualities: humanity, rightness, propriety, and (moral) wisdom (*zhi* 智). These qualities have corresponding natural manifestations in the feeling of commiseration (humanity); the feeling of shame and dislike (rightness); the feeling of modesty and complaisance (propriety); and the feeling of approval and disapproval (wisdom).

Mengzi claims that humans have these four qualities as naturally as one has four limbs. The strongest argument he uses to show this is his famous example of a child about to fall into a well: upon seeing it, without exception, everyone will have a sense of alarm and distress, motivating them to save the child, without any ulterior motives such as gaining the favor of the child's parents, bolstering their reputation among their neighbors and friends, or avoiding the unpleasant sound of the child's crying (*Mengzi* 2A6).

But it is possible for these qualities to fail to be cultivated, or to wither once grown, and a person who doesn't have these qualities is no longer a genuine human being (*Mengzi* 2A6). Mengzi here aims to make two points. First, although humans having these four qualities is similar to humans having four limbs in one sense, they are different in that a human being will not cease to be a human if they lose one or even all of the four limbs, whereas they will cease to be human if they lose these four qualities. In other words, these four qualities are constitutive of human nature.

Second, what Mengzi has in mind when he talks about people without the four qualities is not what we would call sociopaths or psychopaths today; people with inborn deficiencies. He believes that everyone is born with these moral qualities. But Mengzi argues that these inborn qualities may be lost if one doesn't take good care of them. To illustrate, he makes an analogy between a person who has lost their moral qualities and a mountain that has become barren. The latter does so because its beautiful plants were cut by humans and eaten by animals. Similarly, the former does so because the person has not taken good care of their heart-mind (*Mengzi* 6A8).

Xunzi—another important early Confucian—holds the same view. The common conception is that he contradicts Mengzi on this point since he explicitly says that *xing* 性—the same character for human nature in the *Mengzi*—is bad (*xing e* 性惡), whereas Mengzi holds that it is good (*xing shan* 性善). But to identify the unique feature of being human, Xunzi compares humans with other beings in the following way: water and fire possess vital force but lack life; grasses and trees possess life but lack consciousness; birds and beasts possess consciousness but lack the sense of rightness; but humans possess not only vital force, life, and consciousness but also a sense of rightness (see Knoblock 9.16a). In another place, Xunzi asks, "What makes humans human?" and then responds that it is their ability to distinguish between right and wrong (*bian*

辨), something that animals don't have (see Knoblock 5.4). Hence, despite the apparent disagreement between Mengzi and Xunzi as to human nature, it's clear that for Xunzi the distinguishing mark of being human, as for both Kongzi and Mengzi, is the moral quality.

We can now understand that Xunzi, when discussing this unique feature of being human, doesn't use the character for human nature—*xing* 性—in the same sense that Mengzi does. Xunzi uses it to refer to people's inborn love of benefit, something, or the consequence thereof, he considers to be bad (see Knoblock 23.1b). This difference in the understanding of *xing* is the root cause of the common misunderstanding that Xunzi and Mengzi hold contradictory views on human nature: they are simply not using the word *xing* in the same way.

As a matter of fact, Mengzi and Xunzi agree on what humans are born with. Xunzi claims that humans' love for external benefit is inborn, and this is something even sage kings cannot make people free of. But for Xunzi this is not the only thing that humans are born with. Humans are also born with the love of moral rightness, which is something even wicked kings cannot make people get rid of. It is this latter quality, for Xunzi (as for Mengzi), that distinguishes humans from other animals (see Knoblock 27.63).

Similarly, while Mengzi argues that humans are born with the four moral qualities, he also acknowledges that humans are born with what Xunzi calls love of external benefit: good food for their mouth, beautiful colors for their eyes, pleasing sounds for their ears, good smells for their nose, and comfortable feelings for their four limbs (*Mengzi* 7B24). Mengzi and Xunzi agree that what makes humans human—and different from other animals—is their love for moral rightness. The difference is that Mengzi uses the word *xing* to refer to what makes humans human (which even Xunzi agrees is good), while Xunzi uses the same word to refer to the natural tendency of humans to love profit (which even Mengzi agrees will lead to badness).

The Cultivation of Virtues

In Confucian ethics, a good human being is a being in whom the distinguishing mark of being human is fully developed. A virtue, that is, a good character trait, is one that exemplifies a person *as* a developed human being. While Confucians do believe that everyone is born with this distinguishing mark of being human, they also realize that, because humans are also born with the love for external benefit, there is a need to *cultivate* virtues. In terms of the method by which virtues are cultivated, a significant difference *does* exist between Mengzi and Xunzi. Focusing on the four inborn seeds in human beings, Mengzi stresses the importance of taking good care of them so that they can develop into full virtues. By contrast, paying attention to the inborn love for external benefit in human beings, Xunzi emphasizes the need to regulate this love so that it will not lead to chaos.

MORAL CULTIVATION FOR MENGZI

As we have seen, for Mengzi, as for Xunzi, humans are born with the love of morality, which he regards as original human nature or heart-mind and constitutes the only difference between humans and other animals. What makes superior people different from inferior people is that the former preserve it, while the latter abandon it (*Mengzi* 4B19). So moral cultivation lies in preserving and making sure that this heart-mind will not get lost. One way Mengzi says we can do this is by, when someone does something bad to us, instead of condemning this person, asking ourselves: is there anything in our dealing with them that is not humane or morally proper? (*Mengzi* 4B28).

But this heart-mind *can* be lost, and if so, we ought to seek to get it back. While inferior people, after abandoning their original heart-mind, act much like animals, they are still different from animals in the sense that, if willing, they can seek their lost heart-mind. Hence, while animals are not morally responsible for their lack of virtue, inferior people are, in the same way they would seek their lost chicken, and so they are responsible if they don't. It is in this sense that Mengzi says that for such people the way to learn is nothing but to seek the lost heart-mind (*Mengzi* 6A11).

For Mengzi, the original heart-mind can function naturally only when we are interacting with those who are near and dear to us. Moral cultivation also lies in extending this heart-mind where it initially doesn't function so naturally. We all have natural feelings toward our own family members that we don't have toward others. Moral cultivation aims to help us establish analogies between our parents, children, siblings on the one hand, and the parents, children, and siblings of our neighbors, our villagers, our fellow countrypersons, our fellow human beings, and even non-human beings on the other. As a result, eventually we will be able to be affectionate to our family members, humane to all human beings, and kind to all animals (*Mengzi* 7A45). Additionally, as we have the heart-mind that cannot bear to see the suffering of someone in front of us, but not someone we don't see, moral cultivation aims to help us imagine those people who are suffering out of sight as if they were right in front of us, so that we also will not bear to "see" the suffering of others who are far from us (*Mengzi* 1A7, 7B31).

MORAL CULTIVATION FOR XUNZI

Given Xunzi's emphasis on people's inborn love of benefit, for him cultivation lies primarily in following and practicing ritual and moral principles. These rituals and principles were created by sages to prevent the chaos resulting from people's following their inborn love of benefit without restraint.

People are initially motivated to follow ritual and moral principles largely because they enable people to seek benefit more effectively. Xunzi says, "If in seeking to satisfy their desires men observe no measure and apportion things without limits, then it would be impossible for them not to contend over the means to satisfy their desires. Such contention leads to disorder. Disorder leads to poverty" (Knoblock 19.1a). The sages then created the rituals and principles to allow people to seek benefit in a way that doesn't hinder others doing the same. Thus, Xunzi thinks that if you seek benefit, the most reliable bet is to practice humanity, rightness, and virtue; and the surest way to get into peril is to practice baseness, recklessness, and immorality (see Knoblock 4.8).

Of course, Xunzi realizes that being motivated to follow ritual and moral principles by the love of benefit means that people can at most be said to be prudent; they cannot be regarded as virtuous. However, for Xunzi, while it is indeed the case that people initially follow such moral principles only as a more reliable way

to seek benefit, when they keep practicing ritual and moral principle—especially when coupled with some other measures of moral
cultivation, such as reciting Confucian classics (see Knoblock 1.8)
and drawing near the right person to imitate a role (see Knoblock
1.10, 1.11)—people will gradually realize the internal goodness of
these practices. As a result, they will not stop even when doing so
doesn't bring them any benefit. When they reach such a state of
moral perfection, they will take delight in morality. Their eyes are
unwilling to see, their ears are unwilling to hear, and their mouths
are unwilling to say anything against morality. At this point, "the
exigencies of time and place and considerations of personal profit
cannot influence them, cliques and coteries cannot sway them, and
the whole world cannot deter them" (Knoblock 1.14). This is possible, for Xunzi, because in addition to the love of benefit, which
even sage kings would not make people go without, people are
also born with the love for rightness, which even wicked kings
cannot take away from them.

Is Confucian Ethics Self-Centered?

In Confucian ethics, we ought to cultivate ourselves in order to
become a virtuous person. This contrasts with consequentialism—
which enjoins one to produce the best consequence for the largest
number of people—and deontology—which bids one to follow
moral principles. This contrast is unfavorable to Confucianism
because the ideal person in Confucian ethics seems to be self-centered: we do everything in order to become a virtuous person
ourselves. By contrast, the ideal person in consequentialism and
deontology subordinates their interests in order to bring about
good states of affairs or abide by moral principles.

To respond to this charge of self-centeredness, it has to be first
acknowledged that Confucian ethics, as a type of virtue ethics, does
hold that virtue benefits its possessor. It does so in at least three
different senses. First, it pays to be virtuous. Kongzi, for example,
says that while "a superior person seeks the moral way and not the
food . . . If one learns [to be a moral person], emolument will naturally accompany it" (*Analects* 15.32). Similarly, when Mengzi advises
his king to be humane to his people, he draws attention to the fact

that there has never been a case in which the king is humane to his people and yet his people don't obey him (*Mengzi* 6B4).

Second, since human nature consists of virtue, virtue makes its possessor a genuine human being (which is primarily of benefit to that person themselves).

Third, when a virtuous person does moral things, he or she takes delight in them and thus lives a better life than those who have to rely on their will to fight against their natural inclinations in order to do moral things.

However, these three considerations don't mean that a virtuous Confucian is unconcerned with the interests of others. Indeed, the second and third senses in which the virtuous person is self-interested show precisely that the virtuous person *is* other-interested. This is because Confucian virtues—particularly the four cardinal ones; humanity, rightness, propriety, and moral wisdom—are all other-regarding virtues. One cannot have the virtue of humanity, for example, without doing—and *desiring* to do—benevolent things for people in need.

Indeed, this aspect of altruism of Confucian ethics is shared by Aristotelian ethics, which characterizes a virtuous person as a true self-lover: a person who loves the most noble thing in himself or herself, that is, virtue. This self-love then inclines the person to love others. However, a virtuous person in the Confucian tradition is altruistic in a sense in which Aristotle's true self-lover is not. While Aristotle's self-lover does love both himself and others, there is an asymmetry between these two kinds of love. When he loves himself, he is concerned about his internal well-being (virtue); but when he loves others, he is concerned about their external well-being (wealth, health, and honor) (see Aristotle 2014, 173; *Nicomachean Ethics* 1168b25–30). It is in this sense that such a person is criticized as self-centered (see Solomon 1997, 172; Williams 1985, 34, 50).

By contrast, a virtuous person in the Confucian tradition is virtuous not simply because he or she takes care of others' external *well-being*, but also because he or she wants to make others *virtuous*. Kongzi says, "one who wants to get established (*li* 立)[2] ought to help others get established; and one who wants to get completed (*da* 達)[3] ought to help others get completed" (*Analects* 6.30). Hence, when a person wants to get established in her own virtue, he or she should help others get established in their virtue as well.

Even so, one may wonder whether a virtuous person in the Confucian tradition is still self-centered in Thomas Hurka's foundational sense: the reason a virtuous person is concerned about others' well-being, both external and internal, is that he or she wants to be a virtuous person him- or herself. In other words, the person's goal is to become a virtuous person, but because of the special nature of this goal, it cannot be reached unless the person is concerned with others' well-being, with the latter being regarded as an instrument for the former (Hurka 2001, 232).

To such an objection, one might respond that the virtuous person is in fact foundationally or ultimately other-regarding or altruistic. This person acts for his or her own sake only in the sense that he or she seeks to realize her own goal, but that goal itself is to enhance others' well-being. Understood in this way, the good of the virtuous agent is reduced to the good of others. However, instead of self-indulgence (i.e., self-centeredness), a virtuous person now turns out to be self-effacing (see Hurka 2001, 246), which is also arguably something to be avoided in a moral theory.

To avoid the dilemma between self-indulgence and self-effacingness, a proper Confucian response is that virtues naturally benefit both oneself *and* others. We should not see them as independent; a virtuous person cannot have one without having the other, or have one before the other. A virtuous person cannot be an altruist (serving the interests of others) without taking good care of their own internal well-being. In this sense, an altruist has to be an "egoist." However, one cannot be an "egoist" (taking care of one's own internal well-being) without serving the interests of others. In this sense, the Confucian "egoist" has to be an altruist.

If so, on the one hand we can no longer think that such a person is foundationally egoistic, as it is odd to say that the person acts altruistically only because the person wants to be an altruistic person and not because he or she or she really wants to act altruistically. But we also cannot claim that a person truly acts altruistically only when he or she does not want to be an altruistic person. On the other hand, we cannot say that a virtuous person is self-effacing, for being virtuous is the kind of person he or she wants to be.

In short, the virtuous person is completely "egoistic" and completely "altruistic" simultaneously. A virtuous person acts entirely for the sake of their true self and is thus completely ego-istic. However, this is only because the virtuous person defines his or her true self as one concerned with the good of others; he or she is thus entirely altruistic. Altruism and egoism completely overlap. Wittgenstein's famous duck-rabbit image is useful here. A virtuous person looks like an egoist in one way and an altruist in another way. If egoism is taken away, altruism is gone too, and vice versa. Thus, Confucian ethics is immune to the self-centeredness objection.

Summary

Because of its emphasis on virtue, its focus on the goodness of the agent rather than the rightness of the action, the spontaneity and joy when one acts morally, and the primacy of the virtue of the agent over consequences and rules, we take Confucian ethics to be a virtue ethics. For Confucians, what makes humans human is their moral capacity. Everyone is able to be moral and virtuous if they cultivate themselves.

While agreeing on the above, different Confucian philosophers hold slightly different views. Mengzi focuses more directly on the moral qualities and suggests their extension, whereas Xunzi pays more attention to our inborn love for external benefit and suggests the use of ritual propriety to regulate and reshape ourselves.

Finally, Confucian ethics can answer the challenge of self-cen-teredness. The virtuous person is completely "egoistic" and com-pletely "altruistic" simultaneously: it is egoistic acting for his or her true self, while altruistic since his or her true self is taken to be one concerned with others' well-being. Altruism and egoism completely overlap.

Notes

1. The faculty of cognition and affection.
2. Forming one's moral character.
3. This is explained by Kongzi in terms of uprightness (zhi 直) (*Analects* 12.20).

Further Reading

PRIMARY SOURCES

Bloom, Irene, trans. 2009. *Mencius*. New York: Columbia University Press.
Knoblock, John. 1988–1994. *Xunzi: A Translation and Study of the Complete Work*. 3 vols. Stanford: Stanford University Press.
Lau, D. C., trans. 2000. *The Analects*. Hong Kong: The Chinese University Press.
Ni, Peimin, trans. 2017. *Understanding the Analects of Confucius: A New Translation of Lunyu with Annotations*. Albany, NY: State University of New York Press.
Zhu, Xi 朱熹 1994. *Collected Commentaries on the Four Books* 四書章句集注 Taipei: Da'an chubanshe 大安出版社.

SECONDARY SOURCES

Aristotle. 2014. *Nicomachean Ethics*, translated by Roger Crisp. Cambridge: Cambridge University Press.
Geach, Peter. 1956. "Good and Evil." *Analysis* 17, no. 2: 33–42.
Hurka, Thomas. 2001. *Virtue, Vice, and Value*. Oxford: Oxford University Press.
Hursthouse, Rosalind. 1999. *On Virtue Ethics*. Oxford: Oxford University Press.
Solomon, David. 1997. "Internal Objections to Virtue Ethics." In *Virtue Ethics: A Critical Reader*, edited by Daniel Statman. Washington, DC: Georgetown University Press.
Van Zyl, Liezl. 2011. "Right Action and the Non-Virtuous Agent." *Journal of Applied Philosophy* 28, no. 1: 80–92.
Williams, Bernard. 1985. *Ethics and Limits of Philosophy*. Cambridge, MA: Harvard University Press.

3

Virtue Ethics in Early Buddhism

DAMIEN KEOWN

Introduction

Given its distinctive features, many scholars consider Buddhist ethics to be sui generis and are skeptical that it can be assimilated to Western paradigms (Vélez de Cea 2004, 138; Harvey 2000, 49–51; 2010). Contrary to such views, this chapter suggests that Buddhism can be accommodated within the framework of conventional ethical taxonomies as a form of virtue-based eudaimonism. The chapter focuses on the first few centuries of Buddhism in India from its origins in the late fourth century BCE down to the rise of Mahāyāna Buddhism shortly before the turn of the millennium. The primary sources consulted are those belonging to the canon of the Theravāda school, the only early school to have survived down to modern times.

Eudaimonism plays a central role in the ethics of the ancient world, and not only in the West. Confucianism, for example, exhibits similarities to Aristotle's eudaimonism (Sim 2007; 2018; Yu 2007; Angle and Slote 2013; Ivanhoe 2013). Justin Tiwald reports that "the Confucians tend to give shape to their theories of virtue by appealing to the nature of human beings, ideals of human flourishing, and accounts of ideal moral agents, all of these being characteristic ways of justifying or explaining a theory of virtues for Aristotle and later Aristotelians" (2018). For "the Confucians" here we could simply substitute "the Buddhists."[1]

There is much to be learned by triangulating between the teachings of Aristotle, the Buddha, and Confucius, all of whom I regard as exponents of virtue-based eudaimonism. Illuminating though such an exercise might be, however, I confine myself here to Aristotle and the Buddha, both of whom teach that happiness is the highest good and that virtue makes a non-derivative contribution to well-being. As Aristotle observes, "Since happiness is an activity of soul in accordance with complete virtue, we must consider the nature of virtue; for perhaps we shall thus see better the nature of happiness" (NE 1102a5–7).

Given methodological concerns about imposing Western theoretical concepts on the indigenous data, I work from the ground up here in justifying the classification of Buddhist ethics just proposed. This involves reviewing an indigenous formulation of doctrine (the four noble truths) to illustrate the centrality of virtue in Buddhist teachings and its intimate relation to happiness. This task occupies the first half of the chapter. The second explores axiological parallels between the Aristotelian and Buddhist concepts of well-being. On a semantic note, I use the terms *happiness, eudaimonia, nirvāṇa,* and *well-being* interchangeably, reserving *welfare* for conventional or prudential goods like health, wealth, beauty, and reputation.[2]

Virtue

One reason to favor a virtue-based interpretation of Buddhism is that references to virtue are ubiquitous in its teachings. This fact by itself, of course, is not conclusive and may constitute a purely "factoral" feature (Kagan 1998) compatible with a conception of Buddhism as "virtue theory" rather than "virtue ethics" (Driver 1998).[3] As will become clear, however, the *summum bonum* (highest good) of *nirvāṇa*—and the Buddhist saint who attains it—are characterized most fundamentally by virtue. While welfare plays a role in the Buddhist conception of well-being, it is, I suggest, a derivative one.

The most fundamental Buddhist teaching is known as "the four noble truths." The first noble truth observes that suffering (*dukkha*) is endemic in human existence; the second attributes the arising of suffering to desire (*taṇhā*); the third proclaims that suffering can be ended (*nirodha*) by attaining the state known as *nirvāṇa*; and the fourth sets out the path (*magga*) that leads to this elevated state. The Buddha was often compared to a physician, and his teachings to a medicine such that the four noble truths provide a diagnosis and cure for the sickness that afflicts sentient life.

The emphasis on welfare (suffering and its alleviation) in this doctrinal formulation might initially lead us to suppose that consequentialism would provide the best explanatory framework for Buddhist ethics. Thus, Buddhism could be classified as a form of "negative utilitarianism" and its moral teachings understood as an instrumental means to minimize the "disutility" of suffering (Breyer 2015). On this analysis, virtue or moral good would be a means to non-moral or prudential good, as taught, for example, by Epicurus.[4] More sophisticated versions of consequentialism might attribute intrinsic worth to virtue, as in forms of "character consequentialism" (Clayton 2006; 2009; Goodman 2009), but such hybrid strategies face intractable problems of axiological incommensurability. We will return to the relation between virtue and welfare in the second half of the chapter.

While a concern with welfare looms large in the first noble truth, I think we will see from the other three that it is virtue rather than welfare that grounds this doctrinal formula. Like Stoicism, Buddhism attaches relatively little importance to hedonic (pleasure-focused) values. Such things pertain to the "mundane" (*lokiya*) sphere of worldly welfare, in contrast to the supreme or "supramundane" (*lokuttara*) sphere of virtue. Countless passages make clear that the pursuit of prudential values in isolation from virtue subverts the nirvanic *telos* (aim).

Contrary to standard interpretations, then, I suggest that the "disease" for which Buddhism seeks a cure is not suffering. Suffering, rather, is a *symptom* of the disease. But if suffering is not the disease, then what is? The diagnosis is given in the second noble truth, which defines the cause of suffering as *taṇhā*. The familiar translation of *taṇhā* as "desire" requires qualification, for Buddhism does not condemn all desire (Morrison 1997). On the contrary, it values desire for the good, or virtuous desire (Dhp 118). To bring out this contrast, *taṇhā* is better rendered here as "ego-driven desire" or "craving."[5] In Buddhist exegesis, *taṇhā* is identified with the three "roots of evil" (*akusalamūla*), these being three basic vices of greed or acquisitiveness (*rāga*), hatred or aversion (*dosa*), and ignorance or delusion (*moha*). Greed and hatred denote ingrained emotional traits, while delusion signifies intellectual confusion about what is good and true. From this toxic matrix springs a cascade of subsidiary vices like conceit, envy, avarice, sloth, and others familiar from any taxonomy of moral psychology.

The "disease" that gives rise to suffering is thus a form of emotional and cognitive disorder. The dynamic at work here is that ignorance of the good leads to the pursuit of false values (*vipallāsa*) and ultimately to the cycle of disappointment and frustration known as *saṃsāra*. The antidote to suffering, unsurprisingly, is the correction of the maladjustment just described through eradication of the vices that give rise to it. This is why *nirvāṇa* is known as "the extinction of the vices" (*kilesa-parinibbāna*) and is defined as "the end of greed, hatred, and delusion" (SN 38.1). These three vices are also referred to as "fires," and "*nirvāṇa*" is explained etymologically as the "blowing out" of these fires.[6]

As the individual makes progress to *nirvāṇa*, the three root vices are not merely extinguished but replaced by their opposing virtues, namely the three "virtuous roots" (*kusalamūla*), or "cardinal virtues" of unselfishness (*arāga*), benevolence (*adosa*), and understanding (*amoha*). The saint (*arahant*) who attains this state is distinguished from the untutored "worldly" person (*putthujjana*) not so much by the absence of suffering (even saints suffer) as by accomplishment in virtue.

So much for suffering and its cause. What, then, is the "medicine"? The answer is provided in the fourth noble truth, that of the "way" or "path" (*magga*) that leads to *nirvāṇa*. This path consists of eight factors, namely right view, right intention, right speech, right action, right livelihood, right effort, right mindfulness, and right meditation. We see from the prefix "right" (*sammā*) that the eight factors are normative. They derive their normativity from the *telos*: since following the path is something we do, we can do it well or badly. Doing it well means cultivating attitudes and performing actions inspired by the three virtuous roots, and doing it badly means the opposite. The kind of acts typically inspired by these dispositions are codified in action-guiding norms and precepts.

The eight factors mentioned above are grouped into three areas of "training" (*sikkhā*), namely Morality (*sīla*), Meditation (*samādhi*), and Wisdom (*paññā*). The foundational nature of Morality (*sīla*) is signaled by placing this category first in standard formulations of the eightfold path.[7] Morality (Pali: *sīla*; Skt: *śīla*) includes right speech, right action, and right livelihood. It involves the exercise of self-restraint, propriety, and respect for the precepts, combined with the cultivation of a range of virtuous traits and dispositions. This emphasis on self-cultivation reveals that Buddhism views moral conduct primarily from a first-person "agent-centered" perspective; that is, it matters *who* performs an action, not merely that the action is performed *by someone*. This is not to suggest it thinks acts are unimportant (Fink 2013), but merely that it sees good actions as flowing naturally from a virtuous (*kusala*) character. Which traits are to be cultivated? We have already referred to the three "cardinal virtues," and other commonly mentioned virtues are generosity (*dāna*), non-harming (*ahiṃsā*), renunciation (*nekkhamma*), energy (*viriya*), patience (*khanti*), concern (*dayā*), mindfulness (*sati*), and compassion (*karuṇā*).

The second category of the eightfold path, Meditation, includes right effort, right mindfulness, and right meditation. Right effort (*sammā vāyāma*) means developing the mind by practicing mindfulness and mental cultivation and replacing negative thoughts with positive and wholesome ones. Right mindfulness (*sammā sati*) means developing constant awareness in four areas: in relation to the body, feelings, mood or mental state, and thoughts. It also involves eliminating negative traits such as the five "hindrances" (*nīvaraṇa*), namely desire for sensual pleasure, ill will, sloth and drowsiness, worry and agitation, and nagging doubts.

Right meditation (*sammā samādhi*) means developing mental clarity and calm by concentrating the mind through meditational exercises. These exercises develop the mind and the emotions through two dedicated techniques. "Insight meditation" (*vipassanā*) develops the epistemic virtue of wisdom (*paññā*) enabling firsthand validation of the four noble truths. "Calming meditation" (*samatha*) aims at the cultivation of feelings of moral concern and is closely linked to the practice of the four "Divine Abodes" (*brahma-vihāras*), namely loving kindness (*mettā*), compassion (*karuṇā*), sympathetic joy (*muditā*), and equanimity (*upekkhā*). Here we note a discrepancy with Aristotle, for whom contemplation (*theoria*) is passive in nature and as such is a virtuous *activity* rather than a virtue. In Buddhism, by contrast, contemplation (*samādhi*) is a spiritual practice that has a dynamic role in promoting moral and intellectual virtue.

The third component of the eightfold path is Wisdom (*paññā*). This category embraces two items: right view and right intention. Right view (*sammā diṭṭhi*) means accepting the validity of the four noble truths and is explained as at minimum belief in the law of *karma*, respect for parents and religious teachers, and the possibility of personal spiritual progress. Right intention (*sammā saṅkappa*) means making a commitment to attaining freedom from sensual desires (*kāma*), abandoning hatred (*avyāpāda*), and abstaining from causing harm to others (*ahiṃsā*). "Wisdom," then, involves both cognitive and conative elements and embraces "theoretical under-standing, experiential insight, and practical wisdom" (MacKenzie 2018, 164).

With respect to practical decision-making, normative guidance is available from various sources. We have already referred to the existence of action-guiding norms and precepts. Various formula-tions of precepts are available, the most basic being a list known as the "Five Precepts" (*pañca-sīla*), which prohibit taking life, stealing, sexual misconduct, lying, and consuming intoxicants. These precepts are followed by the laity, while monks and nuns follow a more extensive and elaborate code of conduct known as the Vinaya, a monastic code comparable to the Rule of St. Benedict in Christian monasticism. Also important in normative terms is the principle of the "golden rule," which in the Buddhist formulation counsels us *not* to do to others what we would not wish done to ourselves. As Scheible observes: "In Theravāda Buddhism, the Golden Rule is not equivalent to the precept to 'love your neighbor as yourself,' but rather 'do no harm to your neighbor as you would do no harm to yourself.' Love and nonharm are separate paths of action, while they may stem from the same wellspring" (2008, 126). While the above norms and precepts provide general guidance, not all moral decisions are codifiable, and rules cannot be specified in advance for every case. Since Buddhism is a form of virtue ethics, it does not offer a test or "decision procedure" comparable to Kant's "categorical imperative" or consequentialism's principle of utility that can be used as a "tie-breaker" in resolving moral dilemmas. Instead, Buddhism takes the view that the virtuous agent will, like the Aristotelian person of practical wisdom (*phronimos*) or the Confucian sage (*junzi*), develop "a connoisseur-like expertise to perceive order and rightness, and to act accordingly" (Loy 2014, 289). Such a person, as Battaley puts it, "*knows* which actions are conducive to the good life. She deliberates well, judges well and perceives the world as she should" (2014, 180). The intellectual virtue of practical wisdom may be thought of as the hub to which the moral virtues are attached. The two classes of virtue operate in tandem: the moral virtues order the sentiments toward what is conducive to well-being, while the intellectual virtue of practical wisdom selects wise means to attain the desired ends.

The three categories of the eightfold path can be pictured as a triangle in which the three sides brace and support one another. Morality (*sīla*) forms the baseline and is the foundation for religious practice. And just as morality is the foundation for meditation and wisdom, it is strengthened by them in turn since inner calm and clear understanding produce a heightened moral sensibility. Meditation trains the emotions and sharpens the intellectual faculties, making wisdom stronger and more penetrating, and wisdom supports meditation by making clearer and more intelligible the experience of the meditative states. If we understand the interrelationship in this way, we can say that "*nirvāṇa*" is simply a name for the confluence of these three categories. As the Buddha expressed it, "Just as the rivers Ganges and Yamuna merge and flow along united, so too do *nirvāṇa* and the Path" (DN ii.223). As Bhikkhu Bodhi explains, "The two stand together in a bond of reciprocal determination, the path leading to the achievement of the goal and the goal giving form and content to the path" (Bodhi 1980, 17).

Eudaimonia

Having considered the nature of the path, we now turn our attention to the *telos* or goal. An initial observation is that the virtues mentioned above differ to some degree from those mentioned by

Aristotle (and, we might add, Confucius). This is due to different conceptions of the particular human goods that constitute well-being.[8] A further difference is that Aristotle stands within the Socratic tradition that in Cicero's words "called philosophy down from the heavens" (Cicero 2005), so for him the goal of human perfection has no soteriological implications. The comparison that follows, therefore, assumes a "naturalized" understanding of *nirvāṇa* as a state of perfection attained in life (Flanagan 2011; Segall 2020).

The formal similarities between *nirvāṇa* and *eudaimonia* seem clear enough. Aristotle characterizes *eudaimonia* as final (*teleion*), self-sufficient (*autarkes*), and "lacking in nothing" (NE 1097b14–15). He says it is "the end in matters of action" (NE 1097b22) and the "most desirable of all things, without being counted as one good thing among others" (NE 1097b16–17). As Cooper sums up, the final human good has the following characteristics: (a) it is desired for its own sake; (b) everything else that is desired is desired for the sake of it; (c) it is never chosen for the sake of anything else (1975, 92). *Nirvāṇa* seems to fit these formal criteria. Whatever else *nirvāṇa* is, it is indisputably the *summum bonum* of Buddhism and may be characterized, like *eudaimonia*, in the way just described.

As noted, eudaimonists classify and rank human goods in different ways, so disagreements about *eudaimonia* center not on its formal character but its substantive content. Aristotle claimed to offer only a rough outline of *eudaimonia* (NE 1098a20–21), and much ink has been spilt in defending different interpretations of his views. In Book X of the *Nicomachean Ethics*, he appears to suggest that contemplation (*theoria*) is the highest good. Earlier, however, in the main body of the work, he gives the impression that the good life is one of moral virtue. Most commentators take him to mean that both contribute to well-being, while disputing their relative priority. In addition to virtue, Aristotle also holds that conventional or "external" goods are required for happiness.

The intellectual history of Buddhism reveals a similar tension between these rival conceptions of well-being, although less explicitly formulated. Disagreement turns on whether *nirvāṇa* is primarily an intellectual good, a moral good, or a prudential good.[9] The high tradition (scholastics and metaphysicians) unsurprisingly prioritizes intellectual virtue. *Nirvāṇa* is here identified with the epistemic grasp of certain formal doctrines, particularly those concerning causality and the nature of the self. On this view, *eudaimonia* consists in "realizing ourselves as dependently originated, impermanent, and empty" (Snow 2019, 75). It follows that "Unless a person knows something about Buddhist metaphysics she cannot have Buddhist virtue or attain Buddhist *eudaimonia*" (Snow 2019, 87).

This cerebral conception marks one end of a spectrum. At the other end, one clearly visible in the earliest sources, we find a more visceral understanding that discourages interest in views, doctrines, and philosophies. The "Book of Eights" (Aṭṭhakavagga), for instance, according to its translator, "explicitly denies the role of ultimate religious 'truth' and 'knowledge' in attaining personal peace" (Fronsdal 2016, 2). The sage depicted here is not a metaphysician but a meditator who has subdued the passions. Other early sources make scant reference to the epistemological grasp of doctrine that is supposedly an indispensable precondition for well-being.[10] The doctrine of "dependent origination" (*paṭicca-sammuppāda*) so fetishized by later metaphysicians functions here primarily as an illustration of how vice, in the form of craving and ignorance, subverts well-being. Its function is normative and teleological rather than descriptive or phenomenological (Jones 2019).[11]

An authoritative statement by the Buddha, furthermore, makes clear that epistemic virtue is not paramount in the way often portrayed. In the following passage, he declares moral and epistemic virtue to be interdependent and mutually supportive: "Wisdom (*paññā*) is purified by morality (*sīla*) and morality is purified by wisdom. Where one is, the other is, the moral man has wisdom and the wise man has morality, and the combination of morality and wisdom is called the highest thing in the world. Just as one hand washes the other, or one foot the other, so wisdom is purified by morality and this combination is called the highest thing in the world" (DN i.124). The Buddha here defines *eudaimonia* ("the highest thing in the world") as a symbiosis of moral and epistemic virtue. Are we to understand, then, that *nirvāṇa* consists exclusively of these two elements? Such is a common view, supplemented on some accounts by feelings of peace and contentment (Flanagan 2011, 16).[12] On this understanding, the Buddha held a Stoic conception of *eudaimonia* in which external goods play little or no part. This would mark a difference with Aristotle, for whom the possession of external goods makes the life of the virtuous person "better, more attractive, more pleasant as befits a person of excellent character" (Roche 2014, 54).[13]

Buddhist sources contain many Stoic-sounding passages that appear to deny importance to worldly goods.[14] I think it would be a mistake, however, to conclude from this that welfare plays no part in *eudaimonia*, not least because, as we saw from the first noble truth, Buddhism is concerned with suffering. There is, furthermore, a countervailing textual tradition that understands *nirvāṇa* primarily as a "felicity" (Collins 1998) or state of unalloyed welfare of the kind envisaged in utopias the world over.

Perhaps, then, we should understand the Buddha's statement in this way: while the combination of wisdom and moral virtue may be the "highest thing in the world," it does not follow that these are the *only* things in the world that have value. The Buddha's call to adopt a "middle way" followed his realization, after six arduous years of self-mortification, that the rejection of prudential goods was "a blistering way of practice" (*nijjhāmā paṭipadā*) (AN i.295) and as prejudicial to well-being as the overvaluation of the same goods. The post-awakening Buddha is celebrated for his possession of abundant external goods, notably goods of the body like beauty, health, and longevity (Powers 2012; Mrozik 2007), and social goods like honor, reputation, and friendship.

What this suggests is that prudential goods should not be rejected in their entirety, but that prudence must be exercised with respect to them. On this understanding, virtue directs the pursuit and use of external goods, which in turn complete the happiness of the agent. Virtue is thus necessary but not sufficient for happiness. Of course, without virtue, no amount of welfare can help an agent realize happiness, and it would be "ignoble" (unbecoming to the "noble person" or *ariya*) to prioritize welfare over virtue or regard them as of equal worth.[15] The person who pursues prudential good as an end makes a commitment to *saṃsāra* rather than *nirvāṇa* (Dhp 75).

An important final point is that Buddhism teaches that welfare is dependent on virtue and that individuals receive the good or bad fortune they deserve (Dhp 109, 120).[16] Virtuous deeds are said to produce "merit" (*puñña*), a term linked etymologically to the English "boon" and "bounty" (Harvey 2000, 18). Merit manifests itself in "goods of fortune," which complete the happiness of the virtuous agent. The correspondence between the three constitutive elements of well-being is then as shown in table 3.1.

Table 3.1. The Three Components of Well-Being in Aristotle and Buddhism

	Aristotle	Buddhism
1	Moral virtue (*ethike arete*)	Morality (*sīla*)
2	Intellectual virtue (*ethike dianoetike*)	Wisdom (*paññā*)
3	External goods (*ta ektos agatha*)	Merit (*puñña*)

Source: Author's own material.

Summary

In the first half of the chapter, we saw that according to Buddhist teachings, virtue is fundamental to well-being. It was suggested, furthermore, that the relation between virtue and *nirvāṇa* in Buddhism parallels that between virtue and *eudaimonia* as conceived by Aristotle. Despite their cultural and metaphysical differences, it seems fair to say that *nirvāṇa* and *eudaimonia* belong to the family of "natural teleologies" (Flanagan 2014) and share the same ethical architecture or "structural isomorphism" (Flanagan 2011, 155). The central project of both is self-realization through the actualization of natural potential, the parameters of which are defined in Buddhism by the formula of the "five aggregates" (*khandha*). On this account, humans are embodied beings (*rūpa*) who are self-aware (*viññāna*) and endowed with the powers of sensation (*vedanā*), cognition (*saññā*), and will (*saṅkhāra*).[17] *Nirvāṇa* is achieved through the development of these natural capacities, from which we see that human perfection will be complex in nature and extend beyond the actualization of any single faculty, such as the intellect. It will include, for example, goods proper to the body, the sentiments, and the will. On this basis, we can say that Buddhism, like Aristotle, holds a "nature fulfilment" theory of well-being.

In the second half of the chapter, we saw that the *telos* as conceived by Buddhism and Aristotle is constituted by the three components shown in table 3.1. Epistemic virtue, moral virtue, and external goods are individually necessary and collectively sufficient for happiness. We might term this a *"nirvāṇa+"* conception of well-being in contrast to the more familiar moralized version that includes only the first two items in the table. In terms of the medical metaphor mentioned at the start, the healthy (virtuous or excellent) person is free from the symptoms of disease (suffering). Since freedom from suffering is attributable to the "merit" (*puñña*) accrued through virtue, we might say that welfare is an epiphenomenon of virtue. It follows that if virtue or excellence is foundational, *nirvāṇa* is most appropriately classified as an "excellence prior" (Toner 2015) rather than "welfare prior" form of *eudaimonia* (Baril 2013; LeBar 2018); if the four noble truths are understood in the way suggested in this chapter, the motivation to attain *nirvāṇa* is not the avoidance of suffering but the pursuit of excellence. In Buddhism, this excellence extends, as it does for Aristotle, to social engagement, an engagement epitomized in the Buddha's decision to teach the Dhamma and the heroic mission of the *bodhisattva* to save sentient beings.[18]

Notes

1. For parallels between Confucian and Buddhist ethics, see An (1998) and Cokelet (2016).

2. All references to *nirvāṇa* are to "*nirvāṇa* in this life" (*sopādisesa-nibbāna*). This is the state attained by a living human being, as in the case of the Buddha, who is said to have attained it at the age of thirty-five. It precedes the postmortem metaphysical state of "final" *nirvāṇa* (*anup-adisesa-nibbāna*) reportedly attained by the Buddha on his death at the age of eighty.

3. In essence, "Virtue theory is the area of enquiry concerned with the virtues in general; virtue ethics is narrower and prescriptive and consists primarily in the advocacy of the virtues" (Crisp 1996, 5). Alternatively, "Virtue *theories* offer accounts of what virtues are, and can be parts of larger ethical theories, such as Kantianism and utilitarianism. By contrast, virtue *ethics* is a type of ethical theory that prizes virtue as its central concept" (Snow 2018, 321).

4. "By pleasure we mean the absence of pain in the body and of torment in the soul . . . Of all this the beginning and the greatest good is prudence . . . For . . . it is not possible to live pleasantly unless one lives prudently, honorably, and justly" (Miller 2018, 388).

5. Etymologically, *taṇhā* derives from a root meaning "thirst," and thirst (as desire) can be for both good and bad things.

6. *Nirvāṇa* is not, of course, the "blowing out" or extinction of a "self" (*atta*) since a self—understood as an unchanging ego—does not

exist, according to Buddhist teachings. Buddhism nevertheless recognizes the existence of a subsisting moral agent: in the absence of such agency the canonical depiction of *nirvāṇa* as a *telos* attained over time (Dhp 239) would make little sense (Hanner 2018).

7. This heuristic model unfortunately has often been understood in evaluative terms as ranking morality as inferior to wisdom. Thus G. P. Malalasekera writes: "Buddhism has never regarded *Sīla* as an end in itself but only a means to an end. This conception of morality is, I believe, unique in Buddhism" (Horner 1950).

8. As Yu notes, "it remains one of the major tasks for contemporary virtue ethics to work out a relatively undisputed list that can be applied to all human beings" (2007, 162).

9. To take an example from Mahāyāna Buddhism, many sources eulogize *karuṇā*, or moral virtue, while others, like the "Perfection of Wisdom" (*prajñāpāramita*) literature, prioritize epistemic virtue (*paññā*) in a manner similar to the Socratic conception of *eudaimonia*.

10. For example, firsthand accounts of *nirvāṇa* in the Theragāthā (Norman 2015a) and Therīgāthā (Norman 2015b) do not prioritize the role of metaphysics. Greater emphasis is placed on austerity in lifestyle, control of the passions, and exertion in meditation. The same is true of the *Dhammapada*, which is "among the most popular canonical texts in the Buddhist world" (Carter and Palihawadana 2000, xi). The *Dhammapada* makes no reference to dependent origination in its 423 verses and alludes to the selflessness of phenomena only once (Dhp 279). It characterizes the path to *nirvāṇa* primarily as a struggle against the vices. Some scholars (Horner 1936; Burford 1991; Egge 2015) believe this earlier conception of well-being was undermined by a growing pessimism on the part of scholar-monks and a conviction that the problem of suffering could be solved only through epistemic means.

11. It seems worth asking whether an alternative metaphysical underpinning for Buddhist eudaimonism might be possible. Aristotle's eudaimonism is compatible with his metaphysics of actuality and potentiality, form and matter, and efficient causality and teleology. There seems nothing here that contradicts the Buddha's teachings on impermanence and no-self or is incompatible with natural science (Feser 2019). As regards the nature of the self, Flanagan suggests that "a plausible argument can be mounted that the Aristotelian view is the best on offer" (Flanagan 2011, 161).

12. Flanagan defines Buddhist *eudaimonia* as a stable sense of serenity and contentment caused or constituted by wisdom, virtue, and meditation.

13. We may note that the author of one early work on Buddhist ethics favoured the Stoic position and believed that Buddhism—and Indian thought in general—rejected the idea that external goods were

required for happiness. The venerable Saddhatissa saw this as "another basic difference between the line of Indian thought and that of the later Greek ethics from Aristotle onwards, for where the Nicomachean Ethics allows external goods to be necessary in the practical life of combining prudence and moral virtue as instruments of moral action, and in the highest life of the intellect as a means of physical subsistence, Indian thought offered nothing so accommodating" (Saddhatissa 1987, 22).

14. For example, "the eight worldly conditions" are described as follows: "Gain and loss, disrepute and fame, blame and praise, pleasure and pain: these conditions that people meet are impermanent, transient, and subject to change. A wise and mindful person knows them and sees that they are subject to change. Desirable conditions don't excite his mind nor is he repelled by undesirable conditions" (AN iv.157). I see such statements as counseling equanimity toward external goods rather than their rejection.

15. For this reason, it is difficult to see how a consequentialist formulation can capture the required axiological alignment. A purely enumerative "objective list" itemizing virtue and welfare (Goodman 2009) is insufficiently nuanced to reflect the evaluative priority Buddhism attaches to virtue. A related problem for such pluralistic formulations is to explain how virtue and welfare, as incommensurable values, are to be aggregated and "balanced" in the assessment of outcomes.

16. This, of course, is the doctrine of *karma*. Traditional Buddhists understand *karma* as a form of metaphysical causation, whereas "Buddhist modernists" favor a naturalistic interpretation.

17. *Saṅkhāra* is a complex term with many meanings, but in this context it denotes the constellation of psychological factors that constitute the character of an individual. Chief among these factors, because of its role in generating *karma* and shaping character, is *cetanā*, the faculty of intention, volition, or will.

18. Defining *eudaimonia* in terms of excellence blunts the familiar critique of eudaimonism as egoistic. It would be odd, for example, to criticize an athlete who pursued excellence in sport as "egoistic," particularly when participating as a member of a team.

Further Reading

PRIMARY SOURCES / ABBREVIATIONS

AN *Aṅguttara Nikāya*. English translation by Bhikkhu Bodhi. 2012. *The Numerical Discourses of the Buddha: A Complete Translation of the Aṅguttara Nikāya*. Boston: Wisdom Publications.

Dhp *Dhammapada*. English translation by K. R. Norman, 1997. *Word of the Doctrine (Dhammapada)*. Oxford: Pali Text Society.

DN *Dīgha Nikāya*. English translation by Maurice Walshe. 1996. *Long Discourses of the Buddha: Translation of the Dīgha Nikāya*. 2nd rev. ed. Boston: Wisdom Publications.

NE *Nicomachean Ethics*. English translation by Jonathan Barnes and Anthony Kenny. 2014. *Aristotle's Ethics. Writings from the Complete Works*. Princeton: Princeton University Press.

SN *Saṃyutta Nikāya*. English translation by Bhikkhu Bodhi. 1999. *Connected Discourses of the Buddha: A Translation of the Saṃyutta Nikāya*. Boston: Wisdom Publications.

SECONDARY SOURCES

An, Ok-Sun. 1998. *Compassion and Benevolence: A Comparative Study of Early Buddhist and Classical Confucian Ethics*. New York: Peter Lang Publishing.

Angle, Stephen, and Michael Slote. 2013. *Virtue Ethics and Confucianism*. London: Routledge.

Baril, Anne. 2013. "The Role of Welfare in *Eudaimonia*." *Southern Journal of Philosophy* 51: 511–35.

Battaly, Heather. 2014. "Intellectual Virtues." In *The Handbook of Virtue*, edited by Stan Van Hooft, 177–87. Durham: Acumen.

Bodhi, Bhikkhu. 1980. "Transcendental Dependent Arising: A Translation and Exposition of the Upanisa Sutta." *Wheel Publication*: 1–93.

Breyer, Daniel. 2015. "The Cessation of Suffering and Buddhist Axiology." *Journal of Buddhist Ethics* 22: 533–60.

Burford, Grace G. 1991. *Desire, Death and Goodness: The Conflict of Ultimate Values in Theravada Buddhism*. New York: Peter Lang Publishing.

Carter, John Ross, and Mahinda Palihawadana, trans. 2000. *Dhammapada*. Oxford: Oxford University Press.

Cicero, Marcus Tullius. 2005. *Cicero's Tusculan Disputations*. Project Gutenberg. https://www.gutenberg.org/files/14988/14988-h/14988-h.htm.

Clayton, Barbra R. 2009. "Śāntideva, Virtue and Consequentialism." In *Destroying Māra Forever: Buddhist Ethics Essays in Honor of Damien Keown*, edited by John Powers and Charles S. Prebish. Ithaca, NY: Snow Lion.

———. 2006. *Moral Theory in Śāntideva's Śikṣāsamuccaya: Cultivating the Fruits of Virtue*. London: Routledge.

Cokelet, Bradford. 2016. "Confucianism, Buddhism, and Virtue Ethics." *European Journal for the Philosophy of Religion* 8, no. 1: 187–214. https://doi.org/10.24204/ejpr.v8i1.75.

Collins, Steven. 1998. *Nirvana and Other Buddhist Felicities: Utopias of the Pali Imaginaire.* Cambridge: Cambridge University Press.

Crisp, Roger. 1996. *How Should One Live?: Essays on the Virtues.* Oxford: Clarendon Press.

Davis, Leesa. 2014. "Mindfulness, Non-Attachment, and Other Buddhist Virtues." In *The Handbook of Virtue Ethics,* edited by Stan van Hooft, 306–17. Abingdon, Oxon: Routledge.

Driver, Julia. 1998. "The Virtues and Human Nature." In *How Should One Live,* edited by Roger Crisp, 111–30. New York: Oxford University Press.

Egge, James. 2015. *Religious Giving and the Invention of Karma in Theravada Buddhism.* Abingdon, Oxon: Routledge.

Feser, Edward. 2019. *Aristotle's Revenge: The Metaphysical Foundations of Physical and Biological Science.* Neunkirchen-Seelscheid: Editiones scholasticae.

Fink, Charles K. 2013. "The Cultivation of Virtue in Buddhist Ethics." *Journal of Buddhist Ethics* 20: 668–94.

Flanagan, Owen. 2011. *The Bodhisattva's Brain: Buddhism Naturalized.* Cambridge, MA: MIT Press.

———. 2015. "It Takes a Metaphysics: Raising Virtuous Buddhists." In *Cultivating Virtue. Perspectives from Philosophy, Theology, and Psychology,* edited by Nancy E. Snow, 171–95. Oxford: Oxford University Press.

———. 2014. *Moral Sprouts and Natural Teleologies: 21st Century Moral Psychology Meets Classical Chinese Philosophy.* Milwaukee, WI: Marquette University Press.

Fronsdal, Gil. 2016. *The Buddha before Buddhism: Wisdom from the Early Teachings.* Boulder, CO: Shambhala Publications.

Goodman, C. 2009. *Consequences of Compassion: An Interpretation and Defense of Buddhist Ethics.* Oxford: Oxford University Press.

Hanner, Oren. 2018. "Moral Agency and the Paradox of Self-Interested Concern for the Future in Vasubandhu's *Abhidharmakośabhāṣya.*" *Sophia* 57, no. 4: 591–609. https://doi.org/10.1007/s11841-018-0642-0.

Harvey, Peter. 2000. *An Introduction to Buddhist Ethics: Foundations, Values and Issues.* Cambridge: Cambridge University Press.

———. 2010. "An Analysis of Factors Related to the *Kusala/Akusala* Quality of Actions in the Pāli Tradition." *Journal of the International Association of Buddhist Studies* 33, no. 1–2. https://doi.org/175–209. 10.2143/JIABS.33.1.3144320.

Horner, I. B. 1936. *The Early Buddhist Theory of Man Perfected.* London: Williams and Norgate.

———. 1950. *The Basic Position of Sīla.* Colombo: Bauddha Sahitya Sabha.

Ivanhoe, Philip J. 2013. "Virtue Ethics and the Chinese Confucian Tradition." In *The Cambridge Companion to Virtue Ethics*, edited by Daniel C. Russell, 49–69. Cambridge: Cambridge University Press.

Jones, Dhivan Thomas. 2019. "A Teleological Mode of Conditionality in Early Buddhism." *International Journal of Buddhist Thought & Culture* 29, no. 2: 119–49. https://doi.org/10.16893/IJBTC.2019.06.29.2.119.

Kagan, Shelley. 1998. *Normative Ethics*. Boulder, CO: Westview Press.

LeBar, Mark. 2018. "Eudaimonism." In *The Oxford Handbook of Virtue*, edited by Nancy E. Snow, 1–21. Oxford: Oxford University Press.

Loy, Hui-chieh. 2014. "Classical Confucianism as Virtue Ethics." In *The Handbook of Virtue Ethics*, edited by Stan Van Hooft, 285–93. Durham: Acumen.

MacKenzie, Matthew. 2018. "Buddhism and the Virtues." In *The Oxford Handbook of Virtue*, edited by Nancy E. Snow, 153–70. Oxford: Oxford University Press.

Miller, James, ed. 2018. *Lives of the Eminent Philosophers: By Diogenes Laertius*. Translated by Pamela Mensch. New York: Oxford University Press.

Morrison, Robert. 1997. "Three Cheers for *Taṇhā*." *Western Buddhist Review* 2.

Mrozik, S. 2007. *Virtuous Bodies: The Physical Dimensions of Morality in Buddhist Ethics*. Oxford: Oxford University Press.

Norman, K. R. 2015a. *Elders' Verses (Vol. I)*. Oxford: Pali Text Society.

———. 2015b. *Elders' Verses (Vol. II)*. Oxford: Pali Text Society.

Powers, John. 2012. *Bull of a Man*. Cambridge: Harvard University Press.

Roche, T. D. 2014. "Happiness and the External Goods." In *The Cambridge Companion to Aristotle's Nicomachean Ethics*, edited by Ronald Polansky, 34–63. New York: Cambridge University Press.

Scheible, Kristin. 2008. "The Formulation and Significance of the Golden Rule in Buddhism I." In *The Golden Rule. Ethics of Reciprocity in World Religions*, edited by Jacob Neusner and Bruce Chilton, 116–28. London: Continuum International Publishing Group.

Segall, Seth Zuiho. 2020. *Buddhism and Human Flourishing: A Modern Western Perspective*. Cham: Palgrave Macmillan.

Sim, May. 2007. *Remastering Morals with Aristotle and Confucius*. Cambridge: Cambridge University Press.

———. 2018. "The Phronimos and the Sage." In *The Oxford Handbook of Virtue*, edited by Nancy E. Snow. Oxford Handbooks Online. Oxford: Oxford University Press.

Snow, Nancy E. 2018. "Neo-Aristotelian Virtue Ethics." In *The Oxford Handbook of Virtue*, edited by Nancy E. Snow, 322–42. New York: Oxford University Press.

———. 2019. "Metaphysics, Virtue, and *Eudaimonia* in Aristotle and Buddhism." In *Naturalism, Human Flourishing, and Asian Philosophy. Owen Flanagan and Beyond*, edited by Bongrae Seok, 74–91. London: Routledge.

Tiwald, Justin. 2018. "Confucianism and Neo-Confucianism." In *The Oxford Handbook of Virtue*, edited by Nancy E. Snow, 171–89. Oxford Handbooks Online. Oxford: Oxford University Press.

Toner, Christopher. 2015. "Virtue Ethics and Egoism." In *The Routledge Companion to Virtue Ethics*, edited by Lorraine Besser-Jones and Michael Slote, 345–57. New York: Routledge.

Vélez de Cea, Abraham. 2004. "The Criteria of Goodness in the Pāli Nikāyas and the Nature of Buddhist Ethics." *Journal of Buddhist Ethics* 11: 123–42.

Yu, Jiyuan. 2007. *The Ethics of Confucius and Aristotle: Mirrors of Virtue*. New York: Routledge.

4

Communo-Welfarism

An Akan Humanistic Moral Theory

MARTIN ODEI AJEI

Introduction

This chapter examines the moral philosophy of the Akans of Ghana. The Akans constitute a folk group that inhabits much of the south and middle belts of Ghana and the eastern part of the Ivory Coast. Akans are the largest folk group in both countries and account for approximately 40 percent of the population of Ghana and 30 percent of the Ivory Coast.

In this chapter I defend the view that the Akans of Ghana consider communo-welfarism to be of fundamental moral value. By communo-welfarism I mean the pursuit of common human good from the premise of a communalist conception of human nature—that is, of humans as beings for whom relational ties of social organization are natural and indispensable. I approach this thesis by examining conclusions from theoretical deliberations on ethics by Ghanaian philosophers who speak various dialects of *Twi*—the language of Akans—as their first language. Primary among these are the works of J. B. Danquah, Kwasi Wiredu, William Abraham, Kwame Gyekye, and Christian Ackah. These authors endeavor to answer questions related to how best to live from an Akan perspective using reasoned argument. I argue that their views all support the idea that communo-welfarism is the central aim of Akan ethics.

However, my use of the work of the above philosophers in support of a view of Akan ethics in no way implies an intention to proclaim their entire ethical thinking as indexed to the Akan tradition or to unite them as mere narrators and interpreters of the tradition. Each philosopher claimed the task of assessing Akan moral thought as a philosophical responsibility and considered his conclusions as open to examination. For this reason, they deemed their respective contributions and differences among them as meaningful elements in a confluence of thought in quest of the optimal flourishing of a tradition of Akan philosophy. I maintain this as an aspiration as well.

Humanism as the Source and Justification of Moral Standards

Humanism, as a philosophical concept, constitutes an answer to a fundamental question: what is the status of humanity in the cosmic order? Are humans insignificant bipeds foraging on a precariously balanced planet, or the masters of the universe? The moral-philosophical response to this question emphasizes the agency of human beings and their value in relation to other existents in the universe. It conceives the human being, to paraphrase Protagoras, as "the measure of all things."

It is not always obvious that Akan thought is fundamentally humanistic. Opoku, a scholar of religion and ethics, asserts that Akan "morality flows out of religion" (Opoku 1978, 152), and Danquah thinks that all value is determined in relation to the ideal of "the great Ancestor" (Danquah 1968, 3), whom he defines as God.[1] Yet in spite of these views, the humanistic source of moral principles and conduct is well established in Akan thought. Two tenets of this position can be delineated. The first inheres in the conception of humans as the ultimate source of moral value by virtue of the definitive value assigned to human interests, and the second in a universalist conception of humanity.

Justification for the first aspect of humanism can be found in analysis of the Akan phrase *"onipa na ohia: sɛ mefrɛ sika a, sika ngye so; mefrɛ ntoma a ntoma ngye so, enti onipa na ohia"* (literally, "it is the human being that counts, because neither money nor expensive apparel can come to your aid in your need, only a human being can"). Wiredu considers this maxim a basic precept of Akan morality (1992, 193–206, 194, 201). He notes, I think correctly, that *"ohia"* connotes both "value" and "need," and that, accordingly, the adage is best interpreted either as "human interest is the basis of all value" or "human fellowship is the most important of human needs." In my view, his latter interpretation is subsumable under the former; hence my preference for rendering it as "it is the human being's interests that are of ultimate value."

This interpretation highlights Wiredu's ethical humanism, which begins with his belief that "the will of God, not to talk of that or any other extra-human being, is logically incapable of defining the good" (1992, 194). Additionally, his normative theory is humanistic, as it belongs to the set of "theories that define and explain norms in terms of the interests, capabilities, and circumstances (present and primeval) of the human species" (1996, 36). Ackah affirms the humanistic focus of Akan ethics and attributes this to the empirical basis of the standards of this ethical tradition: from relations among persons in communities (1988, 119), which invariably cultivate the postulating of human goods and desires as key ethical ends (1988, 133–34). Gyekye also excludes extra-human beings from moral consideration (1995, 131) and sustains the position that moral value is determined "in terms of consequences for mankind and society" (1995, 132).

The other aspect of Akan humanism, its universalist orientation, is ingrained in the maxim *"honam mu nni nhanoa."* Gyekye interprets the latter maxim as "humanity has no boundary," meaning "all humankind is one species, with shared basic values, feelings, hopes, and desires" (2010), and considers this to sufficiently establish the idea that our common membership of a universal human family constitutes a legitimate basis for universal application of moral ideals. Danquah affirms the significance of communalist values evolved from familial relations as extending to "embrace not only the Akan but the entire . . . family of humanity" (1968, xxix), while Wiredu thinks ethical standards are binding on all human beings in the same manner everywhere (2005, 45–46). For Wiredu, "it is the biological affinity between one person and another that makes possible the comparison of experiences and the interpersonal adjustment of behaviour that constitutes social experience" (1996, 19). Thus, our common human biology grounds common norms of thought that make for viable accounts of the objectivity of concepts and conceptual constructs; hence the universality of moral concepts.[2]

Character and Morality

One may draw a rough and ready distinction between the three foremost normative ethical theories by saying that consequentialists consider the consequence of one's conduct to be the ultimate basis of judging the moral import of that conduct; virtue ethics consider the pursuit of rationally based virtues to facilitate the achievement of happiness—which, in Aristotle, constitutes the enactment of one's ultimate being—to be primary; and deontologists focus on dutiful adherence to principle.

This distinction, if accepted, helps to give some meaning to the centrality that Akan thought accords to character in deliberations on morality. Gyekye suggests that "ethics" may be translated into Akan as *"suban ho nimdee"* (studies on character) or *"suban ho adwendwen"* (reflections on character) (1995, 148), as "good character is the essence of the African moral system, the linchpin of the moral wheel" (2010). Gyekye's conclusions are inferred from the fact that in Akan the judgments "He has no morals," or "He is immoral," or "He is unethical," or "His conduct is unethical" are expressed as *Onni suban* (He has no character) (1995, 147). Thus, discussions about morality turn out to be discussions about character; hence ethics or morality is conceived essentially in terms of character. Furthermore, in moral evaluations, other concepts are rendered as instrumental to the value of character. For instance, a dishonest or cruel person, or one who pursues morally distasteful conduct generally, is judged to be one with a bad character (who has *suban bone*); whereas one judged as a good person—that is, one who displays pro-social virtues and other operative ideals of society such compassion, generosity, and so forth—is described as having good character (*suban pa*) (Gyekye 1995, 148).

Danquah's doctoral thesis (1927)—his most prominent work on ethics—gives additional credence to this emphasis on virtuous character. Danquah discusses the nature of the consciousness that characterizes a developed moral personality. In Danquah's view, a morally excellent character is the outcome of a rationally systematized unity of feelings and reason (1927, 23), and such character is the source of good or bad judgment. Such an optimally coordinated self-conscious agent is the most suitable determinant of the value of the good or good conduct (Danquah 1927, 54). Hence, for Danquah, the moral end is moral excellence, achieved though refinement of moral personality. Human character must strive to attain such excellence, for the definitive human good is an activity that enacts or implies actions performed in accordance with such excellence.

Danquah's discussion of Akan ethics relies on the Akan concept of the feeling of shame—"*adefere*"—as a moral category (1927, 108f1). The relevance of shame, a feeling of loss of dignity and of remorse, is a function of conscience, the morally active element of thought; and thus a function for determination of good and bad, which Akans call *tiboa*: the "animal" in one's head. Ackah likewise emphasizes the cultivation of virtuous character (1988, 79, 80, 111) and conscience (1988, 112–15) as the primary focus of Akan moral education. In his view, the fundamental aim of such education is character building (1988, 79) toward behavior that will elicit praise rather than blame (1988, 119–20). Training of conscience is also pivotal to uphold self-esteem and the repute of family, as "there is practically nothing an Akan does, good or bad, which may not be said to indicate what sort of family he comes from" (1988, 121).

These considerations provide reason for Gyekye's perceiving of similarities between Aristotle's ethics of virtue and Akan ethics (1995, 153). If moral failure is occasioned by lack of a good character, then instruction for developing a virtuous character is necessary (for on Akan terms good character is not innate; Wiredu maintains that at birth, the brain is a tabula rasa for conceptual mapping and merely contains innate conceptual possibilities [1996,

21]). Humans are born with a potential for virtuous character, a capacity that evolves through moral instruction. One enacts virtue by developing the habit of pursuing good deeds, and the more frequently we do so the more habituated we are to performing virtuous acts. It is such progressive habituation that brings one closer to moral excellence.

A synthesis of the reflections so far yields the following perspective: (1) character and consequences are central concepts in Akan thought; (2) virtuous capacity is not innate but evolves as the result of instruction and practice; and (3) virtue is a kind of deliberative action and is thus contingent on the activity of reason (the rationally systematized unity of feelings and reason mentioned previously). These three perspectives are held, in various degrees, by Aristotle (1985, II.4.1105a). Aristotle's ethics considers actions and choices that conduce to a human being's ultimate good—her "intended" life—to be morally right, whereas actions that subvert the ultimate good as morally wrong (Copleston 2003, 333). This ultimate moral end is *eudaimonia*, usually translated (not unproblematically) as "happiness." This end is peculiar to humans among all natural beings, because it consists in activity that accords with reason, the distinguishing feature of being human (Copleston 2003, 334). It is by dint of reason that we move from a habitual disposition to act virtuously to really acting virtuously, because reason develops our capacity to recognize a choice as virtuous in itself (Copleston 2003, 335). Thus, the moral end—happiness—consists in performing acts guided by the consistent deliberation of reason. The virtuous life, a testament of achievement of the human destiny, is a life lived according to reason.

Gyekye's identification of Aristotelian virtue ethics with Akan moral thought is in some ways apt. But this is not because good character is the "linchpin of the wheels" of these moral systems, or because ethics is the "studies or reflections on character." Aristotle defined ethics as a science of human action (Copleston 2003, 333); for him it is a virtuous end, but not virtuous character, that is of ultimate moral value. Gyekye's analogy between Aristotle and Akan ethics has credence because both ethical frameworks are fundamentally aiming at an end. However, Aristotle's end— *eudaimonia*—differs from that found in Akan ethics.

Personhood, Community, and Morality

The notion of moral personhood further strengthens the importance of character in Akan moral thought. A strong consensus exists among African philosophers that African communitarian thought stresses the ontological and moral relevance of community in defining essential attributes of personhood. This ontological thesis is found in John Samuel Mbiti's claim that the African individual can only define herself by saying: "I am because we are, and because we are, therefore I am" (1970, 141). To be human, on this view, is to be by nature inseparable from community ties. This thought is echoed in the Akan maxims *"onipa nye abe na ne ho ahyia ne ho"* (the human is not a palm tree that he should be self-sufficient) and *"onipa firi soro besi a, obesi onipa kurom"* (when a human being descends from heaven, he descends into a human town") (Gyekye 1995, 155). The indissoluble relations that community ties entail invoke visions of mutual interdependence as a human mode of being and the reciprocal responsibility this solicits from everyone as underlying a distinct fact of human life: that in the social setting, to be human is to differ and be different, but not to be indifferent (Masolo 2004, 495). Thus, one's natural membership in community inheres in the fact that human existence necessarily commences in a community of well-defined social affiliations and continues to be embedded in a context of hardly discardable mutual interdependence in order to fulfil its social self: personhood (Gyekye 1997, 39).

Hence, "personhood is something which has to be achieved, and is not given simply because one is born of human seed" (Menkiti 1984, 172). Fulfilling obligations and observing the ideals imposed by human interdependence makes one a "person." These considerations suggest a distinction between "a human being" and "a person," where the former refers to homo sapiens as such and the latter to a human being in whom moral attributes are developed by virtue of her elevated consciousness as a communal being and by her performance of acts that express her commitment to the well-being of community and its members. The concept of a person under consideration is thus normative, in the sense that it underscores a judgment on human character. A human being judged as having bad character (*suban bone*) is taken to be logically equivalent to one who lacks personhood, and such a person is judged to be "*not* a person" (*onnye onipa*); whereas the virtuous person is judged to be "a person" (*oye nnipa*).

That the judgment that a human being is "not a person" is made in the wake of that individual's persistent unethical behavior implies that the practice of moral virtue is considered intrinsic to the conception of a person. What expresses lack of moral personhood is, primarily, a rational and competent person's inability to pursue conduct that promotes the common good. A human being who is "not a person" is one who repeatedly falls short of observing society's cherished moral ideals and standards and thus subverts the ends or capacity of others with whom she relates.

However, not being a "person" does not entail forfeiting one's status as an object of moral value and attention. All *human beings* enjoy all the rights of community membership, but only *persons* retain the status of admirable moral subjects. What this means is that a deficit in personhood need not thwart and stifle the freedoms and action of the individual, as social structures exist between her and the state that are designed to "lighten the weight of the state on the back of the individual" (Abraham 2015, 62). Thus, a "non-person" nevertheless retains the civil, political, and legal rights of citizenship and is as well an object of moral and emotional care. She would, however, unlike a "person," not be an object of veneration and esteem, and is not someone to look up to for character formulation and a source of commendable ideals.

The Akan position is thus similar to what Charles Taylor calls ontological communitarianism, that is, explaining social life and personal identity in terms of shared goods and "irreducibly social" factors—substantive ends that cannot be accounted for by or reduced to individuals—such as community and solidarity (Abbey and Taylor 1996, 3). Akan thought acknowledges that individual goals and communal goals can actually be separate and that there can be tension between these distinguishable goals. One's individual projects, such as economic and political goals, may conflict with pursuit of the moral self—personhood—which requires action that harmonizes with the preservation and the growth of the welfare of the community: the ultimate ethical aim of social life. Gyekye advocates promoting the common good "without violating individual rights or otherwise degrading the dignity of an individual human being" (Gyekye 1997, 270–71), or in a manner that produces a "cramped and shackled [individual] self responding robotically to the ways and demands of the communal structure" (Gyekye 1997, 55–56).

The need for solidarity and interdependence provides no justifiable grounds for forfeiting the moral subject's autonomy. But it provides reasonable grounds for individuals to endeavor to improve the stock of community well-being, since their aspirations are always realizable within a social context. In a situation where a moral choice is required between these goods, individual entitlements should be pursued so as not to detract from the stock of available or prospective communal goods, for choosing otherwise invariably constrains one's prospects as well. From these views, the inference can be drawn that the common good of shared relationships and the realization of human dignity are logically distinct, but morally indistinguishable, concepts. Thus, for advocates of Akan moral personhood and ontological communitarians, the nature of a person is a pivotal starting point of moral and social consciousness.

This is opposed to the starting point in liberal moral theory where the human is conceived as a discreet individual by nature who has social ties for reasons that are constitutive of her being. The obligations of the liberal person's sociality, as Taylor points out, are only contingent on obligations to herself by virtue of her rights as an individual (1992, 38–39). What is morally good is that which allows individuals to determine the basis for right conduct in moral matters and achieve their interests. Distinctive to this position is the view that features intrinsic to individuals are what above all else justify their status as moral subjects. Such a line of reasoning is succinctly stated by Ayn Rand and Nathaniel Branden in their claim that "the first step [in moral reasoning] is to assert man's . . . need of a moral code to guide the course and fulfillment of his own life" and that this code should establish that "his own interests is the essence of moral existence" (Rand and Branden 1964, x).

Teleology and Community

The discussion until now established the teleological leanings of Akan ethics. But while Aristotle's ethics can also be considered a form of teleology (in that it aims at the end of *eudaimonia*), his is a narrower form of teleology than that espoused by Akan ethics.

There are similarities: Aristotle's framework also posits the human as ontologically communitarian by nature and her excellence—personhood—as inhering in promoting this nature. Thus, promoting such excellence is what makes you a good moral being. This view of moral virtue as a property of excellent being is also found in Akan ethics.

But for Aristotle, the end—the excellence—of a knife is to cut well, and such excellence demonstrates the achievement of the purpose of the full being of the knife. For the human, such realization of one's full being—the end of excellence—is happiness. The moral end for humans in Aristotle, then, is a personal good: fulfilment of the self. In this sense, Aristotelian consequentialism is individualist in orientation. But the moral end in Akan ethics is based in the communal nature of a person; it is contingent on the pursuit of conduct that ultimately enacts one's communitarian personhood. The virtues that work toward this end are socially oriented virtues that trump individual ends. When achieved, the end of personhood is at one with the preservation and growth of community welfare and is a valuable moral end distinct from achievement of the ideals of individual selves. Thus the achievement of personhood is not morally intrinsically valuable, for that achievement merely functions to facilitate something else: the welfare of the community. A good society emerges from the striving of individuals to achieve the moral excellence of communal welfarism. Hence, the welfare of the community and the achievement of personhood are interdependent, but not logically equivalent. This makes Akan teleology collectivist, against Aristotle's individualist *eudaimonic* teleology.

Akan Ethics and Deontology

Even though it is not far-fetched to perceive deontological leanings in Akan moral philosophy, it would be incorrect to consider it to be fundamentally deontological. There are tendencies in Wiredu's ethics toward Kant's deontological moral theory. In *Groundwork of the Metaphysics of Morals*, Kant sets out a "supreme principle of morality," the categorical imperative (CI), and sufficient condition for making sound moral judgments. The first of the three formulations of this principle is "act only in accordance with that maxim through which you can at the same time will that it should become a universal law" (4:421). CI forbids having substantive moral commitments and upholds only the duty to pursue morality by appeal to *pure* practical reason. This is hardly controversial, when one considers it in light of Kant's opening statement of the *Groundwork* that nothing can possibly be conceived or called good without qualification except a good will (4:393). The good will is good in itself, unconditionally good, the outcome of the highest function of reason, and implies a duty to act on CI (4:396/7).

Wiredu may be said to be subscribing to this with his claim that morality requires the reasoned (this doesn't mean exclusively rational) pursuit of a supreme principle: sympathetic impartiality (SI) to which other moral rules and patterns of conduct must conform. He formulates this as "let your conduct at all times manifest a due concern for the interest of others" (Wiredu 1996, 31). "Due concern" for the interest of others entails imagining oneself in the position of a person whose interest your act will impact and welcoming that impact. SI, then, implies the golden rule, that one ought not to "do unto others what you would not that they do to you" (Wiredu 1992, 198). Further, Wiredu pursues this conception of morality as implying a duty to act in accordance with principle and illustrates this with the example of borrowing money with a promise to pay it back. Such a promise, he opines, is regulated by SI, which "applies to everyone in the universe," and adherence to which "is absolutely essential for the continuation of human society" (2008, 334).

Additionally, Wiredu agrees with Kant that the highest principle of morality should unconditionally be an imperative, as SI is. But despite these similarities, there are important differences that undermine any claim of conceptual equivalence between CI and SI. Kant forbids a substantive commitment to human interests, which, in Wiredu's view, primarily renders CI non-humanistic, and thus untenable (Wiredu 1996, 95). According to Wiredu, a "dose of compassion" should be germane to moral considerations, for "ability without sentimentality is nothing short of barbarity" (1992, 197),[3] and the absence of such compassion robs CI of worthy moral credentials (Wiredu 1996, 95). It is more plausible to place Wiredu in the consequentialist camp, as he conceives human well-being as an irreducible presupposition of all morality, since every moral endeavor has human well-being as its object (1996, 64). Further, according to him, the communalistic orientation of Akan society, which he affirms, "means that an individual's image will depend rather crucially upon the extent to which his or her actions benefit others than him/herself" (1992, 200).

Communo-Welfarism

Gyekye is also explicitly teleological. He notes that the value of good character in the Akan moral system inheres in its instrumentality to the achievement of other ends (1995, 153). A principal reason for this is that "the views of the traditional thinkers [he consulted] indicate that what is good is constituted by the deeds, habits, and behavior patterns considered by the society as worthwhile because of their consequences for human welfare" (2010); hence "in Akan moral thought, the sole criterion of goodness is the welfare of community" (1995, 132).

Gyekye equates this decisive moral end with the stock of common good, which he defines as "the social conditions that will enable each individual to function satisfactorily in a human society" (1997, 64). This position is affirmed by other Akan philosophers. For Wiredu, a sympathetic adjustment of a moral agent's interests with those of others, even at the cost of a possible abridgement of her own interests (1992, 153), is the means to the end of securing human well-being (1996, 65); while for Ackah it is desirable in moral evaluation that "consequence of acts are stressed, especially those that have implications for the good of the many [over] that of an individual" (1988, 80).

The notion of the common good derives unquestionably from the communalist order of Akan social organization. Social structures and institutions reflect not only a theoretical perspective on human nature, but also ideals and standards that those institutions aspire to serve; and the notion of the common good expresses shared moral aspirations and standards worth pursuing in a communalist setting. It is thus a basic premise of communalist social morality. In Akan thought, the pursuit of such ends is enjoined by social life, which, as seen, is considered natural to the human being (Gyekye 1995, 155; Wiredu 1980, 4).

Both Gyekye and Wiredu uphold the Akan image of a twin-headed crocodile with a single (i.e., common) stomach as symbolizing the moral notion of the common good. According to Gyekye, the common stomach "indicates that at least the basic interests of all the members of the community are identical. It can therefore be interpreted as symbolizing the *common good*, the good of all the individuals within a society" (2010). He goes on to explain that such a good is not equivalent to the utilitarian aggregate of individual goods: "It does not consist of, or derive from, the goods and preferences of particular individuals. It is that which is essentially good for human beings as such, embracing the needs that are basic to the enjoyment and fulfillment of the life of each individual" (2010). The reason for distinguishing the common good from the sum of individual goods is that the former is not contingently common, whereas the latter could be. Rather, the common good is fundamentally common, meaning that it is pursued with the aim of it benefiting members of society collectively. For this reason, its achievement implies the achievement of the individual's good as well; it is not diametrically opposed to individual ends: it spans all individual social and political goods and pro-social values and ideals that make for human flourishing. Hence tension ought not to exist between the common good and the good of individual members of community. Thus, on Akan terms, what expresses moral personhood is a rationally competent person's attitudes and virtues that promote the welfare of others and maximize the common good (which alone is morally significant in itself).

Communo-welfarism and political culture in Africa

Francis Fukuyama's *The End of History and the Last Man* (1992) proclaimed the triumph of liberal democracy and with it, the end of the evolution of political culture. According to this view, liberal democracy is the final form of government for all nations and, as such, represents "the end of history" (Fukuyama 1992, 304). Since this remarkable claim, the global tendency to regard multi-party elections as a necessary condition for successful democratic culture has gained astonishing momentum. The ethical thrust of this claim is that universalizing liberal democratic practice is morally defensible, as this practice supplies the conditions for satisfying the political ends of all people everywhere; and that the most important vehicle for this practice is political partyism. This tendency, in Africa, is exemplified in the practice of electoral democracy in forty-four of the fifty-four African countries.

In the main, the theorists of communo-welfarism question the universality claims of liberal democracy, and the suitability of its concomitant multi-party democratic systems, in Africa. In Abraham's view, "political theory, in so far as it deals with institutions, is quite relative, and by no means to be assumed in any given instance to be simply universal in its applicability" (Abraham 1962 [2015], 20–21). Wiredu's objections are elaborated in his enunciation of his theory of consensual democracy, a political system grounded in Akan concepts of the person and of the legitimation of political authority, which sustains political pluralism and representative government without multiple political parties (Wiredu 1997). Wiredu draws several contrasts between consensual democracy and "majoritarian" (liberal) democracy. The former upholds consensus building as a guiding principle and aim of decision-making, its underlying philosophy is cooperation, and its purpose participation in power to accustom action to the common good (Wiredu 1997, 187). Consequently, policies in government in a consensual democratic system are validated by the entirety of citizens. Conversely, parties in majoritarian political systems comprise citizens with similar interests vying for political power for the sole aim of implementing policies that reflect their sectional aspirations (Wiredu 1997, 186–87). This makes members of the majority party winners invested with legitimate authority and the right to impose their decisions on the minority. Abraham echoes these views in claiming that "well-organized parties, in the plural, are not essential to democracy" (Abraham 1962 [2015], 146); and that prominent among indigenous institutions that can contribute to solving Africa's current political problems is the deliberative democratic system of traditional Africa that aimed at consensus (72–73). Consensual democracy is rooted in the communo-welfarist view of personhood, whereas liberal democracy proceeds from the individualist concepts of man initiated by the political philosophies of Hobbes and Locke.

Summary

I uphold the Akan position that communal welfare is the good toward which moral persons work, and that such welfare is a distinct and ultimate aim of the conduct of morally excellent selves. And I characterize this view of the intrinsic goodness of community welfare as communo-welfarist consequentialism, a moral collectivist theory that rejects all forms of moral individualism. The Akan communo-welfarist moral theory is based in ontological communalism and places intrinsic value on the welfare of community as a whole by means of upholding the adjustment of individual interests sympathetically toward communal harmony and social solidarity. It is a theory that is "latent in common sense" (Rawls 1980, 518)—one that rests on the most essential convictions and traditions—of Ghanaian moral and political history.

Notes

1. This contrasts with his consigning the basis of ethical value in human interests in his PhD dissertation, which is discussed in section 3.

2. Danquah agrees with the claim to language as essential to community and of community as essential to morality. In Danquah's view, "Language is the primordial requisite of social intercourse, and morality is only possible for a rational being in a social community" (*Thesis*, 218). Yet he rejects Wiredu's thesis of the biological foundation of morals.

3. Arguably, the notion "ability" in this affirmation by Wiredu is elliptical. In the context of the quote, it is clear that he understands the term to mean not merely mental aptitude but rather the skill to deploy one's mental faculties toward an end, that is, skillful action toward an end. If so, then the quote can be rendered as "reasonable action without sentimentality is barbarity."

Further Reading

PRIMARY SOURCES

Abraham, William, E. 1962 [2015]. *The Mind of Africa*. Oxford: Oxford University Press [Accra: Sub-Sahara Publishers].

Ackah, Christian Abraham. 1988. *Akan Ethics: A Study of the Moral Ideas and the Moral Behaviour of the Akan Tribes of Ghana*. Ghana: Ghana University Press.

Ajei, Martin Odei. 2019. "Ontology and Human Rights." *South African Journal of Philosophy* 38, no. 1: 17–29

———. 2019. "Toward a Tradition of Ghanaian Political Philosophy." In *The Oxford Handbook of Comparative Political Theory*, edited by Leigh K. Jenco, Megan C. Thomas, and Murad Idris, 125–45. Oxford: Oxford University Press.

Danquah, Joseph Boakye. 1968. *Akan Doctrine of God: A Fragment of Gold Coast Ethics and Religion*. London: Frank Cass.

Gyekye, Kwame. 1995. *An Essay on African Philosophical Thought: The Akan Conceptual Scheme*. Philadelphia: Temple University Press.

———. 1997. *Tradition and Modernity: Philosophical Reflections on the African Experience*. Oxford: Oxford University Press.

———. 2010. "African Ethics." Stanford Encyclopedia of Philosophy, https://plato.stanford.edu/entries/african-ethics/.

Opoku, Kofi Asare. 1978. *West African Traditional Religion*. Singapore: FEP International Private Ltd.

Wiredu, Kwasi. 1992. "Moral Foundations of an African Culture." In *Person and Community, Ghanaian Philosophical Studies I*, edited by Kwasi Wiredu and Kwame Gyekye. Washington, DC: Council for Research into Values and Philosophy.

———. 1980. *Philosophy and an African Culture*. Cambridge: Cambridge University Press.

———.1996. *Cultural Universals and Particulars*. Bloomington: Indiana University Press.

———. 1997. "Democracy and Consensus in African Traditional Politics: A Plea for a Non-party Polity." In *Postcolonial African Philosophy: A Critical Reader*, edited by E. C. Eze, 303–12. Cambridge: Blackwell.

———. 2008. "Social Philosophy in Postcolonial Africa: Some Preliminaries Concerning Communalism and Communitarianism." *South African Journal of Philosophy* 27, no. 2: 332–39. https://doi.org/10.4314/sajpem.v27i4.31522.

SECONDARY SOURCES

Abbey, Ruth, and Charles Taylor. 1996. "Communitarianism, Taylor-Made: An Interview with Charles Taylor." *The Australian Quarterly* 68, no. 1: 1–10. https://doi.org/20634713.

Aristotle. 1985. *Nicomachean Ethics*. Translated by Terence Irwin. Indianapolis: Hackett Publishing.

Copleston, Frederick. 2003. *History of Philosophy Volume 1: Greece and Rome*. London: A&C Black.

Danquah, Joseph Boakye. 1927. *The Moral End as Moral Excellence*. PhD diss., University of London.

Fukuyama, Francis. 1992. *The End of History and the Last Man*. New York: The Free Press.

Kant, Immanuel. 1996. *Groundwork of The Metaphysics of Morals* (1785). Translation by Mary Gregor in *Practical Philosophy (The Cambridge Edition of the Works of Immanuel Kant)*, edited by Mary Gregor. Cambridge: Cambridge University Press.

Masolo, D. A. 2004. "Western and African Communitarianism: A Comparison." In *A Companion to African Philosophy*, edited by Kwasi Wiredu. Malden: Blackwell Publishing. https://doi.org/10.1002/9780470997154.ch41.

Mbiti, John Samuel. 1970. *African Religions and Philosophy*. London: Heinemann.

Menkiti, Ifeanyi Anthony. 1984. "Person and Community in African Traditional Thought." In *African Philosophy: An Introduction*, edited by Richard A. Wright. New York: University Press of America.

Metz, Thaddeus. 2017. "Replacing Development: An Afro-Communal Approach to Global Justice." *Philosophical Papers* 46, 1: 111–37. https://doi.org/10.1080/05568641.2017.1295627.

Rand, Ayn, and Nathaniel Branden. 1964. *The Virtue of Selfishness*. Calcutta: Signet Press.

Rawls, John. 1980. "Kantian Constructivism in Moral Theory." *The Journal of Philosophy* 77, no. 9: 515–72. https://doi.org/10.2307/2025790.

Taylor, Charles. 1992. "Atomism." In *Communitarianism and Individualism*, edited by Shlomo Avineri and Avner de-Shalit. Oxford: Oxford University Press: 29–50.

Wiredu, Kwasi. 2005. "On the Idea of a Global Ethic." *Journal of Global Ethics* 1, no. 1: 45–51. https://doi.org/10.1080/17449620500106636.

Section 2

Consequentialist Moral Theories

Introduction

This section of the book examines "consequentialist" theories of ethics. As the name indicates, consequentialists are fundamentally concerned with bringing about good consequences. This kind of moral theory has a long history and continues to appeal to both moral philosophers and laypeople alike. And it should be clear why: if ethics is not about making the world *better* in some way, then what is it for? After all, once we recognize that some state of affairs is *good*, what could be more obvious than that we ought to try to bring that state of affairs about? (Mulgan 2001, 14). If we have the option to produce more good rather than less, surely we ought to do so (Driver 2012, 5).

However, just as there can be various character-based accounts of ethics, consequentialist theories can differ quite markedly. In this chapter, we will consider some (though not all) of the ways in which consequentialist theories can be distinguished from one another.

But first it is important to know what draws all these theories together: essentially, that the *good* is explanatorily primary. The character-based approaches we looked at in the last section took dispositions to be basic and derived their accounts of the good and of right action from that starting point. But consequentialists take the good to be the starting point and derive from it their accounts of right action and virtue.

We can frame this issue in terms of the relationship between theories of value and theories of the right. A theory of value tells us what is good or bad in and of itself; a theory of the right tells us which actions are right or wrong (Kurka 2006, 357). Consequentialism, as a family of moral theories, is characterized by the idea that the first task of ethics is to develop a theory of value. Only from there can we establish a theory of the right. In other words, consequentialist theories are therefore those in which the good is *independent of* and *prior to* the right.

Consequentialism is usually contrasted with "deontology"—the subject of the third section of the book—since deontology prioritizes the right over the good. In deontology, our options for action are constrained in some way; we cannot simply act to bring about the best consequences. For instance, if the "best" state of affairs involves injustice, then according to many deontological theories we are nonetheless prohibited from acting to bring it about.

We can also contrast consequentialist and deontological theories in terms of their *direction*. Consequentialist theories are wholly forwarding looking, whereas deontological theories are always at least partly backward looking. For example, considering the morality of the death penalty from a consequentialist perspective would involve asking what implementing such a punishment *achieves*. If we allow the death penalty, would this lead to better consequences than if we did not? Would it reduce crime? Would it make society safer and happier? By contrast, a deontological theory would look at the death penalty and ask, for instance, whether the people being so punished *deserve* that punishment. But whether or not someone *deserves* something is a matter of what they have done *in the past*; it is not about the benefits of the action in the *future*.

Decision Procedures

It is not necessarily the case that consequentialist theories have *no* place for deontic concepts such as justice, fairness, and so on. While consequentialism is focused on bringing about the good, it leaves open the possibility that the best way of bringing about that good may be by relying on concepts such as justice and fairness. In this respect, a sophisticated understanding of consequentialism as a moral theory requires distinguishing between consequentialism as a *theory of morality* and consequentialism as a *decision procedure*.

As a theory of morality, what *makes something right* for the consequentialist is the consequences it brings. But the mere fact that the consequences are what makes something right does not directly tell us what we *ought to do*; it is instead about how we *establish* whether something is right or wrong in the first place.

For instance, sometimes being honest brings about the best consequences and sometimes it does not. What makes telling the truth or telling a lie in any particular case right or wrong is a matter of whether it brings about the best consequences. But in practice, we may not always be able to easily tell whether telling the truth or telling a lie will bring about the best consequences. In such situations, we probably need a *rule of thumb* to guide our actions. So, for example, we might adopt a rule of thumb that tells us to be honest in all unclear cases. If this rule of thumb in fact leads to better consequences than trying to evaluate each case individually, then a consequentialist has every reason to live by it. In other words, a consequentialist can recommend *as a decision procedure* that we live by a non-consequentialist moral principle. But this does not mean that being honest is right *because* it is honest; only that being honest leads to the best consequences.

In fact, the questions of what makes something right and what an agent ought to do may come apart entirely. While a naive consequentialist may try to evaluate every decision in consequentialist terms, a sophisticated consequentialism may end up abandoning consequentialism as a decision procedure entirely (Mulgan 2004, 42). The world is so messy, and our knowledge so limited, that calculating consequences on a case-by-case basis is almost certainly not an effective means of bringing about the best states of affairs. If so, the sophisticated consequentialist would live by apparently deontic principles as decision procedures, or focus on developing certain virtues, or both. But the sophisticated consequentialist can do this while holding that it is nonetheless *consequences* that *make* an action right. Principles and virtues are merely *tools*; principles in that they can be more reliable guides to the good consequences, and virtues insofar as they make us more reliable performers of those actions that lead to good consequences (Deigh 2010, 120). Principles and virtues are decision procedures, but consequences are the *criterion of rightness*.

Theory of Value

Consequentialism tells us that our theory of right action should be secondary to our theory of value. But consequentialism—as a family of theories—does not have a single view about what that theory of value should be (Brink 2006, 389). And the possible answers to the question of what has value are numerous.

When we speak about states of affairs having *value*, however, we mean more precisely that they have *intrinsic* value, or that they have value *in and of themselves*. This can be contrasted with having value *instrumentally*. By "instrumentally valuable," we mean that something is valuable because of what *else* it gets us. For instance, an expensive smartphone is certainly valuable. But *why* is it valuable? It seems plausible to think that smartphones have value not merely in virtue of what they are, but rather what further things they get us: they are instruments for achieving what we *really* care about.

How do we establish whether something has intrinsic or instrumental value? Various tests have been proposed. For instance, G. E. Moore suggests the *isolation test* (Moore 1903). In the isolation test, we isolate a thing from the consequences it may bring and ask whether it is still valuable. It seems clear that smartphones fail the isolation test. After all, we value smartphones *only* because of what they do for us. If they did not bring about certain consequences—allowing us to surf the internet, chat with friends, play games, and so forth—what would be the point of them? By contrast, happiness—a popular candidate for having intrinsic value—seems to pass the isolation test. Happiness seems to be an end in itself; happiness is good not because of what it *brings* us, but simply for what it is.

A second test is that of *conceptual primacy* (Driver 2012, 28). According to this test, a thing is intrinsically good if it terminates a series of explanations. For instance, if asked *why* we value our smartphone, we may respond that it allows us to play games. In which case, playing games is more conceptually primary than the smartphone, meaning that smartphones cannot be intrinsically valuable. But then we can ask the further question: why do we value playing games? Presumably we will answer with something like "we enjoy them" or "they make us happy." If so, then enjoyment or happiness is conceptually primary, and playing games is merely instrumental for achieving those ends. If we then ask why we value happiness, typically this question will be met with blank faces or shrugs. There does not seem to be any *further* reason why we ought to value happiness. If so, then happiness is intrinsically valuable according to the test of conceptual primacy, whereas smartphones and playing games are not.

A final test is that of *constancy* (Driver 2012, 28). According to this test, we ask whether the thing is valuable *no matter what* consequences it brings. So, for instance, if using smartphones made us deeply unhappy, would we still value them? Since their value seems to consist only in the fact that they happen to bring about good, rather than bad, consequences, probably not. What about happiness, then? If happiness brought about bad consequences, would we still think it valuable? (Note, the question here is not whether we ought to *pursue* happiness in cases where it brings about bad consequences; perhaps we ought not to in those cases. Rather, the issue is whether happiness *in and of itself* is still considered valuable, despite the bad consequences.) Arguably, happiness passes this test: happiness is still good in itself, no matter what it brings (even if pursuing it in cases where it leads to bad consequences may not be prudent).

Objective versus Subjective, Welfarist versus Non-Welfarist

Accounts of intrinsic value can be divided in at least two overlapping ways: subjectivism versus objectivism, and welfarism versus non-welfarism. For subjectivists about value, intrinsic goods are good insofar as they bring about something that a *subject* values. As David Sobel puts it, according to subjectivism, "valuers create value with their valuing" (Sobel 2016, 16). The objectivist, by contrast, holds that things can be valuable independently of a valuer.

Objectivists and subjectivists can come in both welfarist and non-welfarist variants. For welfarists, only those things that make a person's life go well are of intrinsic value. As Simon Keller describes it, for the welfarist, "facts about the best interests of individuals are, in some sense, the building blocks of morality" (Keller 2009, 82). Of course, this leads to the question of what is, in fact, in a person's best interests, and welfarists disagree among themselves about this issue. For instance, hedonistic welfarists take "best interests" to be about pleasure and (avoiding) pain; desire satisfaction theorists think our bests interests lie in getting what we want; whereas perfectionism is concerned with living an *excellent* life, where excellence is understood as the accomplishment of certain objectively valuable goals or the development of certain capabilities or talents.

Non-welfarists, by contrast, think that there are things that are intrinsically valuable regardless of whether they contribute to the welfare of human beings. For instance, though a healthy biosphere generally does contribute to human well-being, a non-welfarist might think that it would be nonetheless valuable *even if* it did not benefit humans (or other sentient creatures) in any way.

To recap, we have two distinctions: whether value depends on our attitudes (subjectivism vs. objectivism); and whether value depends on its contribution to the welfare of those beings who count morally (welfarism vs. non-welfarism). We can combine these distinctions in four ways. Welfarists can hold, for instance, that only those things that are subjectively valued as a matter of fact can contribute to welfare. Or they might think that something can contribute to our welfare even if we do not subjectively value it as such. Similarly, subjectivist non-welfarists believe that the things that are of value independently of their contribution to our welfare must nonetheless still be valued by us. For instance, putting aside the contributions of a healthy biosphere toward our welfare, they might think that whether a healthy biosphere is valuable depends on whether we subjectively value it. But objectivist non-welfarists hold that things can be valuable independently of whether we value them *or* their contribution to our welfare.

In terms of the theories considered in this book, both the Cārvāka and utilitarians typically have welfarist accounts of value: the Cārvāka take pleasure to be the only thing with intrinsic value, and while utilitarians disagree about precisely what is of value (pleasure, desire satisfaction, the perfection of character, etc.), nonetheless it must contribute to our welfare to be of value.

Mohism is a trickier case: they identify wealth, population, and social order as the goods we ought to pursue, and on the face of it these things do not *directly* relate to the welfare of sentient beings. For instance, increasing the population may or may not make our lives go better. But it is debatable whether Mohists truly considered wealth, population, and social order as *intrinsically* rather than *instrumentally* valuable. This question is simply not one that they seemed interested in discussing (in terms of their extant texts, in any case). However, if pressed on this issue I think they would likely have identified wealth, population, and social order as contributing to some deeper good that *does* relate directly to human welfare. Hence, they are likely also welfarists.

The interpretation of Mahāyāna Buddhism in this section suggests that the goods that a Buddhist practitioner should attempt to bring about—the elimination of suffering, virtue, and *nirvāṇa*/ bliss—are *good for* those who achieve them. But since *nirvāṇa* is a matter of developing certain capacities, this reading of Mahāyāna Buddhism is arguably a perfectionist account of welfare. But while *nirvāṇa* certainly does seem to be a matter of human *excellence* ("human nature perfectionism" [Hurka 1993]), some East Asian Mahāyāna views also think that the entire world, including nature, is objectively valuable. If so, then Mahāyāna Buddhism might be interpreted as objectivist non-welfarism. This latter view is supported by the idea that the achievement of *nirvāṇa* in Mahāyāna Buddhism involves the realization of the *emptiness* of all things, including that there is no meaningful difference between beings capable of subjectivity and everything else: that there is no "I" in the first place. If so, then value *must* be a matter of the achievement of objectively valuable states of affairs, since ultimately there are no subjects, human or otherwise, to "perfect" their "excellences."

Universal versus Non-Universal, Partial versus Impartial

Whereas the previous distinctions related to *what* matters, we can also typologize consequentialist theories in terms of *who* matters (and how much they matter), and we can do so along two dimensions.

The first—the distinction between universal versus non-universal theories—is about who counts in the theory. Should we be interested in the welfare of everyone who will be affected by our actions, or is our concern limited to only certain groups or categories of beings (Timmons 2013, 114)? For instance, say we adopted a hedonistic account of value (a welfarist view according to which only pleasure is of value and pain of disvalue), should we be concerned with *all* beings who experience pleasure and/ or pain? Or do we limit our concern to a subset of those beings, such as human persons? If the former, the theory is universalist; if the latter, non-universalist.

All the theories we consider in this section of the book are universalist. In fact, while we can certainly conceive of non-universalist consequentialist theories, they are hard to motivate, and the universalistic nature of consequentialist theories is often taken to be one of their most appealing features. After all, it seems difficult to draw the line between one group and another in terms of moral concern in a non-arbitrary way.

Where the theories in this section *do* differ is along the axis of partialism versus impartialism. To say that a theory is partial is to say that it weights the good of individuals differently. This distinction is sometimes put in terms of agent-neutral versus agent-relative value (Brink 2006, 382). To say that a value is agent neutral is to say that it does not make any essential reference to an agent; it is *neutral* as to who the agent is. To say "everyone matters equally" is to adopt an agent-neutral attitude. Conversely, agent-relative value essentially makes reference to specific persons (Driver 2012, 22); value is *relative to* that person. To say "my friends (justifiably) matter more than strangers *to me*" is to adopt an agent-relative attitude.

We can combine universalism and partialism in various ways. We can have universalist impartialism, in which everyone matters equally, making no reference to the agent. We can have universalist partialism, in which everyone matters equally, but the agent is justified in favoring those related to them in some way. We can have non-universalist impartialism, in which only some matter (or some matter more), but our concern for those who matter makes no reference to the agent. And we can have non-universalist partialism, in which only some matter (or some matter more), but also from within the limited group who matter, the agent is justified in favoring those related to them in some way.

So how do we categorize the theories in this section in terms of universalism and partiality? Certainly, both utilitarianism and this reading of Mahāyāna Buddhism are universalist and impartial. For Buddhism, all beings capable of suffering are of equal moral concern, and the same is true for all beings capable of experiencing pleasure or happiness, or having their desires satisfied, according to the utilitarian. Both views are also impartial: they deny that we can weight beings differently merely by virtue of their relationship to the agent.

On the other hand, as a form of hedonistic ethical egoism, Cārvāka ethics is clearly universalist and partial. For the Cārvāka, what matters is *my* pleasure, and my pleasure alone. In that sense, the Cārvāka think that value is relative to the agent: the fact that the pleasure is specifically *mine* is what gives me a reason to pursue it. But a Cārvākan is quite willing to credit that while *their* pleasure matters and yours does not *to them*, they also think *you* have good reason to pursue *your* pleasure at the expense of *theirs*. And the same is true for every being capable of experiencing pleasure. Hence, every being is included as an object of concern: it is a universalistic theory.

Mohism is again tricker. It is expressly universalist, but at times does seem to allow that we can treat people closer to us (friends, compatriots) differently than people with more distant relations (strangers). In this sense, a case could be made that it is partial. The central question is therefore how that differential treatment is justified. Rather than being partial, this may be a matter of differential treatment bringing about better consequences than if we were to treat family and strangers alike. If so, this partialism is a decision procedure rather than being a matter of the Mohist theory of morality, and since this procedure is justified in an agent-neutral way, Mohism is fundamentally impartial.

Object of Evaluation

Thus far we have considered *what* matters (objectivity and welfarism/perfectionism) and *who* matters (universality and partiality). A third way of distinguishing consequentialist theories is on the basis what we ought to be *evaluating*. On the face of it, this may

104 | Section 2

seem to be a similar issue to what matters. But the issue of what *matters* (the theory of value) and what a theory is *assessing* is not quite the same. For the former question, we are concerned with whether we should ultimately care about pleasure, or desire satisfaction, or beauty, friendship, virtue, and so forth. For the latter question, we are interested in what thing we are evaluating in terms of its ability to bring about those goods. For instance, we might be concerned with *acts*, but we may instead focus our attention on *rules, character traits, motives, institutions,* and so on (McElwee 2020, 202). After all, acts may have good or bad consequences, but so might rules, character traits, motives, and institutions. So, taking hedonism as our theory of value, we might ask not which *acts* lead to the most pleasure, but instead ask which rules, character traits, motives, or institutions do so.

But we must be careful when trying to answer the question of a theory's object of evaluation. After all, we may care about rules, motives, character traits, or institutions as a decision procedure, but nonetheless hold that what is of fundamental importance is acts. For example, rules might matter because implementing certain rules improves the quality of the acts people perform, which in turn increases the overall good (Rules → Acts → Good). This is a decision procedure. Or we might think that rules matter because of their direct effect on the good, skipping acts as an intermediary (Rules → Good). In this latter view, we are *fundamentally* concerned with right *rules* rather than right *acts*. This distinction is important. For instance, if we were using rules merely as a decision procedure, then those rules can and should be abandoned when *not* following the rule leads to the act that leads to the most good. So, if we are using a rule against lying for profit as a decision procedure, then in those cases where we are quite sure that lying for profit will lead to the most good overall, we are justified in doing so. By contrast, if we are concerned with rules *fundamentally*—if our object of evaluation is right *rules* rather than right *acts*—then *even if* abandoning a rule leads to more good *in that case*, we nonetheless must adhere to it. The rule is not there to get us to *do* the best thing (act): the rule *itself* is what is being evaluated.

In terms of objects of assessment, the fundamental concern of Cārvāka ethics is acts, and the same is true of classical utilitarianism. However, some contemporary versions of utilitarianism, such as "rule utilitarianism," make rules—or moral codes—the object of assessment (Brandt 1959, 253). When it comes to Mohism, there is some dispute about whether it should be seen as ultimately concerned with acts or with rules, though in my view, the central role of *yan* (statements/doctrines 言) in the theory, and its emphasis on *public* morality, strongly suggests that it is fundamentally concerned with the nature of the public moral code, rather than acts. Our consequentialist interpretation of Mahāyāna Buddhism arguably takes character traits as its object of assessment. However, some also claim that Mahāyāna Buddhism has a *global* view; anything and everything is an appropriate object of evaluation in a non-derivative way. So, the Mahāyāna Buddhist evaluates acts *and* character traits *and* motives, and so on.

Summary

In this chapter we have considered consequentialism as a family of moral theories in which the good is more fundamental than the right. We have also looked at the ways that different consequentialist theories can differ from each other: the nature of the good being pursued, who counts and how, and what is being evaluated.

With this in mind, we can characterize the theories in this section of the book in the following way:

Cārvāka ethics: Cārvāka ethics has a subjectivist, welfarist theory of the good focused on pleasure (hedonism). It is universalistic (everyone counts), but partial (only *my* good matters). It evaluates acts.

Utilitarianism: Utilitarianism usually has a subjectivist, welfarist theory of the good, which has classically been hedonistic in character. But other versions see happiness (where happiness is not reducible to pleasure) or desire satisfaction as being of fundamental value. There are also contemporary Western consequentialists who subscribe to perfectionist or objectivist accounts of value. Utilitarianism is decidedly universalistic and impartial and is usually concerned with evaluating acts (though there are more recent versions that diverge on this matter, most prominently rule utilitarianism).

Mohism: The good for Mohists is wealth, population, and social order. However, it is likely that—if pushed on the matter— these goods would be acknowledged as instrumental and would be grounded in a deeper, most likely welfarist value. Mohists are universalist, and *probably* (to my mind) impartialist, though a case could be made that they have elements of partiality. Their object of evaluation is most likely *society's moral code*, though they have also been interpreted as act consequentialists.

Mahāyāna Buddhism: Mahāyāna Buddhists aim to eliminate suffering and achieve *nirvāṇa*/bliss. In this sense, our consequentialist reading of this traditions suggests that they are welfarist, in particular in terms of how *nirvāṇa* contributes to the perfection of human excellences. Mahāyāna Buddhists think that all beings who can suffer matter—or alternatively everything that exists—so they are certainly universalists. They do not accept that we can justifiably prioritize those close to us, so they are impartial as well. Arguably, their object of evaluation is *character*, though they have also been taken to advocate for a *global* account in which absolutely everything is able to be evaluated in terms of its ability to bring about the good.

Further Reading

Arneson, Richard. J. 2000. "Perfectionism and Politics." *Ethics* 111, no. 1: 37–63. https://doi.org/10.1086/233418.

Brandt, Richard. 1959. *Ethical Theory: The Problems of Normative and Critical Ethics*. New Jersey: Prentice-Hall.

Brink, David O. 2006. "Some Forms and Limits of Consequentialism." In *The Oxford Handbook of Ethical Theory*, edited by David Copp, 380–423. New York: Oxford University Press. https://doi.org/10.1093/oxfordhb/9780195325911.003.0015

Deigh, John. 2010. *An Introduction to Ethics*. Cambridge: Cambridge University Press.

Driver, Julia. 2012. *Consequentialism*. Abingdon: Routledge.

Griffin, J. 1986. *Well-Being: Its Meaning, Measurement and Moral Importance*. Oxford: Clarendon Press.

Hurka, T. 1993. *Perfectionism*. New York: Oxford University Press.

Keller, Simon. 2009. "Welfarism." *Philosophy Compass* 4, no. 1: 82–95. https://doi.org/10.1111/j.1747-9991.2008.00196.x.

Kurka, Thomas. 2006. "Value Theory." In *The Oxford Handbook of Ethical Theory*, edited by David Copp, 357–79. New York: Oxford University Press. https://doi.org/10.1093/oxfordhb/9780195325911.003.0014.

McElwee, Brian. 2020. "The Ambitions of Consequentialism." *Journal of Ethics and Social Philosophy* 17, no. 2: 198–218. https://doi.org/10.26556/jesp.v17i2.528.

Moore, G. E. 1903. "Mr. McTaggart's Ethics." *International Journal of Ethics* 13: 341–70.

Mulgan, Tim. 2001. *The Demands of Consequentialism*. Oxford: Clarendon Press.

Sobel, David. 2016. *From Valuing to Value: A Defense of Subjectivism*. Oxford: Oxford University Press.

Suikkanen, Jussi. 2015. *This is Ethics: An Introduction*. Wiley Blackwell.

Timmons, Mark. 2013. *Moral Theory: An Introduction*. 2nd ed. Plymouth: Rowman and Littlefield.

5

The Secular Hedonism of the Cārvākas

PRADEEP P. GOKHALE

The Nature of Cārvāka/Lokāyata *Darśana*

Classical Indian philosophy has developed through systems or schools (*darśana*). A system of philosophy is an interrelated structure of thought in the areas of knowledge, reality, and values of life. Generally, every system of Indian philosophy consists of a source text that is supposed to be foundational to the system. This so-called source text, which is generally in the form of aphorisms (*sutra*) or verses (*kārikā*), is an abbreviation or crystallization of the background literature, which could be scattered and unorganized.

Cārvāka/Lokāyata-*darśana* is an important school of Indian philosophy. The source text of the system is supposed to be the aphorisms of Bṛhaspati. However, identifying the Cārvāka/Lokāyata position is difficult, since (a) there is no full-fledged authentic Cārvāka text; (b) popular expositions of the Cārvāka-*darśana*, such as *Ṣaḍdarśanasmuccaya* and *Sarvadarśanasaṅgraha*, present a narrow and one-sided picture of epistemology (the philosophy of knowledge) and the value system of Cārvākas and do not bring out its diversity; and (c) the scattered statements and views attributed to Cārvākas in the polemical works of different systems of Indian philosophy—one of the main sources of information about the

109

Cārvāka-*darśana*—may be inauthentic and misrepresent the Cārvāka view. Hence true or authentic Cārvāka-*darśana* becomes a matter of reconstruction. Scholarly efforts in the last century have brought forward two such formulae:

(1) Cārvāka as a single materialist system: this is the model of the Cārvāka-*darśana* prescribed by Debiprasad Chattopadhyay and Ramakrishna Bhattacharya, which accepts perception as well as a kind of inference as authentic methods for gaining knowledge. Though materialist in its ontology (philosophy of being), they hold that the Cārvāka is not hedonist in its axiology (philosophy of value).

(2) Cārvāka as a family of systems: in this view, the core feature of the Cārvāka-*darśana* is not its materialist ontology, but its opposition to the otherworldly metaphysics and ethics of other systems. Under this account, the Cārvākas adopted different epistemological strategies for criticizing otherworldly metaphysics, from extreme skepticism to mitigated empiricism. They also held diverse axiological views, including moral skepticism, asceticism, and hedonism. The Cārvākas therefore do not form a uniform single system, but a family of systems (Gokhale 2015).

In this chapter we will pursue the ethical perspective of the Cārvākas against the backdrop of the above complexity regarding the authentic Cārvāka-*darśana*. Diverse ethical perspectives have been attributed to Cārvākas. For example, the seventh-century sceptic Cārvāka Jayarāśi, having refuted basic categories (*tattva*) of knowledge and reality, says at the end of his treatise, "When in this way all essential categories are refuted, all practices are all right insofar as they are beautiful for not being reflected upon (philosophically)" (quoted in Gokhale 2015, 155). This suggests anarchism in the realm of morals. Some Cārvāka thinkers seem to have become ascetics. However, these characterizations of the Cārvāka ethical perspective are exceptional. The more common and dominant characterization is that it is hedonistic. (However, hedonism is not regarded as an authentic characterization of the Cārvāka ethical perspective by some modern scholars, as mentioned above. We will come back to this issue later.)

In spite of its diversity, the common feature of the ethics of the Cārvāka-*darśana* is that it accepts only this world and rejects values related to another world, such as the afterlife. Cārvāka ethics can be called secular in this sense. Hence one part of our task in this chapter is to explore the nature and significance of the secular character of Cārvāka ethics. We will also consider in what sense and to what extent Cārvāka ethics can be called hedonistic.

The Hedonist Ethics of Cārvākas

THE QUESTION OF HEDONISM IN THE CĀRVĀKA-DARŚANA

The ethical perspective of the Cārvākas is popularly identified as hedonism. Philosophically, ethical hedonism is a view according to which only pleasure or happiness is intrinsically desirable and only pain or suffering is intrinsically undesirable. While hedonism is accepted in most systems of Indian philosophy, these systems distinguish among types of pleasures and regard certain types of pleasure as of higher value. Accordingly, different forms of hedonism can be identified in Indian philosophy. The systems that accept liberation (*mokṣa* or *nirvāṇa*) as the ultimate goal of life conceptualize liberation as the purest, eternal state of pleasure (or at least the state in which there is an absolute absence of pain). Since such a state cannot be experienced by an embodied human being, the possibility of a disembodied state is accepted in most of the liberation-oriented systems. The Pūrvamīmāṃsā system, which is known for its justification of Vedic ritualism, regards heaven (*svarga*) as the highest value, which it understands as "pure experience as unalloyed bliss" or "unsurpassable bliss" (Wadhvani 1977–78, 183). Since such bliss is not available in this world, the Pūrvamīmāṃsā system imagines a heaven where it is available.

A form of hedonism that accepts the bliss of liberation or heaven as the highest intrinsic value can be called "religious hedonism." The Cārvākas are opposed to religious hedonism, since the soul and the other worlds presupposed by such a view are not acceptable to them (since such things cannot be empirically verified). Instead, the Cārvākas regard those pleasures that we can be sure are definitely available in this world and this life as intrinsically desirable, and those pains that belong to this world and this life as intrinsically undesirable. Their hedonism in this sense can therefore be called "secular hedonism."

Critics of the Cārvākas often describe Cārvāka secular hedonism as narrow and irresponsible. An oft-quoted verse that presents this form of hedonism attributed to the Cārvākas runs:

While life remains, let a man live happily,
Let him feed on ghee even though he runs in debt;
When once the body becomes ashes,
how can it ever return again? (SDSC, 10)

The second line, which implies that one should enjoy life even by making debts, attributes a selfish and irresponsible hedonism to the Cārvākas. Other such statements include "The only end of man is enjoyment produced by sensual pleasures" (ibid., 3) and "There is no other hell than mundane pain produced by purely mundane causes as thorns etc." (ibid., 4).

The above statements occur in the chapter on the Cārvāka in a sixteenth-century text, *Sarvadarśana-saṅgraha*, by Mādhavācārya. They were received by modern scholars in two diametrically opposite ways: some scholars relied on the picture of Cārvāka ethics presented by such works and described the ethical ideal of Cārvākas as "an unqualified hedonism"; as "sensualism, selfishness and gross affirmation of the loud will" (Radhakrisnan 1923, 281–82); or as "hedonism pure and simple" (Hiriyanna 1973, 194). On the other hand, modern materialist scholars such as Chattopadhyaya and Bhattacharya went to the other extreme by claiming that Cārvāka ethics cannot be called hedonistic at all.

Arguably the truth is between the two extremes. A dominant current of ethical thought in the Cārvāka school is hedonistic. But their hedonism was not "pure and simple hedonism" or "unqualified hedonism." It was very much a qualified hedonism. It was not irresponsible, as made out by their opponents. It was also not restricted to sensualism or egoism: it contained intellectual, social, and universalist concerns.

ENJOY LIFE BY MAKING DEBTS?

Let us first consider the question of whether the statement recommending "eating ghee even by making debts" is an authentic Cārvāka statement. Scholars such as Sadashiv Athavale (1997, 69–70) and Bhattacharya (2012, 201–5) have pointed out that the second line above was not originally part of the verse. In earlier occurrences, the second line is "Nobody is beyond the scope of death," which puts quite a different spin on the passage. In fact, Cārvākas do not advocate enjoying life by making debts, or by

enjoying themselves by any means whatsoever, but rather emphasize undertaking legitimate means of making a living.

For instance, a different text, *Sarvasiddhāntasaṅgraha*, records
their view in the following way: "By adopting only those means
which are seen (to be practical) such as agriculture, the tending
of the cattle, trade, politics and administration etc. a wise man
should always (endeavour to) enjoy pleasures (here) in this world."
(SSS, 6) It is noteworthy here that the Dharmaśāstra texts such as
Manusmṛti (Bühler, 1.89–90, 7.17–19) assigned these means of making
a living to specific castes, the first three to the merchant caste and
the fourth to the warrior caste. By contrast, the Cārvākas regarded
these means as open to all without discrimination. Moreover, the
Cārvākas pointedly did not include in the list of acceptable means
of making a living the ritualistic methods used by the priest class,
or those used by ascetics. In fact, the Cārvākas are critical of such
means: "The ritual of Agnihotra, the three Vedas, the (ascetic's)
triple staff, the smearing of one's self with ashes are all (merely)
means of livelihood to those who are destitute of intelligence and
energy. So opines Bṛhaspati" (SSS, 6).

While recommending a rational and practical way of life,
Cārvākas accepted a social order maintained by a political authority. This is suggested by their statement "The only Supreme is the
earthly monarch, whose existence is proved by all the world's eye-
sight" (SDSC, 4). This, however, does not mean that the Cārvākas
accepted all aspects of the social order as it was traditionally
understood. For instance, the Cārvākas were critical of the hierarchical *varṇa* caste system and the gender discrimination advocated
by the Vedas and Dharmaśāstra. Hence, though the Cārvākas held
that there should be law and order, it should not be based on an
otherworldly, dogmatic, or discriminating worldview; it should
be a secular order based on a rational and egalitarian outlook.
Moreover, while traditionally the social order was governed by a
monarch, the Cārvāka do not necessarily advocate for monarchy
as the highest political system. Rather, they merely hold that there
should be order rather than chaos.

IN DEFENSE OF SENSUOUS PLEASURE

The charge that Cārvāka hedonism is merely of a sensualist sort
also needs to be examined. It is true that the Cārvākas are gen-

erally disposed to welcome or celebrate sensuous pleasure. But this view should be interpreted in contrast with the ascetic and orthodox ritualist approaches.

Ascetic systems generally condemn sensuous pleasures. According to such systems, sensuous pleasures are often associated with, or are conducive to, pain. Hence, one should abandon them and focus on the bliss of a liberated state that is eternal and absolutely free from suffering. But the Cārvākas deny the possibility of the bliss of absolute or disembodied liberation. If so, we are left only with mundane pleasures, which are inevitably mixed with suffering. According to the Cārvākas, the mixing of pleasures and pains in this world is simply a brute fact that we need to accept. Hence, they argue,

> The pleasure which arises to men from contact with
>   sensible objects,
> Is to be relinquished as accompanied by pain—such is
>   the reasoning of fools;
> The berries of paddy, rich with the finest white grains,
> What man, seeking his true interest, would fling away
>   because these are covered with husk and dust?
>   (SDSC, 4)

According to the Cārvākas, then, wisdom lies in enjoying pure pleasure and in avoiding the pain that accompanies it as far as one can. There is no wisdom in throwing away pleasure simply because it is accompanied by pain. Hence, the maximization of pleasure and the minimization of pain is the goal.

SECULAR HEDONISM VERSUS RELIGIOUS HEDONISM

The advocates of Dharmaśāstra do not condemn sensuous pleasures altogether. But they maintain that sensuous pleasure should always be kept under the control of religious obligations. By following religious obligations, one accumulates merit and attains heavenly pleasures—which are far more intense and abundant than sensuous pleasures—after death. But the Cārvākas deny the existence of heavenly pleasures and instead replace the imaginary heavenly pleasures with the intense pleasures available in this world.

However, this does not mean that the Cārvākas cherish sensuous pleasures alone. What seems to be important for them is the maximization of *worldly* pleasures and the minimization of *worldly* pains. But "worldly pleasures" is a broad category that includes, along with sensuous pleasures, aesthetic, mental, and intellectual pleasures. In this sense, though Cārvāka hedonism should not be labeled as sensuous hedonism, it is accurate to call it a "this-worldly," or secular, hedonism.

The Secular Ethics of Cārvākas

Is Secular Ethics Possible?

Non-Cārvākas in the Indian tradition believed, based on scriptures, that moral values such as truthfulness and non-injury have their ultimate justification in the doctrines of *karma*, rebirth, and other worlds. Since Cārvākas do not accept these doctrines, the non-Cārvākas claim, Cārvākas cannot have any moral concern at all. Hence Jayantabhaṭṭa says in *Nyāyamañjarī*: "In Lokāyata doctrine no obligation is instructed, it is just a talk of baseless disputants (*vaitaṇḍikakathā*). There is no scripture (that they accept)" (quoted in Gokhale 2015, 149).

In Theravāda Buddhist literature this view is called annihilationism (*ucchedavāda*). Annihilationism has two aspects: ontological and moral. Ontologically it holds that after death there is no continuation of sentience. Morally it means that morally good or bad actions performed during life have no adequate consequences. Hence there is no point in behaving morally. The negation of the afterlife and the negation of morality were joined together in the notion of annihilationism. Non-Cārvākas generally therefore held that one cannot possess a moral perspective without believing in an afterlife (though the Buddha sometimes seems to make an exception [Gokhale 2017]). The Cārvākas stood against this general misconception of the religious philosophers of India and claimed that they did have a moral perspective, one concerned with leading a happy life in this world.

Otherworldly Religious Ethics

That the Cārvāka system accepted this world and no other world, this life and no life after death, is its unique feature, not shared by other systems of Indian philosophy. All other systems accepted some transcendent entities, those that are said to exist beyond this world and this life. The Vedānta school accepted the transcendent Brahman as the ultimate reality. The Nyāya and Vaiśeṣika accepted God (Īśvara) as the maker of the world. These systems also accepted an individual self that can exist without the body and can transmigrate. The Sāṃkhya, Yoga, Pūrvamīmāṃsā, and Jain schools accepted neither Brahman nor God, but they accepted a self that can exist without the body. Buddhism accepted neither Brahman, nor God, nor self, but it accepted the existence of "mind-series" (citta-santāna) that can undergo a process of transmigration. These transcendent entities—namely God, self, or mind-series—were supposed to provide for an explanation of how rules of conduct operate. According to the theistic systems, God stipulates the rules of conduct through scriptures and distributes the fruits of actions in accordance with those rules. The other (non-Cārvāka) systems, which did not accept the existence of God, held instead that an action itself yields its fruit by some unseen mechanism.

Rules of conduct were therefore ultimately justified in these systems on the basis of the doctrine of *karma*. The doctrine of *karma* consists of two kinds of relation between action and consequence: (1) Every action, good or bad, must result in reward or punishment to the agent herself; (2) Every experience of pleasure or pain must be the fruit of the action performed by the agent herself. The doctrine therefore holds that the fruits of an action must be experienced by the agent, if not in this world and this life, then in the next life in some other world. Hence the doctrines of other worlds and rebirth are the corollaries of the doctrine of *karma*.

The Cārvākas rejected the doctrine of *karma* along with its implications in terms of other worlds and life after death, since such things cannot be empirically verified. This does not mean that they were critical of morality as such. Their concern for morality is suggested, for instance, by their criticism of the custom of animal sacrifice. The Cārvākas were opposed to animal sacrifice primarily because it involved violence and destruction of nature. Hence, they argue, "If one goes to heaven by cutting wood for sacrificial posts, killing animals and causing the mud of blood, how does one go to hell?" (quoted from *Viṣṇupurāṇa* in Athavale 1997, 49). The advocates of Vedic ritualism argue that sacrificial violence is not violence at all. They claim that the animal killed in a sacrifice goes to heaven. So the performer of animal sacrifice really helps the animal by sending it to heaven. But the Cārvākas think otherwise. They expose Vedic hypocrisy when they ask: "If the beast slain in the Jyotshṭoma rite will itself go to heaven, why then does not the sacrificer forthwith offer his own father?" (SDSC 10).

The epistemological view of the Cārvākas (that there is nothing beyond what is given by experience or by empirical reasoning) therefore had direct implications for their ethical perspective. They were opposed to dogmatic beliefs or blind beliefs that could not withstand the test of empirical justification. For instance, according to Vedic ritualism, one is supposed to offer food to Brahmin priests in the *śrāddha* ritual. It was believed that when the priests eat it, it reaches the ancestral world, and the ancestors are satisfied. The Cārvākas argue that this dogmatic belief leads to absurd results: "If a man is truly satiated by food that another person eats, then *śrāddhas* should be offered to people who are travelling abroad" (Chattopadhyay 1990, 354). Similarly, they point out that "If beings in heaven are gratified by our offering the *Śrāddha* here, then why not give the food down below to those who are standing on the housetop?" (SDSC, 10)

CRITICISM OF CASTE AND GENDER DISCRIMINATION SUPPORTED BY SCRIPTURES

The Cārvākas exposed the irrationality of the hierarchical system of caste and gender discrimination advocated by the Vedas and the Dharmaśāstra. For example, in a dialogue between the orthodox sage Bhṛgu and the rationalist-materialist Bharadvāja, Bhṛgu claimed that God created the four classes (*varṇa*) as having four colors, representing intrinsic differences and the hierarchy among them. Bharadvāja counters this position as follows: "If the four *varṇa*s differ because of their different colours, then (the problem is that) we do observe the admixture of colours among *varṇa*s. Desire, anger, fear, greed, sorrow, worry, hunger and exertion, they apply to all of us. How are *varṇa*s different from each other then? The bodies of all of us release sweat, urine, stool, phlegm, bile and blood. How are *varṇa*s different from each other then?" (*Mokṣadharma* 181.6–8). Another example: the Dharmaśāstra of Manu held that "day and night women must be kept in dependence by the males (of their families)" (Bühler, 9.2). It attributes vices to women such as "passion for men, a mutable temper, natural heartlessness and disloyalty towards her husband" (Bühler, 9.15). However, men are not similarly discredited in these Dharmaśāstra texts. In the *Naiṣadhīyacarita*, the representative of the Lokāyata notices this discriminating attitude to women expressed in the Dharmaśāstra and responds, "Shame on them, who have a hypocritical approach to the family status of women, who out of envy are protective about women but not so protective about men, in spite of there being no difference between their weakness for erotic desire" (NC 17.41). The above instances throw light on the anti-otherworldly, anti-violence, anti-hypocritic, and anti-dogmatic aspect of Cārvāka ethics. By implication. the Cārvākas emerge as supporting non-violence, truth, rationality, and justice.

THE THEORY OF HUMAN GOALS (*PURUṢĀRTHA*)

The philosophy of life in the Indian tradition acknowledges four types of human goals (*puruṣārtha*): pleasure (*kāma*), wealth (*artha*), religious obligations (*dharma*), and liberation (*mokṣa*). Pleasure and wealth are considered mundane goals, whereas religious obligations and liberation are regarded as trans-mundane goals. Though schemes of the first three goals (*trivarga*) and of the four goals (*caturvarga*) were primarily introduced through Vedic philosophy, we find different configurations of the four value categories prescribed by different systems of Indian philosophy, including heterodox ones (such as Jainism and Buddhism) (Gokhale 2002). But which of these goals were acceptable to the Cārvākas? Some statements imply that pleasure (*kāma*) alone is the end of life (Bhattacharya 2012, 128), whereas some others speak of both pleasure (*kāma*) and wealth (*artha*) as the twin ends of the Cārvākas (ibid.). But despite this disagreement, religious obligations and liberation—the trans-mundane goals—are not acceptable to the Cārvākas.

Vātsyāyana, the author of the *Kāmasūtra*, presents the Lokāyatika (Cārvāka) argument against *dharma* (religious obligations):

The Lokāyatikas say—Religious obligations should not be pursued, for their fruits are supposed to be due in the future, and at the same time it is also doubtful whether they will bear any fruit at all.

What foolish person will give away that which is in his own hands into the hands of another? Moreover, it is better to have a pigeon today than a peacock tomorrow; and a copper coin which we have the certainty of obtaining, is better than a gold coin, the possession of which is doubtful. (KS, 9, with minor modification)

In other words, religious obligations are not acceptable to the Cārvākas, because their alleged results are remote and uncertain.

Similarly, liberation is also not acceptable to the Cārvākas. The other systems of Indian philosophy, which universally accepted liberation as the ultimate goal of life, generally regarded liberation as a disembodied and eternal state of the soul. This liberated state of the soul is regarded as a state full of bliss, or at least as absolutely free from suffering. But the Cārvākas do not accept the existence of the eternal soul. While Buddhists also do not accept the existence of the soul, they accept instead the existence of a series of momentary consciousness, which cease at the time of liberation (nirvāṇa). Hence, according to the Buddhists, everyone undergoes a beginningless cycle of birth and rebirth. Nirvāṇa is the stoppage of this cycle. But the Cārvākas do not accept the cycle of birth and rebirth. Hence, they do not accept any form of liberation, whether it be mokṣa or nirvāṇa.

DHARMA AND LIBERATION AS THIS-WORLDLY HUMAN GOALS

We have seen that among the four goals, Cārvākas accept the first two—which are secular—and deny the last two—which are religious. But the so-called religious goals can also have secular counterparts. Hence, we find that though the Cārvākas deny dharma and mokṣa as religious goals, they seem to accept their secular counterparts in some form. In this way Cārvākas did not accept dharma in its transcendental form but accepted it in the form of a secular human value conducive to social order. Cārvākas did not explain their notion of dharma in terms of transcendent entities like non-Cārvākas did, but as Guṇaratna (the commentator of Ṣaḍdarśanasamuccaya) observes, they identified it with kāma (pleasure or desire) (Bhattacharya 2012, 128, fn. 21). *Dharma* in the sense of obligations is an other-regarding value, whereas *kāma* in the sense of desire (for pleasures and removal of pains) is a self-regarding value. Now Cārvākas are suggesting that while pursuing one's own *kāma*, one should also recognize the *kāma* of others. In this way only one acknowledges one's obligations to others. Pursuing *dharma* in this sense consists of recognizing the others' pursuits of *kāma* while pursuing one's own *kāma*. *Dharma* as a secular human value becomes explainable in terms of *kāma* in this way. The order in society can be maintained by pursuing *dharma* in this form.

It should be noted here that though Cārvākas can accept *dharma* as the concern for the *kāma* of others, they would not recommend it to be pursued at the cost of one's own *kāma*. On the other hand, when they recommend *kāma* as the pursuit of one's own pleasure, they do not fix any measure of it. It can vary from person to person, as freedom of choice is an important value for the Cārvākas. By accepting *dharma* as a value, Cārvākas are only saying that one should also acknowledge similar pleasure-pursuits of others.

Similarly, Cārvākas did not accept liberation in its transcendental form, but tried to secularize it. Two statements are ascribed to Cārvākas in this context. One statement says, "The only Liberation is the dissolution of the body" (SDSC, 4), which only implies that the so-called disembodied liberation, which is attained after death, is not admitted by them. The other statement gives a positive account of liberation and says, "The only bondage is dependence on another and therefore independence is the true liberation" (SDSC, 169). Here independence (*svātantrya*) refers to human freedom rather than freedom of the soul. Freedom of the soul is essentially "freedom from." It is freedom from bondage, suffering, and so forth. But a free or liberated soul is free from actions also. Hence it does not have "freedom to." Human freedom has two aspects: "freedom from" and "freedom to." A free human being is free from bondage, constraints, and so forth. But she is also free to choose courses of action. This twofold freedom is an important prerequisite of the hedonistic pursuit of pleasure.

There is a popular saying in Sanskrit: "Everything that depends on others (gives) pain, everything that depends on oneself (gives) pleasure; know that this is the short definition of pleasure and pain" (Bühler, 4.160). This substantiates the importance of human freedom as a hedonistic value. Though this verse is included in

Manusmṛti, which is a Dharmaśāstra text, the human freedom praised in it does not have the same status in the Dharmaśāstra framework that it does in the Cārvāka theory of values. In the Dharmaśāstra it becomes restricted because of the hierarchical framework of caste and gender. Hence high-caste persons were supposed to enjoy more freedom than low-caste ones, and men more freedom than women. Similarly, the systems oriented to disembodied liberation gave subordinate status or even the status of disvalue to "human" freedom. But in the Cārvāka theory it is an ideal state indiscriminately prescribed for all.

CĀRVĀKA HEDONISM: EGOISTIC OR UTILITARIAN?

One of the charges against the Cārvāka ethics is that it is just egoistic hedonism and contains no altruistic element in it. The ground of this charge is that Cārvākas accept pleasure (*kāma*) and wealth (*artha*) as the human goals that are essentially egoistic and reject obligations (*dharma*) as the goal that is essentially altruistic or universalistic. But we have seen that though Cārvākas reject *dharma* as a ritualistic and otherworldly goal, they do accept it as a secular goal. Their recognition of the legitimate ways of livelihood, political authority, and governance shows their concern for social order and well-being. This concern does not seem to be about the well-being of human beings only, but about living beings in general. This is suggested by the concluding statement of the chapter on Cārvāka-*darśana* in *Sarvadarśanasaṅgraha*: "Therefore one should adopt the view of Cārvākas for favor of living beings at large" (SDS). It is noteworthy that the chapter talks here of living beings (*prāṇinām*) and not just human beings.

In this way the Cārvāka hedonism can be called utilitarian in the sense of being concerned with general good (that is, the good of living beings at large). This also explains their concern about the slaughter of animals and destruction of nature caused by sacrificial rituals enjoined by orthodox religious philosophies.

Summary

In spite of diversity in the epistemological, ontological, and axiological positions of the Cārvāka system, one common feature of

122 | Pradeep P. Gokhale

all the members of the Cārvāka family is that they were opposed to the transcendental and otherworldly views of other systems. Hence, their this-worldly, secular approach to ethics is a distinguishing mark of the Cārvāka system. Its other dominant aspect, though not upheld by all Cārvāka philosophers, is that it is a form of hedonism. The Cārvākas pleaded for sensuous pleasure against its condemnation and subordination by religious systems. Despite this, their hedonism cannot be reduced to sensualism and egoism, as it frequently is by critics. Their motto, "While life is yours, live joyously" (SDSC, 2), expresses their concern with a happy life in this world. We can also say that Cārvākas pleaded for pursuit of happiness not just as egocentric well-being, but as a part of well-being of all beings.

As suggested in the beginning, there is no full-fletched authentic Cārvāka text, and the accounts of the Cārvāka view given by the rival schools that are the main sources for understanding it are many times exaggerated or distorted. Hence presenting the Cārvāka view in its authentic and reasonable form becomes a matter of reconstruction. Such a reconstruction has its limitations because, although it can provide a strong formal structure, it cannot fill up much positive and substantial content in it. Despite these limitations, the secular hedonism of Cārvākas remains important, as it has survived as a constant challenge before the dominant tradition of the religious philosophies of India.

Further Reading

PRIMARY SOURCES

Chattopadhyaya, Debiprasad (in collaboration with Mrinal Kanti Gangopadhyay). 1990. *Cārvāka/Lokāyata*. New Delhi: ICPR Publications.
Gokhale, Pradeep P. 2015. Lokāyata / Cārvāka: A *Philosophical Inquiry.* New Delhi: Oxford University Press.

SECONDARY SOURCES

Athavale, Sadashiv. 1958 / 1997. *Cārvāka, Itihāsa Āṇi Tattvajñāna.* Wai: Prājñapāṭhaśāḷā Maṇḍaḷa.

Bhattacharya, Ramkrishna. 2012. *Studies on the Cārvāka/Lokāyata*. Delhi: Anthem Press India.

Brandt, Richard B. 1963. "Hedonism." In *The Encyclopedia of Philosophy*. Vol. 3, edited by Edward Paul, 432–35. New York: Macmillan Publishing Company.

Bühler, G. 1886. *The Laws of Manu*. Oxford: Clarendon Press.

Franco, Eli. 1987. *Perception, Knowledge and Disbelief (A Study of Jayarāśi's Scepticism)*. Delhi: Motilal Banarsidass.

Gokhale, Pradeep P. 2002. "Some Remarks on the Nature of *Puruṣārtha*s and the Buddhist Approach to Them." In *Studies in Indian Moral Philosophy, Problems, Concepts and Perspectives*, edited by S. E. Bhelke and P. P. Gokhale, 105–15. Pune: IPQ Publication Pune University.

———. 2017. "The Possibility of Secular Buddhism." *Proceedings of the Institute of Oriental Studies, RAS. Issue. 1:* Moscow: Institute of Oriental Studies, RAS, 160–72

Hiriyanna, M. 1973. *Outlines of Indian Philosophy*. Bombay: George Allen & Unwin.

KS. 1925. *Kamasutra of Vatsyayana*, translated from Sanskrit by The Hidoo Kamashastra Society. Benaras, NY: The Friends of India Society.

Mokṣadharma. 1954. "Part III: Mokṣadharma, A." In *The Śāntiparvan*, edited by S. K. Belvalkar. Poona: Bhandarkar Oriental Research Institute, 1954.

NC. 2015. *Naiṣadhīyacaritam of Śrīharṣa, With Dīpikāṭīkā of Narahari*. Delhi: Bharatiya Vidya Prakashan.

Radhakrishnan, S. 1923. *Indian Philosophy*. London: George Allen and Unwin.

SDS. 1978. *Sarvadarśanasaṅgraha of Mādhavācārya*. Edited by Vasudevshastri Abhyankar. Poona: Bhandarkar Oriental Research Institute.

Mādhava Ācārya. 1882. *Sarva-Darśana-Saṃgraha or Review of the Different Systems of Hindu Philosophy* (SDSC). Translated by E. B. Cowell and A. E. Gough. London: Trübner.

SSS. 1909. *Sarvasiddhāntasaṅgraha of Śaṅkarācārya*. Edited and translated by M. Rangacarya. Madras: Government of Madras.

Wadhwani, Yashodhara. 1977–78. "Heaven and Hell in the Pūrvamīmāṃsā and the Nyāya-Vaiśeṣika systems." *Bulletin of the Deccan College Post-Graduate and Research Institute 37*, nos. 1/4: 182–86.

6

Utilitarianism

NICHOLAS DRAKE

Introduction

Utilitarianism is an ethical theory that was first systematically developed in England in the late eighteenth century. Utilitarianism is the view that an action is right to the extent that it promotes well-being. (Well-being is what you have if your life is going well.) When you're deciding what the ethically right thing to do is, you should choose to do what promotes well-being the most, and no one's well-being matters more than anyone else's. (There are several kinds of utilitarianism that vary with that description in different ways, which we'll look at later.)

Utilitarianism can be viewed as the combination of two ideas, *consequentialism* and *welfarism*. Consequentialism is the view that an act is right to the extent that it has the best consequences, and welfarism is the view that the only thing that ultimately matters ethically is well-being. So utilitarians think you should do what has the best consequences, and that the kind of consequences that matter are promoting well-being.

Utilitarianism is for many people a commonsense idea: when we're thinking about the ethically right thing to do, what matters is which action will help people (and animals) and which will harm them. The more an action helps people, the better it is; the more an action harms people, the worse it is. Utilitarianism does a good job of capturing the idea that what's central to ethics is treating others well, and it also does a good job of expressing an intuitive view of what treating others well means: promoting their well-being. The basic idea is that what matters is making the world a better place, which means helping people's lives go well.

Utilitarianism is also attractive in giving a clear criterion for right action. Under some ethical theories, what makes an action right or wrong is complex to explain, and it can be hard to see how to work out whether an action is one you should do. Utilitarianism is relatively straightforward: you work out which action is going to do the most good for everyone by promoting their well-being, and you do that.

Utilitarianism is also attractive in offering an ethical view that works at a political level, not just a personal level. Many ethical theories say how *individuals* should act, but not how we should act as a society. Utilitarianism says we should choose those laws and policies that best promote well-being, treating everyone equally. That's an intuitive idea for deciding what to do as a society, and one that in principle is relatively straightforward to apply: when considering whether to introduce a law or policy, work out whether it will make people's lives better or not, and introduce it if it does. In fact, as we'll see, utilitarianism was initially developed more as a political and legal theory than as a personal moral code.

Despite these attractive features of utilitarianism, there are some strong arguments against it, which we'll look at in the section on objections.

Early Utilitarians

BENTHAM

The philosopher who coined the term "utilitarianism" and first gave a systematic account of the view was Jeremy Bentham (1748–1832). By "utility," Bentham meant "the quality of being instrumental for well-being"; something has utility just if it will promote well-being. Utilitarianism, then, is the view that actions are right to the extent they have utility.

"Utilitarianism" is a famously bad name for the theory, as it makes it sound dull and joyless; we use the word to describe buildings or objects that are practical and useful but not attractive or interesting. That's unfortunate, as utilitarians usually think of well-being as pleasure or happiness, and their notions of pleasure and happiness can be rich and broad.

Bentham lived in England and spent his life trying to reform legal and political systems. Bentham described the English legal system as a "fathomless and boundless chaos" that denied justice to people (quoted in Judson 1910, 42). He saw utilitarianism as a rational, practical basis for laws and policies to replace the ad hoc and arbitrary way they were created and maintained at the time. Simply, he thought legislators should evaluate laws and policies by whether or not they promoted people's well-being.

Bentham was a *hedonist* about well-being. Hedonism is the view that the only thing that contributes to well-being is pleasure, and the only thing that detracts from it is pain. How great a pleasure is, Bentham thought, depends on its intensity, duration, certainty (how likely it is to occur), propinquity (how soon it will occur), fecundity (how likely it is to be followed by other pleasures), purity (how likely it is to *not* be followed by pain), and extent (how many people will be affected by it). What makes *no* difference to how great a pleasure is, Bentham thought, is its source—he said it makes no difference whether pleasure comes from poetry or from push-pin (a children's game of the time).

The practical implications of Bentham's theory were progressive or even revolutionary at the time. One of these was the idea that the purpose of criminal punishment should only be deterrence, not retribution; it is bad if criminals suffer, and they should be made to suffer only to prevent the occurrence of worse suffering. Another view of Bentham's, very controversial at the time, was that animals should be protected by law from mistreatment. Animals are afforded less protection than people in law, and the reason given is usually that animals have lower moral status as they lack humans' powers of reasoning. Bentham argued that this was not a morally relevant difference when causing pain and wrote that "the question is not, Can they *reason*? Nor, can they *talk*? But, can they *suffer*?" (Bentham 1789, 283n). Bentham also believed that the vote—permitted only for certain men at the time—should be extended to all adults, including women.

MILL

John Stuart Mill (1806–73) was Bentham's godson (Bentham and Mill's father, James Mill, were close friends). Mill was well-known as a philosopher in his lifetime, but, like Bentham, was also a social and political reformer and was a British MP from 1865 to 1868. Mill did much to popularize utilitarianism, not least by publishing Bentham's work, which wasn't well-known in his own lifetime. Something that helped Mill's popularization of utilitarianism is that, although he wrote a huge amount, his book *Utilitarianism* is only about seventy pages long, easy to read, and was first published as a series of magazine articles (J. S. Mill 1863).

Mill's utilitarianism differs from Bentham's mainly in their views of well-being. While both were hedonists, believing well-being consists just in pleasure, Mill disagreed with Bentham's view that the *source* of a pleasure makes no difference. He believed there are higher and lower pleasures, and that higher pleasures contribute more to well-being. Higher pleasures include things like intellectual and profound emotional pleasures and pleasures achieved through activity rather than experienced passively. Famously, he wrote, "It is better to be a human being dissatisfied than a pig satisfied; better to be Socrates dissatisfied than a fool satisfied" (J. S. Mill 1863, 10). We know the difference between the quality of higher and lower pleasures, Mill thought, because anyone who has experienced both prefers the higher ones.

Mill thought that, as the only thing that matters is well-being and everyone's well-being is equally important, people should be guaranteed the basics of life, such as food, shelter, and freedom. He believed people are the best judges of what contributes to their own well-being, and so they should be free to live how they like if it doesn't harm others. His book *On Liberty*, which includes that argument, remains extremely influential in political thought (J. S. Mill 1859).

HARRIET TAYLOR MILL

Mill met Harriet Taylor (1807–1858) in 1830, and although she was already married, they soon fell in love. Taylor's husband died in 1849, and she and Mill married in 1851. Taylor Mill was not only a major influence on Mill, but also a collaborator. Mill wrote, "not only during the years of our married life, but during many of the years of confidential friendship which preceded it, all my published writings were as much my wife's work as mine; her share in them constantly increasing as years advanced" (J. S. Mill 1873, 251).

Taylor Mill also published, under her own name, the essay "The Enfranchisement of Women" in 1851 (H. T. Mill 1998, 51–73). This was a very important early work in feminist philosophy. At a time when women were not allowed to vote and married women could not legally own property in their own names, Taylor Mill argued for full social and political equality for women and that married women should work outside the home. She heavily influenced an important essay of Mill's on the subject, "On the Subjection of Women" (J. S. Mill 1869).

During the twentieth century, many kinds of utilitarianism were developed, often in response to arguments against the views of Bentham, Mill, and other early utilitarians. At this point it is easier to talk about the different types of utilitarianism than about particular philosophers. Before doing so in the section on types of utilitarianism, we'll look at a couple of the ways utilitarianism works in practice.

Utilitarianism in Practice

We'll look at how utilitarianism works in practice by discussing the treatment of two topics in ethics by the best-known living utilitarian philosopher, Peter Singer. Utilitarianism says that the only thing that matters is well-being and that everyone's well-being matters equally. We saw that the early utilitarians thus thought their society needed to change the way it treated women, who were not afforded many of the basic rights men enjoyed; gay people, who were punished harshly for actions that harmed no one's well-being; and animals, the treatment of which in ways that caused them great suffering was considered ethically permissible.

Singer's 1975 book *Animal Liberation* takes up this last theme (1975). Singer argues that it's wrong to treat the interests of animals differently from the interests of people (though of course, those interests are different; it's not in the interests of animals to have education, for example). It's in the interests of all sentient beings, whether human or not, to have well-being, including feeling pleasure and not feeling pain. So, it's just as wrong to cause a certain amount of suffering to an animal as it is to cause that same amount of suffering to a human.

Some opponents of this argument say that the interests of humans matter more because they have greater cognitive abilities than animals. However, Singer points out that there are a lot of humans who *don't* have greater cognitive abilities than some animals; an adult chimpanzee has the intelligence of a four-year old child, for example. Babies and people with some severe cognitive disabilities have lesser cognitive abilities than some animals. This suggests a test for whether it's permissible to do something to an animal: you should consider whether you think it's okay to do that thing to a human with the same cognitive abilities as the animal, and if it isn't okay to do it to the human, it isn't okay to do it to the animal. (These examples are often unpleasant to think about, because we're used to thinking of animals and humans so differently.) For example, babies and some adults with severe cognitive disabilities have cognitive abilities and abilities to feel pleasure and pain that are no greater than those of a cow. So, if it is wrong to kill those humans or conduct scientific experiments on them, it's wrong to kill a cow or experiment on it. Animals are bred and killed for food in huge numbers, generally living in conditions bad for their well-being, even though nutritional alternatives are available. They're also used in scientific experiments that offer little benefit. Singer says that as these practices cost far more in well-being than they contribute, they're wrong.[1]

Another topic on which utilitarianism has been influential is our behavior toward the world's poor. In a famous article, Singer asks us to imagine passing a child drowning in a pond (1972). If you can save the child, it would be wrong not to, even if you suffer some inconvenience or ruin your clothes. As it happens, there are children dying of starvation and easily preventable diseases whom we can save just as easily by making donations to aid organizations. Just as it is wrong to let the child drown in the pond if we can save her, it is wrong to let a child far from us die of starvation or disease if we can save her. There is no ethically relevant difference between the child in the pond and children dying of starvation. The children dying of starvation are far away, but it isn't obvious why this matters ethically. So, Singer argues, we should be making substantial donations to aid organizations. This argument led people to establish groups like Giving What We Can, which encourages people to pledge to give 10% of their income to the most effective charities.

These arguments that we should change how we treat animals and respond to severe poverty are good examples of how utilitarianism works in practice. Although utilitarian theories developed a great deal between Bentham and Singer—we'll see several variations in the next section—we can see the continuity between Singer and Bentham's saying that "each is to count for one, and no one for more than one" (J. S. Mill 1863, 257). The utilitarian idea is still that we should make the world a better place by improving well-being, and that everyone's well-being matters equally.

Types of Utilitarianism

TYPES OF UTILITARIANISM WITH DIFFERENT THEORIES OF WELL-BEING

Utilitarianism says that what matters, ethically, is well-being. Well-being is what you have that makes your life go well: what's ultimately good for you. But philosophers of well-being disagree about what the correct theory of well-being is—about what it is that's ultimately good for you—and utilitarianism isn't committed to any particular view. One way of dividing types of utilitarianism is therefore by the theory of well-being they hold to be correct.

One view of well-being we've already encountered is hedonism, the view that well-being is a matter of having pleasure and not having pain or suffering. This was Bentham and Mill's view. Theories of well-being are concerned with what well-being *ultimately* consists in, so hedonists can think lots of different things can contribute to well-being that aren't pleasurable themselves if they *result* in pleasure. Exercising might contribute to your well-being, for example, even if you don't enjoy it. If being fit and healthy gives you pleasure, and exercise makes you fit and healthy, then exercise contributes to your well-being.

An objection to hedonism is that it makes all well-being a matter just of having certain experiences, regardless of whether those experiences are based in reality. If there was an "experience machine" that gave you great pleasure by making you think you were experiencing the life most pleasant for you, when in reality you're just immobile and hooked up to a machine, many people think hooking up to the machine wouldn't be good for your well-being (Nozick 1974, 43). But in this example, the person inside the machine is experiencing as much as or more pleasure than she would outside it. So, if you think that being in the machine wouldn't be good for your well-being, you can't think hedonism is correct.

The *desire-satisfaction* (also called *preference-satisfaction*) theory of well-being holds that well-being is a matter of having satisfied desires: getting what it is in life you want or prefer, whether or not that gives you pleasure. The word "desire" can make us think of pleasures like food or sex, but desires include things like wanting world peace, wanting to be kind, and wanting your loved ones to be safe. The stronger and more important a desire is to you, the more its satisfaction contributes to your well-being.

Some desire satisfaction theorists think that satisfying *any* desire you have contributes to your well-being, while others think that only satisfying *certain* desires matters. Some of your desires might be ones you wish you didn't have, like a regretful smoker's desire for a cigarette; and other desires might be ones that you have because you're not thinking clearly or you're misinformed, like your desire to quench your thirst by drinking what you think is water but is actually gin. The view that all your desires matter for your well-being is the *unrestricted* desire-satisfaction theory, while the views that say only some desires matter are *restricted* desire-satisfaction theories.

An objection to desire-satisfaction theories is that even if a person is thinking clearly and is well-informed, her deepest desires might be for a life that *can't* be good for her. Perhaps, for example, she wants more than anything to spend her life counting grass (Rawls 1971, 432). Another objection is that some desires don't seem to affect your well-being even if you endorse them and they're well-informed. For example, you might desire that a stranger you meet on the train has a good life, and she might go on to have a good life without you ever hearing of her again. It seems strange, at least, to think that this would contribute to your well-being, as it will never have an effect on you that you'll be aware of.

Utilitarians tend to endorse either hedonism or a desire-satisfaction theory. Some, though, hold an *objective list* theory. These theories are called "objective" because they say well-being doesn't depend on your attitudes, such as desiring things; and they're called "lists" because they usually say well-being consists of having several different things that are good for you. Things on the list might include health, knowledge, good relationships, and freedom. Having pleasure and having some satisfied desires can also be on the list. Whereas hedonism says that *only* pleasure matters, and desire-satisfaction theories say *only* satisfied desires matter, objective list theories can include some kinds of pleasures and satisfied desires on their list.

One difficulty with objective list theories is that they say that things you don't care about in the slightest can determine whether you have well-being or not, which seems wrong. For example, an objective list theory might have knowledge on the list. If someone has great knowledge about something they don't care about in the slightest, it is odd to think that this adds to their well-being. Another is that some objective list theories don't have an explanation for what does and doesn't go on the list. For example, a theory might have health, good relationships, knowledge, accomplishment, and acting well toward others on the list. But what do those things all have in common that makes them constituents of well-being?

There's a huge literature on theories of well-being, and each theory has responses to the objections I've mentioned (and to the many objections I haven't mentioned). For our purposes, what matters is that there are different theories of well-being, any one of which a utilitarian might think gives the right account of what it is we should promote in the world. Importantly, it's no objection to utilitarianism to argue that a particular theory of well-being is wrong; everyone thinks there's *some* correct theory of well-being, and whatever it says well-being is, that's what we should promote. An argument against the particular theory of well-being a utilitarian view uses is only an objection to a *particular kind* of utilitarianism, rather than utilitarianism as a whole.

Types of Utilitarianism with Different Theories of Right Action

Another difference between utilitarian theories is what exactly they say makes an action right. The simplest utilitarian criterion of right action is that an action is right if and only if, and because, it has consequences for well-being at least as good as any other act. This is called *act utilitarianism*. Put simply, what makes an act right or wrong is just the consequences for well-being it has.

A problem with act utilitarianism is that we can think of situations in which it recommends acts that seem deeply wrong. In a famous example, we're asked to imagine a sheriff in a small town with a Black minority and a White population hostile toward them (McCloskey 1957). The White population believes that a particular Black man committed a rape when he's in fact innocent. The sheriff cannot find out who committed the rape, and if no one is convicted of it, the White population will riot against the Black population and likely kill several people. The sheriff can frame and punish the person the White population suspects, and that will avert the riot. Act utilitarianism seems to say that the right thing for the sheriff to do is to frame the person. But this seems deeply wrong to many people.

In response to problems like the sheriff example, some utilitarians reject act utilitarianism in favor of *rule utilitarianism*. According to rule utilitarianism, an act is right if and only if, and because, it's in accord with one of the right ethical rules, and the right ethical rules are the ones that have the best consequences for well-being overall if people generally internalize and follow them (Hooker 2000, 32). Put simply, what makes an action right or wrong are the consequences for well-being of following the rule that says to do it. In the sheriff case, rule utilitarianism would say it's wrong for the sheriff to frame the innocent man because doing so would breach the rule that you should only punish people for things they've done. That's one of the right ethical rules because people generally following it has good consequences; almost always, punishing people for what they *have* done wrong and not what they *haven't* promotes well-being.

Act utilitarians argue that rule utilitarianism is wrong because, they say, it doesn't make sense to follow a rule in those exceptional cases when doing so won't have good consequences and might even cause misery. The act utilitarian J. J. C. Smart called always sticking to the rules "rule worship" (1956, 349). If rule utilitarianism *does* allow exceptions, act utilitarians say, then it's actually just act utilitarianism after all, as this would mean that it is ultimately the consequences of acts that matter, not the consequences of rules. For example, a good rule is to save people from drowning if you can. But what if the person is a murderous dictator, whose death will free a nation from terrible suffering? If rule utilitarians permit an exception in this case because the consequences of saving the dictator would be so bad, it seems rule utilitarians are evaluating the consequences of individual actions after all, rather than thinking in terms of rules.

However, some utilitarians have a different criterion for right *action* than they have for right *decision making*. For example, you might think that what *makes* an action right or wrong is the consequences it has for well-being. But you might also think that *deciding what to do* by working out the consequences of each act is a bad way to do things, and so you should follow rules instead. After all, it is almost certainly impractical to calculate—case by case—the consequences of every action we perform. Hence, we can accept *act utilitarianism* as the *criterion* for right action, while using *rule-following* as the decision-making *procedure*. This kind of theory is called *indirect utilitarianism* because you don't work out what to do by directly working out what the right action is.

The difference between indirect utilitarianism and rule utilitarianism can be confusing when indirect utilitarianism says the right decision procedure is to follow rules. The difference is that although rule utilitarianism and this kind of indirect utilitarianism both say you should follow the rules, rule utilitarianism says what makes an act right is that *it's in accordance with the right rules*. But indirect utilitarianism says that what makes an act right is that *it has the best consequences*. So indirect utilitarianism can sometimes seem odd, in that it can say that sometimes the act you should perform isn't actually the right act. The reason indirect utilitarianism says that is because it says you shouldn't be *thinking about* which act has the best consequences, just which act fits the best rules. (See table 6.1.)

Indirect utilitarianism can help with objections to act utilitarianism like the sheriff example, while avoiding the problems that rule utilitarianism has. It can say that the right action in the sheriff case is to frame the innocent person to avoid the deadly riot. But it also says that the sheriff should *not* decide to do that,

Table 6.1. Rule Utilitarianism and Indirect Utilitarianism

	Rule utilitarianism	Indirect utilitarianism
What makes an act right?	The act fits the set of rules that have the best consequences.	The act has the best consequences.
How do you decide what to do?	Follow the right set of rules (the rules that have the best consequences).	Follow the right set of rules (the rules that have the best consequences).

Source: Author's own material.

because the sheriff shouldn't be thinking about which act has the best consequences. Instead, he should be making decisions according to the best rules, which say *not* to frame innocent people. Although following those rules means the sheriff won't perform the best act *in this case*, over the course of the sheriff's life he'll do more good this way.

Objections

As with other ethical theories, a wide range of arguments have been made against utilitarianism. Utilitarians have responded to these objections by adjusting their theories or arguing that the objections fail. This prompts a new round of objections and yet more responses to those objections, generating a large literature. Here we'll look at just three objections and the most common utilitarian responses to them.

THE CLUELESSNESS OBJECTION

One objection to utilitarianism is that we can't be sure what the consequences of our actions will be, and so if utilitarianism is the right ethical theory, we can never know what the right action is. If utilitarianism is right, the objection says, then we're ethically "clueless." Utilitarians, though, say that we know well enough the *likelihood* of various consequences of our actions. For example, it's possible that killing someone just because he annoys you might have good consequences overall, but very unlikely; and it's possible that saving a drowning child will have bad consequences overall, but very unlikely. We can't *always* know what the right action is under utilitarianism, but that's the case for ethical theories in general.

The other two objections we'll look at are more important than the cluelessness objection. One of these objections is that if utilitarianism is correct, then we're obliged to do things that seem to be very wrong; this can be called the *injustice* objection (Mulgan 2007, 93). The other objection is that if utilitarianism is correct, then we're obliged to do things that ask far too much of us; this is called the *demandingness* objection.

THE INJUSTICE OBJECTION

We've encountered an example of the injustice objection, the sheriff case. Another common example is a surgeon who has five patients who need different lifesaving organ transplants and one healthy patient with all those organs. The surgeon could save the five sick patients by killing the healthy patient and transplanting her organs to the others. Utilitarianism seems to say the surgeon ought to do that, which seems wrong.

We also saw earlier a possible utilitarian response to such injustice objections, which was to change from act utilitarianism to rule utilitarianism. The rules with the best consequences say sheriffs should only charge people they believe are guilty (or the legal system would collapse) and surgeons shouldn't deliberately kill their patients (or people wouldn't go to the hospital).

But there are ways to respond to the injustice objection while sticking to act utilitarianism. One way is to admit that act utilitarianism requires the action that *seems* unjust, but to deny that it *is* unjust. For example, utilitarians might say that it *feels* very wrong for the sheriff to frame the innocent person, but ask, is it *really* better to let several people be killed by rioters instead? Part of this utilitarian response can be arguing that our intuitions about these cases aren't reliable; that those intuitions are shaped by what's *usually* the right thing to do or are something we have because of humans' early evolutionary history, and they don't reliably work in societies like ours where we have well-developed legal systems and people can do things like organ transplants.

Another response to the injustice objections is to say that the examples are too unrealistic to matter. Utilitarians might say, for example, that circumstances in which a surgeon can kill a person and successfully transplant five of their organs into five other patients, while being certain those five people's lives will be saved, are too unlikely to worry about. And if a surgeon thinks she is in these circumstances, the chances that she's got something wrong and wouldn't make things better by killing the healthy patient are high enough that she should play it safe and just care for her patients in the normal way. Although Bentham and Mill didn't encounter these kinds of objections, this kind of response seems in keeping with their emphasis on real, practical matters.

THE DEMANDINGNESS OBJECTION

The demandingness objection is that if utilitarianism is right, then there are some things we're obliged to do, but we *can't* be obliged to do them because they ask too much of us. For example, think of Singer's argument that we ought to save children's lives if we can, even if they're in distant countries. There are so many children whose lives we can save by making donations that Singer's argument seems to mean that we should radically change our lives. Any money we spend on luxuries, even small ones like a trip to the movies, could instead go toward saving people's lives. And as our luxuries don't make as much difference to our well-being as staying alive does to the well-being of people facing death from curable disease or starvation, utilitarianism seems to require us to give up all our luxuries. We'd not only have to live extremely simply, but also give up on our important plans in life—for example, going to university—which don't contribute more to our well-being than using our resources and time to save others contributes to theirs. But, the objection goes, this *can't* be right—if an ethical theory asks this much of us, it must be wrong.

One utilitarian response to the demandingness objection is to accept that utilitarianism is this demanding but deny that means it's wrong. We happen to live in a world that's very unjust and in which we're able to make a difference to the lives of suffering people not geographically close to us (something that just happens to be true at this point in history). In these circumstances, it happens that we can save others from death or disease instead of indulging in luxuries for ourselves, so we should do so. Utilitarians can, again, question the reliability of our intuitions that utilitarianism is too demanding, as we evolved those intuitions when we couldn't affect distant strangers.

Utilitarians can also soften the demandingness of the theory in a couple of ways. One way is to abandon the distinction between *right and wrong* in favor of a distinction between *better and worse*: we should think of actions as being on a scale of worse to better. This is called *scalar utilitarianism* (Norcross 2006). This means we can think of someone giving some of her income and time to people in need, but still spending time on her own plans and enjoying some indulgences, as not doing what's *wrong*, just not doing what's *best*. Another thing that can soften utilitarianism's demandingness is to distinguish between *doing something wrong* (or not doing what's best) and *doing something blameworthy*. Although utilitarianism might mean that people should ideally be giving a great deal of their money and time to others, it doesn't necessarily mean that people should be blamed for not doing that. Utilitarianism only supports blaming people when that has the best consequences.

Summary

Utilitarianism has waxed and waned in its popularity since its inception. It was the dominant ethical theory for much of the twentieth century before falling out of favor in the second half, as duty-based and virtue-based theories became more widely accepted. However, Western philosophers are strongly divided on which ethical theory is correct, and utilitarianism retains a strong following. There are no indications of this changing, and utilitarianism will continue to have strong support—and to have a strong influence on many non-utilitarian theories—as long as people find appealing the ideas that what matters ethically is making the world a better place, and that what makes the world a better place is the well-being of everyone in it.

Notes

1. Singer has been accused of seriously devaluing the lives of disabled people in some such arguments.

Further Reading

PRIMARY SOURCES

Bentham, Jeremy. 1789/1970. *An Introduction to the Principles of Morals and Legislation.* In *The Collected Works of Jeremy Bentham,* edited by J. H. Burns and H. L. A. Hart. Oxford, UK: Clarendon Press.
———. 1830. *Rationale of Reward.* London, UK: Robert Heward.
Hooker, Brad. 2000. *Ideal Code, Real World: A Rule-Consequentialist Theory of Morality.* Oxford, UK: Oxford University Press.

This is the leading presentation of rule utilitarianism.

McCloskey, H. J. 1957. "An Examination of Restricted Utilitarianism." *The Philosophical Review* 66, no. 4: 466–85.
Mill, Harriet Taylor. 1998. *The Complete Works of Harriet Taylor Mill,* edited by Jo Ellen Jacobs. Bloomington: Indiana University Press.
Mill, John Stuart. 1873/1964. "Autobiography." In *The Collected Works of John Stuart Mill, Volume 1,* edited by J. M. Robson. Toronto, Canada: Toronto University Press.
———. 1859/2003. *On Liberty.* London, UK: Penguin.
———. 1869/1984. "On the Subjection of Women." In *The Collected Works of John Stuart Mill, Volume xxi—Essays on Equality, Law, and Education,* edited by J. M. Robson. Toronto, Canada: University of Toronto Press.
———. 1863/2001. *Utilitarianism.* Indianapolis: Hackett Publishing.
Norcross, Alastair. 2006. "The Scalar Approach to Utilitarianism." In *The Blackwell Guide to Mill's Utilitarianism,* edited by Henry West, 217–32. Malden, MA: Wiley-Blackwell, 2006.
Nozick, Robert. 1974. *Anarchy, State, and Utopia.* Oxford, UK: Basil Blackwell.
Rawls, John. 1971. *A Theory of Justice.* Cambridge, MA: Harvard University Press.
Sidgwick, Henry. 1874/1981. *The Methods of Ethics.* 7th ed. Edited by John Rawls. Indianapolis, IA: Hackett.
Singer, Peter. 1975. *Animal Liberation: A New Ethics for Our Treatment of Animals.* New York: HarperCollins.
———. 1972. "Famine, Affluence, and Morality." *Philosophy and Public Affairs* 1, no. 3: 229–43.

————. 1979. *Practical Ethics*. Cambridge, UK: Cambridge University Press.

This is a good introduction to modern utilitarian approaches to a range of practical issues.

Smart, J. J. C. 1956. "Extreme and Restricted Utilitarianism." *Philosophical Quarterly* 6, no. 25: 344–54.

————, and Bernard Williams. 1973. *Utilitarianism: For and Against*. Cambridge, UK: Cambridge University Press.

This is a short book with one section by a prominent utilitarian and the other by a prominent opponent of utilitarianism.

Secondary Sources

*These are good general introductions to utilitarianism.

*Bykvist, Krister. 2009. *Utilitarianism: A Guide for the Perplexed*. London, UK: Continuum.

*de Lazari-Radek, Katarzyna, and Peter Singer. 2017. *Utilitarianism: A Very Short Introduction*. Oxford, UK: Oxford University Press.

Judson, Frederick N. 1910. "A Modern View of the Law Reforms of Jeremy Bentham." *Columbia Law Review* 10, no. 1: 41–54.

*Mulgan, Tim. 2007. *Understanding Utilitarianism*. Stocksfield, UK: Acumen.

*Nathanson, S. 2014. "Act and Rule Utilitarianism." In *Internet Encyclopedia of Philosophy*. https://iep.utm.edu/util-a-r/.

7

Mozi and Inclusive Care

MICHAEL HEMMINGSEN

Introduction

Mozi (originally called Mo Di) was an ancient Chinese philosopher who lived during the Warring States period (475–221 BCE). He is considered the founder of the philosophical school that bears his name and is credited as the author of the text *The Mozi* (almost certainly incorrectly, as *The Mozi* was more likely an edited collection of chapters by like-minded authors and members of the Mohist school).

Mohism offers a communitarian, public-facing moral philosophy grounded in the benefit of all. It eventually withered away as an independent philosophical school. However, to some extent the disappearance of Mohism can be attributed to its success, in the sense that its most significant ideas were absorbed into rival schools such as Confucianism. Mozi can also be thought of as China's first philosopher, in that *The Mozi* was the first attempt in that tradition to offer explicit arguments for a view, provoking rival schools to do so in turn and inaugurating China's rich history of philosophical disputation. Despite being nearly two and a half thousand years old, Mohism is a sophisticated philosophy that offers insights into ethics that have relevance to this day.

Doctrines

For Mohists, unless we affirm the correct views, we will not act morally. Hence, Mohist ethics revolves fundamentally around words. The *dao* (道)—the "Way" of morality—should be *explicitly* articulated in what are called *yan* (statements/doctrines 言). Affirming righteous (*yi* 義) doctrines will lead to morally correct action, whereas affirming unrighteous doctrines will lead to the opposite. As a result, of central importance to ethics is the identification of the correct *yan*. Mohist ethics is therefore less about the development of the right character (unlike the rival school of Confucianism) and more about knowing and adopting the correct moral view.

Importantly, *yan* are not merely private guides for behavior; they are not a personal moral code. *Yan* are statements that should be publicly shared and followed by all. If a *yan* cannot be consistently followed by all without causing problematic or self-defeating consequences, this is clear evidence that it is not a correct *yan* (Fraser 2013). Mozi expresses this idea in a conversation with the egoist Wumazi, who asserts a *yan* under which he would willingly kill another to benefit himself:

> Master Mo Zi said: "Is your way of thinking to be kept secret or is it to be told to others?"
>
> Wu Ma Zi replied: "Why should I keep my way of thinking a secret? I shall tell others."
>
> Master Mo Zi said: "In that case, then, if one person agrees with you, one person will want to kill you to benefit himself. If ten people agree with you, ten people will want to kill you to benefit themselves. If [everyone in] the world agrees with you, [then everyone in] the world will want to kill you to benefit themselves." (46.19)

In other words, Mozi points out that Wumazi's *yan* cannot be applied universally and should therefore be rejected. If Wumazi alone were to follow his *yan*, it might benefit him. But if he were to publicize his *yan*, as Mohists think he ought to—and if everyone were to follow it—it would end up being self-defeating. Others following Wumazi's *yan* would be inclined harm *him* to benefit themselves, precisely the opposite of what his *yan* was intended to accomplish. Mohist ethics therefore advocates for a single, unified moral code across society, a set of standards that *everyone* ought to—and can consistently—follow. Any candidate model of ethics must be able to be universalized in this way if it is to provide a legitimate foundation for action.

Universalization and Benefit

But what tests must a *yan* pass if we are to declare it successfully "universalized"? What are the standards that a *yan* must meet to be considered *yi* (righteous)? Mohists propose several "gauges" (*biao* 表) by which they determine the correctness of a *yan*. They ask (1) whether the *yan* agrees with the practices of the sage kings—the ancient rulers who are taken to be a model for righteous governance; (2) whether the *yan* corresponds to common experience; and (3) whether the *yan* leads to benefit (*li* 利).

The main focus of Mohist ethics is arguably about the third of these gauges: whether the *yan* leads to beneficial consequences. But what counts as "beneficial consequences"? In the Mohist view, benefit consists in wealth, population, and social order. In other words, if a *yan* increases wealth or population or contributes to social order, then we ought to affirm that *yan*.

But why the emphasis on wealth, population, and social order? Unlike utilitarians, Mohists did not engage in a debate about the fundamental goods that constitute benefit. As far as we know, they were not concerned with justifying wealth, population, and social order by reference to anything more fundamental (such as happiness or pleasure). This lack of concern with the foundations of benefit is unlikely to be because Mohists were unsophisticated in their thinking. Rather, Mohists saw themselves above all as social reformers. They identified clear problems—war, poverty, and so on—and developed their philosophical system as an attempt to overcome those problems. In other words, instead of developing positions on abstract philosophical questions, the answers to which are unlikely to have any direct bearing on the issues they were concerned about, first and foremost Mohists wanted to offer a practical solution to the challenges facing society (Loy 2008). Hence, they simply assumed—not unreasonably—that the audience they were addressing would agree with them that wealth, population, and social order were valuable.

When speaking about "wealth," however, Mohists did not consider it in the abstract, in the sense of increasing a society's prosperity with no reference to *who* benefits. Mohists were concerned with the poverty of the common people, and the pursuit of wealth was aimed primarily at meeting people's basic needs. In fact, Mozi clearly spoke out *against* the pursuit of wealth for entertainment and war. He pointed out that

> The people have three hardships: to be hungry and not find food; to be cold and not find clothing; to be weary and not find rest. These three things are great hardships for the people. If this is so, then suppose we strike the great bells, beat the sounding drums, strum lutes, blow pipes, and brandish shields and battle-axes. Will this enable the people to find the materials for food and clothing? I certainly don't think this will ever be so. (32.4)

In other words, we ought not to spend money on entertainment or weapons while the people are still hungry, cold, and weary.

With a global population of 8 billion, the assumption that increasing the population is a benefit often seems strange to a modern audience. However, given the very different conditions at the time—for instance, the constant need for farmers to cultivate the land and produce enough food, and the loss of able-bodied citizens to war between states—it is not hard to imagine why increasing the population may have seemed obviously beneficial at the time.

Inclusive Care

What *yan* leads to wealth, population, and social order? To answer this, we need to consider what kind of *yan* leads to the opposite: poverty, low population, and disorder. Though the term itself is never used explicitly in *The Mozi*, a reasonable candidate for this contrary *yan* is *bie ai* (別愛), or exclusive/partial care. To follow the *yan* of *bie ai* is to include some people in our circle of moral concern while excluding others. In other words, it is to hold that while some people matter, morally speaking, others do not; or that (like Wumazi) those close to us simply deserve greater concern than those further away. Being willing to benefit fellow countrymen by harming those who live elsewhere indicates an attitude of *bie ai*, as is being willing to ignore the suffering of others so long as one's own family is doing well. It is not, then, a wholly uncommon *yan* in modern society, as I am sure it was not in Mozi's time. In Mozi's view, the evils of the world are the result of this kind of attitude—of being willing to harm others to benefit ourselves (or those close to us)—being a regularly followed, universalized model for conduct (Loy 2013).

In contrast to this attitude, Mozi offers the *yan* of *jian ai* (兼 愛). Precisely how this term ought to be translated is a matter of disagreement among scholars of Mohist philosophy, and the specific English terms used typically correspond to different ways in which Mohist ethics is interpreted. For our purposes, I translate the term as "inclusive care," though alternatives to *jian* include "universal" and "impartial," and *ai* is sometimes translated as "love" or "regard" rather than "care."

For Mohists, the *yan* of inclusive care ought to replace that of *bie ai*. If this happens, poverty, low population, and disorder will be reduced or eliminated. If inclusive care is the model for our collective conduct, then "there would not be savage battles . . . [or] mutual usurpation," "there would be kindness and loyalty . . . compassion and filial conduct . . . [and] harmony and accord," and "the strong would not dominate the weak, the many would not plunder the few, the rich would not despise the poor, the noble would not scorn the lowly, and the cunning would not deceive the foolish." If all follow inclusive care, then "Within the world, in all cases, there would be nothing to cause calamity, usurpation, resentment and hatred to arise" (Mozi 15.3).

What, then, does it mean to act according to a *yan* of *jian ai*? The second term, *ai*—which we are translating here as "care"—is less an emotional attitude than it is a disposition to act to benefit the recipient of our care. In other words, for the Mohists, to "care" about someone means to be inclined to benefit them and disinclined to harm (*hai* 害) them. This, I think, is captured in our everyday use of the term, in that to claim to care about someone while not being willing to actually help that person—to benefit them—seems confused (Martinich and Tsoi 2015). To reduce "care" to a mere emotional stance—feeling strongly positive toward them—while disentangling it from a disposition to benefit misses something essential about what it *means* to care (Robins 2012). In other words, caring for the Mohists is not simply talk, and it is not primarily a feeling. If we care about someone, then we are disposed to *act* by doing things we identify as beneficial to that person, while avoiding or opposing things that we take to be harmful to them (Fraser 2016). This does not mean, of course, that our disposition to benefit that person cannot be *accompanied* by affection and emotional attachment. Merely that, for the Mohists, it is the disposition to act that most fundamentally constitutes caring (Fraser 2016).

As for *jian*, Mohist ethics is focused on providing standards that can be publicly followed and regularly practiced. Hence, to understand this term, we should situate it in a social context. In other words, *jian ai* is not about individuals acting in isolation from each other but is rather focused on the way that we can *all* include one another in a system of *mutual* care. There is no expectation that we should include others in a purely one-directional, altruistic way; acting to benefit others while they take advantage of our generosity. Instead, the background for our actions is that *jian ai* is a *yan* that is followed by all—or at least most—people in a society. As such, when we act to benefit others, they will behave the same way. They may not benefit us directly; *jian ai* at a social level does not necessarily require one-to-one reciprocity. However, our care for others will be returned to us, if not from the person we benefit specifically (they may not, after all, be able to benefit us in return), then from others participating in our shared system of mutual care.

In saying that we have no obligation to act in a purely altruistic way, however, there are two caveats. First, Mohists do think, quite plausibly, that people tend to return the treatment that they are shown. Hence, if we treat others according to a *yan* of *ex*clusive care, they will treat us in the same way. Similarly, if we treat them according to a *yan* of *in*clusive care, they are likely to reciprocate. Acting altruistically toward others is therefore recommended to spread the *yan* of *jian ai* and help it to become society's standard.

Second, while following *jian ai* in a system of mutual care is the minimum required of us—it is the standard of righteousness (*yi*)—the sage, as well as perhaps the ruler (Back 2017), acts according to a higher standard: benevolence (*ren* 仁). This standard *does* involve altruism. However, at least in the case of sages, *ren* is supererogatory. That is, it is morally *praiseworthy*, but is not a basic moral *obligation*.

Equal Concern versus Equal Treatment

The *"jian"* in *"jian ai"* is about *who* we should include in our system of mutual care, and its answer to this question is "everyone." That is, we should not limit our relations of mutual care to only our family, or the people in our neighborhood or country, but instead should consider ourselves to be in relations of mutual care—at least in principle—with absolutely everyone, everywhere. Being in relations of mutual care with everyone, however, does not mean that we ought to treat everyone the same. We can therefore separate *jian ai* into two dimensions: *whom* we ought to care about, and *how* we ought to care about them. Hence, the fact that Mohism thinks that we should care about *all* people does not *necessarily* entail that the *way* we care about everyone must be identical. Though Mozi certainly thinks that we ought to "regard the person of my friend as I regard my own person, or regard my friend's parents as I regard my own parents" (Mozi 16.5), *jian ai* is not a matter of equal *treatment*.

Mozi tends to emphasize our obligations to those with whom we are in relationships. I can care about someone on the other side of the world in the sense that, *if* we were to interact, I would be disposed to benefit and not harm them. However, this is quite different from saying that, regardless of such a relationship, I ought to act to benefit complete strangers. In this sense, then, Mozi's focus seems to be not on some abstract sense of equality between people, but rather on how we ought to conduct ourselves in respect to those with whom we are in particularistic relationships: friends, family, fellow citizens, and so on.

Since Mohist ethics is fundamentally social, it does not merely govern how we treat others in individual interactions, but also engenders more general obligations to support social institutions that benefit others, such as by ensuring that those in our society who struggle to fend for themselves are taken care of (Back 2017). In fact, Mozi explicitly states that inclusive care entails that [people] will use their acute hearing and keen sight to help each other see and hear; they will use their strong and powerful limbs to help each other in action; and they will use principles to encourage mutual instruction. As a result, those who are old, without wives and children, will have the means of support and nourishment through their old age, and those who are young and weak, or who are alone without a father or mother, will have the means of help and support while they grow into adulthood. (Mozi 16.4)

But what about complete strangers, citizens of other countries, and so on? Can those who have no relationship to us whatsoever be disregarded? For Mohists, even complete strangers must be included in our care. But if we recall the earlier contrast of *jian ai* with *bie ai*, the fundamental moral mistake that Mohists identify is to act to *harm* others to *benefit* ourselves (or our family, country, etc.). As applied to strangers, we might therefore say that *jian ai* is less about being disposed to positively benefit others at one's own expense, and more about never *harming* others for one's own benefit. Hence, while our obligations under *jian ai* to particular others are positive, our obligations to non-particular others should properly be understood as negative, in the sense that *jian ai* forbids actions such as attacking other states for the benefit of our own, or stealing from others to benefit ourselves or our family (Back 2017).

In summary, we might understand *jian ai*—the inclusion of all others in our sphere of moral concern—as entailing three different kinds of behavior. First, we should be trying to actively benefit those with whom we are in direct, particular relationships. For instance, we should act in a filial way to our parents, care for our children, show loyalty to our friends, and so on (Back 2017). Second, we ought to help those in special need, such as the hungry, disabled, elderly, and so forth. We are not expected to treat people in those positions like friends or family members, in the sense that *jian ai* does not require that we care for another person's parents in the *same way* we would care for our own. However, we do have obligations, as part of a collective, to act in ways that ensure that those with special needs are taken care of and that everyone is able to live a life of dignity. Third, we must ensure that our actions do not *harm* non-particular strangers (Back 2017). Hence, not-harming is the fundamental principle that applies to all actions, with our obligations becoming more stringent as our relationships become more concrete (Loy 2013).

While the above certainly describes a form of differential treatment, it is arguably showing all people equal consideration. The difference in treatment from person to person is not an indication that some are deserving of more consideration than others. Rather, it arises from the fact that equal consideration can take different forms, depending on how and why we interact with others.

But how is it possible for a theory grounded in *benefit* to distinguish responsibilities based on relationship? To say that my obligations to friends and family are different to my obligations to strangers suggests, on the face of it, that either benefit is not the most important criterion of morality (in the sense that having a certain relationship to someone—a decidedly non-consequentialist factor—is just as, or more fundamental than, benefit). Or that there is a difference between the individuals I interact with themselves that justifies differential treatment. But my family being *my* family should not matter in an objective sense. After all, they may be complete strangers to *you*; and someone who is a stranger to me might be *your* family member. If I am concerned with performing the actions that bring about the most benefit, then it should not matter *who* benefits. After all, sometimes the action that brings about the most benefit overall will involve sacrificing my own family for the sake of a stranger. But Mohists do not require this.

To make sense of differential treatment, despite the fundamental role of benefit, we should understand Mohism as a form of rule consequentialism. Given the emphasis on *yan* (doctrine), as well as the Mohists' constant justification of principles in terms of benefit, such a reading of Mohist ethics is a natural one.

Put simply, rule consequentialists hold that while *ultimately* we ought to be concerned with bringing about the most benefit overall, this goal should be mediated through a set of rules. To find out how we ought to act, we need to first work out what set of rules—if generally followed—would bring about the best consequences. In other words, we do not act to bring about benefit directly—through calculating the benefit of each act individually—but rather act according to those rules that lead to the most benefit.

According to the Mohists, *jian ai* is one such rule; differential treatment is another. After all, a society in which people treat family and friends like strangers—in the sense that they do not go out of their way to help them—is likely to involve less benefit than the opposite. Conversely, a society in which strangers are treated like family members is also likely to be worse, in that it requires an impractical level of self-sacrifice. Hence, Mohists do not claim that strangers are objectively any less important than family members; rather, they simply think that a rule that allows for us to treat those two groups differentially leads to greater benefit overall.

Consequentialism versus Divine Command Theory

As discussed earlier, *jian ai* is—Mohists think—supported by the three gauges: correspondence to the words and actions of the ancient sage kings; its agreement with empirical observation; and the benefits it brings. However, Mozi also separately raises another potential source of justification for *jian ai*: that it reflects the will of Heaven (*tian* 天).

While the correspondence of *jian ai* to the words and actions of the ancient sage kings is more clearly a secondary justification for *jian ai*—and while empirical observation is more relevant to factual rather than moral matters—there is disagreement among interpreters of *The Mozi* as to whether the *fundamental* justification for *jian ai* should consist in benefit or Heaven's will. Certainly Mohists assume that there is no *practical* inconsistency to holding that both benefit *and* Heaven's will support *jian ai*: as a matter of fact, they think, what is beneficial is what Heaven wills, and what Heaven wills is always beneficial. Mozi holds that "only when there is clear compliance with Heaven's intention, and obedience to Heaven's intention is widely practised in the world, will the administration be well ordered, the ten thousand people harmonious, the country wealthy, materials for use sufficient, and the ordinary people all obtain warm clothes and enough food so they will be at peace and free from anxiety" (Mozi 27.3). Nonetheless, *philosophically* holding to both sources of justification raises some difficult issues. Unlike in contemporaneous philosophical schools, which saw Heaven in a naturalized way, as non-personal—more or less equivalent to the natural world, without beliefs and desires—Mohists believed that Heaven was at least a quasi-personal entity with a will that it expressed in action. It is from these actions that Mohists inferred support for *jian ai*, since Heaven clearly acts, they think, to care and benefit all people in an inclusive way. After all, nature provides everything we need to sustain our lives, and does so without favoritism. As Mozi describes it, "Heaven is broad and unselfish in its actions, and is generous in its bestowing without considering itself virtuous" (Mozi 4.3).

The difficulty with using Heaven's will to support *jian ai*, however, is that it is at least *in principle* possible for Heaven—as a *person*—to will something *other than* our benefit. Hence, though Heaven is assumed by Mohists to will benefit, it is conceivable that it may do otherwise. If so, we are faced with the question of which of the two sources of grounding is more fundamental. That is, if Heaven wills other than benefit, then what moral standard should we follow? Should we follow Heaven's will (and thereby not bring about benefit), or should we try to bring about benefit (and thereby fail to follow Heaven's will)?

If Heaven's will is primary, then Mohism is a form of deontology: our duty to Heaven is prior to the good. On the other hand, if benefit is the ultimate principle, then Mohism is a form of consequentialism: the good is prior to our duty; for example, we first establish what is good (wealth, population, and social order) and from there can work out what we are obligated to do. These are two extremely different accounts of morality, and at most only one of them can be held consistently by the Mohists.

Which way to go on this question is still a matter of dispute among scholars of Mohism, since Mozi at times seems to imply that *both* sources of justification are fundamental. He says on the one hand that "righteousness undoubtedly comes from Heaven" (Mozi 27.1), which certainly suggests that benefit is good *because* Heaven wills it. On the other hand, Mozi frequently speaks about Heaven's righteousness in a way that indicates that its promoting benefit is *evidence of* its righteousness, which only makes sense if we take benefit as the more fundamental standard.

Aside from assuming that Mozi was simply confused, we therefore have two main options: 1) Mozi thought that beneficial results is the fundamental standard of morality, making him a consequentialist; or 2) Mozi thought that following the commands—or will—of Heaven is the fundamental standard of morality, making him a Divine Command Theorist (DCT).

We can think through this problem by considering Mozi's comparison of Heaven to measuring devices. For instance, he says that

> Heaven's intention is no different to a wheelwright having compasses or a carpenter having a square. Now a wheelwright takes hold of his compasses in order to determine whether things in the world are round or not, saying: "What accords with my compasses is called round and what does not accord with my compasses is called not round." In this way the roundness or non-roundness of all things can be ascertained and known. Why is this so? It is because the standard for roundness is clear. Also a carpenter takes hold of his square in order to determine whether things in the world are square or not, saying: "What accords with my square is called square and what does not accord with my square is called not square." In this way the squareness or non-squareness of all things can be ascertained and known. Why is this so? It is because the standard for squareness is clear. (Mozi 27.10)

This kind of comparison can be taken in two ways. One reading is that Mozi sees Heaven as *establishing* a standard: something is round *because* it accords with the compass. The relevant kind of analogy is to something like a meter or a gram. While distance or weight are objective qualities, *measurements*—such as meters or grams—are not objective. There is no natural fact of the world that a certain distance is a meter: that a certain length can be referred to as "one meter" is something that human beings have decided on. Hence, the creation of the standard comes first, and whether a thing in the world matches the standard comes second.

This first interpretation of this passage therefore accords with DCT, in that it is taking Heaven to be *creating* what is right or wrong. Just as we cannot call something "round" unless it accords with the compass, we similarly cannot call something "good" unless it accords with Heaven's will. Heaven's will establishes the standard of goodness first, and only after that can we determine whether something in the world meets that standard.

However, we can read the compass metaphor in a slightly different way. After all, we typically would not say that according with a compass *makes* something a circle. A circle *just is* a circle, and it is so whether we use a compass to establish that fact or not. Rather than *creating* the circleness of the circle, a compass is instead a tool we can use to *determine* whether something *already is* a circle. Under this interpretation, benefit is a good independently of our ability to measure this fact. Heaven's will should therefore be understood merely as a useful device—like a compass—for working out, in practice, what things *are* good in and of themselves, since as a matter of fact Heaven always wills the good. Under such an interpretation, the good—the beneficial consequences—come first.

While the matter of how to interpret this metaphor—and the grounding of Mozi's ethics more generally—is still a matter of debate, the use of the compass metaphor and the reference to tools like set squares suggests that the consequentialist interpretation of Mozi's ethics is the more plausible one. After all, Mozi could have chosen to use as his metaphor measures that are determined by human beings, such as distances or weights. But instead, he used examples such as circles and squares, which more plausibly exist prior to our measuring of them. Unlike scales or meter-rules, compasses and set squares *determine* but do not *establish* standards. Hence, for the Mohists, Heaven acts to *illustrate* Mohist ideals and can provide a compelling rhetorical justification for *jian ai*. But Heaven does not create those ideals.

Under this view, Heaven is what we might refer to as an "epistemic authority," such as scientists or historians. For instance, as a layperson I will generally trust a physicists' determination of matters relating to physics. However, this is not because I think the physicist *makes* physics facts true with her declarations. Rather, I merely think that physicists are reliable guides to what is true and what is not when it comes to that field. Similarly, Heaven is the highest authority when it comes to moral matters. If we use Heaven as our guide, we will almost certainly end up making the correct decision. However, it is benefit, rather than Heaven's will, that fundamentally *grounds* Mohist ethics.

Summary

Mohism is a rule consequentialist moral philosophy in that it justifies its fundamental principle—*jian ai*, or inclusive care—on the basis of the consequences it brings. Mohists advocate that we ought to affirm *yan*—or doctrines—that can be followed by everyone consistently and that will lead to wealth, population, and social order, and they argue that *jian ai* is just such a doctrine. If everyone follows it, we will all be better off than if we were to exclude others from our care. For instance, we might follow a doctrine of exclusive care, and care for only our own parents, but not for the parents of others. However, if we were to do so, then just as we have no disposition to benefit our neighbor's parents, *they* will have no disposition to benefit *ours*, and if our parents are ever in need of care that we cannot provide on our own, no one will step in to assist. By contrast, if we are disposed to benefit everyone's parents, and everyone else is disposed to benefit ours, then we do not have to worry, since their well-being rests on a secure foundation.

Nevertheless, *jian ai* does not entail complete equality of treatment. For instance, though we should have the same *care* for the parents of others that we do for our own, since they stand in a different relationship to us than our own parents, the form our care takes is different. We ought to positively benefit our own parents, whereas we are merely obliged to help our neighbor's parents when they are in need of assistance. As for complete strangers, since we are not in a concrete relationship with them, our obligations end at ensuring that our actions do not bring them harm. In this respect, then, Mohist ethics is a system of mutual care in which we ought to have equal *consideration* for all, but in which our *treatment* of others differs depending on how they are related to us.

Though benefit is usually taken to be the fundamental criterion of morality for Mohists, they also exhort us to follow Heaven by taking the way Heaven's will is expressed in nature as a standard for governing our actions. For instance, Mohists think it is illustrative that nature provides the necessities of life—sunlight, water, and so on—in an indiscriminate, inclusive way, and they think that we ought to emulate this attitude. However, though we must follow Heaven, it is most likely that we ought to respect Heaven's will not because it issues commands that generate moral obligation in and of themselves, but rather because Heaven is a reliable guide as to what is morally correct. Hence, Mohism is *foundationally* a form of consequentialism; the exhortation to follow Heaven's will operates merely as an example to follow, required because of our lack of knowledge of what is good.

Further Reading

PRIMARY SOURCES

Mozi. 2010. *The Mozi: A Complete Translation*. Translated by Ian Johnston. Hong Kong: Chinese University of Hong Kong Press.

SECONDARY SOURCES

Ahern, Denis M. 1976. "Is Mo Tzu a Utilitarian?" *Journal of Chinese Philosophy* 3, no. 2: 185–93. https://doi.org/10.1111/j.1540-6253.1976.tb00388.x.
Back, Youngsun. 2017. "Reconstructing Mozi's Jian'ai." *Philosophy East and West* 67, no. 4: 1092–1117. https://doi.org/10.1353/pew.2017.0095.
———. 2019. "Rethinking Mozi's *Jian'ai*: The Rule to Care." *Dao* 18: 531–53. https://doi.org/10.1007/s11712-019-09685-0.
Chiu, Wai-wai. 2013. "*Jian ai* and the Mohist Attack of Early Confucianism." *Philosophy Compass* 8, no. 5: 425–37. https://doi.org/10.1111/phc3.12031.
Defoort, Carine, and Nicolas Standaert, eds. 2013. *The Mozi as an Evolving Text: Different Voices in Early Chinese Thought*. Leiden: Brill.
Duda, Kristopher. 2001. "Reconsidering Mo Tzu on the Foundations of Morality." *Asian Philosophy* 11, no. 1: 23–31. https://doi.org/10.1080/09552360120048825.
Fraser, Chris. 2016. *The Philosophy of the Mòzǐ: The First Consequentialists*. New York: Columbia University Press.
Hemmingsen, Michael. 2020. "The Tension Between Divine Command Theory and Utilitarianism in Mozi and George Berkeley: A Comparison." *Philosophy East and West* 70, no. 3: 740–56. https://doi.org/10.1353/pew.2020.0052.
Johnson, Daniel M. 2011. "Mozi's Moral Theory: Breaking the Hermeneutical Stalemate." *Philosophy East and West* 61, no. 2: 347–64. https://doi.org/10.1353/pew.2011.0021.
Lai, Whalen. 1993. "The Public Good That Does the Public Good: A New Reading of Mohism." *Asian Philosophy* 3, no. 2: 125–41. https://doi.org/10.1080/09552369308575379.

Loy, Hui-Chieh. 2008. "Justification and Debate: Thoughts on Most Moral Epistemology." *Journal of Chinese Philosophy* 35, no. 3: 455–71. https://doi.org/10.1111/j.1540-6253.2008.00491.x.

———. 2011. "The Word and the Way in *Mozi*." *Philosophy Compass* 6, no. 10: 652–62. https://doi.org/10.1111/j.1747-9991.2011.00426.x.

———. 2013. "On the Argument for *Jian'ai*." *Dao* 12: 587–604. https://doi.org/10.1007/s11712-013-9346-x.

Lu, Xiufen. 2006. "Understanding Mozi's Foundations of Morality: A Comparative Perspective." *Asian Philosophy* 16, no. 2: 123–34. https://doi.org/10.1080/09552360600772769.

Martinich, A. P., and Siwing Tsoi. 2015. "Mozi's Ideal Political Philosophy." *Asian Philosophy* 25, no. 3: 253–74. https://doi.org/10.1080/09552367.2015.1079936.

Robins, Dan. 2012. "Mohist Care." *Philosophy East and West* 62, no. 1: 60–91. https://doi.org/10.1353/pew.2012.0005.

Soles, David E. 1999. "Mo Tzu and the Foundations of Morality." *Journal of Chinese Philosophy* 26, no. 1: 37–48. https://doi.org/10.1111/j.1540-6253.1999.tb00531.x.

van Norden, Bryan. 2007. *Virtue Ethics and Consequentialism in Early Chinese Philosophy*. Cambridge: Cambridge University Press.

Vorenkamp, Dirck. 1992. "Another Look at Utilitarianism in Mo-Tzu's Thought." *Journal of Chinese Philosophy* 43, no. 1: 423–43. https://doi.org/10.1163/15406253-01904004.

Wu, Yun, and Amin Ebrahimi Afrouzi. 2020. "The Mohist Notion of Gongyi." *Dao* 19: 269–87. https://doi.org/0.1007/s11712-020-09722-3.

8

Why Would a Buddha Lie?

Varieties of Buddhist Consequentialism

GORDON F. DAVIS

Introduction

"Buddhism" can have a loaded meaning; someone who self-declares as "Buddhist" has either envisaged a path to becoming enlightened or aspires to such an awakening. After all, the linguistic root of *"buddhist"* refers to being awake, and terms derived from it refer to the attainment of wisdom—including ethical wisdom, which is our focus here. In a more descriptive or historical sense, though, "Buddhism" is a long and complex tradition of thought and practice. And in this sense, Buddhism is more a family of traditions than a single religion or a single philosophy or a single set of doctrines.

Nonetheless, it is common to simplify the family lineage by highlighting two main traditions: the Theravada and the Mahāyāna. Sometimes Theravada is called "Southern Buddhism" and sometimes its textual and philosophical roots are said to represent "Early Buddhism" (Sri Lanka and India, for example, having older associations with Buddhism than Japan or Korea to the northeast). Correspondingly, Mahāyāna Buddhism is sometimes called "Northern Buddhism," but this is obviously of less importance to its adherents than its inherent meaning of "great (*maha*) vehicle (*-yana*)." The historical details of its development may also be of marginal importance. But for Mahāyāna philosophers, it has often been stressed how their "vehicle" overtook or even upended the earlier understanding(s) of suffering, impermanence, emptiness, compassion, and liberation.

On any philosophical question, then, we would naturally expect two different sets of ideas and doctrines from these two different traditions. However, there may be a couple of exceptions where a deep convergence remains. Arguably, first of all, there is a broadly similar understanding of "middle way" in both traditions (if not in detail). Second, the philosophical traditions on both sides share a similar degree of skepticism about selfhood and identity—replacing *ātman* with *anātman*, or *no-self*—even if the nature of this "skepticism," as I put it, does differ in many ways.[1] (These exceptions also happen to be relevant to our ethical topic here.)

Another possible exception is a kind of *consequentialism*, at least if taken in a broad and loose sense. In contemporary philosophy, "consequentialism" usually has a narrow sense, referring to the claim that ultimately *only* consequences matter in the final evaluation of decisions and actions. In a looser sense—not always welcome in purely theoretical contexts—some are willing to speak of consequentialism as coming in varying degrees. In this sense, it is *mainly* consequences that matter in evaluation. An ethicist like Kant may be seen as deeply non-consequentialist because on his view there are norms and principles that must be strictly honored no matter the cost or consequence (even though he admits that if, and only if, virtue and justice are fully attained, more happiness is better than less), and all these are grounded in a foundational categorical imperative. A more pluralist-minded ethicist may instead be *generally* or *largely* consequentialist if they would guide our choices according to the results of the (optimal) choice, with only a few weak constraints on optimization playing an occasional, or occasionally legitimate, role in our moral decision-making.

It is worth mentioning here, before we proceed, why we focus on "consequentialism" rather than "utilitarianism"—even though the latter is consequentialism's most famous family member by far. With some exceptions, utilitarianism is focused on a certain type of result—happiness—and often this "happiness" is reduced to pleasure. This is only one part of the utilitarian view (others having to do with impersonal aggregation, optimization or maximization, and instrumentalized agency and decision-making). But because the nature of "pleasure" is often approached through a modern—or even scientific—lens, it can be difficult to compare utilitarianism with kindred ethical ideas from non-Western traditions of thought.

The main advantage of discussing consequentialism instead is that this broader view equally stresses optimal results but without always having to specify what kinds of results are the intrinsically valuable ones. A view can be fully consequentialist while adopting a pluralist conception of what has final or intrinsic value—for example, along with pleasure, there can be intrinsic value accorded to knowledge, love, and achievement. A practical consequentialist may wish to employ some kind of common scale to allow judgments about such goods to inform decision-making. But the kind of *ideal* consequentialism that we may encounter in pure theory, on one hand, and in religion, on the other, need not pin down such standards and measurements, and there could be a variety of reasons for leaving those open.

Returning to the "loose" sense of consequentialism, we might think of this as a highly pragmatic mindset, focused on results and intent on letting bygones be bygones, but leaving open a possible role for—occasionally warranted—constraints on maximization. In that sense, arguably *both* of the above traditions of Buddhism, at least in their respective textual foundations, show signs of a deeper commitment to consequentialism than most of the Western religious traditions.[2]

I begin by highlighting two particular Buddhist ideals of consequentialism (in the loose sense), one from each of the major traditions. These are, respectively, the "raft-releasing" ideal of Theravada Buddhism and the "skillful means" ideal of Mahāyāna Buddhism. Actually, *all* the traditions know the image of the raft crossing a turbulent river as a metaphor for the hard work of the path that leads to *nirvāṇa*. The traditional parable warns against fetishizing the raft; that is, even though the raft is honored as indispensable, one should ultimately be pragmatic, to the point of leaving it behind once its work is done. This parable is familiar to Mahāyānists as well, but it is often generalized. A major ideal in Mahāyāna ethics is that of skillful means (*upāya* in Sanksrit—a hallmark of the *bodhisattva*, the revered figure who stops just short of *nirvāṇa* to help others). This permits advanced moral agents not only to distance themselves from path/raft constraints, but even to violate moral precepts in particular instances if this would serve the greater good. The precept that forbids lying can be broken, for example, but only if doing so optimally benefits those deceived, or rather all those affected by the transgression. (The phrase *"advanced moral agents"* reflects the idea of *skillful* means; such transgressions are only justified if the greatest possible benefits are achieved.)

The difference between seeing things from the raft and seeing things from the far shore is sometimes expressed in terms of the "Two Truths Doctrine," based on a distinction between conventional truth and ultimate truth. Though this is not the place to defend such doctrines—or, for that matter, to defend consequentialism against other moral theories—it is worth noting that a full defense of the latter may require something like the former. Thus, instead of dismissing conventional moral rules (as an act-utilitarian might), a sophisticated consequentialist can admit a role for conventional rules insofar as they are justifiable in terms of the "ultimate" moral standard. This two-level approach echoes Hemmingsen's point in the section introduction: there is a difference between a *theory of morality* and a moral *decision procedure*. If someone wisely avoids modeling a decision procedure on consequentialism, such wisdom does not necessarily cast doubt on the consequentialist theory; in fact, overall consequences might constitute the foundational *reason* why moral decision-making works best when framed by common "conventions." As *sangha* rules illustrate, effective cooperation requires common norms, but the norms should hardly include the standard—let alone the theory—by which effectiveness is ultimately judged. (Instead of "theory," some Buddhists might prefer a term like "foundation"; hence the corresponding reason—*hetu*—could be grounded in *parinispanna-svabhāva*, for instance.)[3]

A Robust Consequentialist Interpretation:
Goodman's *Consequences of Compassion*

Charles Goodman's book *Consequences of Compassion* (2009) represents the first intensive, full-length treatment of consequentialist ideas in the Buddhist tradition.[4] Though mainly Mahāyānist in orientation, Goodman leads up to his ideal formulation(s) of Buddhist ethics by noting the foreshadowing of those ideas in Theravada contexts. Notably, he presents some reasons for framing Theravada ethics in terms of a theoretical framework known as "rule consequentialism."[5]

Rather than delving into the nuances of rule consequentialism, however, it would be worth contextualizing Goodman's project in terms of a much simpler theme that is more integral to Buddhism's own traditional framing: suffering. This is understood via the "four noble truths:" the truth of suffering, the truth of the cause of suffering, the truth of the end of suffering, and the truth of the path that leads to the end of suffering. Goodman discusses the issue of suffering, but pivots from the "negative" ideal of simple cessation of suffering toward a quite striking emphasis on *positive* goods such as enjoyment, flourishing, and happiness.

The foundational discourse in which the Buddha presented the four "noble truths" lends itself to a consequentialist interpretation. It clearly presents a guide for incrementally improving the well-being of practitioners. Meanwhile there is little in the four noble truths that sounds deontological or virtue oriented. The one possible exception is the mention of "moral discipline" (*sila*), consisting of right speech, right action, and right livelihood. But Goodman (2009, 222, n. 10) shows that, from the Mahāyānists' viewpoint, this element of practice cannot coherently be equated with all of morality, since they accept that ethics also encompasses generosity and compassion, which are not covered by "moral discipline."

In any case, Goodman does not dwell for long on the four "noble truths," because demonstrating a role for consequentialist reasoning in Buddhist ethics requires much more. Showing that Buddhism is consequentialist requires parsing any statements of Buddhist doctrine along the lines of "end justifies means." Goodman suggests that, for both Theravada and Mahāyāna, the ends include a plurality of positive attainments, including joy, material well-being, character development, and spiritual attainment.

But merely highlighting end(s)—whether simple, single or plural—does not make a theory consequentialist. After all, virtue theories are also "teleological," that is, they pursue an end, and deontological theories often have a place for goal-directed action.

The key question therefore seems to be whether Mahāyānists would nonetheless reject such non-consequentialist views, perhaps implicitly, by holding that (a) any rule that regulates a Buddhist's own practice may be broken on some occasions, and that (b) trade-offs between the well-being of different groups of people are justified (e.g., sacrificing some to save others), when required for the sake of the greater good. Both of these features are characteristic of consequentialist ethics, but not of virtue-based or deontological ethics.

To determine whether Mahāyānists subscribe to (a) and (b), Goodman relies on classical texts in the Buddhist tradition rather than on surveys of contemporary Buddhist attitudes, and he highlights one author in particular: Śāntideva, the eighth-century monk who wrote a revered work called the *Bodhicaryāvatāra* (2006). Goodman argues persuasively that Śāntideva's view permits—and even requires—the kind of assessment that implies both (a) and (b). That is, the view requires not only a pragmatic readiness to adapt rules skillfully (at least for advanced practitioners), but also requires transgressive actions in suitable circumstances.

Such permissible—and sometimes *required*—transgressions have long been envisaged in Mahāyāna texts under the heading of "skillful means" (*upāya*), noted earlier. But Goodman argues that Śāntideva understood how such transgressions can be theorized systematically in relation to an impartial concern for all sentient beings (something that is also characteristic of many consequentialist ethical theories). The idea is that *bodhisattvas* reshape their moral agency in the form of constant service to all others. On this view, for example, not only *kind* lies may be justified, but also some *calculated* ones, that is, lies intended to bring about certain desirable consequences. This idea of calculating outcomes applies to other so-called "transgressions."

But a problem seems to arise immediately: in Buddhism, whereas most sentient beings are deluded and require help, the *bodhisattva* is a specially qualified agent, guided by advanced practical wisdom. Is there not then something special about *bodhisattvas*? Could they have a status or importance that others lack (whereas a commitment to consequentialism would have ruled out such preferential treatment)? One of the most interesting aspects of Goodman's discussion of Śāntideva is his teasing out, from the latter's texts, a number of indications that Śāntideva would *not*, in fact, prioritize his own agency or that of any *bodhisattva*, or give either any special status. This may sound simply equitable in spirit, but there is more to this move than meets the eye.

Goodman connects this to another theme in Buddhist philosophy—one clearly signaled in Śāntideva—namely, the ethical significance of the no-self insight, or *anātman*. This insight casts doubt not only on the so-called "seat of consciousness" (e.g., *self* as underlying *substance*), but also on the notion of a unified *agent*.[6] If we accept this insight, then not only do "one's own" benefits matter no more than any other's; but also, one's ability to perform a good deed is not to be cherished, especially whenever some other agent is in a better position to deliver the best result, and yet not to be cherished in other cases, either, insofar as people often—and often deleteriously—indulge an illusory "sense of agency." In this way, Goodman explains how the Buddhist no-self insight can justify what is called "agent-neutrality" (rather than "agent-relative" priorities), even in moral contexts.[7] And agent-neutrality is sometimes taken as the hallmark of consequentialist morality.

In the spirit of Goodman's approach, it is worth emphasizing that these consequentialist themes are not merely a few minor considerations lurking in specialized contexts or in a few selected texts. A case could be made that they are key to the deepest message of Mahāyāna philosophy. No-self is liberating; all Buddhists accept that. But in recommending the path to liberation, earlier Buddhists implied that an enlightened person should never sacrifice their spiritual attainments. But should they not—on the contrary—be willing to sacrifice anything "of their own" to help others access similar attainments? Such sacrifices—for lack of a better word—seem to follow from accepting the no-self insight; in other words, one's *"own"* status cannot stand in the way, as there is really no such thing. It is not that taking oneself out of the picture is a way of "annihilating" an existing thing; *emptiness* means that "oneself" was never there in the first place, and thus could never have justified any agent-relativity.

However, the robust consequentialism defended by Goodman—which is arguably both a *strict* and a *direct* consequentialism—is not welcomed by all Mahāyānists, let alone all Buddhist philosophers . . . let alone all Buddhists and all ethicists! Some argue that the Mahāyānist permission that is granted to certain *bodhisattvas* (to make certain exceptions to otherwise weighty moral constraints) is a permission that depends on particular features of particular circumstances, rather than any generalizable guideline such as the principle of utility or some other form of consequentialist rationality. Michael Barnhart (2012), for example, argues that Buddhist ethics tends to be *particularist*, rather than consequentialist. Others argue that it is, or ought to be, virtue-oriented in a more constrained sense—that is to say *aretaic*, but not any kind of aretaic consequentialism (Keown 2001). Instead of exploring those views here, we can now turn to consider alternative interpretations of Mahāyāna ethics that are at least quite *close* to the consequentialist approach.

Mitigated Roles for Consequentialism in Other Interpretations of Mahāyāna Ethics

It is worth noting that, according to philosophical consequentialism, *any* kind of action might be justifiable—or indeed morally *required*—under circumstances where performing that action would bring about the best outcome. After all, how could a consequentialist justify a firm line marking off certain kinds of action as taboo after having disqualified taboos in the name of practical flexibility?[8] For instance, while honesty may be a sound general rule, would a Buddha—facing limited options—honor the rule in a case where doing so would preclude the compassionate saving of lives? An enlightened transgression, involving so-called "lying"—or worse, as far as "dishonorable" action-types are concerned—could indeed be the right course of action. Goodman, for example, alludes to the violence of Padmasambhava's legendary *upāya* to acknowledge that his consequentialism recognizes no limits on acceptable action-types; that is, that there are no action-types (lying, killing, stealing, etc.) that are wrong in themselves, or wrong in absolutely every possible scenario. But are there no justified constraints of any kind, even in hard cases?

In this section we will consider two possible ways of constraining consequentialism (for better or worse), one based on the idea of *bodhisattva* "stages" of development, and another based on a somewhat egalitarian notion that we must all become *bodhisat-*

tvas, each contributing equally to collective liberation. These would seem to both qualify as Mahāyāna ideals, but, depending on the conclusions one draws from issues raised in the first section above, it is an open question whether these views should count as fully consequentialist.

In her book *Moral Theory in Śāntideva's* Śikṣāsamuccaya (2006), Barbra Clayton places greater emphasis on the development of *virtue* as a key ethical concern for Śāntideva.[9] She acknowledges that, on Śāntideva's account, the behavior of a *bodhisattva* "comes increasingly to resemble utilitarianism," but the upshot for his ethical system as a whole, in her view, is not utilitarianism as an overarching principle, but rather a "hybrid form of virtue ethics" (Clayton 2006, 117).

In fact, as Goodman's accommodation of virtue suggests, it may not be *virtue* that pulls this approach away from strict consequentialism. Rather, it is the notion of "graduated" moral standards that apply differently to different groups of people. Somewhat akin to the way different moral standards can apply to monks and laypeople (as in Theravada), the idea here is that *most* people should follow firm moral rules, whereas *bodhisattvas* are uniquely able to make exceptions to such rules in their direct pursuit of maximal well-being (for all). The practical result would be the same as that sought by strict consequentialism if—and only if—the practical limits imposed on non-*bodhisattvas* indirectly led to the best possible result, when conjoined with the saving graces of occasional *bodhisattva* improvisation. In other words, the best consequences are achieved by insisting that non-*bodhisattvas* follow moral rules (because they do not have the insight that allows them to appreciate the exceptions where not following the—generally beneficial—rules would maximize the good), while allowing *bodhisattvas* to break the rules when their superior judgement indicates that doing so would maximize well-being.

However, insofar as that rationale is not specifically offered as the *reason* for the limits imposed on non-*bodhisattvas*, this view seems not to qualify as full-fledged consequentialism, either practically or theoretically. All things considered, this is not necessarily a weakness in this view (let alone a weakness as an interpretation of Śāntideva). Indeed, some non-consequentialists may welcome it, even though it appears to clash with what is often considered a paradigm of an enlightened value, namely the idea of equal status among moral agents.

A different—and perhaps opposite—kind of qualification has been suggested by the present author, resulting in what might seem a "Kantian" sort of consequentialism (Davis 2013).[10] It is easiest—and more fitting—to approach this not via Kant, but via Buddhist concepts. Some say there are three kinds of *bodhisattva*: (1) those who reach liberation and inspire others to follow after them (the "king's way"); (2) those who delay their own liberation until after they have ushered every other being into *nirvāṇa* ahead of them (the "shepherd's way"); and (3) those who wait for others on the near shore, and then having crossed to the far shore, resolve to disembark simultaneously along with all others (the "boatman's way").

What would a consequentialist say about these various ways of being a *bodhisattva*? Which model should a *bodhisattva* follow? A direct consequentialist can only say that it depends on how many beings they are in a position to help, and by what means. Based on these factors, some should take the king's way (whenever optimal); some should take the shepherd's way (whenever optimal); and perhaps for whoever is left in *saṃsāra*, it may work best to serve as boatmen.

But what if the heart of the Mahāyāna creed is embodied in the boatman's way, and what if it should take some kind of priority? It would after all seem to be the *middle way* relative to the other models. Moreover, this model would seem to cohere with the Mahāyānist "postponement of *nirvāṇa*" and also with the notion, present inter alia in Śāntideva, that the highest good involves the entire chain of being(s) gathering, as *bodhisattvas* one and all, around a sort of round table of equals. (Hence the tempting comparison with Kant's ideal of a "realm of ends.")

Once again, this could be reconciled with a robust consequentialism, or it could go in a slightly different direction. If the implication is that a *bodhisattva* must hold her own spiritual progress in check, in a spirit of solidarity, even when s/he could deliver optimal results (for all) with the "king's way," then this ethic legitimizes an exception to what strict consequentialism would entail—and thereby jettisons any such consequentialism. I say this is only "slightly" different, because the solidarity becomes a kind of framing constraint within which, after all, the aim is still the greatest overall well-being in the long run.

However, this view could instead be adapted to, or collapsed into, full consequentialism if the assembly of equal *bodhisattvas* were counted as part of the end rather than an obligatory means to an end. (In other words, equality would then not be a moral constraint—and perhaps nothing would so qualify—but would rather be part of the ideal ultimate outcome.) In that case, its priority over the ways of kings and shepherds would be due not so much to any greater effectiveness in liberating the multitude, but rather to its having intrinsic value, perhaps not only through the joy of fellow-feeling but also through equality per se. This would not make an imperative of equality *absolute*, however; *bodhisattvas* may still be justified in occasionally violating "rights"—and in compromising the equal provision of rights and benefits—to achieve that final equality. Of course, one of the main objections to consequentialism is that it fails to respect human rights; but, other than offering some reflections in this note,[11] I leave it to other contributors to discuss how "rights" and associated "duties" might feature in various non-Western ethical systems.

Objections to the Idea of Consequentialism being "Buddhist"

I close by considering a few other objections to consequentialist interpretations of Buddhist ethics. One concerns the role of compassion in Buddhist ethics and poses the question of whether these theoretical frameworks may ultimately misunderstand the true meaning of *karuṇā* (which encompasses both "compassion" and "care"). Imbuing the concept with a very wide scope, Buddhism counsels *karuṇā*, not only toward sufferers who merit immediate attention, but also toward anyone whose well-being may be sacrificed in the aftermath of that attention, for example, as a result of any trade-off that might be necessary to alleviate the greater initial suffering. For that matter, *karuṇā* also goes out to those who benefit materially but remain blithely unaware of their spiritual or existential blind spots. In light of this, some Buddhists would object that an exclusive focus on positive consequences might prevent us from recognizing those other occasions for compassion, which are nonetheless as justified as any others. Hence a consequentialist focus turns out to be a step in the wrong direction, on this view.

But this objection may only undermine consequentialism if compassion is thought to be intrinsically good as well as instrumentally effective in alleviating suffering. Otherwise, if only alleviation matters intrinsically (and if the focus on suffering justifies "any means necessary"), then the key point would have been conceded to the consequentialist. Despite the initial impression, then, there may not be a real disagreement here. On the other hand, even if we grant that compassion is intrinsically good in some sense, consequentialists need not retreat. Many would point out that something's being intrinsically good does not guarantee that it is intrinsically *right*. These consequentialists could agree that we should cultivate as much compassion as possible within the practical bounds set by consequentialism. And Mahāyānist consequentialists could make this same point; after all, their skeptical view of *nirvāṇa* (as construed by what they call *Śrāvakayāna*) can be summed up this way: such bliss is intrinsically *good*—to a point—but not intrinsically *right*. And when it prevents the enlightened person from helping others on the path, it is not right at all, on this account of Mahāyāna ethics. The same could be said for compassion and other virtues,[12] but admittedly there is more to be said about this complex topic.

We should also consider a couple of concerns that one hears quite often in discussions of these "theoretical" moves in comparative ethics. Some are open to the possibility that general moral principles may lie buried in ancient Buddhist texts, but they would prefer to identify those principles as belonging to their source(s) rather than using contemporary "isms." And they might wonder why Westerners such as Goodman and Clayton should receive the kind of credit that I have given them here. A related concern stems from doubts about such principles playing any role in those texts or any ancient traditions at all. There is a worry, in other words, that we are simply imposing an adventitious grid on a deeply different worldview and confusing the grid for the real thing. There might even be a patronizing double standard at work, whereby we let the Western philosophers of the past speak for themselves but fail to extend the same courtesy to ancient Buddhist writers.

These are live—and quite general—issues in the contested field(s) of comparative and/or cross-cultural philosophy. In a partial, and tentative, defense of both of the aspects just noted, we might point out that similar dilemmas give rise to similar problems even within the Western philosophical tradition. Hume, for example, had no word for "utilitarianism," but this term is often used for a family of approaches to interpreting his ethics. And it does seem possible that Hume was really a utilitarian "in all but name." The interpretive grid would then turn out to be more than a grid; instead, it serves as a clarification or even a discovery.[13] Even if this, and other similar cases, helps to remove the suspicion of a double standard being at work here, there remains the key question as to whether anything like consequentialism is verifiably present in the writings of ancient writers such as Śāntideva. Therein, indeed, lies the hard work of translation and intensive textual analysis, which an introductory chapter such as this must, alas, forgo. The plausibility of any readings such as those outlined above will naturally depend on those more detailed investigations. I end here with a note that highlights some secondary sources that offer ample testimony from primary sources.[14]

Summary

Theravada Buddhism may lend itself to a consequentialist interpretation at the level of underlying ethical principles, but the latter are probably underdetermined in that doctrinal context. Charles Goodman's pioneering work on comparative ethical philosophy opens up some lines of inquiry in that regard, but he plausibly sees a deeper and more explicit role for consequentialist ideas in a different strand of Buddhist tradition, that of Mahāyāna Buddhist philosophy. Even there, scope for divergent interpretations remains, and ideals other than optimization in the alleviation of suffering—ideals such as virtue and equality—can be combined with elements of consequentialism to bring out other ways of systematizing Mahāyāna ethics. These other ways may be alternatives to strict theoretical consequentialism, which continues to be dogged by objections—not only philosophical objections, but methodological ones from various Buddhist points of view.

Notes

1. On this, and issues surrounding terms and concepts related to *anātman* (e.g., "no-self," "not-self" and "emptiness"), and contested terminology in the philosophical context (e.g., "skepticism"), see Davis (2018). Also see n. 6 below.

2. Philosophical traditions are another matter, but from many religious perspectives, there are things long gone that are *not* relegated to "bygones"; thus many Western traditions focus on the moral imperative of rectifying some past transgression. Consequentialism focuses on melioration, not rectification.

3. Embodying non-dual ultimate truth, according to certain sub-traditions of Mahāyāna, the notion of *parinispanna-svabhāva* does not belong to "theory" in any familiar sense, but insofar as it means something like the *perfected ground* of enlightened being, it may be seen as a foundational axiological standard. There is of course the common theme in Mahāyāna philosophy: how to square non-duality with a "doctrine" of duality. For those who approach this in terms of ethics, there is a tempting solution: instead of a two-level account, it can be *multi*-level; after all, "theory of morality" has multiple layers of its own, e.g., a "criterion of rightness" can have separate epistemic, ontic, and conative levels.

4. Kalupahana (1976) was among the first—to my knowledge—to discuss utilitarianism as a candidate for the foundations of Buddhist ethics; other antecedents prior to Goodman include Siderits (2000), Donner (2006), and Clayton (2006).

5. My aim here is to not overcomplicate characterizations of consequentialism, so I do not fully explain how a rule-based version differs from generic consequentialism. Suffice it to say that, in some ways, rule consequentialism is potentially more complex than any simple (or "direct") consequentialism; and it would be interesting to discover—as Goodman claims we can—that over time, Buddhist moral philosophy transitioned from a more complex to a less complex form of ethical theory. If so, the reason may well be, as Goodman argues, that the more direct form is a more defensible one, philosophically speaking (see ch. 3 in Goodman [2009]).

6. For some different interpretations of *anātman* (no-self/not-self) and their potential ethical implications, see the diverse range of viewpoints—including some critiques of related views—in Davis, ed. (2018).

7. "Agent-neutrality" qualifies moral reasons that bear no essential reference to an agent; agent-*relativity*, by contrast, involves treating at least some of our moral reasons as fundamentally relational. For instance, I would be positing an agent-relative reason if I were to say, despite others

being in a better position to help, "I ought to help her because we have (such-and-such) relation"; whereas we could focus on an agent-neutral reason by saying, "those ought to help who happen to be in a position to resolve things for the best." The latter makes no reference to any agent *in particular*.

8. It is interesting to notice how, outside of philosophy, by contrast—in political theory, for example—people discussing "Machiavellian consequentialism" tacitly assume some unspecified limit to acceptable tactics, taking it for granted that some violations of rights or decency would be so "beyond the pale" that even some Machiavellians would balk. For better or worse, strict moral consequentialism recognizes no such limits, with this one exception: a quite severe limit to the normative weight of self-interest (showing, in fact, how far it is from any Machiavellian view).

9. As I indicated when including "character development" among the ends that Goodman acknowledges, he too stresses the importance of virtue—but as a desideratum rather than an absolute constraint on *upāya*. That is, virtue is something that is important for morality, but dispensable when *upāya* demands it.

10. The "Kantian" label can be misleading, though, if it leads us to preclude the possibility that ancient and medieval texts in the Mahāyāna tradition already constrained consequentialism in the way suggested here—in which case a Buddhist would hardly need Kantian language to make the following point.

11. We can find counterparts in ancient Buddhist texts for several familiar notions, perhaps especially those familiar from ancient Greek ethics, but also some others in the Western tradition. It is much harder, however, to find any explicit reference to "rights" in the Buddhist tradition. There is a close counterpart to "having a right" in Sanskrit—*adhikāra*—but while used in Hindu texts, I am not aware of any significant appeal to this concept in classical or medieval Buddhist texts. (Some may regret this as an oversight; but it is an interesting question whether no-self views justify this omission, especially with respect to rights that presuppose agent-relative reasons.)

12. This may sound odd, given that proper compassion is focused on others, by its very nature. The consequentialist will note, however, that the point can apply to anything, including anything that is *ceteris paribus* good.

13. Something similar is worth keeping in mind when we consider "Buddhist ecology." McMahan (2008) may be right that ancient Buddhist texts offered very little in the way of theorizing about ecology, and yet he may be underestimating the close relevance of Buddhist axiological themes to philosophical ecology. In any case, Buddhist environmental ethics is a

thriving field, and it would be unfortunate if aborted because of narrow views as to how much can permissibly be "read into" (or extracted out of) classical texts.

14. E.g., Clayton (2006), Cowherds (2015), and—in addition to chapters 4 and 5 in Goodman (2009)—especially Goodman (2016).

Further Reading

PRIMARY SOURCES

Śāntideva. 2006. *The Way of the Bodhisattva (Bodhicaryāvatāra)*. Rev. ed. Translated by Padmakara Translation Group. Boston: Shambhala. (From Tibetan)
———. 1997. *A Guide to the Bodhisattva Way of Life*. Translated by Vesna A. Wallace and B. Allen Wallace. Boulder: Snow Lion Press. (From Sanskrit)

SECONDARY SOURCES

Barnhart, Michael. 2012. "Theory and Comparison in the Discussion of Buddhist Ethics." *Philosophy East and West* 62, no. 1: 16–43. https://doi.org/10.1353/pew.2012.0001.
Clayton, Barbra R. 2006. *Moral Theory in Śāntideva's Śikṣāsamuccaya: Cultivating the Fruits of Virtue*. London: Routledge.
Cowherds. 2015. *Moonpaths: Ethics and Emptiness*. Oxford: Oxford University Press.
Davis, Gordon F. 2013. "Traces of Consequentialism and Non-Consequentialism in Bodhisattva Ethics." *Philosophy East and West* 63, no. 2: 275–305. https://doi.org/10.1353/pew.2013.0015.
———, ed. 2018. *Ethics without Self, Dharma without Atman: Western and Buddhist Philosophical Traditions in Dialogue*. Cham: Springer.
Donner, Wendy. 2006. "The Bodhisattva Code and Compassion." In *Comparative Philosophy and Religion in Times of Terror*, edited by Douglas Allen. Lanham: Rowman & Littlefield.
Goodman, Charles. 2009. *The Consequences of Compassion: An Interpretation and Defence of Buddhist Ethics*. Oxford: Oxford University Press.
———. 2016. *The Training Anthology of Śāntideva: A Translation of the Śikṣāsamuccaya*. Oxford: Oxford University Press.
Kalupahana, David. 1976. *Buddhist Philosophy: A Historical Analysis*. Honolulu: University of Hawai'i Press.

Keown, Damien. 2001. *The Nature of Buddhist Ethics.* 2nd ed. New York: Palgrave.

McMahan, David. 2008. *The Making of Buddhist Modernism.* Oxford: Oxford University Press.

Siderits, Mark. 2000. "The Reality of Altruism: Reconstructing Śāntideva." *Philosophy East and West* 50, no. 3: 412–24.

Section 3

Deontological Moral Theories

Introduction

In the third section of the book, we consider "deontological" moral theories. We can understand deontological theories as those that ground morality in *principles*. However, *most* moral theories involve principles. Consequentialist theories,[1] for example, will often utilize principles as rules of thumb, or decision procedures, and at a deeper level consequentialists are quite happy to say that the principle "maximize the good" is of fundamental importance. The key difference between deontology and consequentialism is not therefore the *importance* of principles, but rather the *relationship* principles bear to the ends that we pursue (Freeman 1994).

As we saw when discussing consequentialism, one way of understanding and categorizing moral theories is through the relationship between the right and the good (Rawls 1999), the good being a matter of what is valuable and the right a matter of what actions we ought to (or ought not to) perform. In consequentialist theories, the good is *independent* of the right, both in the sense that the *nature* of the good is not *determined* or *influenced* by the right, as well as in the sense that our pursuit of the good is not *constrained* by the right. What makes a theory "deontological," by contrast, is that it constrains our pursuit of the good and/or what goods are legitimately allowed to be pursued in the first place (Ronzoni 2010, 470).

177

"Rights" are a deontological notion. For example, Jack might need to decide whether to torture someone to get information that would help prevent a bombing. If Jack were a consequentialist, he would evaluate the situation wholly in terms of which action—torturing or not torturing—would lead the best consequences overall. If the harm of the torture was outweighed by the good of preventing the bombing, Jack would be justified in torturing the person. By contrast, if Jack held that human beings have a *right* to freedom from torture, the option of torturing would no longer be on the table *regardless* of whether it would bring about the best consequences. Jack's range of morally permissible actions is *constrained* by that right.

For instance, consider the famous "Transplant" thought experiment: In Transplant, a patient arrives at a hospital complaining of a minor ailment (a sore knee, for example). There are five other patients in the hospital, all of whom are in dire need of transplanted organs, and all of whom will certainly die without them. As it turns out, the patient with the sore knee's blood type matches that of those in need of the transplants. The doctor who treats the first patient therefore has a decision to make: should she treat the person with the sore knee and send him on his way, or should she murder him and use his organs to save the five lives? (We can stipulate here that the doctor can do this in secret and will never be found out—so there will not be any confounding reputational or trust issues—and that there is nothing unusually important about the first patient, or anything unusually bad about the five transplant patients, so that the calculus really does come out in favor of the murder option.)

When I give this example to students, most of them say that the doctor ought not to kill the patient with the sore knee to save the lives of the five. But since the murder option is the option that leads to the best state of affairs—five lives are surely more valuable than one—killing the patient cannot be wrong because of the consequences it leads to. Rather, to students it is *just wrong*; the *action* of murdering an innocent person is wrong *in itself*. In this sense, while consequentialists take as their fundamental concepts "good" and "bad," and character-based theorists "virtuous" and "vicious," deontologists are fundamentally interested in "right" and "wrong": they focus on the nature of the *action itself* (Tännsjö 2008, 56).

Obligatory, Prohibited, and Permitted Actions

Because of the maximizing logic of consequentialism, there is always the best state of affairs (which we are *obliged to* try to bring about) and all lesser states of affairs (which we are *prohibited* from trying to bring about). All actions are *either* prohibited *or* obligatory, with nothing in the middle (except in the rare case when two or more actions lead to exactly equally good states of affairs).

For deontological theories, there are certain actions you *must* perform—such as helping someone in serious need. And there are actions you *must not* perform—such as torture. But since principles act as *constraints* rather than *goals*, deontological theories can accommodate more easily a third category of actions that are neither obligatory *nor* prohibited but instead merely *permitted*. These are actions that you *can* but do not *have to* perform. In this way, deontological theories are arguably closer to our common sense; in our daily lives, we assume that there is significant scope for us to make our own decisions about how to live and what to value. Hence, while some consequentialist theories claim to make a role for permitted actions (see satisficing utilitarianism, for example [Slote 1984], or scalar utilitarianism [Norcross 1997]), deontological theories have a much easier time making sense of the commonsense distinction between the obligatory, prohibited, and permitted.

The addition of *permitted* actions makes possible the further idea of "supererogatory" actions. A supererogatory action is one that you are not *obligated* to perform, but that would be a (morally) good thing to do nonetheless. For instance, we probably have a moral obligation to help others in need, such as by donating to charity. But this obligation has limits: beyond a certain point, we can say we have done what is morally required of us. But we could nonetheless *choose* to do more, and if we did, that would be a morally good thing. Such an action is described as "supererogatory."

Special Commitments and Agent Relativism

One key place where deontology provides scope for our own goals and values is in "special commitments." These are obligations that we have to *specific* others, such as to our family and friends; or to those we have entered into agreements with or made promises to; or arguably to compatriots (Miller 2004; Miller 2007; Rawls 1999).

Consequentialism can certainly make sense of special commitments. However, the way that it does so is in conflict with our commonsense understanding of such obligations. For the consequentialist, special commitments arise from a concern with bringing about the most overall good. It may well be, for instance, that recognizing special commitments *as a decision procedure* leads to more good. After all, if everyone prioritizes their own family and friends, it is possible that this would lead to an overall better state of affairs than if we had no special concern for our family members and friends. Similarly, a world in which people go back on their word whenever the consequentialist calculus demands it, or a world in which we had no fellow-feeling with our compatriots, is quite likely a worse one.

But, as Bernard Williams points out, such a justification for special commitments seems to involve "one thought too many" (Williams 1973). That is, we usually take our obligations to our parents, for example, to exist simply in virtue of the fact that they are our parents. The additional step of reasoning that we take to justify those obligations in consequentialism—the contribution of those obligations to the greater good—seems not just *unnecessary*, but *inappropriate*. For example, I do not care for and prioritize my son in my deliberations because of some abstract concern with impartial justice; I act to benefit him because he is my son, I am his father, and I care for him. Similarly, friends do not expect loyalty from each other because being loyal leads to some greater good; they expect it merely *because* they are friends—there is something inherent in the nature of *that relationship* that gives rise to an obligation to be loyal (McNaughton and Rawling 2006, 442). The special commitments we have should not therefore be thought of as being *derived* from any further consideration such as "the greater good": they inhere in the relationships we are in directly.

From a deontological perspective, special commitments are another kind of constraint on our pursuit of the good. As constraints, they differ from rights in that they are owed specifically to individuals with whom we stand in certain kinds of relationships, rather than to everyone generally (McNaughton and Rawling 2006, 425), but they constrain us in similar ways. For instance, a person could choose to either use their limited resources to send their own daughter *or* their friend's daughters to a private school. If we were to adopt an impartial consequentialist perspective, and if their friend's daughter is likely to benefit more from attending the school than their own daughter, they may be obliged to use the money to help their friend's daughter instead of their own. But the deontologist recognizes a special obligation to support the education of their *own* daughter, *even if* this does not lead to the most good overall. The option of bringing about the most good by supporting their friend's daughter instead is not open to them: their possible (morally acceptable) actions are constrained by this commitment.

Both rights and special commitments illustrate the *agent-relative* nature of deontology. We have already come across this term discussing consequentialist ethics—in particular contrasting the agent-relative consequentialism of the Cārvāka with the agent-neutral consequentialism of utilitarianism, Mohism, and Mahāyāna Buddhism. To recap, an agent-neutral theory is one in which the description of the right action makes no essential reference to an agent. For instance, the utilitarian tries to bring about the most pleasure, but it does not matter *whose* pleasure they are bringing about, only how much overall. By contrast, an agent-relative theory makes essential reference to the agent. For example, from a Cārvākan perspective, the fact that the pleasure is *mine* rather than someone else's is what gives me a reason to try to bring it about.

While consequentialism comes in both agent-neutral and agent-relative varieties, deontology is always agent relative, in large part because of the way that it sees principles as constraints rather than as values to pursue.[2] For instance, imagine a scenario in which a kidnapper says that they will kill two innocent people unless *we* kill one innocent person ourselves. If the deontological theory in question prohibits—constrains us from—killing innocent people, we should not kill the one. But this prohibition is not because the death of innocent people *in general* is a bad state of affairs. The issue is rather that *we*—the agent—are forbidden from killing innocents *ourselves*. Hence, a description of this situation in moral terms includes an *essential* reference to an agent: *I*—the agent—*must not* kill innocents. Similarly, the fact that my son is *my* son is what gives me a special moral reason to prioritize his interests: the word "my" is essential here for making sense of what I ought to do.

The Moral Law

Constraints are usually thought of in terms of law-like prohibitions, and as such deontological moral theories often see themselves as attempts to specify the "moral law." But there are important differences between ordinary law and the moral law, most especially in terms of what *motivates* us to *follow* the two different kinds of law. Ordinary laws motivate us *externally*, whereas morality motivates us *internally*. That is, when we follow laws, we do so ultimately because they are backed with the threat of force. The costs or benefits of following the law provide our motivation.

Now, what I am *not* saying here is that we *only* follow laws because of the threat of punishment, for instance, but rather that we only follow laws *as laws* for such a reason. Take the example of murder: hopefully everyone reading this book is motivated to follow the law prohibiting murder. But at the same time, I would hope that their reason for this is not because of the threat of punishment, but simply because killing is wrong. But if so, we would not kill other people regardless of whether there was a law prohibiting it. It is only in those cases where a person *fails* to be motivated by a moral reason where the law becomes relevant as a way of dissuading them. And in those cases, the reason to follow the law is external: the punishment. In other words, either we are motivated by morality to perform or not perform a certain action, and the law is irrelevant to our motivations; or we are not motivated by morality, and the threat of punishment standing behind the law is our motivation.[3]

However, our motivation to follow *moral* laws does not seem to be external. We are not *coerced* in any way to follow moral laws; we follow them for their own sake. But this leaves us with the question of where precisely the *authority* of moral laws come from. For what reason are we obligated to follow them for their own sake? The answer to this question is in some ways what distinguishes the different deontological theories in this book from each other.

Most of the theories we consider—Kantianism, Scanlon's contractualism, and Habermas's discourse ethics—are all *procedural*. This means that, just as ordinary laws only have authority if they pass through the proper procedures (for instance, if they are consistent with the Constitution or Bill of Rights, have a majority of members of Congress or Parliament vote in favor of them, and so on), it is the passing of moral principles through the correct *moral procedures*—whatever they may be—that gives them their authority.

A classic—and relatively simple—example of proceduralism is the golden rule. According to the golden rule, we work out whether an action is permitted by asking whether we would want others to treat us in the way that we treat them: "do unto others as you would have them do unto you." If an action passes that test, it is permissible; if not, it is prohibited. While none of the proceduralist theories in this section of the book subscribes to the golden rule, in certain respects they try to capture the same basic idea.

According to Kantian ethics, we are all self-legislators, in the sense that we live according to law-like principles—maxims—that we give ourselves. But these maxims must pass a certain test to be legitimate—what Kant calls the categorical imperative—that ensures that the maxims are *universalizable* (that they are able to consistently be followed if they were made into universal laws). If they can be, the maxim is legitimate; if not, it is illegitimate. We are *internally* motivated by the categorical imperative because we are fundamentally rational beings, and the universalization procedure is an inherent law of reason itself (just like the laws of physics are laws of nature). For Kant, then, the motivation to follow the moral law comes from our nature as rational self-legislators.

Scanlon's contractualism claims that our actions are always instances of more general principles. So, for instance, when we steal from others, the individual act is an expression of the principle that it is okay to steal. Scanlon then asks us to consider whether the principle governing that action could be reasonably rejected by others "as a basis for informed, unforced general agreement" (Scanlon 1998, 153). The issue here is one of fundamental moral recognition. What motivates us is the sense that acting on principles that others could reasonably reject puts us in relation to others in which they are not considered persons, beings that can choose how to live their lives in an autonomous manner as we do. And insofar as we would expect others to act according to principles that we could not reasonably reject, they have a right to expect the same of us.

For Habermas, morality is built into the practice of argumentation, or reason-giving: so long as we engage in the practice of

argumentation, his basic principle of morality—the universalization principle—must be accepted. This principle is presupposed
in the very activity of reason-giving in the first place. And the
exchange of reasons is the inherent *telos* of language; insofar as
we are language-users, we cannot help but understand our actions
as justified by reasons that we assume to be warranted, but that
can in principle be shown to be mistaken in argumentation. If we
do not engage in discourse (idealized argumentation) with others,
we have no reason to be confident that the reasons on which we
are acting are valid. But it is irrational to be unconcerned with
whether we are acting on the basis of valid reasons.

There are clearly similarities between Kant, Scanlon, and
Habermas's views. These theories were all developed in the modern era, and they all have a distinctively modern understanding
of moral equality. While earlier versions of deontology involve an
authoritarian understanding of law—in Divine Command Theory,
for instance, God passes down the law from on high, and human
beings are simply expected to follow it—these modern theories have
a certain kind of republican sensibility, in that laws are valid only
through the consent of those subject to them. In other words, these
approaches are an extension of the concept of popular sovereignty
to the moral realm (Deigh 2010, 180).

The Moral Community

In a democracy, the laws we live by are not just made by us, but
also apply impartially, to the pauper and the ruler alike. In current
deontological moral theories, the moral law operates in a similar
manner. The principles that are uncovered in subjecting them to
the appropriate procedure apply to all persons in an impartial way.
Or at least, they apply equally to every being who is a member
of the *moral community*.

The idea of the moral community is another parallel between
ordinary law and the moral law. Democratically valid laws are
limited in their application to those who have consented to them
(either in practice or tacitly). So, for instance, New Zealand law
applies to people in New Zealand, and not to people living in

Taiwan. There is a community of people who consented to New Zealand law[4] and to whom the law applies, and then there are those outside that community.

Proceduralist deontological theories usually do not think of moral laws in precisely this way. They usually hold that the moral law is *universal*, and that it applies regardless of whether you actively assent to it or not. Nonetheless, the moral law is like ordinary law in that for both there is an inside and an outside: there are those who count and those who do not. The criterion for membership in a national legal community is citizenship. But membership in the moral community is not a matter for people to merely *decide*—we should not imagine a committee or governing body choosing who is in and who is out of the moral community or passing judgments on requests to join. Membership in the moral community is instead a simple fact that is determined by the possession of capacities that allow a person to participate in the practice of morality in a reciprocal way. These capacities might be a matter of being able to formulate and act on maxims, or being capable of recognizing and abiding by those principles that no one can reasonably reject, or being capable of justifying our actions to others with reasons in public discourse. Regardless of the specifics, a being is or is not included in the moral community as a brute fact because of their inherent capacities.

However, beings excluded from the moral community usually still have some kind of status, albeit as moral *patients* rather than moral *agents*. For instance, animals and children arguably do not have fully developed capacities that allow them to participate in the moral community in a reciprocal way. When animals and children factor into moral deliberations, they do so as beings who may be *objects* of moral concern, but who cannot fully participate in the moral community as equals. In other words, we have obligations *to* them—there are restrictions in how we might treat them. But they do not have moral obligations to us in turn since they are simply not—or not yet—the kinds of being capable of fully understanding and living by moral principles. This is similar again to ordinary law: we may have laws that restrict how children or animals can be treated, but, lacking certain capacities, they have no right to participate in the process of *creating* laws (in other words, voting).

Intuitionalism, Pluralism, and Non-Absolutism

In all of the above theories, rationality or reason has a central place: immoral conduct is a form of irrationality (Shafer-Landau 2012, 161). But the two remaining deontological views in this section—W. D. Ross's pluralism and Mou Zongsan's Kantian Confucianism—do not think that morality is a matter of our ability to reason (or, at least, not in quite the same way).

According to these versions of deontology, moral principles come from our *intuition*. For Mou, this is because moral principle is found within us, not outside us. Mou develops the Confucian School of Mind's idea that our heart-mind is itself a manifestation of universal principle—the same principle that underlies everything else, including morality. We all have the capacity for *liangzhi* (conscience 良知) that allows us to look inward and gain knowledge of that universal principle directly, so long as selfish desire is not clouding our internal sight.

The nature of the heart-mind and our relationship to it also explains our moral motivation. In fact, Mou sees his view as making an advance on that of Kant. For Kant, we have our intellectual understanding of moral principle on the one hand, and our motivation to follow that moral principle on the other. The moral person understands both what their duty is vis-à-vis moral principle, and at the same time sees the legitimacy of that principle in terms of their own will and is therefore motivated to live by it. But these two things can come apart. For Mou, by contrast, coming to know moral principle from within our Original Mind (the heart-mind of universal principle) is inherently motivating: there is no separation between intellectual understanding and feeling; feeling moral principle *is* understanding it, and understanding it is feeling it.

For Ross, moral principles come from intuition in an analogous manner to mathematical principles. For example, when we are learning addition as a child, we start by noting that if we put together a pile of two blocks and a pile of three blocks, we get a pile of five blocks. Here, we are observing a specific instance of addition. Once we have engaged in this process a few times, we start to come to understand the principle that governs how addition works *in general*—we extrapolate a principle from the individual examples—and we can then start to apply this principle to other cases.

Similarly, for moral principles, we simply *see* that we ought not to harm *this person here* and *that person there*—individual instances of non-harming—and from that we generalize to an appreciation of the moral principle that we ought not to harm others *in general*. Moral principles are therefore not about our rationality per se, but more about our capacity for *insight* into the nature of specific cases, as well as our ability from there to understand them as instances of a more general principle.

Ross's deontological theory is also distinctive in two other ways. First, it is *pluralistic* (as compared to the *monism* of the other views). For Kant, Scanlon, Habermas, and Mou, ultimately there is a single basic rule that governs the moral acceptability of all other principles. For Kant, this is the categorical imperative; for Scanlon, the idea of reasonable rejection; for Habermas, the universalization principle; and for Mou, universal principle. But Ross does not accept the idea that there is one ultimate principle. For Ross, we have duties to be just, to be grateful, to keep promises, and so on, and all these duties are basic; none can be reduced to or derived from any other. Hence, there is a *plurality* of duties, rather than one (mono) single, ultimate duty. And we can see why Ross might think this, given his intuitionism. After all, our intuition that we have a duty to keep our promises in various concrete cases (thereby giving rise to a more general duty of fidelity) seems grounded independently from our intuition that we ought to avoid harming in various concrete cases (giving rise to the general duty of non-harm). Both fidelity and non-harm are moral duties, but our justifications for thinking we have a duty to be honest on the one hand, and a duty to not harm on the other, do not seem to have anything in common. Each of these considerations seems to matter for its own sake.

Secondly (and relatedly), Ross is non-absolutist about moral principles. Whereas for Kant, Scanlon, Habermas, and Mou their ultimate moral principles are *absolute*—they cannot be broken for any reason—for Ross the principles that underlie our moral duties *can* be broken. And given his pluralism, it should be easy to see why: our various basic duties will inevitably come into conflict. For instance, sometimes it is more important to be honest than to avoid harming, and at other times the reverse is true. But if so, then both principles, at different times, can be justifiably broken. In fact, it seems unlikely that *any* of the various fundamental moral duties that Ross identifies will *always* come out on top. If so, then every moral principle is non-absolute.

Summary

In this chapter we have seen how deontological theories are concerned fundamentally with *actions* rather than states of affairs or dispositions. They prioritize the right over the good, in that the right constrains our pursuit of the good in certain ways. By seeing moral principles as constraints on how we go about trying to achieve the good, deontological theories are able to more easily make sense of the category of "permitted" actions—actions that we are legitimately able to choose to perform or not. We also get an agent-relative theory of ethics concerned with what actions *we* perform specifically, and that can make room for special commitments, such as to our family, friends, and compatriots.

Deontological theories typically have a quasi-legal character. Just as ordinary laws do not tell us what we should value or how we should live our lives, but rather restrict how we go about accomplishing our own aims, moral principles also act as prohibitions on how the good can be pursued. But unlike ordinary laws—which are backed by the threat of force and are externally motivating—deontologists claim that we are motivated to follow deontological moral laws for their own sake. Quite why we ought to do so is a matter of disagreement between the different deontological theories under consideration. Most offer a proceduralist account of the authority of moral principles, usually tied in some way to our natures as rational beings capable of understanding and acting on 'principles. By contrast, Mou sees the motivation to follow moral principle as inherent in our coming to know the content of the principle itself: knowing and feeling moral principle are one and the same. Lastly, Ross's pluralism justifies the motivating force of principles in terms of the fact that they are generalizations from moral qualities that we directly intuit in concrete cases.

Whatever the particular explanation, one central concern for deontologists is precisely where our moral motivation comes from. While this issue is pressing for all moral theories, this is particularly so for deontological theories because of their law-like nature. After all, we may be able to recognize the *content* of the moral law, but can always ask why—absent coercive force, as in the case of ordinary laws—we ought to *abide* by those moral laws. The various deontological views in this section can be understood—at least partly—as differing ways this question of how the moral law can be *internally* motivating.

Notes

1. Consequentialism—and especially universalist, impartialist consequentialism—is a common foil for deontological theories. So most of the time it is used as a contrasting example in this chapter.

2. Though Tom Dougherty disagrees: see Dougherty 2013.

3. There is, of course, a third possibility: that we follow the law out of respect for the law *as* the law. This is particularly important in democratic contexts, where we understand the law as being in some way a matter of the collective will of society. However, this itself is a deontological reason to obey the law, so for our purposes here we can think of this option as a variant of following the law for "moral" reasons.

4. That citizens in a country *have* consented to the laws is, of course, debatable.

Further Reading

Deigh, John. 2010. *An Introduction to Ethics*. Cambridge: Cambridge University Press.

Dougherty, Tom. 2013. "Agent-Neutral Deontology." *Philosophical Studies: An International Journal for Philosophy in the Analytic Tradition* 163, no. 2: 527–37. https://doi.org/10.1007/s11098-011-9829-8.

Freeman, Samuel. 1994. "Utilitarianism, Deontology, and the Priority of Right." *Philosophy & Public Affairs* 23, no. 4: 313–49. https://doi.org/10.1111/j.1088-4963.1994.tb00017.x.

Miller, David. 2007. *National Responsibility and Global Justice*. Oxford: Oxford University Press.

Miller, Richard W. 2004. "Moral Closeness and World Community." In *The Ethics of Assistance: Morality and the Distant Needy*, edited by Deen K. Chatterjee, 101–22. New York: Cambridge University Press. https://doi.org/10.1017/CBO9780511817663.007.

McNaughton, David, and Piers Rawling. 2006. "Deontology." In *The Oxford Handbook of Ethical Theory*, edited by David Copp, 424–58.

New York: Oxford University Press. https://doi.org/10.1093/oxfor dhb/9780195325911.003.0016.

Norcross, Alastair. 1997. "Good and Bad Actions." *Philosophical Review* 106, no. 1: 1–34. https://doi.org/10.2307/2998340.

Rawls, John. 1999. *A Theory of Justice*. Rev. ed. Oxford: Oxford University Press.

Ronzoni, Miriam. 2010. "Teleology, Deontology, and the Priority of the Right: On Some Unappreciated Distinctions." *Ethical Theory and Moral Practice* 13: 453–72. https://doi.org/10.1007/s10677-009-9209-z.

Scanlon, T. M. 1998. *What We Owe to Each Other*. Cambridge: The Belknap Press of Harvard University Press.

Shafer-Landau, Russ. 2012. *The Fundamentals of Ethics*. 2nd ed. Oxford: Oxford University Press.

Slote, Michael. 1984. "Satisficing Consequentialism." *Proceedings of the Aristotelian Society* 58. https://doi.org/139-163. 10.1093/aristotelian supp/58.1.139.

Tännsjö, Torbjörn. 2008. *Understanding Ethics: An Introduction to Moral Theory*. 2nd ed. Edinburgh: Edinburgh University Press.

Williams, Bernard. 1973. "A Critique of Utilitarianism." In *Utilitarianism: For and Against*, edited by U. C. Smart and B. Williams, 75–150. Cambridge: Cambridge University Press. https://doi.org/10.1017/CBO9780511840852.002.

9

Immanuel Kant and Deontology

LUCAS THORPE[1]

Introduction

This chapter has two main sections. In the first section I briefly sketch Immanuel Kant's moral theory as laid out in his *Groundwork of the Metaphysics of Morals* (1785). I explain Kant's claim that morality must be grounded on what he calls a categorical imperative and examine his three formulations of this categorical imperative. In the second section I explain the distinction between "deontological" and "teleological" ethical theories. Kantian ethics is often presented as the paradigm example of a deontological ethical theory, but I question whether Kant's ethics should be understood as purely deontological.

Kant's Ethics

Many people think that what is really important in life is to be, say, clever or brave or happy. But Kant thinks that none of these things is good if one lacks a good will: "It is impossible to think of anything at all in the world, or indeed even beyond it, that could be considered good without limitation except a *good will* . . . a good will seems to constitute the indispensable condition even of worthiness to be happy" (*Groundwork* 4:393). For Kant, the most important question in moral philosophy is therefore not "What is it to be happy?" but the question "What is it to have a good will?" And a "good will" is understood not in terms of what it achieves or what it aims at, but the fact that it is moved by—or governed by—reason.[2]

But Kant thinks that human beings are imperfectly rational beings, and as such our reason is always potentially in conflict with our inclinations. For morally imperfect beings like ourselves, morality is therefore always a matter of *duty*.[3] Truly moral behavior involves acting *from* duty and not merely acting *in accordance with* duty (4:397). Take the example of promising to meet my friend at a certain place to help them study for an exam. Perhaps I really enjoy spending time with them, even helping them study for an exam. In such a case I am doing what duty demands, but I am not necessarily doing it *from* duty. But if I were to still come and help, even if I was not in the mood and would much rather be going to a party, then this would be an example of acting *from* duty and not merely *in accordance with* duty.

It is important to note that Kant is not saying here that it would be morally better to help one's friends without enjoying it. Instead, he is merely pointing out that a good person is one who would choose to keep their promise *even if* they were not so inclined. It is therefore possible, and desirable, to act from duty *and* from inclination simultaneously. Ideally a good person does the right thing *and* enjoys doing it. It is just that a good person would still do the right thing *even if* they did not have the inclination to do so. This is what it is to act *from* duty. The person who merely acts *in accordance with* duty would forget about their duty if their inclination changed. They might keep their promises if they enjoy doing what they promised to do but will break their promises if they thought they would not enjoy keeping them.

Kant further argues that the obligation of duty is to be thought of in terms of an imperative or command. Thus he says, "The representation of an objective principle, insofar as it is necessitating for a will, is called a command (of reason), and the formula of the command is called an *imperative*. All imperatives are expressed by an *ought* and indicate by this the relation of an objective law

of reason to a will that by its subjective constitution is not necessarily determined by it (a necessitation)" (4:413). The point Kant
is trying to make here is quite simple. Morality is something that
binds and constrains us; when we recognize the call of duty, we
recognize that there is something that we *should* do. And the fact
that I *should* do something is not a mere subjective preference, but
an objective command. Because of its objective law-like character,
then, the demand of morality cannot be explained purely in terms
of satisfying one's desires, because our desires are contingent and
subjective, whereas laws are necessary and objective.

Although the content of the moral law is necessary and objective, it does not have the same status as a law of nature. Laws of
physics tell us what *will* be the case; laws of morality only tell us
what *should* be the case. And because we are imperfectly rational
and have free will, the fact that we recognize that we *should* do
something does not mean that we *will* do it. Thus, although the
moral law is objectively binding on us, the "subjective constitution"
of our will is "not necessarily determined" by the law. In other
words, we do not always in fact do what we recognize we ought to.

But what does morality command? To answer this question,
Kant distinguishes between what he calls hypothetical imperatives
and categorical imperatives. A hypothetical imperative is a conditional (if-then) command. For example, a hypothetical imperative
may say: If you want to pass your class, do your homework! Or,
If you want to be happy, spend time with your friends! Such
hypothetical imperatives only command conditionally. If you
do not want to pass the class, then you do not need to do your
homework. If you do not want to be happy, you do not need to
spend time with your friends. Kant believes, however, that moral
obligations cannot be conditional in this way: morality commands
absolutely, not conditionally. Thus Kant claims that

> Since every practical law represents a possible action
> as good and thus as necessary for a subject practically
> determinable by reason, all imperatives are formulae for
> the determination of action that is necessary in accordance
> with the principle of a will which is good in some way.
> Now, if the action would be good merely as a *means to
> something else* the imperative is *hypothetical*; if the action

is represented as *in itself good*, hence as necessary in a will in itself conforming to reason, as its principle, then it is *categorical*. (4:414)

Morality, Kant thinks, must be based on a categorical imperative rather than a hypothetical one.

Kant then argues that merely reflecting on the concept of what a categorical imperative is allows us to grasp what such an imperative must demand. Thus, in one of the most difficult and most famous paragraphs in the *Groundwork* Kant argues:

When I think of a *hypothetical* imperative in general I do not know beforehand what it will contain; I do not know this until I am given the condition. But when I think of a *categorical* imperative I know at once what it contains. For, since the imperative contains, beyond the law, only the necessity that the maxim be in conformity with this law, while the law contains no condition to which it would be limited, nothing is left with which the maxim of action is to conform but the universality of a law as such; and this conformity alone is what the imperative properly represents as necessary. There is, therefore, only a single categorical imperative and it is this: *act only in accordance with that maxim through which you can at the same time will that it become a universal law*. (4:420–21)

The argument in this paragraph is quite abstract, but the basic idea is quite simple: As an objective command, a categorical imperative must be a law. However, as categorical, it must be an *unconditioned* law. It must be a command that cannot command us to do anything in particular; it can only be a command the only content of which is that it is commandlike. In other words, the categorical imperative must be a purely formal and contentless law, as any content over and above its form would make it conditioned. The only thing that a law whose content is merely the form of being lawful could command is that one act lawfully. So the categorical imperative tells us that an action is only moral if the underlying motivation (maxim) is such that it could serve as a universal law.

Immediately after claiming that there can only be a single categorical imperative, Kant proceeds to introduce what he calls three formulations of this imperative. There has been much debate as to how, or whether, these distinct formulations can be thought of as formulations of a single imperative. I finish this section by explaining each of these formulations, and then in the final section of the paper I say something about the relationship between them.

In the course of explaining the three formulations of the categorical imperative, Kant uses four concrete examples to illustrate each formulation. These are examples of duties that his contemporaries would have accepted as obvious moral duties. The examples are not chosen randomly, for Kant thinks that there are two ways we can divide duties: between duties to oneself and duties to others, and between what he calls perfect and imperfect duties. Perfect duties command us to perform specific actions. For example, Kant thinks that repaying a debt when asked is a perfect duty, because one has a particular duty to perform a specific action—pay back that particular debt to a particular person. Imperfect duties, by contrast, do not demand specific actions. For example, Kant thinks that we have a duty to promote the happiness of others, but because this duty does not tell us specifically *whose* happiness to promote and precisely *when* to do so, it is imperfect. Given these distinctions, we can categorize duties into four classes. Kant discusses one example from each class:

(1) **Perfect duties toward oneself:** The duty not to commit suicide.

(2) **Perfect duties toward others:** The duty not to make a promise with the intention of breaking it. (The duty to not make a "lying promise.")

(3) **Imperfect duties toward oneself:** The duty to develop one's talents.

(4) **Imperfect duties toward others:** The duty to care about the happiness of others. (The duty of beneficence.)

Formulations of the Categorical Imperative

I now briefly explain each formulation of the categorical imperative. The first formulation of the categorical imperative is the

formula of universalizability. This formulation states: "act as if the maxim of your action were to become by your will a *universal law of nature*" (4:421). Simply, Kant thinks that whenever we act, we have some subjective principle of action (what he calls a "maxim") that lies behind our action. The formula of universalizability asks us to try and imagine a world in which everyone acted on the same subjective principle that we did; that is, he asks us to imagine that the subjective principle of our action was an objective law.

Kant thinks that in some cases it is not even possible to conceive of a world in which our subjective principle was an objective law. This can be called a **contradiction in conception**. For example, suppose I am tempted to make a lying promise, with the maxim of my action being the following subjective principle: "when I believe myself to be in need of money, I shall borrow money and promise to repay it, even though I know that this will never happen" (4:442). It is possible for me *individually* to act on such a maxim, in isolation. But if I try and conceive of a world in which everyone acted on such a maxim, I can see that such a world would not be possible. The ability to make a lying promise presupposes a world in which the institution of promise making exists. If *everyone* made lying "promises" whenever it was convenient, there could not really be any such thing as promise making. So, Kant concludes, a world in which such a maxim was a universal law is inconceivable, and this formula of the categorical imperative therefore suggests that acting on such a maxim would be immoral.

It is important to stress here that Kant is not saying that maxim is immoral because the consequences of everyone following the rule would be bad, but that it is simply impossible to conceive of a world in which the rule were a law that everyone followed.

There are also **contradictions in willing**, of which beneficence is a good example. Consider a maxim of never willing to help others when they are in need. Imagine a world in which everyone acted in this way. Although such a world is conceivable, Kant thinks that nobody could will such a world. For we are all beings who are sometimes in need of help from others, and willing a world in which no one was motivated to help others would involve willing a world in which we were never helped when we needed it to achieve our own goals. Such willing would be self-defeating. For when we aim to achieve something (when we "will an end"), we also will the means to that end. But to will a world in which no one ever helps anyone else would be to will a world in which certain means to our ends (help from others) are not possible. In willing such a world together with willing particular ends, we both will the means to our ends and will that such ends are not available. Hence, our willing is contradictory.

The second formulation of the categorical imperative is the **formula of humanity**, which states: "So act that you use humanity, whether in your own person or in the person of any other, always at the same time as an end, never merely as a means" (4:428). Kant introduces this formulation by distinguishing between what he calls subjective ends and objective ends. He argues that moral principles, insofar as they involve ends, have to involve *objective* ends—ends that hold necessarily for all rational beings. Subjective ends, such as satisfying one's desires, are ends that depend on the contingent nature of particular agents and as such are ends that can only serve as the basis of hypothetical imperatives. Appealing to such subjective ends, then, can "furnish no universal principles, no principles valid and necessary for all rational beings" (4:428). But, Kant asks, "suppose there were something the *existence of which in itself* has an absolute worth, something which as *an end in itself* could be a ground of determinate laws; then in it, and in it alone, would lie the ground of a possible categorical imperative" (4:428). Kant argues that rational beings are such ends in themselves.[4] That is, rational beings are *persons* who demand respect, not mere *things* to be used for our own purposes.

To illustrate what is involved in treating others as ends and never merely as means, Kant returns to his four examples. For instance, respecting the humanity of others is not compatible with making a lying promise, as the other person "cannot possibly agree to my way of behaving toward him" (4:430). Kant's discussion of this example suggests that respect for the humanity of others involves only treating them in ways that they could, at least in principle, agree to.

But, Kant thinks, respect for the humanity of others involves more than just treating people in ways that that they can possibly consent to: one must also have some concern with promoting the happiness and well-being of others. Kant also thinks we have a duty to develop our own talents and moral character, and a duty not to commit suicide, for committing suicide is to fail to treat oneself as an end in itself.

The third formulation of the categorical imperative is sometimes referred to as **the formula of the realm (or kingdom) of ends** and sometimes as **the formula of autonomy**. Kant's discussion of the realm of ends and his introduction of the notion of autonomy is influenced by Jean-Jacques Rousseau's account of the idea of an ideal republic in his *Social Contract*. In such a republic, each individual member is a citizen, and the laws are made by and endorsed by all citizens. As such, each individual citizen is both the source of the laws that govern the community and a subject of those laws. In the *Groundwork*, Kant takes Rousseau's political ideal of a republic and turns it into his ethical ideal of a realm of ends. Thus Kant explains that "a rational being belongs as a *member* to the realm of ends when he gives universal laws in it but is also himself subject to these laws" (4:433).

The third formulation of the categorical imperative says that we should act in a way such that we could be a citizen in such an ideal community. This involves only acting on maxims that could potentially be laws in such a community and respecting other human beings as if they were fellow citizens within such a moral community. This is what Kant means when he claims that "morality consists, then, in the reference of all action to the lawgiving by which alone a realm of ends is possible" (4.434). When we evaluate the maxims behind our actions, we must think of ourselves, and all other human beings, as constituting a single community potentially governed by laws that all could will, and we should ask when evaluating our own maxims whether they could serve as laws for such a community.

Like Rousseau, Kant identifies the idea of being a member of a realm of ends with possession of a certain type of freedom, which he names "autonomy" (from the Greek: *autos* = self; *nomos* = law). An individual is autonomous if they are subject to a law they have made themselves. So being a member of a realm of ends is the same as being an autonomous individual who possesses moral freedom. This is why this formulation is sometimes called the **formula of autonomy**.

Is Kantian Ethics Deontological?

Today, especially among Anglo-American ethical theorists, it is common to contrast deontological with teleological ethical theories, and to suggest that all ethical positions can be classified as either deontological or teleological. Thus, for example, William Frankena offers the following influential definition:

> Deontological theories deny what teleological theories affirm. They deny that the right, the obligatory, and the morally good are wholly, whether directly or indirectly a function of what is nonmorally good or of what promotes the greatest balance of good over evil for self, one's society, or the world as a whole . . . For them the principle of maximizing the balance of good over evil, no matter for whom, is either not a moral criterion or standard at all, or, at least, it is not the only basic or ultimate one. (1973, 15)

This way of classifying ethical theories is, however, relatively recent. The word "deontology" seems to have been coined in the early nineteenth century by the utilitarian philosopher Jeremy Bentham, with its roots coming from the Greek *deont-* ("that which is binding" or "duty") and *-ology* (*logos*, which means "science" or "theory of"). So based on its etymology, it literally means the science of what ought to be done. Through much of the nineteenth century and into the early twentieth century, the word deontology was just used as a posh way of saying "ethical theory." In the late nineteenth century, however, many philosophers attempted to introduce ways of categorizing moral theories into broad opposing camps. By the 1930s, many philosophers in the English-speaking world came to think that the broadest distinction was between what they named teleological and deontological theories.

Understood in negative terms, the distinction between deontological and teleological moral theories has to do with their understanding of the relationship between the good and the right. Teleological moral theories start out with some understanding of what is good, and they give an account of what is right in terms of this good. But the deontologist denies this claim, arguing that there are some things that are right or wrong regardless of whether they promote or produce anything good.

Deontology can also be defined positively in terms of picking out those ethical theories that place moral rules at the center of morality. A deontological moral theory is therefore one that says that morality is a matter of obeying moral rules or principles, such as "do not lie!" or "do not kill!" These principles or rules are a source of obligation even if obeying them will not promote or maximize the good.

Kantian ethics is often presented as the paradigm case of a deontological ethical theory in the Western tradition. Kant places the notion of duty or obligation at the center of his ethics and rejects consequentialism. But should Kant be understood as offering a fully deontological ethics? Although Kant is clearly not a consequentialist, it is not obvious that his theory is completely non-teleological. After all, the concept of a good will, humanity, and the realm of ends are central to his ethical theory, and all seem to be, in a sense, ideas of the good.

Kant certainly does think that moral principles and rules are important: a virtuous individual is one who recognizes and abides by the rules of morality. However, as we have seen, there is a lot more to his ethical thought than merely following rules or principles, and there are disagreements among Kant scholars about the degree to which moral rules and principles play a foundational role in his ethical system.

Perhaps the most influential recent interpretation of Kant's ethics is offered by John Rawls, who offers a strongly deontological reading of Kant's ethics. He names this interpretation "Kantian constructivism." A central commitment of the constructivist position is the deontologist's claim that the "the right is prior to the good." To understand what this slogan means, we can contrast the constructivist position with that of the utilitarian, who believes, in contrast, that the "good is prior to the right." Thus Rawls explains that "Utilitarianism starts with a conception of the good given prior to, and independent of, the right (the moral law), and it then works out from that independent conception its conceptions of the right and of moral worth, in that order" (1989, 92). In other words, first the utilitarian works out what goods we should be aiming at. Once she knows this, she can then discover what we ought to do (what is "right") by seeing whether the action brings about those goods.

A Kantian constructivist, by contrast, starts with a conception of the right and defines the good in terms of the right: a state of affairs is good if it was (or perhaps could have been) chosen in the right way. This disagreement can be understood as a disagreement about what it is to be reasonable. The utilitarian will define reasonableness in terms of the good, whereas the constructivist will define the good in terms of the reasonable.

For instance, imagine a group of individuals who wish to share a cake. The utilitarian will argue that the procedure we use to determine how to divide up the cake is reasonable if it is intended or likely to produce the best decision; that is, a decision that maximizes total happiness. The constructivist, by contrast, will argue that a decision is good if the procedure used to make the decision was a reasonable one. On this approach, what it is to be reasonable must be defined independently of, and prior to, any conception of the good or the desirable.

Rawls's constructivist interpretation is based on an account of the relationship between the first and third formulation of the categorical imperative. He interprets the first formulation as providing an account of the right and the third formulation as providing an account of the good.

A constructivist ethics starts by providing an account of the "reasonably willable." This is precisely what Rawls believes Kant is trying to do when he introduces the first formulation of the categorical imperative in the *Groundwork*. Rawls argues that the first formulation of the categorical imperative should be understood as introducing a procedure to test the reasonableness of maxims, which he calls the CI-Procedure (2000, 181). According to Rawls, the first formulation of the categorical imperative is an attempt to give an account of what it is to be reasonable in purely deontological terms, terms that make no reference to the good or the morally desirable. To be reasonable is to implicitly follow a certain procedure—the CI-Procedure—and the good or morally desirable is to be defined in terms of this procedure.

If the first formulation of the categorical imperative specifies a procedure to test the reasonableness of our maxims, the second two formulations specify the objects that such a reasonable person should value (or find good). A reasonable person will value the humanity of herself and others and will value the idea of being a member of a realm of ends. The notions of "humanity" and "a realm of ends" are concepts of the good. Given his reading of Kant as a moral constructivist, Rawls believes that Kant is committed to the position that these two ideas must be defined in terms of the procedure introduced in the first formulation. In other words, he believes that the second and third formulations of the categorical imperative are dependent for their content on the first formulation. Rawls and his followers, then, read Kant as committed to a strongly deontological position in both the negative sense of rejecting teleology and in the positive sense of putting moral rules (the CI-procedure) at the heart of his ethics.

Critics of such a strongly deontological interpretation tend to stress the second and third formulations of the categorical imperative, arguing that these formulations offer some notion of the good independent of the right. Such approaches stress the idea that Kant thinks that human beings are ends in themselves and are deserving of respect regardless of whether anyone actually chooses to show such respect. According to this more teleological interpretation, Kantian ethics presupposes the value of humanity and the value of being a member of citizen in a moral community.

Kant begins the *Groundwork* by examining our everyday ethical commitments. He thinks that it is a part of our commonsense morality that we should only act on principles that can be universalized. But then he asks: why do we care about universalizability? And his answer is that we care about universalizability because we care about other human beings and about standing in the right sort of relationship with them. According to this more teleological interpretation of Kant's ethics, the structure of the argument has to do with uncovering what we ultimately value. We do not construct an idea of the good from a set of (meaningless) moral rules. Instead, we care about certain moral rules because we recognize the value of other human beings and our standing in the right sort of relationship to them. If this interpretation is correct, then Kantian ethics is ultimately teleological (and not fully deontological) because the value of humanity and the value of being a member of a realm of ends are conceptions of the good and are foundational for his ethics.

There is, then, disagreement between scholars about the degree to which Kantian ethics should be understood in purely deontological terms, and to what degree notions of the good play a foundational role in his ethical theory.[5]

Summary

Kant's argument in the *Groundwork* that morality must involve a categorical imperative, and his account of the three formulations, has probably been his most influential contribution to ethics in the Western tradition. His appeal to universalization as a criterion to judge the validity of principles of action has become one of the most influential alternatives to utilitarian accounts of morality. And Kant's appeal to the value of humanity has played a large role in the development of thinking about human rights, with many defenders of human rights attempting to ground such rights in Kantian terms: in the dignity of human beings. In addition, many have found the idea that we should treat others as ends rather than means an attractive moral ideal; for example, feminist critiques of the "objectification" of women can be understood in such Kantian terms. Finally, Kant's appeal to the value of autonomy has also been extremely influential. However, there has been a regrettable tendency to understand Kant's notion of autonomy in individualistic terms (as a capacity for self-determination) rather than in social terms (as a capacity to be a citizen in an ideal moral community).[6]

Notes

1. Support for work on this paper was provided by Boğaziçi University Research Fund Grant Number 15681. Thanks to Michael Hemmingsen for comments on various drafts of this chapter.

2. What exactly Kant means by reason is a bone of contention among Kant scholars, and much of his practical philosophy can be understood as an attempt to clarify what is involved in being governed by reason. Some understand reason primarily in terms of a capacity of rationality

and rules. Others understand reason to involve a capacity to set ends and pursue them. I take practical reason to essentially involve a (moral) capacity to interact with others on the basis of mutual respect. See Thorpe (2018).

3. Kant often imagines the idea of a perfectly rational being, which he calls the idea of a holy will. For such a being morality would *not* be a matter of duty; a morally perfect individual would just act morally with no inner conflict.

4. There is debate over why Kant thinks that human beings are ends-in-themselves. One suggestion is that what makes us ends in ourselves is our capacity to set ends, for only a being that has value has the capacity to make decisions about what has value.

5. See Tilev (2021) for an account that tries to combine deontological and teleological conceptions of autonomy.

6. See Thorpe (2011) and Vatansever (2021) for a further discussion of this point.

Further Reading

PRIMARY SOURCES

Kant, Immanuel. (1785) 1996. *Groundwork of The Metaphysics of Morals*. Translation in *Practical Philosophy (The Cambridge Edition of the Works of Immanuel Kant)*. Edited by M. Gregor. Cambridge: Cambridge University Press.

———. (1788) 1996. *Critique of Practical Reason*. Translation in *Practical Philosophy (The Cambridge Edition of the Works of Immanuel Kant)*. Edited by M. Gregor. Cambridge: Cambridge University Press.

———. (1797) 1996. *The Metaphysics of Morals*. Translation in *Practical Philosophy (The Cambridge Edition of the Works of Immanuel Kant)*. Edited by M. Gregor. Cambridge: Cambridge University Press.

There are so many editions of the *Groundwork* that it is not very helpful to give the page number of a particular English edition. Instead, when scholars want to refer to a particular page in Kant's work, we refer to the volume number and the page number of the German edition of Kant's complete works. So a reference to the Groundwork of the form 4:443 means volume 4, page 443 of the German Academy edition. Most English editions of the *Groundwork* have these numbers down the side of the page—so whatever English edition you are using, you should be able to find the passage referred to.

SECONDARY SOURCES

Foot, Philippa. 1972. "Morality as a System of Hypothetical Imperatives." *The Philosophical Review* 81, no. 3: 305–16. https://doi.org/2184328.

Frankena, William K. 1973. *Ethics*. 2nd ed. Hoboken, NJ: Prentice-Hall.

Guyer, Paul. 1993. *Kant and the Experience of Freedom: Essays on Aesthetics and Morality*. New York: Cambridge University Press.

Louden, Robert B. 1998. "Toward a Genealogy of 'Deontology.' " *Journal of the History of Philosophy* 34, no. 4: 571–92. https://doi.org/10.1353/hph.1996.0070.

Moran, K. 2022. *Kant's Ethics (Elements in Ethics)*. Cambridge: Cambridge University Press.

Mudd, Sasha. 2018. "The Good Will and the Priority of the Right in Groundwork I." In *Natur und Freiheit: Akten des XII. Internationalen Kant-Kongresses*, edited by Violetta L. Waibel, Margit Ruffing, and David Wagner, 1993–2000. Berlin: De Gruyter.

Rawls, John. 2000. *Lectures on the History of Moral Philosophy*. Cambridge, MA: Harvard University Press.

———. 1989. "Themes in Kant's Moral Philosophy." In *Kant's Transcendental Deductions*, edited by Eckart Förster, 81–113. Stanford, CA: Stanford University Press.

Rousseau, Jean-Jacques Rousseau. 2002. *The Social Contract and The First and Second Discourses*, edited by Susan Dunn. New Haven: Yale University Press.

Saunders, Joe. 2021. "Recent Work on Freedom in Kant." *British Journal for the History of Philosophy* 29, no. 6: 1177–89. https://doi.org/10.1080/09608788.2020.1865268.

Sticker, Martin. 2019. "A Funeral March for Those Drowning in Shallow Ponds?: Imperfect Duties and Emergencies." *Kant-Studien* 110, no. 2: 236–55. https://doi.org/10.1515/kant-2019-0001.

Thorpe, Lucas. 2019. "What's Wrong with Constructivist Readings of Kant?" In *The Philosophy of Kant*, edited by Ricardo Gutierrez. Aguilar: Nova Science Publishers.

———. 2018. "Kant, Guyer and Tomasello on the Capacity to Recognize the Humanity of Others." In *Kant on Freedom and Spontaneity*, edited by Kate Moran. Cambridge: Cambridge University Press.

———. 2014. *The Kant Dictionary*. London: Bloomsbury.

———. 2011. "Autonomy and Community." In *Kant and the Concept of Community*, edited by Lucas Thorpe and Charlton Payne. Rochester: University of Rochester Press.

———. 2006. "What Is the Point of Studying Ethics According to Kant?" *Journal of Value Inquiry* 40: 461–74. https://doi.org/10.1007/s10790-006-9002-3.

Tilev, Seniye. 2021. "Two Conceptions of Kantian Autonomy" In *The Court of Reason: Proceedings of the 13th International Kant Congress*, edited by Beatrix Himmelmann and Camilla Serck-Hanssen, 1579–85. Berlin: De Gruyter, 2021.

Uleman, J. 2010. *An Introduction to Kant's Moral Philosophy*. Cambridge: Cambridge University Press.

Vatansever, Saniye. 2021. "Kant's Coherent Theory of the Highest Good." *International Journal for Philosophy of Religion* 89: 263–83. https://doi.org/10.1007/s11153-020-09782-8.

Wood, Allen W. 1999. *Kant's Ethical Thought*. New York: Cambridge University Press.

10

Mou Zongsan and Moral Feeling

WING-CHEUK CHAN AND MICHAEL HEMMINGSEN

Introduction

Mou Zongsan (牟宗三) (1909–1995) is arguably the most important Chinese philosopher of the twentieth century. In claiming to return to Mencius's (372–289 BCE) original position, Mou singles out the Song-Ming (宋明) Neo-Confucian School of Mind (*xinxue* 心學) as represented by Lu Xiangshan (陸象山) (1139–1193) and Wang Yangming (王陽明) (1472–1529) as the "orthodox" lineage on which he bases his interpretation of Confucianism, and as a major founder of Modern New Confucianism, Mou tries to reconstruct these traditional Confucian ethics in terms of Immanuel Kant's (1724–1804) moral philosophy. Mou identified the heart-mind with Kantian practical reason—our ability to guide our actions according to principle—and claimed that the Confucian idea of the immanence of benevolence (*ren* 仁) and righteousness (*yi* 義) is equivalent to Kant's concept of autonomy.

The School of Mind and Moral Feeling

Mou provided a threefold typology of Song-Ming Neo-Confucianism: (1) The School of Principle (*lixue* 理學), as represented by Cheng

Yi (程頤) (1033–1107) and Zhu Xi (朱熹) (1130–1200); (2) the School of Mind, as represented by Lu Xiangshan and Wang Yangming; and (3) the School of Being (*xingxue* 性學), as represented by Hu Wufeng 胡五峰 (1105–1162) and Liu Zongzhou 劉宗周 (1578–1645). Mou especially singled out the School of Mind as his own predecessor. In Mou's eyes, only the School of Mind represents orthodox Confucianism. Mou's ethics therefore results from a synthesis of the traditional School of Mind and Kant's moral philosophy.

According to *xinxue* philosophers Lu Xiangshan and Wang Yangming, the slogan of the School of Mind is "Mind is Principle." By this they mean that the very same pattern that underlies the universe (*li* 理) is found in the human heart-mind (*xin* 心). In fact, they claim that the heart-mind fundamentally *is* this universal principle, the same universal principle found in all things, meaning that the human heart-mind forms "one body" (*yiti* 一體) with everything else in the universe. Because universal principle is inherently good, the heart-mind of human beings is also good. As such, human beings are born with innate moral knowledge and virtue as well as an innate faculty of "pure knowledge" (*liangzhi* 良知) that gives them access to this innate moral knowledge. Human beings only fail to act morally when their selfish desires interfere with their faculty of *liangzhi*. Moral cultivation is therefore a matter of removing selfish desires to better access the heart-mind of universal principle and its innate moral knowledge.

For Mou, the School of Mind's identification of the heart-mind with principle is a faithful articulation of Mencius's thesis of the "immanence of benevolence and rightness" (*renyi neizai* 仁義內在). Mencius spoke of the "four beginnings" or inborn seeds of morality: the feeling of commiseration, the feeling of shame, the feeling of resignation, and the feeling of right and wrong. Each of these seeds gives rise to a different moral virtue. For Mencius, these seeds were understood as the "criteria" of morality (Chan 1963, 54–55), in the sense that anyone who lacks these basic feelings is condemned to lack morality and therefore be "inhuman."

Non-Sensible Moral Feeling

Traditionally the four beginnings were thought of as *feelings*. But contrary to this, Mou thought of the four beginnings instead as "reasons." What is the difference between the two? The four beginnings are somewhat equivalent to the concept of *conscience* in Kant. But conscience does not give us a reason to act; rather, it is merely a faculty that allows us to be receptive to the commands of duty (arising from the moral law). In other words, for Kant the source of our moral reasons is not found in our conscience. For Mou, by contrast, the four beginnings themselves contain reasons for action; they can provide the content of our duty, not merely a motivation to perform it. The four beginnings are the manifestation of mind, and since mind is equated with universal principle itself, the four beginnings are not merely a *response* to principle but are themselves manifestations of principle.

Mou therefore developed his own idea of moral feeling to challenge Kant's ethics. In his Chinese translation of Kant's *Critique of Practical Reason*, Mou remarks:

> Kant only addressed the influence of laws on feeling so that the special feeling of respect arises—moral feeling. This can be *a priori* known, for this is a result in feeling. This is not "sensible," but rather "practical." Nonetheless, he failed to recognize that such non-sensible feeling can be "reversed" to be the "ground," and this is the "feeling of the Original Mind." Since it, as the feeling of the Original Mind, can function as the ground, it can also function as the "foundation of laws." (2003, v.15, 286)

In other words, the Kantian feeling of conscience—or respect—plays a much more limited role than the equivalent feeling in Mou's system. Whereas Kant thinks that knowledge of the moral law can give rise to the special moral feeling of respect, Mou thinks that the feeling of respect can itself be "reversed" to become the *source* of moral law.

This does not mean that the idea of respect was not important to Kant. As John Drummond observed,

> First, respect is the only emotion that has a relation to cognition, and second, respect is the only emotion that serves as an incentive for morally praiseworthy action . . . Respect is similar to all other emotions as an affective response. This accounts for its negative

moment, namely, the pain and humiliation produced by the thwarting of our inclinations by the moral law. But respect also has a positive moment: insofar as the moral law commands our respect for its power to humiliate us when we compare the law to the inclinations present in our physical natures, respect enables us to love its role as a moral incentive. Respect for the law, in other words, is the recognition of the law's nature as positive, determining principle of the will. (2003, 1)

To put this another way, of all our emotions, only respect arises directly from our cognition of the moral law, and only respect can *motivate* us to *follow* that law. It also plays a special role in allowing us to love the part the moral law plays in determining our will, even when the moral law leads us to act against our inclinations.

However, despite the importance of respect for Kant, beginning with his *Groundwork for the Metaphysics of Morals*, Kant nonetheless denied the foundational role of moral feeling. Instead, practical reason—our rational capacity—was understood as the only source of the moral law. Respect as moral feeling was "regarded as the *effect* of the law on the subject and not as its cause" (2002, 17). In other words, *first* we come to understand the moral law through practical reason. *Then* our knowledge of the moral law causes us to have a feeling of respect for this law. In short, this view denies that moral feeling has any power to determine the moral law; it can only ever be a product of it. As Kant declared: "[M]oral feeling . . . cannot yield an equal standard of good and evil, nor can one validly judge for others at all through his feeling" (2002, 60). In short, in Kant there is an essential distinction between practical reason and moral feeling. Moral feeling cannot tell us what is good or evil or divulge what we ought to do in any given case. It can only arise once we have already determined good and evil, which we do via the exercise of our capacity for practical reason.

However, for Mou, moral feeling *can* function as the "cause" of morality. The key to this lies in the possibility of "non-sensible moral feeling." In other words, Kant originally saw moral feeling as merely "sensible"—that is, just a special kind of feeling relating to morality and the moral law, but not itself a fundamental part of what *grounds* morality. It is an "affective *response*" that recognizes the moral law's authority over our will and allows us to positively love the moral law.

By contrast, for Mou respect is a "non-sensible" moral feeling, a feeling that is not a reaction or response to other things—the laws of morality that are independently determined via reason—but is rather a source of moral knowledge in and of itself. Mou even speaks of respect as the "feeling of the Original Mind" in Mencius's sense—the mind with innate moral knowledge. In this context, Mou identifies the four beginnings in Mencius as "non-sensible moral feelings":

> Mencius spoke of "mind" in terms of *li* (principle). It is neither Hume's "moral sense," nor Kant's "moral feeling" or "moral sense." In Kant, moral feeling and moral sense are the same. Even moral feeling in Kant's sense is different from the four beginnings in Mencius. The latter is rather reason. Insofar as the four beginnings as reason are the foundation of the moral law, moral feeling in Kant's sense, though differing from moral sense, is only the effect. More precisely, it results from the influence of the moral law upon our mind. In regard to the question: "Where does the moral law come from?" Kant's answer is as follows:
>
> It does not come from moral feeling, for moral feeling merely perceives the moral law, but it cannot establish any moral law. Moral laws are entirely established by reason. This is nothing but the autonomy of the will. (2019, 69)

This means that for Mou, in Kantian terms, the heart-mind (which is essentially the Original Mind) not only *appreciates* morality, but also actually grounds moral action itself. The heart-mind is the dynamic source of moral action. Hence, for Mou there is identity between the "non-sensible moral feeling" of respect and the will. In essence, Mou interprets Mencius's thesis of the "immanence of benevolence and rightness" as a counterpart of the Kantian idea of autonomy. For Kant, to be autonomous is a matter of acting on those laws that a person has given to themselves (rather than being bound by laws given by others or by nature). Similarly, for Mou, since benevolence and righteousness are immanent in the heart-mind, then benevolence and righteousness are not moral concepts given by others but are given to the self *by* the self: the Original Mind.

The Identity of Reason and Feeling

Mou's view relies on the possibility of "non-sensible" moral feeling, as well as the "identity" of reason and feeling. How does he explain these ideas? First of all, Mou sees Mencius's four beginnings as constitutive elements of human nature. Mencius's beginnings—as feelings—are purely good. While the beginnings may or may not develop into full-fledged virtues (humanity, righteousness, propriety, and wisdom) depending on the efforts of the individual and the situation they find themselves in, the beginnings are nonetheless always morally good themselves. Whether or not a person develops the virtue of humanity, for instance, the raw feeling of commisera-tion—the seed and prerequisite of this virtue—is always positive. Hence, the four beginnings play a "foundational role" in terms of the Original Mind's "loving good and hating evil."

In other words, since human beings' Original Mind always has the four beginnings, and since those four beginnings are always morally good, then the Original Mind is innately disposed toward good and against evil. These moral feeling are grounded in the very being of humans. In other words, they are "ontological feelings." These feelings also connect human beings—via universal principle—with the fundamental nature of things. Accordingly, they are "non-sensible" moral feelings in the sense that their source is principle itself, rather than existing as a response to things (such as moral laws), as with Kant.

In explaining the relationship between reason and feeling, Mou further writes: "The illuminating awareness of the Original Mind itself is 'reason' (principle/law), and 'enlightenment feeling' (*juejing* 覺情) (moral feeling), and also 'purely intellectual intuition.' As reason or principle/law, it is practical reason (moral reason). It differs from the rough speech of the practical use and discursive use of the same reason . . . As enlightenment feeling, it is as such self-gathering, self-caring, and self-respect without indulgence. Enlightenment feeling, reason, and principle/law are three in one" (2003, v.15, 334). In other words, our basic moral feelings are intellectual (non-sensible); they are reason (the faculty that allows us to make judgments, including moral ones); and they themselves contain the moral law, since they are an expression of universal principle.

In claiming the identity of enlightenment feeling, reason, and principle/law, Mou also tries to illustrate how each of them is related to one another. He continues: "This is not to first establish a special type of moral feeling as the ground of principle/law—as what is opposed by Kant. Rather, reason itself is enlightenment feeling. Since it is non-sensible, it is called 'enlightenment feeling' or 'intellectual feeling.' Enlightenment feeling is also reason: it is 'not prior to reason,' nor is it 'after reason.' It is identical with reason. Therefore, the Original Mind loves principle/law, principle/law and righteousness please the mind" (2003, v.15, 335). In other words, reason is an "intellectual feeling"—what Mou refers to as "enlightenment feeling"—and enlightenment feeling is itself reason. It is not that we reason to the moral law, which in turn gives rise to an intellectual, non-sensible feeling. Nor is it that we have enlightenment feeling, which then provides some kind of special content for our capacity of reason to process. Rather, to reason and to experience a non-sensible enlightenment feeling is one and the same thing.

Respect for the Moral Law

Mou's disagreement with Kant can be clearly shown in Mou's following observation:

> [Kant] separated "reason" and "feeling of respect" into two layers. As a result, "feeling of respect" is an effect only, and it is "acquired afterward." But then it is impossible to explain why reason's principle is dynamic and

> how is it possible to generate such feeling of respect. It is due to the fact there is "no intuition" of such law as well as the will responsible for the self-legislation of such law. If so, then human mind's loving of law in producing the feeling of respect will become contingent. Namely, it can love or not love, and it can respect or not respect [the law]. The law is given over there. Only when I respond to its affection, I would generate the feeling of respect. If I reject or accept it, then it can do nothing to me. Then the matter of whether I accept or reject it would lack of any criteria. It would be only up to the contingency of human mind. It is because the human mind is purely sensible (belonging to material force, *jaizhizhiqi* 材質之氣). (2003, v.15, 335)

For Kant, we may or may not have respect for the moral law. The feeling of respect is merely an *effect* of the moral law, so the feeling of respect only occurs if a person happens to respond to their intellectual apprehension of the moral law that is given to them by reason. There is no guarantee that they will do so, and hence no guarantee that a feeling of respect for the moral law will arise *even if* a person knows the moral law through their reason. Mou goes on:

> However, if "consciousness of the law" is affirmed as a "fact of reason," then even the illiterate is capable of knowing it. In this way, human mind "must be able to love," and "must be able to respect" [it]. If so, then such a mind that is capable of knowing and respecting [the law] is identical with our illuminating awareness of the Original Mind. Insofar as such a mind is "non-sensible" (not belonging to the material force), how can one say that it is necessarily an effect, and hence deny its possibility of being converted to be a "cause" and becoming identical with reason? (2003, v.15, 335)

In short, Mou is arguing here that if we understand the feeling of respect as identical to reason, then *knowing* the moral law is the same thing as *respecting* it. The basic moral feelings illuminate us as to *what* is good (since they are inherently good) while at the same time consisting in a *respect for* that good. So, unlike Kant, for whom respect for the moral law is a contingent effect of understanding, for Mou understanding and respect always go together. In other words, our Original Mind is simultaneously both an intellectual source of the content of morality and a feeling of respect for that morality.

Mou explains the transformation of Kant's concept of respect or conscience into a ground of morality in the following way:

> The will is the essential function of the mind. The intelligible understanding is also its essential function. It does not have any sensible object outside itself as the object of its desire. As a result, it desires the self-legislative law only. This is nothing but the self-determined direction of ought to do—it is identical with the principle. The principle is not outside the mind itself. As such, the will *is* the principle. It can establish this principle by itself, namely, to desire this principle means to be fond of this principle; only in this way it is truly its own autonomy: the will is not merely determined, but is rather determined by this principle, it also self-determinately determines this principle. (2003, v.15, 286)

In other words, because our heart-mind is fundamentally principle, and because the heart-mind is also the source of our will, we cannot separate our desire to follow principle from the identification of the principle itself. Our *will* or *desire* to follow principle and our knowledge *of* the principle itself are one and the same thing. The principle itself is a motivating force.

Mou further states: "With the returning to the feeling of the Original Mind, it knows immediately that 'the pure practical principle itself functions as a power of the *Bewegung* [motivating force].' It is because the pure principle is identical with the Original Mind. While the Original Mind establishes this principle by itself, it is fond of this principle. At the same time, it respects this principle" (2003, v.15, 287). Simply *knowing* what is right is enough in itself to motivate us to *do* what is right. In other words, the Original Mind discloses what we ought to do—it is itself principle, which is inherently moral—and simultaneously provides the reason for doing that good thing. There is no separation between *knowing* and *doing*—no possibility of "weakness of will," in which we know what we ought to do but do not have the will to do it—since knowing and willing are both inherent in the universal principle of the Original Mind, which all human beings are born with.

Freedom of the Will

In accounting for the possibility of morality, Kant understood the "freedom of the will" as merely a postulate. In other words, we need to *assume* that we have freedom of the will in order to make sense of morality. After all, if our wills are not free, our decisions are not free either. And if our decisions are not free, we can never be responsible for what we do, and the idea of moral action becomes nonsensical (or so Kant says). Yet we clearly live in a phenomenal world in which everything is caused—a world in which it is not at all clear that our will, understood as a phenomenal thing (a thing in the world) can escape cause-and-effect, and thus be truly free. As such, freedom of the will must be what Kant refers to as *noumenal*: something that exists independently of our sense perception (the faculties that take in information from the phenomenal world). And the noumenal is, for Kant, fundamentally unknowable for human beings. Hence, while we can *postulate* freedom of the will, we cannot ever really *grasp* it. To make sense of moral action, we need to assume the existence of freedom of the will while at the same time recognizing that it is beyond our ability to sense or comprehend.

But for Mou, our inability to intuitively grasp the freedom of the will in Kant's sense is due to his failure to appreciate the existence of the Original Mind implicit in the autonomy of the will. In other words, since Kant does not appreciate that the moral law arises from within ourselves—from our Original Mind, as expressed in Mencius's idea that human beings possess inherent benevolence and righteousness, he does not see that our freedom is in-separate from ourselves. But armed with Mencius's doctrine of the Original Mind—which gives us direct access to the universal principle shared by all things—Mou holds that human beings even have the capacity of "intellectual intuition." That is, they have the ability to know even things such as freedom of the will merely by examining the universal principle within the Original Mind that is their birthright. This *procedure* is called by Mou as "concretely witnessing by means of inward awareness" (*nijuetizheng* 逆覺體證).

Universal Law versus Particular Feeling

To be critical, one might still not be convinced regarding his account of the "identity" between reason and feeling, for rational principles/moral laws are "universal," whereas the "non-sensible" moral feeling is "particular." In other words, while moral laws can be *applied* to concrete cases, the moral laws themselves always have a universal character. This is central to Kant: moral laws are those maxims that we can "at the same time will that it become a universal law." Moral laws do not merely state that *this* instance of lying (for instance) is wrong, but that *all* instances of lying are wrong. By contrast, non-sensible moral feelings are always particular in character, in that they are concrete feelings directed to a specific object. To put it another way, when you feel respect for the moral law, the feeling of respect is a particular instance of feeling, whereas the moral law you are feeling respect *for* is *not* an *instance*, but rather a universal truth given by reason.

The problem identified here, then, is that Mou seems to be saying that a particular thing—the specific instance of the feeling of respect—is literally identical to a universal thing—the moral law that is being respected. But the particular and universal are two entirely different categories. So, while we may be able to claim identity between two particular things—the current prime minister of New Zealand and Jacinda Ardern are the same entity, for instance—or two universal things—for instance, uniting separate laws of nature about electricity and magnetism into the laws of electromagnetism—how can we claim that a universal thing is identical to a particular thing? It would be like saying that an apple falling from a tree *literally is* the law of gravity, rather than just an instance of it.

At this juncture, it might be helpful to turn to his close colleague Tang Junyi (唐君毅: 1909–78) for a solution. For Tang, rational principle is nothing but universalization of feeling, while feeling is nothing but particularization of rational principle.[1] In other words, our moral feelings are universal moral principle as expressed in a particular instance, and universal moral principle is those same feelings extended generally. Feeling is a concrete manifestation of the moral law.

Summary

In short, our heart-mind is itself universal principle. We have direct access to the moral knowledge contained in the universal principle found in our heart-minds via our innate faculty of pure knowledge (*liangzhi*). This moral knowledge is then grasped as "ontological feelings," which not only give us intellectual knowledge of the moral law, but at the same time motivate us to act on it. As with the other School of Mind philosophers, then, knowledge and action are one. Our goal is to remove selfish desires so as to gain the right knowledge—the knowledge of universal principle found in our Original Mind. Once we have this knowledge, we cannot fail to act morally. So, unlike in Kant, where the source of our knowledge of morality (reason) is independent of the motivating emotion of respect (meaning that it is possible to have one without the other), for Mou our feeling of respect is identical to reason. The feeling of respect can therefore be "reversed" so as to not merely play the role of a "sensible" feeling that takes the moral law as its object, but instead to act as the ground of morality as a "non-sensible" feeling. As a result, we gain knowledge of the moral law and are motivated to act on the moral law at one and the same time. One does not follow or precede the other: knowledge of morality and moral motivation are literally the same thing.

Note

1. From class notes in Tang's 1973 course on metaphysics at the Chinese University of Hong Kong.

Further Reading

PRIMARY SOURCES

Chan, Wing-tsit. 1963. *A Source Book in Chinese Philosophy*. Princeton: Princeton University Press.
Mou, Zongsan 牟宗三. 2003. *Mou Zongsan xiansheng quanjie* 牟宗三先生全集 (Collected Works of Mou Zongsan). 25 vols. Taipei: Lienjing chupan gongsi.
———. 2004. *Song-Ming ruxue de wenti yu fazhan* 宋明儒學的問題與發展 (The Problems and Development of Song-Ming Neo-Confucianism). Shanghai: Huadong shifan daxue chubanshe.
———. 2019. *Mou Zongsan xiansheng jiangyan lu* 牟宗三先生講課錄 (Lectures of Mou Zongsan). 10 vols. New Taipei: Dongfeng Renwen jijinghui.

SECONDARY SOURCES

Billioud, Sébastien. 2011. *Thinking through Confucian Modernity: A Study of Mou Zongsan's Moral Metaphysics*. Leiden: Brill.
Bunnin, Nicholas. 2008. "God's Knowledge and Ours: Kant and Mou Zongsan on Intellectual Intuition." *Journal of Chinese Philosophy* 35, no. 4: 613–24. https://doi.org/10.1111/1540-6253.12065.
Chan, N. Serina. 2003. "What Is Confucian and New about the Thought of Mou Zongsan?" In *New Confucianism: A Critical Examination*, edited by John Makeham. New York: Palgrave Macmillan: 131–64. https://doi.org/10.1057/9781403982414_6.
———. 2011. *The Thought of Mou Zongsan*. Leiden: Brill.
Chan, Wing-cheuk, 2000. "Leibniz and Chinese Philosophy of Nature." *Studia Leibnitiana, Supplementa* 33: 210–23.
———. 2005. "Mou Zongsan on Zen Buddhism." *Dao: A Journal of Comparative Philosophy* 5, no. 1: 73–88. https://doi.org/10.1007/BF02857005.
———. 2006. "Mou Zongsan's Transformation of Kant's Philosophy." *Journal of Chinese Philosophy* 33, no. 1: 125–39. https://doi.org/10.1111/j.1540-6253.2006.00340.x.
———. 2011. "Mou Zongsan and Tang Junyi on Zhang Zai's and Wang Fuzhi's Philosophies of Qi: A Critical Reflection." *Dao: A Journal of Comparative Philosophy* 10, no. 1: 85–98. https://doi.org/10.1007/s11712-010-9200-3.
———. 2013. "Mou Zongsan's Typology of Neo-Confucianism: Its Hidden Sources." In *Inter-culturality and Philosophic Discourse*, edited by Yolaine Escande, Vincent Shen, and Chenyang Li, 147–62. Cambridge: Cambridge Scholars Publisher.

Clower, Jason, ed. 2014. *Late Works of Mou Zongsan: Selected Essays on Chinese Philosophy*. Leiden: Brill.

Drummond, John. 2006. "Respect as a Moral Emotion: A Phenomenological Approach." *Husserl Studies* 22: 1–27. https://doi.org/10.1007/s10743-006-9001-z.

Guo Qiyong. 2007. "Mou Zongsan's View of Interpreting Confucianism by 'Moral Autonomy.'" *Frontiers of Philosophy in China* 2, no. 3: 345–62. https://doi.org/10.1007/s11466-007-0022-2.

Kant, Immanuel. 2002. *Groundwork for the Metaphysics of Morals*. Translated by Allen Wood. New Haven: Yale University Press.

Li Jingde 黎靖德. 1986. *Zhuzi yulei* 朱子語類 (Topically Arranged Conversations of Master Zhu). 8 vols. Beijing: Zhonghua shuju.

Liu, Zongzhou 劉宗周. 2007. *Liu Zongzhou quanji* 劉宗周全集 (The Collected Works of Liu Zongzhou). 8 vols. Hangzhou: Zhejiang guji chubanshe.

Shi, Weimin. 2015. "MOU Zongsan on Confucian Autonomy and Subjectivity: From Transcendental Philosophy to Transcendent Metaphysics." *Dao* 14: 275–87. https://doi.org/10.1007/s11712-015-9434-1.

———, and Chiulo Lin. 2015. "Confucian Moral Experience and Its Metaphysical Foundation: From the Point of View of Mou Zongsan." *Philosophy East and West* 65, no. 2: 542–66. https://doi.org/10.1353/pew.2015.0027.

Schmidt, Stephan. 2011. "Mou Zongsan, Hegel, and Kant: The Quest for Confucian Modernity." *Philosophy East and West* 61, no. 2: 260–302. https://doi.org/10.1353/pew.2011.0029.

Tang, Junyi 唐君毅. 1975. *Zhongguo zhexue yuanlun: yuanjiao pian* 中國哲學原論: 原教篇 (The Primordial Doctrine of Chinese Philosophy: Yuanjiao pian). Hong Kong: New Asian Research Institute.

Tang, Refeng. 2002. "Mou Zongsan on Intellectual Intuition." In *Contemporary Chinese Philosophy*, edited by Chung-Ying Cheng and Nicholas Bunnin, 327–46. Malden, MA: Blackwell. https://doi.org/10.1002/9780470753491.ch17.

Zheng, Jiadong. 2004–5. "Mou Zongsan and the Contemporary Circumstances of the Rujia." *Contemporary Chinese Thought* 36, no. 2: 67–88. https://doi.org/10.1080/10971467.2004.11040596.

———. 2004–5. "Between History and Thought: Mou Zongsan and the New Confucianism That Walked Out of History." *Contemporary Chinese Thought* 36, no. 2: 49–66. https://doi.org/10.1080/10971467.2004.11040597.

11

Contractualism

JUSSI SUIKKANEN

Introduction

There is a long historical tradition of trying to understand morality in terms of a contract. The core idea in this tradition is that what is right and wrong is in some way grounded in either what we have agreed to do or in what we could be expected to agree to in some hypothetical circumstances. This contractualist way of thinking goes back to at least Ancient Greece (Plato, *The Republic*, 358e–59b), but it really became the prominent way of thinking especially about our political obligations during the Early Modern period through the social contract theories of Thomas Hobbes (1996 [1651]), John Locke (2002 [1689]), and Jean-Jacques Rousseau (1997 [1762]).

Contractualism is not, however, merely a historical tradition, but rather it continues to be a popular approach. In political philosophy, many debates concerning justice still tend to take John Rawls's (1971) contractualism as their starting point. Similarly, in moral philosophy, different ways of developing the basic contractualist insights are at the center of several key theoretical debates (Gauthier 1986, Scanlon 1998, Southwood 2010, and Parfit 2011). That so many people have approached morality through the idea of a contract for more than two millennia suggests that the contractualist framework must be getting something right. Yet, as we will see below, the devil will be in the details.

For the sake of simplicity, this chapter focuses on just one contemporary formulation of contractualism—the version outlined by T. M. Scanlon in his 1998 book *What We Owe to Each Other*. This view is often considered to be the paradigmatic version of contractualism—a pinnacle in the long tradition of contractualist thinking. It's also one of the clearest, most appealing, and most debated formulations of contractualism.

The next section provides an outline of Scanlon's theory. The following section then explains how contractualism differs from classical utilitarianism especially in its treatment of cases that involve different-sized groups. After this, I outline a key internal debate in contractualist ethics today to do with how the view should be formulated with respect to time. Finally, the last section focuses on two traditional objections to contractualism—the redundancy objection and the question of whether the view can explain our obligations toward non-human animals and cognitively impaired human beings.

Outline of Scanlon's Contractualism

According to Scanlon (1998, 147–53), ethical theories must be able to answer the following two questions:

1. Which actions are right and wrong?

2. What good reasons do we have for not doing the actions that are wrong?

When it comes to the first question, we are looking for a theory of right and wrong that would fit our carefully considered moral convictions about individual cases (Scanlon 2003, 149). Thus, a theory that entails that we should keep our promises and not be rude to our friends will be much more plausible in this respect than a theory that entails that it would be morally permissible to harm innocent babies for fun.

In the case of the second question, Scanlon emphasizes that a plausible ethical theory should be able to answer that question in an informative way (Scanlon 1998, §4,3; Prichard 1912). For this reason, a theory that claims that we should do right actions merely because they are right will be less plausible. In addition, if a theory claims that we should avoid doing wrong actions because acting in those ways will make us worse off (because of, for example, the disapproval of others), that theory too fails to provide a satisfactory answer to the second question. The reason offered here is a wrong kind of reason—not a moral reason but rather one based on selfishness. We expect, after all, that good moral agents do what is right for some other reason than merely their own selfish interests.

Let us then consider how Scanlon's contractualism tries to answer the previous two questions. At the heart of his view is the following principle (see Scanlon 1998, 153): an action is wrong if and only if it is forbidden by the set of principles no one could reasonably reject (and right if it is authorized by those principles). Notice that the view is not formulated in terms of which principles individuals actually agree to accept or could accept. There are two reasons for this. First, it is questionable whether there ever is or could be principles that everyone would accept at the same time—there just seems to exist too much moral disagreement for that to be possible. Second, Scanlon (1998, 155) worries that some self-sacrificing individuals will agree to principles that would be very bad for them, because those principles benefit others. If we understood right and wrong in terms of actual contracts, then it would be right to treat those individuals badly, which still seems objectionable.

So, instead of an actual agreement, Scanlon formulates his view in terms of principles no one could reasonably reject. What are they then? Scanlon (1998, 195) thinks that we should first consider what the consequences would be of adopting together different sets of moral principles. Different principles would, of course, make a difference to what kind of lives different individuals would come to live. We can then call the lives that individuals would come to live under the different principles their "standpoints" (Scanlon 1998, §5.4). Here some elements of those standpoints will be good and make the lives choice-worthy, whereas other elements will be different burdens the individuals occupying those standpoints will have to bear as a result of the moral principles they live under.

Scanlon (1998, §5.2) then claims that individuals can make objections to the principles we could adopt together on the basis of the personal burdens they would have to bear under them. What are these burdens? Scanlon (1998, 204) suggests that we cannot understand them on the basis of people's personal tastes or specific interests, but rather we need to focus on what "generic reasons" individuals would have for objecting to the principles on the basis of their own personal standpoints. For example, we can ask whether the principles entail that individuals would be physically harmed, unable to trust other people or to form personal relationships with them, suffer from poverty or ill health, unable to be autonomous or to make free choices, have limited opportunities to engage with education, art, sciences, and so on.

Scanlon's (1998, 195) contractualism then focuses on the individuals who can make the strongest personal objections to the principles they live under based on the burdensome elements of their personal standpoints. Those individuals can reasonably reject a set of moral principles they live under if there is an alternative set to which no one has an equally serious personal objection. The set of principles no one can reasonably reject is then the one where some individuals have stronger personal objections to all other sets (ibid.). According to this view, the actions that are authorized by that non-rejectable set are then the morally right things to do for us, whereas the actions that are forbidden by it are wrong. This is Scanlon's answer to the first question above. I use a concrete example in the next section to illustrate how the previous test works in practice, and the later sections also consider how well the view fits our moral intuitions. Before that, let me introduce Scanlon's answer to the second question.

Why should we then follow the non-rejectable principles? The key claim here is that by doing so you can justify your actions to others on defensible grounds (Scanlon 1998, §4,3). By contrast, if you do not follow these principles, you are telling other people that you are willing to overlook their serious objections to your way of treating them. This is because, by violating the non-rejectable principles, you are expressing to others that you would rather follow some other principles that cause wholly unnecessary serious burdens to some individuals, burdens that no one would need to bear if you followed the non-rejectable principles. Furthermore, those who will be the victims of your unjustifiable actions will take the fact that you don't care about their objections to indicate that you are not willing to grant them the same equal moral status as for others, and this they will see as a serious moral harm done to them. In Philip Pettit's words, for this reason we tend to "shrink from the gaze of another when we realise that it is impossible for us to justify our behaviour to someone else" (Pettit, 2000, 231).

On the positive side, if you follow the non-rejectable principles and thus show that you care about whether you can justify your actions to others on grounds no one could reasonably reject, this will allow you to form valuable moral relationships with others—the kind of relationships we have good reasons to be in for their own sake. Scanlon (1998, 162) calls these relationships ones characterized by "mutual recognition." In them, we can wholeheartedly stand by our actions knowing that no one could reasonably reject the principles we act on. Generally, this will also lead to an atmosphere of trust and mutual cooperation, which will also be in our interests in other ways too. Thus, to summarize, in this way Scanlon believes that there is a close connection between (i) his account of right and wrong in terms of the principles no one could reasonably reject and (ii) his story of why we ought to avoid acting wrongly based on the valuable moral relationships avoiding those actions will enable us to have.

Contractualism, Utilitarianism, and Aggregation

To see how the previous view works, let us consider an example Scanlon (1998, 235) uses both to illustrate the view and to compare it with classical utilitarianism. According to classical utilitarianism, an action is right if and only if it would lead to a higher total amount of general happiness than any other alternative available to you in the situation you are in. Consider then the following case.

It's the World Cup final—a match watched by millions of people. Unfortunately, there is an accident at the transmitter room, and some crucial electronic equipment has fallen on Jones's arm. This is giving him extremely painful electric shocks, but the only way to save Jones would be to cut off the transmission for fifteen minutes. The problem is that doing so would deny millions of people the enjoyment of watching the match for that time. What is the right thing to do?

Classical utilitarianism's answer to this question is that we should continue the transmission despite the suffering this would cause to Jones. After all, if we cut the transmission, we will lose millions of fifteen-minute-long periods of enjoyment added together, and this would be a worse loss in terms of the total amount of happiness than if Jones has to suffer for the rest of the match.

Scanlon's (1998, 235) contractualism, in contrast, entails that we should stop the transmission and save Jones. It makes us focus on the most serious objections that individuals would have to different solutions to the dilemma. If we continue the transmission, Jones will have a very strong objection to this based on the extremely painful electric shocks. Yet if we stop the transmission, the strongest objection any one individual will have to this will be the loss of fifteen minutes of enjoyment. If we compare these two personal objections pairwise, it is evident that Jones's objection is stronger. This is why, on Scanlon's view, Jones can reasonably reject the principles that would authorize continuing the transmission, whereas no one can reasonably reject the principles that require us to save him.

Most people here share the intuition that saving Jones would be the right thing to do. Consequentialist views, such as classical utilitarianism, that allow us to aggregate the minor benefits of many people together appear to let us sacrifice few individuals for the sake of the common good. They allow using minorities as a means to the happiness of the majority in a way that we tend to find objectionable. One motivation for Scanlon's (1998, 234–35) contractualism thus is that it offers individuals "anti-utilitarian" moral protections because of the "individualist restriction" built into it. This is the core idea that we can compare only the personal burdens and the objections people have to different principles pairwise and never aggregate them together.

This important motivation for contractualism, unfortunately, also seems to lead to problems in the cases in which aggregating the objections seems quite appealing. For example, consider a case where you can save either one person from a certain death or a large group of people from something almost as bad, for example from permanent blindness or paralysis (Scanlon 1998,

§5.9). In this case, no matter how large the group (say, millions), Scanlon's view seems to entail that we still ought to save the one individual from the slightly more serious harm. This is because her personal objection (death) to not saving her will be stronger than the personal objections the individual members of the large group (blindness or paralysis) have to saving the one individual, and we are not allowed to add those objections together. As a result, Scanlon's contractualism appears to require us to always save the one individual from a serious harm rather than a very large group from a slightly less serious harm.

Scanlon (1998, §5.9) tried to address this concern already in *What We Owe to Each Other*. First, he suggested that different harms belong to "broad categories of moral seriousness" (Scanlon 1998, 238). This allows us to think that harms that are almost as serious really belong to the same category, and so they can be treated as comparable to one another. Thus, in the previous example, blindness and paralysis would belong to the same category as death. Scanlon (1998, 232) also suggested that, even if we are not allowed to aggregate the objections of different individuals together, we should still always save the larger group in the cases where the harms on both sides belong to the same category of seriousness. This is because, if the larger group is not saved in those cases, each member of that group can object not only to the harm they would suffer but also to the unfairness of the fact that their additional presence in the larger group is not making any difference to what we are to do in the case. Scanlon then suggests that this additional consideration counts as a tiebreaker when we must choose between saving a smaller group and saving a larger group where the personal objections on both sides are roughly equally strong. Whether these responses work continues to be debated intensively.

Ex-Post versus *Ex-Ante* Contractualism

This section introduces a more recent lively debate about how Scanlon's contractualism should be formulated with respect to from which temporal perspective we should consider the personal objections to different moral principles. The way I formulated Scanlon's contractualism above is today known as *ex-post* contractualism (*"ex-post"* is Latin and means "after the fact"). According to this type of contractualist views, when we compare different moral principles, we focus on what we can predict would actually happen to specific individuals as a result of the adoption of those principles. Here we are imagining a process where the moral principles are first adopted by everyone and then, because of this, different things happen to different individuals. After all of this has happened in the imagined process, we then retrospectively collect information about what happened to different individuals and how those individuals can now object to the principles they have lived under. Because of this temporal perspective of looking backward, one thing that we will not take into account is how likely it was that any one individual had to bear the burdens he or she came to bear.

The other alternative is *ex-ante* contractualism (*"ex-ante"* means "before the event"). According to such theories, we are to consider objections that individuals would have to the adoption of different principles from a temporally antecedent perspective, from before those principles are adopted. From that perspective, individuals cannot object to the principles based on what actually happens to them as a result of their adoption. Such consequences, after all, haven't been produced yet by the principles, and it might be uncertain and unpredictable how different individuals will be affected. Because of this, from the temporally antecedent perspective, individuals can object to the principles only based on what kind of *prospects* the principles give to them. This means that individuals can object to the principles based on different potential burdens the principles might produce, but, importantly, these objections must be discounted by how improbable the relevant burdens are.

In this framework, everyone can thus object to the principles based on the risks the principles impose on them. These risks can be understood more technically in terms of what is called an individual's "burdensomeness expectation" for a given set of principles. To get that expectation, an individual can multiply each personal burden a given principle could produce with its probability, and then these products are summed up. The thought then is that the non-rejectable set of principles is such that all other principles create higher burdensomeness expectations for some individuals.

To see what these two alternatives mean in practice, let us consider two examples—one that supports the *ex-post* views and another that supports the *ex-ante* views. The first example is Scanlon's (1998, 208–9) own original reason for formulating his view in the *ex-post* way. Consider a health-care policy that would require "us to impose very severe hardship on a tiny minority of people, chosen at random (by making them involuntary subjects of painful and dangerous medical experiments, for example), in order to benefit a much larger majority" (Scanlon 1998, 208). According to *ex-post* contractualism, this policy is clearly reasonably rejectable. We know that when we adopt the principle, there will be some individuals who will be coercively subjected to painful medical experiments. After the principle has been adopted, these individuals can reasonably reject the principle given that there are alternative principles under which no one has to bear equally serious burdens. This is why the *ex-post* views get this case intuitively right.

By contrast, the *ex-ante* views seem objectionable here because the policy's burdensomeness expectation for each individual will actually be quite good from the temporally antecedent perspective. For any individual, the policy has two possible outcomes: the very likely outcome that you will benefit from the policy and the very unlikely outcome that you will have to suffer because of the painful medical experiments. If we assign the positive outcome for you the value of 100 and a probability of 0.999 and the bad outcome for you the value of –1000 and the probability of 0.001, then the policy's burdensomeness expectation for you would be $(100 \times 0.999) + (-1000 \times 0.001) = 99.9 + -1 = 98.9$. This could well be a better expectation for you than if the policy were not adopted. For this reason, the *ex-ante* versions seem to support objectionable policies that will in the future sacrifice some random individuals for the sake of minor benefits for everyone else.

There are, however, also cases where the *ex-ante* views work better. Consider the case of social risk imposition first described by Johann Frick (2015, 181). In it, a terrible virus will kill one million young children if we do nothing. Fortunately, there are two vaccines we could produce (even if we cannot produce both). Vaccine 1 will save every child from death, but it does not offer complete protection. Every child is still certain to get one of their legs paralyzed. By contrast, the Vaccine 2 gives every child a 0.999 chance of surviving the virus completely unharmed. This means that every child has a 0.001 chance that the Vaccine 2 they take does not work for them, in which case the child will sadly die. Furthermore, whichever of these two vaccines we produce, that vaccine will then be given to all the one million children. Which of the vaccines should we then produce?

Here the *ex-post* views have implausible consequences. According to them, we should produce the Vaccine 1 even if we know that the consequence of this policy will be that every one of the million young children will have a paralyzed leg. This is because the *ex-post* views direct us to compare the most serious personal objections the children will eventually have because of the adoption of the two different policies. In the scenario where we produce the Vaccine 1, the strongest objection any one child has to this policy will be that one of their legs gets paralyzed for the rest of their life. By contrast, in the scenario in which we produce the Vaccine 2, the strongest personal objections few children will have to this policy will be that because of the policy they die very young. Because these latter personal objections to the production of the Vaccine 2 are stronger, the principle that we ought to produce the Vaccine 1 cannot be reasonably rejected. This is why the *ex-post* views entail that producing the Vaccine 1 is the right thing to do, but this is intuitively wrong.

By contrast, from the temporally antecedent perspective, it seems like for every individual child the policy that requires producing the Vaccine 2 will offer them better prospects. From this perspective, each child will compare the certainty of having one of their legs paralyzed to getting a 0.999 chance of surviving unharmed and a 0.001 chance of dying. Here most of us would rather take the second option, as it seems to us that it is worthwhile to take the small chance of dying in order to escape the certainty of getting one of your legs paralyzed. This is why, according to the *ex-ante* views, the policy that requires producing the Vaccine 2 cannot be reasonably rejected, which intuitively seems to get things right.

Interestingly, we then have one case that supports the *ex-post* views and one that supports the *ex-ante* versions, even if both views cannot be true. As a result of this standoff, the defenders of the *ex-ante* views have tried to develop their views further so as to find a version that would not entail that we should adopt the policy that permits subjecting some individuals to painful medical experiments in the first case. Likewise, the defenders of the *ex-post* views have tried to develop their views further so as to avoid the objectionable consequence that we should produce the Vaccine 1 in the second case. At this point, it still seems an open question which of these versions of contractualism will turn out to best fit all our carefully considered moral convictions about different cases.

Objections to Contractualism

This final section finally considers two common objections to contractualism. According to the first and the most frequent one, contractualism is theoretically redundant—a spare wheel in the machine of ethical theorizing that does no genuine work but rather merely whizzes around. According to the second objection, contractualism fails because it cannot ground our obligations to treat non-human animals and cognitively impaired human beings well.

The basic assumption of the first traditional objection is that, as an ethical theory, contractualism is an attempt to explain something important about right and wrong actions—be this (i) which actions are right and wrong, (ii) what makes those actions right and wrong, or (iii) what it is for them to be right and wrong. At least three reasons have then been given for why the contractualist explanations for these things would be bad explanations (Southwood 2009, §3.5).

First, it has been argued that there are always better explanations available (McGinn 1999, 35–36). For example, what explains why harming an innocent baby for fun is wrong must be how much the baby would suffer and how monstrous the action would be. This seems like a much better explanation than the one based on the idea that the potential baby-torturer could not justify his or her actions to others on grounds no one could reasonably reject.

Secondly, it has also been argued that the contractualist explanation would be circular—it is presupposing things that it is supposed to try to explain (Hooker 2000). For example, it could be claimed that, when we consider the different objections individuals can make to different principles, at this point we smuggle in prior features of morality (that is, objections already based on what is right and wrong) that are not validated by the contractualist theory.

Finally, the most common version of the objection is that the contractualist explanations are redundant (Blackburn 1999). Whenever someone can reasonably reject a principle allowing some action, for example, because of the harm that those kinds of actions cause to them, that relevant harm itself seems enough to explain the wrongness of the actions in question. Going in the explanation first from the harms to reasonable rejection and then from reasonable rejection to wrongness is just an unnecessary detour where the middle stage can be cut off without a loss.

Contractualists have, of course, tried to address these concerns. The main line of response is based on the thought that contractualism is needed to do genuine explanatory work to get us from other people's potential personal objections to your actions to the reasons you personally have for acting in certain ways (Ridge 2001). For example, in the social risk imposition case described above, the theory is needed to explain how we get from what different objections each child would have for producing either the Vaccine 1 or the Vaccine 2 to the conclusion that you have most reason to produce the Vaccine 2, as that is not obvious before we compare the different objections the children have. Whether this line of response works is something that continues to divide opinions.

The second common objection concerns our duties toward non-human animals and cognitively limited human beings such as infants or severely disabled individuals (Phillips 1998; Hooker 2000, §2.9; Nussbaum 2006). The problem is that Scanlon's contractualism understands right and wrong in terms of the reasons individuals have for objecting to different principles. Yet having a reason to make an objection seems to require (i) being able to evaluate how strong reasons different burdens provide for making objections, and (ii) being able to make the objection in question. These things, however, are something that non-human animals and cognitively limited human beings cannot do. For this reason, both groups do not seem to have any reasons to object to the principles that would permit mistreating them, and so contractualism seems unable to explain our obligations toward non-human animals and cognitively limited human beings.

Several contractualist responses to this objection have been offered, but these responses remain controversial too. First, it could be suggested that many of us who can evaluate and make objections deeply care about non-human animals and cognitively impaired human beings, and so at least we have reasons to reject the principles that permit mistreating them. The problem is that this response only gives non-human animals and cognitively limited human beings an objectionably indirect moral status—they would only matter morally because they happen to matter to us (Hooker 2000, 68). It has also been suggested that we can imagine that non-human animals and cognitively limited human beings would have trustees, who could then reasonably reject principles on their behalf (Scanlon 1998, §4.8). It has likewise been thought that contractualism is only attempting to capture a core part of interpersonal morality—what we owe to each other—and so it is no surprise that some other theory is required to explain the other parts of the moral reality (ibid.).

Summary

This chapter has tried to introduce contractualism in a positive light. Whilst doing so, it has also tried to be open about the main problems of the theory. The first section explained how, according to contractualism, what is right and wrong is determined by the principles no one could reasonably reject, where these principles are a function of the personal objections individuals can make to different alternatives. This section also introduced how, according to Scanlon, we ought to follow the non-rejectable principles because of the valuable personal relationships this enables us to form with others.

The second section then used the television transmitter case to illustrate how contractualism differs from classical utilitarianism. After this, I explained how there are two different versions of contractualism depending on from which temporal perspective we consider the relevant objections. Finally, the last section introduced the redundancy objection and the challenges contractualists face when they try to explain our obligations toward non-human animals and cognitively impaired human beings. I can only hope that this brief introduction inspires a new generation of ethicists to explore the contractualist tradition further.

Further Reading

PRIMARY SOURCES

Darwall, Stephen. 1988. *Contractarianism/Contractualism*. Oxford: Blackwell.
Gauthier, David. 1986. *Morals by Agreement*. Oxford: Oxford University Press.
Hobbes, Thomas. 1996 [1651]. *The Leviathan*. Edited by Richard Tuck. Cambridge: Cambridge University Press.
Locke, John. 2002 [1689]. *Two Treatise of Government*. Edited by Peter Laslett. Cambridge: Cambridge University Press.
Parfit, Derek. 2011. *On What Matters*. Vol. 1. Oxford: Oxford University Press.
Plato. 2000 [circa 380 BC]. *The Republic*. Edited by G. R. F Ferrari, translated by Tom Griffin. Cambridge: Cambridge University Press.
Rawls, John. 1972. *A Theory of Justice*. Cambridge, MA: Harvard University Press.
Rousseau, Jean-Jacques. 1997 [1762]. *The Social Contract and Other Later Political Writings*. Edited by Victor Gourevitch. Cambridge: Cambridge University Press.
Scanlon, T. M. 1998. *What We Owe to Each Other*. Cambridge, MA: Harvard University Press
Southwood, Nicholas. 2010. *Contractualism & the Foundations of Morality*. Oxford: Oxford University Press.

SECONDARY SOURCES

Ashford, Elizabeth. 2003. "The Demandingness of Scanlon's Contractualism." *Ethics* 113, no. 2: 273–302.
Blackburn, Simon. 1999. "Am I Right?" *New York Times*, February 21, 1999, 24.
Frick, Johann. 2015. "Contractualism and Social Risk." *Philosophy & Public Affairs* 43, no. 3: 175–223. https://doi.org/10.1111/papa.12058.
Hooker, Brad 2000. *Ideal Code, Real World*. Oxford: Oxford University Press.
———. 2003. "Contractualism, Spare wheel, Aggregation." In *Scanlon and Contractualism*, edited by Matt Matravers, 53–76. London: Frank Cass.

Kumar, Rahul. 1999. "Defending the Moral Moderate: Contractualism and Common Sense." *Philosophy and Public Affairs* 28, no. 4: 275–309. https://doi.org/10.1111/j.1088-4963.1999.00275.x.

McGinn, Colin. 1999. "Reasons and Unreasons." *The New Republic,* May 24, 1999, 34–38.

Nussbaum, Martha. 2006. *Frontiers of Justice: Disability, Nationality, Species Membership.* Cambridge, MA: Harvard University Press.

Pettit, Philip. 2000. "A Consequentialist Perspective on Contractualism." *Theoria* 66, no. 3: 228–45. https://doi.org/10.1111/j.1755-2567.2000.tb01165.x.

Phillips, David. 1998. "Contractualism and Moral Status." *Social Theory and Practice* 24, no. 2: 183–204. https://doi.org/10.5840/soctheorpract19982421.

Prichard, H. A. 1912. "Does Moral Philosophy Rest on a Mistake?" *Mind* 21, no. 81: 21–37.

Ridge, Michael. 2001. "Saving Scanlon: Contractualism and Agent-Relativity. *Journal of Political Philosophy* 9, no. 4: 472–81. https://doi.org/10.1111/1467-9760.00137.

Scanlon, T. M. 2003. "Rawls on Justification." In *The Cambridge Companion to Rawls.* Edited by Samuel Freeman, 139–67. Cambridge: Cambridge University Press.

Southwood, Nicholas. 2009. "Moral Contractualism." *Philosophy Compass* 4, no. 6: 926–36. https://doi.org/10.1111/j.1747-9991.2009.00256.x.

Suikkanen, Jussi. 2019. "Ex Ante and Ex Post Contractualism: A Synthesis." *Journal of Ethics* 23, no. 1: 77–98. https://doi.org/10.1007/s10892-019-09282-6.

———. 2020. *Contractualism.* Cambridge: Cambridge University Press.

Wallace, Jay. 2002. "Scanlon's Contractualism." *Ethics* 112, no. 3: 429–70. https://doi.org/10.1086/338481.

12

Jürgen Habermas and Discourse Ethics

MICHAEL HEMMINGSEN

Introduction

Jürgen Habermas, born in 1929, is a German philosopher and
social theorist. Habermas's moral theory, called "discourse ethics,"
is a deontological theory in a broadly Kantian mode. That is, it
is a theory concerned at the fundamental level with moral principles (or, in Habermas's terminology, moral "norms"). However,
discourse ethics develops and extends Kant's basic approach in
significant ways. In developing his theory, Habermas draws on
a wide range of thinkers in various fields: German philosophical
theory, including Georg Hegel, and Hans-Georg Gadamer; Karl
Marx and the Frankfurt School of critical theory, particularly Theodor Adorno, Max Horkheimer, and Herbert Marcuse; sociologists
such as Max Weber, Émile Durkheim, and George Herbert Mead;
the philosophy of language of J. L. Austin and John Searle; and
American pragmatist philosophers such as Charles Sanders Peirce
and John Dewey. In synthesizing and further developing these
disparate thinkers, Habermas has created a unique and fascinating
moral theory. Habermas's discourse ethics is merely one piece of
Habermas's broader philosophical system, which includes his social
theory (particularly Habermas's theory of modernity: he takes

discourse ethics, in fact, to be a characteristically *modern* moral theory), psychology, philosophy of language, and epistemology (philosophy of knowledge).

Discourse Ethics and Language

The starting point for discourse ethics is the nature and purpose of language. It is a "reconstruction" of the rules underlying linguistic communication, and particularly the application of language Habermas refers to as "discourse."

Discourse is an activity involving an exchange of reasons. When the speaker makes an assertion and is challenged, they "redeem" the claim by providing a "warrant" for it in the form of a reason. In fact, for Habermas being able to provide a warrant for a claim is essentially what it means to understand that claim in the first place. When I assert something—and genuinely mean what I say—I must have a *reason* to believe that my assertion is valid. When questioned, I must in principle be able to provide that reason (or at least understand what it would take to provide such a reason). The ability to justify validity claims is the fundamental skill that makes one a competent social agent.

Drawing on the philosophy of language of J. L. Austin, this account of what it means to *understand* a claim allows us to divide speech acts (the things we *do* with language) into two kinds: illocutionary and perlocutionary. Illocutionary speech acts are those in which the meaning is internal to the proposition itself, and which are intended to *communicate* that meaning to the listener. In this sense, we might say that illocutionary speech acts are "self-sufficient." By contrast, perlocutionary speech acts are those that aim to have an effect in the world. In other words, they are statements that do not aim to reach understanding with the listener via an exchange of reasons but are instead attempts to bring about certain states of affairs by *causing* the listener to *do* (or not do) something. Unlike illocutionary speech acts, perlocutionary speech acts rely on details of the situation external to the proposition itself to fully make sense of them. For Habermas, illocutionary and perlocutionary speech excludes one another: you can express a proposition as an illocutionary *or* perlocutionary speech act, but never as both (1998, 128).

The illocutionary/perlocutionary distinction maps onto another important distinction for Habermas, that of communicative action (illocutionary speech acts) versus strategic action (perlocutionary speech acts). Communicative action is when we relate to others with the intention of reaching mutual understanding. Strategic action, by contrast, is when we aim solely to influence how others act. Strategic action is therefore a form of "instrumental" action—that is, action with the aim of accomplishing something in the world. Strategic action is wholly oriented to *success* and treats other human beings as social "objects" to be manipulated to achieve our ends, just like we manipulate physical objects to achieve our ends in the natural world. In other words, it treats other *people* purely as *instruments* for the accomplishment of our own goals.

By contrast, communicative action is aimed at achieving mutual understanding: what Habermas refers to as a "rationally motivated" consensus. Rather than trying to realize our chosen goal via whatever means are available to us, communicative action is a way of *mutually* coordinating our actions. This coordination involves "rational motivation" in the sense that the acceptance of an illocutionary speech act at the same time involves an understanding and acceptance of the justifications for that speech act (recall that for Habermas, meaning is tied to our ability to justify claims with reasons). If we manage to successfully reach understanding with others, then at the same time we have come to agree on the claim under dispute and, most importantly, we have done so on the basis of the *shared* understanding of the reasons for accepting that claim. In this sense, the mutual understanding that arises from communicative action is a matter of *voluntary consent*; unlike with strategic action, our subsequent behavior is not based on force or manipulation, but rather than fact that we *accept*—internally, rather than grudgingly in our actions alone—that a particular action is appropriate, or that a particular assertion about the world is true.

Rules of Discourse and Performative Contradiction

Discourse is the process by which we engage with others communicatively, and as a practice it is structured by certain fundamental principles. At the very least, Habermas thinks that discourse requires that the following conditions be met.

First, discourses can only be legitimate if "[e]very subject with the competence to speak and act is allowed to take part in discourse" (Habermas 1990, 89). The basic idea is that an agreement that arises as the result of a discourse in which relevant individuals have been excluded cannot be said to be rationally motivating.

Second, "(i) Everyone is allowed to question any assertion whatsoever; (ii) everyone is allowed to introduce any assertion whatever into the discourse; (iii) everyone is allowed to express his attitudes, desires, and needs" (Habermas 1990, 89). This rule (or set of rules) captures the idea that if we place certain ideas beyond criticism, prevent certain ideas from entering in discourse in the first place, or disallow certain individuals from fully expressing their own points of view, then the discourse cannot be rationally motivating.

Third, "No speaker may be prevented, by internal or external coercion, from exercising his rights as laid down in [the first and second rules]" (Habermas 1990, 89). In other words, the outcome of discourse is not rationally motivating insofar as power has played a role in reaching that agreement. For instance, if I make threats, either explicit or implicit, that prevent you from participating fully in discourse, this undermines our confidence in the validity of the outcome. Essentially, any factor that influences acceptance, and that is external to the illocutionary force of the claim, contravenes this rule.

But why these rules? Certainly they *sound* nice. Nonetheless, do we have any reason—beyond our positive feelings toward them—to agree that these rules are required for agreement in discourse to be rationally motivating?

The answer to this question is the move that grounds Habermas's entire project of discourse ethics. Habermas considers these rules justified by what he calls a "transcendental pragmatic argument." This argument is "transcendental" in that it takes a certain feature of our experience for granted, specifically here the absolute *necessity* of communication and discourse to our existence. Communication and discourse therefore "transcend" all humans, in that they are a condition for a recognizably human existence. But the argument is also "pragmatic" in that what is taken for granted is a real-world practice: argumentation. In other words, insofar as we engage in the practice of argumentation (which underlies discourse), Habermas thinks that we *must* accept these rules (1990, 80–81).

Habermas's transcendental pragmatic argument makes use of a technique called "performative contradiction." A performative contradiction is when the *act* of denying a certain proposition presupposes what is being denied. For instance, imagine I made the following statements: "By excluding contrary perspectives, I became convinced that N is a justified norm"; "We validated the truth of N by preventing those with differing views from participating in the conversation"; "I justified N by coercing the assent of all those who disagreed." The issue here seems to be that, insofar as I am attempting to justify a claim, the act of excluding individuals or perspectives, or coercing participants, undercuts that aim. If I engage in such activities, I thereby undermine any reason I might have to have confidence in the outcome of the discourse.

To put the issue simply, the very aim of justifying validity claims *presupposes* these rules, and I can no longer claim to be genuinely *convinced* of the validity of a claim if I contravene them. They therefore attempt to articulate the difference between mere de facto agreement—that we *verbally assent*—and genuine agreement—that we are truly persuaded, and come to share the same view, for the same reasons, with our discourse partners. These rules therefore *constitute* argumentation, and abandoning them means abandoning both argumentation and communicative action (since communicative action is fundamentally premised on our ability to achieve mutual understanding via argumentation).

As Habermas puts it, "Anyone who seriously engages in argumentation must presuppose that the context of discussion guarantees in principle freedom of access, equal rights to participate, truthfulness on the part of participants, absence of coercion in adopting positions, and so on" (1994, 31). In this sense, these rules are not *external* to discourse: they are implicit in it, and Habermas's transcendental pragmatic argument ultimately gives us nothing more than an explicit articulation of the constitutive rules of a practice that we are already engaged in. It is a formal theorization of the "pre-theoretical" knowledge and competencies that, as beings who engage with each other communicatively as a matter of fact, we already possess.

Justifying Discourse

We might then ask why we should engage in argumentation in the first place? After all, could we not simply opt out of the entire practice of communicative action? Is there any reason why we could not engage with other people purely strategically?

Habermas's response to this concern draws once again on performative contradiction. If you ask *why* we ought to engage in communicative rather than strategic action, then you have already entered argumentation. After all, if you expect your interlocutor to justify the value of argumentation to you, then you must already accept that justification matters (otherwise, what is the purpose of asking "why"?). But if so, then you are *in your actions* demonstrating the importance of argumentation. That is, the very act of questioning the importance of discourse is only possible if you *in practice* already accept its importance. You cannot *argue* against *argument*.

Of course, we might nonetheless try to drop out of practical discourse entirely, with a mute refusal to engage with others communicatively. However, practically speaking such a strategy is impossible. In Habermas's view, we are fundamentally linguistic beings: consciousness and thought itself is structured by language. But language is inherently intersubjective. Our very socialization as a thinking being—as an individual—occurs via the shared activity of language use. In Habermas's words, "Individuation is merely the reverse side of socialization. Only in relations of reciprocal recognition can a person constitute and reproduce his identity. Even the innermost essence of a person is internally connected with the outermost periphery of a far-flung network of communicative relations. Only in the aggregate of his communicative expressions does a person become identical with himself" (1994, 130–31). To put this another way, human beings cannot become individuals without society: individual identity itself is a fundamentally social creation. It is "structured by social meanings [that are] matters for communal determination through public processes of interpretation" (Cronin 1994, xii).

Hence, "The integrity of individual persons requires the stabilization of a network of symmetrical relations of recognition in which nonreplaceable individuals can secure their fragile identities in a *reciprocal* fashion only as members of a community" (Habermas 1994, 109). The alternative to communicative action is therefore "suicide or serious mental illness" (Habermas 1990, 100). Consequently, while it is *logically* possible to drop out of communicative action by relating to others in a purely strategic way, Habermas thinks that such a life is at the very limit of human conceivability.

Ethics and Morality

At this point, we have established general guidance on how we ought to relate to others when we communicate with them (as well as the necessity of communicating with others in the first place). But we have not yet reached a *moral theory*, which Habermas, as a deontologist, sees in terms of the justification of norms. In other words, our approach so far is too broad, since discourse is not limited to the justification of norms, but also applies to justifying truth claims (about the objective world) and truthfulness claims (about the subjective world of our own experiences and values).

In terms of the justification of norms, then, Habermas spells out a basic principle: the Discourse Principle (D). According to (D), "Only those norms can claim to be valid that meet (or could meet) with the approval of all affected in their capacity as participants in a practical discourse" (Habermas 1990, 66). However, (D) in many ways simply formalizes what we have already discussed, as applied to norms specifically. It tells us that norms can only be valid if all affected can agree (in the strong sense of "agree," i.e., rationally motivated agreement). It therefore assumes the rules of discourse, in that rationally motivated agreement cannot occur if the practical discourse (discourse about what we ought to do, normatively speaking) is not open, equal, and inclusive. But it still leaves open *how* the justification of norms actually takes place *within* discourse. That is, when we are discussing the validity of norms, what kinds of reasons can be raised for or against certain norms? What does it *take* for us to reach mutual understanding about norms?

One reason for the vagueness of (D) when it comes to these kinds of questions is that, for Habermas, the category of "norms" is wider than the category of "morality." Habermas separates *ethical* norms from *moral* norms, and discourse ethics is primarily (though not solely) interested in the justification of the latter (the term "discourse *ethics*" is therefore actually a rather misleading term for Habermas's theory).

What is the difference between ethics and morality? To put it simply, morality focuses on questions of *justice*. By contrast, ethics is about how we ought to live, or what a good society would be like. Ethics is therefore about *value*. While ethical questions are framed in terms of "What kind of life should I live?" or "Who do we want to be?," moral questions are instead focused on questions like "What behavior can we legitimately expect of one another?" In this sense, ethical questions are limited to those who share the values or ideals in question, while moral questions have universal import. As Habermas puts it, "The peculiarly moral problematic detaches itself from the egocentric (or ethnocentric) perspective of each individual's (or our) way of life and demands that interpersonal conflicts be judged from the standpoint of what *all* could will in common" (Habermas 1994, 24). This is one reason that Habermas takes discourse ethics to be a characteristically modern theory: it is a brute fact of the modern world that we must interact with others who do not share our values and therefore can no longer resolve disagreements by resorting to ethical discourse. Hence, we can either relate *strategically* to those who do not share our values, or we can engage with them communicatively, using discourse ethics as a means of coming to mutual understanding about what we owe each other *despite* our lack of agreement about specific values.

Morality and ethics, along with practical questions of efficiency, form a hierarchy. Questions of efficiency are at the lowest level. Actions that contravene ethics or morality, even if they are the most efficient means of achieving our ends, are impermissible. Similarly, our ethical values are permitted *only* insofar as they do not contravene universal moral norms. If ethical values conflict with moral norms, we are obliged to modify the former in light of the latter. Each level therefore constrains the ones below, with morality at the highest level, and practical means-end reasoning at the lowest.

The Universalization Principle

This distinction between ethics and morality has helped us to see how *some* norms can be justified in discourse. Ethical norms—being teleologically oriented toward values—can be justified in terms of how well they are able to bring about the ideals or values of the individual or group.[1] But *moral* norms require participants to *"transcend* the social and historical context of their particular form of life and particular community" (Habermas 1994, 24); they are not teleological—in the sense of aiming toward shared values—but deontological—in the sense of placing constraints on permissible action. Hence, we are still left with the question of how moral norms can be justified. It is here that Habermas introduces the universalization principle (U). (U) states that, for a *moral* norm to be justified: "All affected can accept the consequences and the side effects its general observance can be anticipated to have for the satisfaction of everyone's interests (and these consequences are preferred to those of known alternative possibilities for regulation)" (Habermas 1990, 65). Habermas considers this principle the *sole* principle of morality.

It is with (U) where we can most clearly see Habermas's debt to Immanuel Kant. Kant, too, has a universalizability test by which we can evaluate candidate norms—the categorical imperative—and in many ways (U) can be seen as Habermas's version of this principle. For Kant, those norms (or maxims) that we can will as a universal law are legitimate, whereas those norms that cannot be so willed are not. Similarly, for Habermas those norms that can be willed by all affected in discourse are legitimate, and those than cannot are not.

However, while Habermas takes up Kant's project in certain ways—particularly in aiming to establish an impartial point of view from which we can evaluate the appropriateness of moral norms—he also departs from him significantly. Specifically, whereas Kant provides a *monological* universalization principle, Habermas's principle is *dialogical*. Put simply, for Kant it is possible to undertake the testing of norms *on our own*, as an isolated reasoner. For Habermas, however, monological reasoning is not enough. Instead, we must offer our claims to others in order to justify them *dialogically*.

That is, we must engage in *discourse* to determine whether a norm is justified. Identifying correct moral principles is an inherently collective project that involves *real* (and not merely imaginary) discourse (Habermas 2000, 67).

Relying on discourse to establish moral principles also leads Habermas toward a different conception of the moral point of view than Kant. Both Kant and Habermas see the moral point of view in terms of impartiality, but Kant's approach to impartiality means abstracting ourselves away from the concrete, contingent facts of our lives—those characteristics that constitute our identity—in order to adopt a decontextualized perspective: that of pure reason.

By contrast, with Habermas's dialogical approach to reasoning—which takes place between real, concrete individuals—detachment is not the goal. Instead, discourse involves a genuine attempt to see things from other people's points of view. After all, as William Rehg points out, if our aim is to establish moral principles that are "equally good for all" or that have "acceptable consequences for the satisfaction of *each* individual's interests," then we *must* have some sense of the situation of those with whom we engage (1994, 101). (U) requires that we try to take the perspective of all other participants in discourse—what Habermas refers to as "ideal role taking"—in order to properly understand the consequences proposed norms have for those others, as well as the interests, needs, and values that are at stake in that discourse. As Habermas puts it, "If [participants] do not bring with them, and into their discourse, *their* individual life-histories, *their* identities, *their* needs and wants, *their* traditions, memberships, and so forth, practical discourse would at once be robbed of all content" (Habermas 1982, 255). This process can nevertheless be said to be "impartial" in the sense that there is no perspective that can claim for itself a privileged position. Instead of being an *abstraction* from concrete individuals and their identities and concerns, Habermas's impartiality is therefore situated in the space *between* them: it is an *intersubjective* impartiality. To adopt the moral point of view is therefore nothing more than giving oneself over to a "process of dialogical interchange . . . the give-and-take of opinions striving toward consensus" (Rehg 1994, 76).

But how does (U) operate in practice? Since it is a fundamentally deontological principle, we should not take "consequences and the side effects" to refer *solely* to outcomes (though, unlike Kant,

Habermas does think that outcomes matter in the justification of moral norms). In other words, we should not interpret (U) merely as a dialogical formulation of rule utilitarianism. Instead, when discussing the validity of a moral norm, we first need to consider the "roles" that the norm contains. How do the obligations, responsibilities, and benefits of the norm fall differentially on people who fill those roles? "Consequences and side effects" therefore refers *both* to the logical implications of a norm for different roles (action constraints), as well as the practical consequences the norm will have (impacts). We engage in the process of ideal role taking to ask whether we, if we were in those other positions, could reasonably accept those action constraints and impacts. If all can agree to this after adopting the impartial perspective of ideal role taking, then the norm is valid. If they cannot, it is not.

Justifying (U)

But why (U)? Whereas the rules of discourse and (D) can be justified through performative contradiction, Habermas denies that this is possible in the case of (U). So why should we accept it?

Essentially, Habermas thinks that (U) can be justified *abductively*. Unlike *deduction*, in which conclusions follow logically from premises (All men are mortal. Socrates is a man. Therefore Socrates is mortal) and *induction*, in which we generalize from specific cases (All swans I have observed have been white. Therefore, all swans are [likely] white), abduction operates by observing a phenomenon and then offering the best explanation for that phenomenon.

In this case, it is very clear that moral normativity exists. What is more, moral normativity has certain features. For instance, moral norms (unlike ethical norms) are characteristically universal. We do not typically take a norm such as "do not kill" to be relative to cultural circumstances. Instead, it is treated as a norm that is binding no matter where you happen to be from. For instance, if a stranger attempted to kill us, we would hardly find "in my culture, killing is okay" as a persuasive justification for allowing them to continue.

Moral norms are also *cognitivist*. They are not mere subjective preferences. We can tell this by the fact that we treat a norm such as "do not kill" very differently from preferences such as which flavor of ice cream we prefer. There is little to say to someone who prefers strawberry ice cream over chocolate ice cream, even if we feel very strongly that chocolate ice cream is better. But we are able to *argue* with someone who prefers killing over not killing. We can *criticize* their belief, and it is possible that they (or we) might be *wrong* about their view. This does not seem to be the case with purely subjective matters such as ice cream preference.

Given these features—along with the background rules of argumentation and (D), justified by performative contradiction—Habermas argues that (U) is simply the best explanation for moral norms. It underwrites *why* we take moral norms to be binding (we are persuaded of their validity through discourse) and explains the particular characteristics that moral norms have (that they are universal and cognitive). In other words, as with much of Habermas's philosophy, rather than reasoning from first principles, Habermas has taken as his starting point a real-world phenomenon and has reasoned from there. As an abductive inference to explain that phenomenon, (U) is subject to revision or, if a better explanation is proposed, rejection. However, Habermas thinks that, when trying to ground or explain morality, abductive inference is simply the best we can do, and that (U) is the best explanation currently on offer.[2]

Contextualism, Justification, and Application

As a deontological moral theory in the Kantian mode, we might worry that discourse ethics suffers from some of the same problems as Kantian ethics. Habermas has, like Kant, provided an extremely abstracted formal principle of morality. It is not immediately obvious how to connect such a principle to our everyday experiences, or how it could take into account the concrete, contextual circumstances within which we make moral decisions in the real world.

But such criticisms miss several key features of discourse ethics. For one thing, Habermas never claims to *derive* morality from his discourse ethics. (U) does not play the role of an ultimate foundational principle that—on its own—can guide us in concrete situations. In this sense we can characterize discourse ethics as a "minimal ethics." Philosophers cannot *use* (U) to develop any specific moral guidance through deductive reasoning. Instead, discourse ethics merely a) offers a description of the *moral point of view* and b) provides a formal process through which we can *test* norms to ensure that they are fair and just. In other words, as Andrew Edgar puts it, discourse ethics "is not an algorithm through which a set of definitive moral principles could be generated" (2005, 161). Hence, in addition to being universalist and cognitivist, discourse ethics is a *procedural* account of morality.

So where *do* norms come from, if not (U)? For Habermas, they come from the lifeworld, or the background of taken-for-granted practices, roles, and meanings that underwrite our everyday interactions. While mostly our interactions take place without difficulty, sometimes the resources of the lifeworld fail us, and the smooth consensus between individuals or groups that it makes possible breaks down. When such a breakdown occurs, agents must draw on the lifeworld in a more explicit way, by formulating and expressing the norms that were previously implicit in it. Often this alone is enough to restore consensus and allow communicative action to proceed. However, if merely making the implicit norms explicit is not enough to restore consensus, then the formerly uncontested, taken-for-granted norms are made the subject of discourse. It is only at this point that (U) potentially comes into the picture. In other words, (U) merely tests norms that we propose; it does not create them on its own.

Discourse ethics is also very much concerned with the concrete, situated, and specific problems that confront us in our lives. Inflexibility is an oft-cited difficulty with Kantian ethics: in trafficking in abstract, universal principles, Kant ends up with counterintuitive outcomes in cases like the famous "murderer at the door," where his absolute prohibition on lying seems to suggest that we are obliged to tell a murderer that his victim is hiding in our home. Discourse ethics avoids this difficulty by dividing practical discourse into two separate but complementary modes: discourses of justification (where we test norms) and discourses of application (where we apply them in concrete cases).

This division reflects the fact that the question of which norms are *valid* is analytically separate from the question of which norms are *appropriate*. That is, establishing that a norm is valid *does not* tell us that a *particular* action violates that norm, or how to balance conflicting norms in a specific case.

Discourses of application involve a dialogical evaluation of "which of the norms already accepted as valid is appropriate in a given case in the light of all the relevant features of the situation conceived as exhaustively as possible" (Habermas 1994, 14). By taking into account the perspectives of all affected, we settle on a shared description of the situation. That shared description then tells us which of the prima facie valid norms—norms that have been vindicated beforehand through discourses of justification—ought to apply in that specific case.

While we certainly often engage in *both* discourses of justification and discourses of application in any given conversation, as Habermas puts it, we cannot "justify norms and defend concrete actions *in the same breath*" (1994, 128). We cannot at the same time ask whether a norm is valid at all *and* whether or how it applies to a concrete case.

At the same time, application discourses feed back into justification discourses by further specifying and qualifying our norms on the basis of the concrete situations in which we apply them. Initially our norms apply only in standard, foreseeable cases. They are therefore only provisionally justified based on our existing knowledge and our understanding of the typical situations in which we anticipate the norm to apply. Discourses of application help us to see the implications of the norm in unexpected contexts, which can lead us to modifying the norm (Habermas 1994, 39). For instance, "do not lie" is a norm with prima facie plausibility. However, Kant's murderer at the door scenario shows us that we will need to qualify "do not lie" with something like "unless it saves someone's life" for it to be plausible. Of course, any qualifications we make to a norm must also be consistent with our other prima facie valid norms as a system, and we may therefore need to make further changes to other norms as the result of a discourse of application (Rehg 1994, 192–93).

This circle of justification and application allows Habermas to respond to concerns that discourse ethics is insensitive to context. We do not simply apply abstract norms to concrete situations in a thoughtless, dogmatic way. Instead, our careful consideration of the specific problems we face in discourses of application in turn allows us to modify norms in light of concrete moral problems.

Summary

Habermas's discourse ethics is a sophisticated attempt to explain the bindingness of moral norms. Starting with the nature and purpose of language, Habermas builds a theory that reconstructs the implicit rules of argumentation and discourse and demonstrates the essentially dialogical nature of normative justification. He then offers the universalization principle as the best explanation for the phenomenon of moral normativity. This principle provides the procedure by which we both do and ought to test the validity of moral norms in discourse. Since discourse ethics is a minimal ethics, (U) is not a first principle from which we can derive other moral principles. Rather, it is the method by which we test norms that arise from our lifeworld as the result of real-world disagreements. Furthermore, Habermas distinguishes between discourses of justification and discourses of application and thinks that moral norms can be revised in light of discourses of application. His dialogical, minimal, and contextually sensitive moral theory therefore overcomes some of the more significant problems with Kantian deontological ethics, while keeping the more plausible aspects (such as Kant's universalist, cognitivist, and formalist approach to moral justification). Hence, discourse ethics is a significant improvement on Kant's ethics, while also being an innovative new moral theory in its own terms.

Notes

1. We have not at this point touched on debates over which values or ideals we *ought* to have, which is important part of ethical discourse. Such discussions also draw on a group's traditions, albeit in a slightly differently way, but a full discussion of this issue is outside the scope of this chapter.

2. It is here where Habermas's other commitments, e.g., his social theory and theory of modernity, end up doing a lot of work. But this is beyond the scope of our current discussion.

Further Reading

PRIMARY SOURCES

Habermas, Jürgen. 1982. "A Reply to My Critics." Translated by Thomas McCarthy. In *Habermas: Critical Debates*, edited by John B. Thompson and David Held, 219–83. Cambridge: MIT Press.

———. 1984. *The Theory of Communicative Action: Volume 1: Reason and the Rationalization of Society*. Translated by Thomas McCarthy. Boston. Beacon Press.

———. 1985. *The Theory of Communicative Action: Volume 2: Lifeworld and System: A Critique of Functionalist Reason*. Translated by Thomas McCarthy. Boston. Beacon Press.

———. 1989. "Justice and Solidarity: On the discussion Concerning 'Stage 6.'" *The Philosophical Forum* 21, no. 1: 32–52.

———. 1990. *Moral Consciousness and Communicative Action*. Translated by Christian Lenhardt and Shierry Weber Nicholsen. Cambridge, UK: Polity Press.

———. 1994. *Justification and Application: Remarks on Discourse Ethics*. Translated by Ciaran P. Cronin. Cambridge, MA: MIT Press.

———. 1995. "Reconciliation and the Public Use of Reason: Remarks on John Rawls's Political Liberalism." Translated by William Rehg. *The Journal of Philosophy* 42, no. 3: 109–31.

———. 1998. *On the Pragmatics of Communication*. Edited by Maeve Cooke. Cambridge, MA: MIT Press.

———. 2003. *Truth and Justification*. Translated by Barbara Fultner. Cambridge, MA: MIT Press.

———. 2020. "From Formal Semantics to Transcendental Pragmatics: Karl-Otto Apel's Original Insight." *Philosophy and Social Criticism* 46, no. 6: 627–50. https://doi.org/10.1177/0191453720930837.

SECONDARY SOURCES

Abdel-Nour, Farid. 2004. "Farewell to Justification: Habermas, Human Rights, and Universalist Morality." *Philosophy & Social Criticism* 30, no. 1: 73–96. https://doi.org/10.1177/0191453704039393.

Clement, Grace. 1989. "Is the Moral Point of View Monological or Dialogical? The Kantian Background of Habermas' Discourse Ethics." *Philosophy Today* 33, no. 2: 159–73. https://doi.org/10.5840/philtoday198933221.

Cronin, Ciaran P. 1994. "Translator's Introduction." In *Justification and Application: Remarks on Discourse Ethics*. Cambridge, MA: MIT Press, 1994.

Edgar, Andrew. 2005. *The Philosophy of Habermas*. Chesham: Acumen Publishing Ltd.

———. 2006. *Habermas: The Key Concepts*. London: Routledge.

Fultner, Barbara. 2011. *Jürgen Habermas: Key Concepts*. Abingdom: Routledge.

Gilabert, Pablo. 2005. "A Substantivist Construal of Discourse Ethics." *International Journal of Philosophical Studies* 13, no. 3: 405–37. https://doi.org/10.1080/09672550500169232.

Heath, Joseph. 2003. *Communicative Action and Rational Choice*. Cambridge, MA: MIT Press.

———. 2014. "Rebooting Discourse Ethics." *Philosophy and Social Criticism* 40, no. 9: 829–66. https://doi.org/10.1177/0191453714545340.

Heller, Agnes. 1985. "The Discourse Ethics of Habermas: Critique and Appraisal." *Thesis Eleven* 10, no. 1: 5–17. https://doi.org/10.1177/072551368501000102.

Ingram, David. 2010. *Habermas: Introduction and Analysis*. Ithaca, NY: Cornell University Press.

Johri, Mira. 1996. "On the Universality of Habermas's Discourse Ethics." PhD Thesis, McGill University.

MacKendrick, Kenneth. 2000. "The Moral Imaginary of Discourse Ethics." *Critical Horizons* 1, no. 2: 249–69. https://doi.org/10.1163/156851600750133360.

McMahon, Christopher. 2000. "Discourse and Morality." *Ethics* 110, no. 3: 514–36. https://doi.org/10.1086/233322.

Mahoney, Jon. 2002. "Proceduralism and Justification in Habermas's Discourse Ethics." *Philosophy Today* 46, no. 3: 300–12. https://doi.org/10.5840/philtoday200246336.

Niemi, Jari Ilmari. 2008. "The Foundations of Jürgen Habermas's Discourse Ethics." *The Journal of Value Inquiry* 42: 255–68. https://doi.org/10.1007/s10790-008-9119-7.

Pamerleau, William C. 1996. "Can Habermas's Discourse Ethics Accommodate the Feminist Perspective." *Social Philosophy Today* 12: 235–52. https://doi.org/10.5840/socphiltoday19961225.

Papastephanou, Marianna. 1997. "Communicative Action and Philosophical Foundations: Comments on the Apel-Habermas Debate." *Philosophy & Social Criticism* 23, no. 4: 41–69. https://doi.org/10.1177/019145379702300403.

Payrow Shabani, Omid. 2003. *Democracy, Power, and Legitimacy: The Critical Theory of Jürgen Habermas*. Toronto: University of Toronto Press.

Powell, Brian K. 2009. "Discourse Ethics and Moral Rationalism." *Dialogue* 48, no. 2: 373–86. https://doi.org/10.1017/S0012217309090301.

Rehg, William. 1994. *Insight and Solidarity: The Discourse Ethics of Jürgen Habermas*. Berkeley: University of California Press.

Thomassen, Niels. 1992. *Communicative Ethics in Theory and Practice*. Translated by John Irons. New York: Palgrave Macmillan.

Wright, Charles. 2004. "Particularity and Perspective Taking: On Feminism and Habermas' Discourse Theory of Morality." *Hypatia* 19, no. 4: 49–76. https://doi.org/10.1111/j.1527-2001.2004.tb00148.x.

13

Rossian Deontology

PHILIP STRATTON-LAKE

Introduction

Very often when philosophers talk of "modern moral philosophy"
they have in mind utilitarianism and Kantianism. Both these views
are monists about the right—that is to say that, on both views,
all duties are grounded in a single foundational principle. For
utilitarianism, that principle is good-maximization, and for Kant
it is the categorical imperative. Kant is sometimes contrasted with
utilitarianism on the ground that he believes that there are absolute
prohibitions. An absolute prohibition is one that prohibits doing a
certain action under every set of circumstances, so that it is always
wrong. Kant famously thought that there is an absolute prohibition on lying, so for him, lying is always wrong, no matter what.
But utilitarians also endorse absolute prohibitions. On their view,
it is always wrong to fail to produce the best outcome in terms
of utility, no matter what. So, on this picture, all modern moral
philosophy is monistic about the right, and endorses at least one
absolute prohibition.

   But this picture of modern moral philosophy excludes one
very important view: intuitionism. Intuitionism is sometimes portrayed primarily as an epistemic and metaethical view, according

to which certain moral propositions are self-evident, and rightness and goodness are regarded as simple non-natural properties. But another strand in intuitionism is as a pluralistic, first-order moral theory, and the most developed version of this view is laid out in W. D. Ross's *The Right and the Good*. In contrast to utilitarianism and Kant, Ross's deontology is both pluralist and non-absolutist. It is pluralist in the sense that it claims that there is an irreducible plurality of basic principles of duty, and it is non-absolutist in the sense that it denies that any type of action is always wrong no matter what.

That Ross was a pluralist does not mean that he had abandoned the project of trying to find foundational principles of right action from which all duties could be derived. Rather, he thought that all duties could be derived from no fewer than five basic principles: fidelity to promises, reparation for past wrongs or harms, gratitude for past benefits, promoting the good, and avoiding harm (non-maleficence). If he could have subsumed these principles under more fundamental ones without distortion, he would have done. But his view was that these five principles cannot be derived from fewer, more fundamental principles (1930, 27).

Ross's most important contribution to deontology is that his basic principles are principles of what he calls "prima facie duties" rather than those of "duty proper." But the term "prima facie" duty is doubly misleading. First, it suggests something that is morally relevant *at first sight* (the literal translation of "prima facie"), but which may turn out to be illusory. But what Ross wanted to draw attention to is not an apparent fact about the nature of the situation, but a real fact about it, albeit a partial fact. Therefore, most contemporary philosophers instead use the term *"pro tanto"* (which means "as far as that goes") rather than "prima facie."

That is the first clarificatory point. The second is that prima facie duties are not really a type of duty at all, which is presumably why he contrasted it with "duty proper." Duty proper is a verdictive consideration—that is, something that applies at the *all things considered* level. At the all things considered level, for Ross there is almost always only one act you ought to do. (The exception is where there is a moral tie, in which case what you ought to do is either one of the acts most favored.) Prima facie rightness, by contrast, is a contributory notion—it is some partial feature of the action that matters morally, and which contributes to determining whether that act is your duty proper.

I think principles of prima facie duty are best understood as specifying facts about an action Φing, such as the fact that doing Φing would be the keeping of a promise, for instance. The prima facie rightness of these facts lies in that each morally counts in favor of Φing, and thus contributes to Φing being your duty proper. Typically, there will be some other action Ψing that is also prima facie right, perhaps because it falls under the prima facie duty to maximize the good. The fact that Ψing would produce the best outcome is prima facie right in the sense that this fact morally counts in favor of Ψing. Our duty proper, that is, what we actually ought to do, is determined by whether the prima facie rightness of Φing outweighs the prima facie rightness of Ψing. If the prima facie rightness of Ψing outweighs the prima facie rightness of Φing, then our duty proper is to do Ψ.

Ross's deontology is non-absolutist in the sense that any one of his basic principles can outweigh any other. None of them always wins out in a conflict situation. Sometimes the prima facie duty of fidelity will win out, in which case your duty proper is to keep your promise, even if you can do more good by breaking it. Sometimes the prima facie duty to promote the good will win out. In such cases your duty proper will be to promote the good, even if that involves breaking a promise. It all depends on the weight of the competing prima facie duties.

It is because he rejects absolute prohibitions that he rejects the view that there can be strictly universal principles of duty proper. It is just not the case that your duty proper is *always* to promote the good. Similarly, it is not the case that your duty proper is *always* to keep your promises. But although he thought that there are no strictly universal principles of duty proper, there are, he claims, strictly universal principles of prima facie duty (1930, 30). Even though sometimes you ought to break your promise, the fact that you would be breaking your promise always counts against the act. It is not the case that you ought always to do the grateful act, but the fact that an act would express gratitude always counts in favor of it. Sometimes you ought not to do the act with the best consequences, but it is always the case that an act would produce the best outcome counts in favor of doing that act, and so on.

But it should be noted that it is only the *basic* prima facie duties that are strictly universal. Derivative prima facie duties are not strictly universal. Because derivative prima facie duties depend on basic ones for their deontic status, if those basic prima facie duties are absent, the derivative duties will be absent also. To see this, consider the prima facie duty not to lie. Ross regarded this as derived from the more basic prima facie duties of fidelity to promises and non-maleficence. Lying is prima facie wrong, Ross thinks, for two reasons. First, he thinks that the act of communication involves an implicit promise to say only what you genuinely believe to be true, and so falls under the basic prima facie duty of fidelity. Second, lying tends to harm the deceived person, and so falls under the basic prima facie duty of non-maleficence (1930, 54–55).

However, because the prima facie wrong of lying depends for its deontic status on these more basic prima facie duties, in cases where the basic duties do not apply, there will be nothing wrong at all, not even prima facie wrong, about lying. Consider a scenario where you are playing a game where deceiving your opponents is part of the game. In this context there is no expectation at all that you will say what you believe to be true, and so the prima facie duty of fidelity does not apply. And since no one is hurt by playing the game, the prima facie duty of non-maleficence does not apply either. Since the prima facie wrong of lying is derived from these two more basic considerations, in this context there is nothing wrong at all with lying. Hence derivative prima facie duties are not universal in that there will be situations where there is nothing at all that morally counts against them.

The merit of Ross's deontology is, then, that it can get strictly universal moral principles without the implausible absolutism of Kantian or utilitarian theories. There is a cost to this, in that it tells you only about what things morally count in favor of actions and what things count against: we have to work out for ourselves what we ought to actually *do*. While Ross thinks there is always an objective right answer about what we ought to do, all his theory allows us to do is weigh up the competing moral considerations and come to a fallible judgment—what Ross calls a "probable opinion"—about what we ought to do. We can know what counts in favor and against doing certain acts (our prima facie duty), but we cannot know our duty proper.

What Makes this View a Deontological Theory?

What makes a first-order normative theory deontological is hard to pin down. But people often have a set of features in mind when they think of a theory as deontological. Here is a list of some of these features:

1. It is anti-utilitarian

2. It focuses on the intention or motive of action, rather than the consequences

3. It claims that certain acts are absolutely prohibited

4. It distinguishes between doing and allowing harm

5. It endorses the doctrine of double effect

6. It endorses the intrinsic moral importance of personal relationships

Now one might think that Ross's theory is only weakly deontological because, although it is anti-utilitarian, it still retains a utilitarian principle, and in any case being anti-consequentialist is not sufficient for being a deontological theory. Virtue ethics is anti-utilitarian, but is not a deontological theory. Furthermore, Ross's theory does not endorse 2–5. It endorses 6, but once again, that is not sufficient for being a deontological theory, as virtue ethics also emphasizes the moral importance of personal relationships. But it is worth looking at some of these features to see whether Rossian ethics can capture distinctively deontological sentiments.

We have already seen that he rejects the idea of absolute prohibitions, and so would reject 3. But he would also reject 2, or at least a part of it. He would allow that one's *intention* in doing some act can have deontic relevance, but he explicitly rejects the view that one's motive is relevant to the rightness of one's act

(1930, 6). Intention may be relevant insofar as it can determine what your act is. For instance, we cannot know whether an act of killing is manslaughter or murder until we know whether the agent *intended* to kill the other person. So one's intention is relevant to the deontic status of killing. But Ross would deny that one's intention is all that matters in assessing the rightness or wrongness of some act. If some act is your duty proper, then it is not good enough that you intend to do it. You've got to actually do it for your act to be right (1930, 46–47).

He explicitly rejects the view that one's motive is relevant to the morality of right and wrong. He offers a number of reasons, but the main one stems from the principle that "ought implies can." As he understands it, you can do some act in the relevant sense if you would do it if you chose to do it. But our motives are not, he argues, under the control of the will. You cannot choose to act from a certain motive if you do not have that motive, and if you do have it you cannot choose to act from it rather than from some other motive you may have (1930, 5). All you can chose to do is some act, where "act" is understood as distinct from its motive. His view has the implication that someone's motive just doesn't matter for assessing whether they acted rightly. Keeping your promise would be the right thing to do whether you did this from a sense of duty or from self-interest.

This brings us to 4 and 5—the doing-allowing distinction (DAD) and the doctrine of double effect (DDE). DAD is the view that it is a greater wrong to do harm than merely to allow harm. Suppose that if you were to give one hundred pounds to a certain charity, you would save someone from death. If you do not give this money, you would have allowed a preventable harm to occur—the harm of death. But to fail to save a stranger from death is one thing: it is quite another to kill that person. So even if it is wrong not to give the money in this case, it is a much lesser wrong than killing. A utilitarian would deny this, pointing out that in both cases the consequences are equally bad. Since consequences are all that matters in relation to right and wrong, they say, allowing a certain harm and inflicting that same harm are equally wrong.

We have already seen that Ross has a utilitarian principle on his list of basic prima facie duties. Since the utilitarian principle denies DAD, it may look as though Ross would deny it too. It is hard to know what Ross would have said about this, since he does not discuss DAD. But some of the things he does say look as though they fit with DAD. Remember that, for Ross, producing good outcomes and avoiding harm are distinct principles. The latter is the only negative prima facie on his list of basic principles, and it is separated from the prima facie duty to promote the good because he acknowledges that harming people matters more than an equal but opposite benefit.

For instance, suppose you were in a position to give John an extra year of life at the cost of depriving Jim of eleven months of life (and all other things are equal). Since doing this makes the world a better place, a utilitarian would claim that we ought to kill Jim to benefit John. Ross would not agree, because he has a distinct prima facie duty of non-maleficence, and this is more stringent than the utilitarian prima facie duty (1930, 21). Although the prima facie duty of good promotion favors harming Jim to benefit John, the prima facie duty of non-maleficence counts against doing this. And because the additional benefit for John is not significantly higher than the cost to Jim, Ross would, I think, claim that harming Jim to benefit John is wrong.

Ross would, of course, deny that it is *always* wrong to harm someone to benefit others. The wrong of harming is more stringent than the right of benefiting but is not more stringent in the sense that it always outweighs benefiting. If, for instance, you could give one hundred people an extra year of life by depriving Jim of eleven months of life, Ross may well conclude that your duty proper is to benefit those others by harming Jim. Even if he thought that that would still be wrong, there would be some number of beneficiaries, perhaps two hundred, perhaps a thousand, where the amount of good produced would tip the scales, making the act required rather than wrong. So, although Ross does not make explicit reference to DAD, his distinct, and more stringent, prima facie duty of non-maleficence goes some way to capturing DAD.

That leaves us with 5—the doctrine of double effect (DDE). Sometimes one's act has two effects with very different values: one effect may be very good and the other very bad. This is what happens in a standard trolley case, where one diverts a trolley that would otherwise kill five people onto a spur track where one person would be killed. One's action has two effects—saving the five, which is good, and killing the one, which is bad. DDE allows one to do this act, even if the bad effect is foreseen, so long as it is not *intended*. Since in the trolley case mentioned one does not intend to kill the person on the spur track—even if he were not on the spur track, you would still divert the trolley—one may divert the trolley.

Things are different in the bridge version of the Trolley Problem, where the subject saves the five by pushing a fat man off a bridge, thus stopping the runaway trolley, killing the man in the process. Here killing the man is part of your plan and is so intended as a means to your end of saving the five. DDE would prohibit this act, even though it shares the feature of the first case in that it is killing one person to save five. According to DDE, that you *intend* to kill the one person in the bridge case makes an important moral difference.

Ross makes no use of this principle, and it is not clear what he would say about it. Ross was very keen to have a theory that captured our commonsense verdicts as well as possible. It is an interesting question whether his theory has the resources to capture the difference between the first and second trolley cases without DDE. At first sight, it may not seem as though it does. The inclusion of a distinct, more stringent principle of non-maleficence doesn't seem to help, as the harms and benefits are the same in both trolley cases. So if the benefit to the five is great enough to outweigh the harm to the one in the first trolley case, it would seem that it is great enough in the second. That would mean that his theory would entail that we ought to push the fat man off the bridge to save the five. Can Ross avoid this conclusion without DDE?

I think he may be able to do this if he regards being treated as a mere means to someone else's end as a harm. Both the man on the spur track and the fat man on the bridge suffer the harm of being killed. But in addition to this, the man on the bridge suffers the harm of being treated as a mere means. If that is correct, then the harms are not the same in both cases, and that may explain the different verdicts about the permissibility of each act.

This is further supported if we change the bridge scenario. Suppose that the man on the bridge realized that he could save the five at the cost of his own life. Suppose further that he could not bring himself to jump. Instead, he turned his back on you and asked you to push him off to save the five. If you do as he asked, you are still treating him as a means, but you are not treating him as a *mere* means, since he has consented to be treated in this way. It may be argued that it is the latter that is the real harm, as treating someone as a *mere* means is treating them as a mere thing, regardless of what they want. So the fat man's consenting to be used in this way looks morally relevant. If he did not consent, you would have harmed him by failing to respect him as a person with free choice, rather than as a thing to be used for your own ends. And because treating someone as a mere means fails to respect personhood and autonomy, it is plausible to suppose that treating them in this way is a distinct harm. That brings treating others as mere means under Ross's prima facie duty of non-maleficence, and that can explain the difference in our moral judgments in the two trolley cases without reference to DDE.

But there are other deontological-seeming elements in Ross's theory. Ross tries to capture the intrinsic moral importance of personal relations, and his main criticism of utilitarianism is that it fails to do justice to this element of morality (1930, 22). When I promise to benefit you in some way—say, by giving you fifty pounds—the relation of promisor-promisee in which we now stand makes a difference to what I ought to do. Prior to the promise, if I had to choose between giving you the fifty pounds and giving it to someone who would benefit more from it, such as a beggar, then, absent other competing moral considerations, I ought to give it to the beggar. But once I have promised you the money, although the beggar would still benefit more from the money, it may be the case that I ought to, nonetheless, give it to you, because I promised to. But utilitarianism ignores the special relation in which I stand to you; for utilitarians, the promise does not change anything morally.

The same would be true if I had a choice between saving the life of a stranger or of my loving parent. Assuming the benefit of being saved is the same for each, utilitarianism would conclude that it is permissible to save either. But Ross would argue that the family relation makes a huge difference here, and that that relation would make it impermissible to save the stranger. This may be because of the debt of gratitude I owe to my loving parent, which generates a special obligation—that is, an obligation owed to a specific person rather than to all people. Or if we are talking about the special responsibility I have for *my* children, rather than for children generally, that some act would benefit my child gives me a special reason to do it that is weightier than the moral reason I have to benefit the children of strangers.

Ross regards the prima facie duties of fidelity, reparation, and gratitude as special in this way—that is, as owed to specific individuals or groups—and contrasts this with the general prima facie duty to promote the good, impartially considered. This is his main objection to utilitarianism and, along with his focus on duty and obligation, as well as the special weight he gives to the prima facie duty of non-maleficence, makes up his main claim to be regarded as a deontologist.

Some Internal Disagreements among Rossians

As noted earlier, Ross thought that he could ground the whole of the morality of right and wrong in five basic principles. That view raises two questions:

1. Are there too few basic moral principles?
2. Are there too many basic principles?

One might think that there are too few basic moral principles for one of two reasons:[1] the first is that some obligations are unable to be accounted for with Ross's five principles; and the second is that his subsumption of some obligations under these five leads to distortion.

Regarding the first point, one obligation that may not be able to be accounted for is the special obligation a parent has to their child. This is a special, rather than a general, obligation, so it cannot be accounted for by the duty to promote the good. Parents need not actually promise their children they will take special care of them to acquire the special responsibilities they have to do so, and acquiring those responsibilities are clearly not the result of reparation for past wrongs, or gratitude. So, it looks like something else is needed on the list to account for these parental obligations.

Thomas Hurka lists some other omissions. For instance, it is not clear that Ross's theory can account for the wrong of paternalistic actions when those actions will benefit the other person (2014, 190). Since such paternalistic actions would benefit them, they cannot fall under the prima facie duty of non-maleficence and may be required by the duty to promote the good.

Another example Hurka identifies is wrongs relating to property (2014, 191). Often when I violate your property rights I harm you, so this falls under the duty of non-maleficence. But this cannot explain why it would be wrong to use your house while you were away without your consent. If I do not damage the property, and the owner never finds out, it is not clear that this harms the owner. But it seems wrong nonetheless.

The second reason to think there are too few basic principles is that some of Ross's reductions lead to distortion. David Wiggins illustrates this concern by considering a situation in which the only way to promote the virtue of ethnic non-quarrelsomeness (which, qua virtue, would be an intrinsically good thing) would be by ethnic cleansing. "Let us suppose," he writes,

> that ethnic non-quarrelsomeness is a moral virtue. And let us suppose that in the Balkans somewhere some reflective, self-conscious person, a patriot of some sort, possessing both determination and armed power, deliberates as follows: "The only way out of the present situation is to bring into being communities which do not see themselves as ethnically divided and in which the issue of ethnicity can be allowed to go to sleep. That is the essential prerequisite of their becoming communities in which questions of race can be discounted and the positive virtues can eventually be cultivated of ethnic non-quarrelsomeness and non-factiousness. That is for the long run. But now, in the real world of 1997, the only way in which even the first step can be achieved is at cost of a certain minimum of rearrangement, even at the cost of measures of partition or of ethnic cleansing,

266 | Philip Stratton-Lake

as some call it. And that, alas, is what must happen now . . . I can see no alternative." (1998, 267)

We should also suppose that the patriot's deliberation is factually fully informed and correct about the only means to bring about the intrinsically good virtue of non-quarrelsomeness. If this course of action would produce the most intrinsic good, then the principle of good promotion would mean that, absent special relations, the patriot is obligated to pursue this policy. And if beneficence can be reduced to good promotion, then beneficence would require this also. It would require agents in the patriot's position to ask, "how many objects of virtuous concern it is right for them to sacrifice in order for them to promote some larger and more widespread future virtue" (1998, 267). In this picture—which Wiggins thinks is implied by Ross's view—things have gone very wrong.

So there are a number of reasons to suppose that Ross's list of basic principles is too parsimonious. But there are also reasons to suppose that there are too many basic principles on his list. For instance, Brad Hooker (1996, 2003) argues that Ross's five basic principles can be grounded in a single, rule consequentialist principle.

In his article "Ross-style Pluralism versus Rule-consequentialism," Hooker argues that a certain version of rule consequentialism can do better than Ross's irreducible pluralism. He proposes an account that has all the commonsense appeal of Ross-style pluralism, plus a consequentialist principle that justifies all the first-order prima facie duties that are constitutive of the Rossian approach and hence can be used as a guide to their selection. Prima facie duties should, he maintains, be selected on the basis of how much fairness and well-being would result from their internalization by the overwhelming majority. The idea is not that agents' deliberation about which acts are right or wrong in particular circumstances be informed solely by this consequentialist principle. Deliberation about this is guided by the sort of prima facie duties listed by Ross. The consequentialist principle works only at the second-order level of deliberation about which first-order principles should guide one's deliberation and action.

Hooker claims that this version of rule consequentialism has all the commonsense appeal of Ross-style pluralism, but with certain theoretical and practical advantages. Its theoretical advantage is that it is more systematic in the sense that only one principle is regarded as basic. And it is a better guide to action because it includes not only a list of principles by means of which particular acts can be morally assessed, but also a principle by means of which these first-order principles can be morally assessed. Thus, Hooker claims, this version of rule consequentialism is a better theory than Ross-style pluralism. If Hooker is right, then the best version of Rossian ethics will not be deontological at all.

The appeal of Hooker's view is that it can keep all of the appealing features of Ross's original view and just add a unifying rule-consequentialist principle grounding Ross's principles. But it is not clear that adding this grounding principle leaves everything (grounded) unchanged. Remember, Ross claimed not only that considerations of fidelity, gratitude, reparation, and so forth are morally relevant, but also that they have an *independent* moral relevance. This means that, for example, the fact that one has made a promise counts in favor of doing what one has promised no matter what. But on the rule consequentialist revision of Ross, that is not true. On this view promises only matter when and because the principle of fidelity is one of a set of principles that, if internalized by most people, would have the best outcome. But this makes fidelity to promises a derivative principle, which is not how Ross regarded it.

The way to get around this is to maintain that rule conse-quentialism only requires that we *believe* that the items on Ross's list have independent moral relevance, even though they do not. It is believing this by enough people that has the best consequences. It doesn't matter whether these beliefs are true. But if Ross's basic principles are false, because they claim independent relevance they do not have, what are the basic moral principles? All Hooker offers us is a list of principles that, if enough people *believe* they are independently morally relevant, will make the world a better place. But that leaves open what the basic principles are.

There is also an issue of whether we can coherently get our-selves to endorse this view. The problem is that we would have to believe that Ross's set of principles has independent moral salience, when *by our own theory* it does not. The principles do not have this salience because their being regarded as independently salient is required when and because believing this by enough people has the best outcome. But then their salience is not independent. It looks, then, as though Hooker's view requires us to believe certain things that according to that very theory are false. It is not clear that that is psychologically possible.

Summary

In sum, Ross's view is a pluralistic, non-absolutist deontological view. It is pluralistic because he rejects the idea that all our obligations can be grounded in a single universal principle. It is non-absolutist in the sense that he denies that any one moral consideration always wins out in a conflict of prima facie duties. His may be regarded as a deontological view for the intrinsic moral importance he gives to personal relations in determining what we ought to do, and because he regards the prima facie duty of non-maleficence as more stringent than the prima facie duty of maximizing the good. His ethic of prima facie duty offers a unique and important alternative to other dominant forms of modern moral philosophy, which enables deontologists to resist criticisms from other theories, such as virtue ethics and feminist ethics, while remaining true to our deepest moral convictions.

Note

1. I leave aside the more radical critique from particularists that there are no strictly universal principles.

Further Reading

PRIMARY SOURCES

Ross, W. D. (1930) 2002. *The Right and the Good*. Edited by Philip Stratton-Lake. Oxford: Oxford University Press.

SECONDARY SOURCES

Audi, Robert. 1996. "Intuitionism, Pluralism, and the Foundations of Ethics." In *Moral Knowledge? New Readings in Moral Epistemology*, edited by Walter Sinnott-Armstrong and Mark Timmons, 101–36. New York: Oxford University Press.

————. 2001. "A Kantian Intuitionism." *Mind* 110, no. 439: 601–35. https://doi.org/10.1093/mind/110.439.601.

————. 2004. *The Good in the Right*. Oxford: Oxford University Press.

Dancy, Jonathan. 1991. "An Ethic of *Prima Facie* Duties." In *A Companion to Ethics*, edited by Peter Singer. Oxford: Wiley Blackwell.

————. 1998. "Wiggins and Ross." *Utilitas* 10, no. 3: 281–85. https://doi.org/10.1017/s095382080000621x.

Darwall, Stephen. 1998. "Under Moore's Spell." Utilitas 10, no. 3: 286–91. https://doi.org/10.1017/S0953820800006221.

Gaut, Berys. 1993. "Moral Pluralism." *Philosophical Papers* 22, no. 1: 17–40. https://doi.org/ 10.1080/05568649309506391.

Hooker, Brad. 1996. "Ross-Style Pluralism Versus Rule-Consequentialism." *Mind* 105, no. 420: 531–52. https://doi.org/10.1093/mind/105.420.531.

————. 2003. *Ideal Code, Real World: A Rule-Consequentialist Theory of Morality*. Oxford: Oxford University Press.

Hurka, Thomas. 2014. *British Ethical Theorists from Sidgwick to Ewing*. Oxford: Oxford University Press.

McNaughton, David. 1996. "An Unconnected Heap of Duties?" *Philosophical Quarterly* 46, no. 185: 433–47. https://doi.org/10.2307/2956354.

Pietroski, Paul M. 1993. "Prima Facie Obligations: Ceteris Paribus Laws in Moral Theory." *Ethics* 103, no. 3: 489–515. https://doi.org/10.1086/293523.

Skelton, Anthony. 2022. "William David Ross." *The Stanford Encyclopedia of Philosophy*. https://plato.stanford.edu/entries/william-david-ross/.

Shaver, Robert. 2011. "The Birth of Deontology." In *Underivative Duty: British Moral Philosophers from Sidgwick to Ewing*, edited by Thomas Hurka, 126–45. Oxford: Oxford University Press. https://doi.org/10.1093/acprof:oso/9780199577446.003.0008.

Sturgeon, Nicholas. 2002. "Ethical Intuitionism and Ethical Naturalism." In *Ethical Intuitionism: Re-evaluations*, edited by Philip Stratton-Lake, 184–211. Oxford: Oxford University Press.

Stratton-Lake, Philip. 1997. "Can Hooker's Rule-Consequentialist Principle Justify Ross's *Prima Facie* Duties?" *Mind* 106, no. 424: 751–58. https://doi.org/10.1093/MIND/106.424.751

Strawson, P. F. 1949. "Ethical Intuitionism." *Philosophy* 24, no. 88: 23–33. https://doi.org/10.1017/S0031819100006756.

Wiggins, David. 1998. "*The Right and the Good* and W. D. Ross's Criticism of Consequentialism." *Utilitas* 10, no. 3: 261–80. https://doi.org/10.1017/S0953820800006208.

Section 4

Particularist, Anti-Theoretical, and Other Approaches to Morality

Introduction

While the character, consequences, and deontology sections were organized around what they *accept*, the theories in this section are drawn together more in terms of what they *reject*. And just as there can be various independent reasons to reject something, so do the theories in this section differ in significant respects. Nonetheless, there are three main views covered in this part of the book. The first is *anti-theory*, which denies the value of theorizing about morality in the first place. The second is *particularism*, which rejects the existence and/or the value of moral principles of any kind (this is not quite the same as anti-theory, as we will see, though particularism can often overlap with anti-theory in some ways). The third consists in the Yoga school of Indian philosophy, which is argued here to be a non-particularist moral theory that is nevertheless not character based, consequentialist, or deontological.

Anti-Theory

Anti-theorists reject discussions about morality—in terms of both normative ethics *and* meta-ethics—in theoretical terms. However, anti-theorists do not simply fall silent when it comes to the nature of morality—they do not meet questions about morality with a mute refusal to engage. It is therefore not that anti-theorists have no *interest* in morality, nor that they are in any sense *a*moral. Rather, they think that all attempts to systematize morality are going to lead us astray (Hämäläinen 2009, 542).

Daoism, Zen Buddhism, and Advaita Vedanta can be plausibly conceived as anti-theoretical. Daoism, for its part, is deeply skeptical of any attempt to offer a comprehensive account of morality. Any attempt to try to pin ethics down in judgments of right and wrong will inevitably lead a person astray. Instead, moral virtuosity requires attaining a state of emptiness in which we *forget* moral ideas. Only in forgetting morality can our heart act like a "mirror" that reflects back to the world only what is found in it, rather than imposing on it our preexisting (and inevitably mistaken) moral judgments (Fraser 2014, 198).

Zen Buddhism shares a similar sentiment, though for different reasons. For Zen, everything that exists is empty of self-nature. That is, there is no *essence* to things that gives them their natures and that allows us to *conceptualize* them as objects that exist independently of other objects. In fact, Zen Buddhism rejects all concepts—including all moral concepts—as ultimately empty and lacking in self-nature. Hence, insofar as we attempt to talk about the world, in both everyday and moral terms, we are mistaken as to the true (empty) nature of things. As a result, moral concepts inevitably lead us astray.

However, Zen Buddhists do not think that the world is *illusory*. The things we encounter may be empty, but they still exist. The Zen insight is rather that all things *dependently co-originate* with all other things, and that as a result there "is ultimately nothing more to a thing than its suchness; its absolute uniqueness" (Hemmingsen 2022). To put it another way, things are what they are and nothing more. This is the thought behind the following famous Zen passage: "Thirty years ago, before I began the study of Zen, I said, 'Mountains are mountains; waters are waters.' After I got insight into the truth of Zen through the instruction of a good master, I said, 'Mountains are not mountains; waters are not waters.' But now, having attained the abode of final rest [that is enlightenment], I say, 'Mountains are really mountains; waters are really waters'" (Quoted in Abe 1985, 4). An ordinary person sees mountains and rivers as having a self-nature: in this case the concepts of mountainness and riverness. A practitioner of Zen realizes that the mountains and rivers are empty: they do not have a self-nature, there is no such thing as mountainness or riverness by virtue of which mountains are mountains and rivers are rivers. But an enlightened Zen master takes things one further step, recognizing that while the mountains and rivers are empty, they nonetheless exist as unique particulars that are just what they are, no more and no less.

Hence, for Zen Buddhism, like Daoism (and likely influenced by it), the enlightened person completely abandons all moral talk, including moral theorizing. Instead, they respond to things in the world wholly in terms of their absolute uniqueness; in terms of what they are and nothing more.

Finally, Advaita Vedanta subscribes to a metaphysics in which the only thing that is *ultimately* real is Brahman (ultimate reality). Everything that exists is identical to Brahman. As such, the distinctions between things—including self and other—are illusory and are caused by cosmic ignorance (*maya*). All moral talk is not of what is ultimately real, but rather of the illusory world of *maya*, and is therefore a misapprehension.

Anti-Theory and Moral Talk

Even though Daoism, Zen Buddhism, and Advaita Vedanta are anti-theoretical, they nonetheless *do* seem to talk about morality. After all, there are chapters on each of them in this book. On the face of it, this seems to directly refute the claim that they are anti-theoretical, and this contradiction requires an explanation.

In the case of Daoism, this seeming contradiction is explained by the fact that moral talk is intended to be therapeutic rather than doctrinal. In other words, moral talk does not capture the way things *really are*; this is impossible to do in words. Rather, moral theorizing is a tool that assists the practitioner along the path to a state of sageliness in which the truth of things is directly apprehended, at which point the moral theorizing can and should be abandoned.

In Buddhist terms, moral theorizing can be an *upāya*—skillful means—an ultimately false doctrine that is nonetheless of some pedagogical use. Like Daoism, moral theorizing is misguided—it does not reflect anything real—but as a means of advancing the Zen practitioner along the path toward the state of enlightenment, in which the unique *suchness* of things is perceived directly, it can have some benefit.

For the Advaita Vedanta, while the world around us is *illusory*, it is not *nonexistent*. When we realize the truth of Brahman—that our selves (*ātman*) along with everything else are identical to it—we are not realizing that the world is not there, but that it is just not what we thought it was. The idea of the illusory world is sometimes captured with the metaphor of the snake-rope illusion: if we mistake a rope for a snake, we are not making up the snake out of whole-cloth. Rather, the illusion is only possible because the rope is there to act as a substratum. Similarly, the fact that we can mistakenly think that the world around us is the way it is, is only possible because of the very real substratum of Brahman that lies under it. But unless we have genuinely achieved *mokṣa* (the enlightened realization of the truth of Brahman), we cannot help but take the world around us as real. And since that world rests on a real foundation—Brahman—then our moral theorizing about it is not completely mistaken. Hence, insofar as we have not yet reached *mokṣa*, moral theorizing has a place.

In common among all three of these views is what we might call a two-level view: there is the ultimate reality (in which moral theorizing is mistaken) and non-ultimate reality (in which moral theorizing can be useful). So ultimately these approaches are anti-theoretical, but at the everyday, mundane level they are not, and therefore can also engage in moral talk.

Particularism

Moral particularists have a lot in common with anti-theorists. In fact, we might categorize Daoism and Zen Buddhism as *both* anti-theoretical and particularist. The difference between anti-theory and particularism is that the anti-theorist thinks that all systematization and theorization in morality is ultimately mistaken—including metaethical theorizing—whereas the particularist engages in systematic meta-ethical theorizing in support of their view that we ought to abandon principles and generalization in ethics (Hämäläinen 2009, 542).

Particularism is best understood in contrast with *generalism*, or the idea that there are general principles of one kind or another (Leibowitz 2009, 189). At the very least, then, particularism rejects what Mark Lance and Margaret Little refer to as "classical principles," which are "universal, exceptionless, law-like moral generalizations" (2006, 570). For consequentialists and (most) deontologists, so long as we apply these classical principles properly, they guarantee that we will end up doing the right thing. For example, consequentialism tells us that we ought to maximize the good. If we implement this principle—if we really *do* act to maximize the good—then we can be sure that we will do the morally right thing. Similarly, Scanlon's contractualism requires that we subject our principles of action to the test of whether they can be reasonably rejected by all. If they pass this test, we can be certain that we are doing a morally permissible thing (Lance and Little 2006, 570).

Classical principles, then, can tell us *what* is right, they can tell us *why* that thing is right, and in doing so they draw connections across a wide range of cases (Raz 2000, 50). The fact that it brings about the most good, for instance, is *why* an action is good for the consequentialist, and this fact holds across all actions in which the good is maximized: it is a general claim. What is more, classical principles form theoretical systems of interconnected propositions that all support one another and explain any unexpected divergences from what we would expect the right action to be (Lance and Little 2006, 571). No right action *just is* right; if one action is right in one case, but a different action is right in what seems to be similar case, this is always explained by some difference between the two cases that the system of principles accounts for (Raz 2000, 50).

In short, classical principles are "exceptionless, explanatory, interrelated moral generalizations" (Lance and Little 2006, 571), and the central task of moral theory is to establish precisely what those principles are and how we can use them to work out what to do in any given situation. Lance and Little compare this vision of moral theory to Newtonian physics: "Moral theory is supposed to offer us up various morally salient "forces" . . . each of which pushes in the direction of one of the moral verdicts, and to provide us with some sort of algorithm or moral calculus . . . for combining these moral forces into a resultant moral verdict" (2006, 573).

Understood in this way, it is not only the theories in this section of the book that can be considered in some sense particularist. Character-based approaches also reject the existence of classical principles, holding instead that there is an irreducible element of judgment on the part of the virtuous person that does not come down to the mere application of principles or rules. Similarly, in its non-absolutism, Rossian pluralism is an exception to the generalist consensus in deontology. In Ross's view, our pro tanto duties can come into conflict—for instance, we must sometimes choose between being honest and non-harming—and when they do, we have to make a judgment about which duty comes out on top. However, as a non-absolutist, there is no higher-level principle that allows a person to "read off" the right answer (McNaughton and Rawling 2006, 433). For Ross, too, then, we cannot get to right action by algorithmically applying a system of principles.

Holism and Anti-Foundationalism

Holism versus Atomism

While many of the ethical theories in this book are particularist in the sense that they do not think there are ultimate principles that can *fully* explain why an action is right or wrong, arguably Daoism and Zen Buddhism offer a version of particularism that takes anti-generalism in a more radical direction; what we might call "anti-foundationalist particularism."

To understand anti-foundationalist particularism, we need to first distinguish two separate issues: the question of the moral *inputs* on the one hand, and the question of our *all-things-considered* judgments on the other (Hooker 2008, 13).

The issue of moral inputs is sometimes put in terms of *holism* versus *atomism*. In Western philosophy, the strongest proponent of holism is Jonathan Dancy (1993; 2004). Holism is a denial of atomism. Atomism holds that features carry their moral qualities in isolation. So, for instance, pain is always a moral minus, and we can understand each instance of pain as a moral minus before we enter that consideration into any concrete moral deliberations for determining the all-things-considered right action. By contrast, holism suggests that the moral valence of a property can only be determined holistically, from the context in which we find it: in Dancy's words, "a feature that is a reason in one case may be no reason at all, or an opposite reason, in another" (Dancy 2004, 7). So, to use a common example, we usually assume that the fact that something is pleasurable counts in favor of doing it. But if the pleasure is sadistic—if it arises from hurting others—then the property of pleasure in that case switches valence: it ceases to count *toward* doing a thing, and instead counts *against* it. For holists like Dancy, the moral valence of a property is determined by its context; it does not possess a clear moral valence in isolation, that is, atomistically (McKeever and Ridge 2006, 28).

It is important here to be clear that this valence switching happens at the level of moral properties and not at the level of judgments. For instance, an atomist could happily agree that sadistic pleasure is wrong. However, the explanation for this will typically be that the pleasure gained by the sadist is outweighed by the pain of those they harm. But if so, both pleasure and pain have fixed valences (the pleasure always counts for, and the pain always counts against). By contrast, for the holist, the fact that the pleasure is sadistic means that it is sometimes no reason *at all* in favor of the action.

Rossian pluralism, despite being particularist in that it denies that we can use a codifiable set of rules to work out what we should do in concrete cases (our all-things-considered moral judgments), is nonetheless atomistic when it comes to moral inputs. Our various pro tanto duties always count the same way: the fact that an action is honest *always* counts in favor of it; and the fact that it is dishonest *always* counts against it. The fact that our pro tanto duty to be honest is "trumped" by some other pro tanto duty does not mean that our duty to be honest loses its force (Hooker 2008, 13). So even when pro tanto duties come into conflict, they nonetheless always "point" in the same direction. For Ross, one moral duty can be "outweighed" by another. But when something is outweighed, this does not mean its weight changes, simply that the other thing is heavier. By contrast, a holist claims instead that there are no properties that always have the same moral valence, the same "weight."

FOUNDATIONALISM VERSUS NON-FOUNDATIONALISM

The atomism/holism distinction is not the only thing we can say about moral inputs. Even if moral valences change depending on context, they might nonetheless change in predictable ways. For the foundationalist, there is always an explanation as to why something has the moral valence it does (Kagan 1998, 190). As Benedict Smith puts it, "a judgement about a particular moral state of affairs is essentially related to some general piece of knowledge and is derivable from it" (2001, 4). In other words, if something counts morally, there is always a reason why it does, and we can in principle *codify* when, how, and why moral valences switch. But for the non-foundationalist, there is simply no further explanation as to why a particular factor counts morally in the way that it does (Kagan 1998, 190).

Sometimes holists take their view to entail non-foundationalism. For instance, Roger Crisp puts Dancy's view in the following terms: "Any feature that is a reason in one case may be no reason at all, or an opposite reason, in another. *So* there can be no general or universal principles stating the reason-giving status of any such feature" (Crisp 2007, 42, italics mine). Here, the "so" suggests that Crisp attributes to Dancy the belief that holism leads directly to non-foundationalism. But in fact, there is no reason why we could not agree that moral valences switch because of context (holism) but also think that we can codify precisely how and why they do so (McKeever and Ridge 2006, 27–28). If so, we have come right back around to a form of generalism. Radical particularism, then, requires that there be no deeper, generalist explanation as to why a property's polarity changes when it does: radical particularism is non-foundationalist (Leibowitz 2009, 184).

There are therefore three separate issues at play here. First, the matter of our all-things-considered moral judgments; second, the variance/invariance of moral properties; and third, whether there is an explanation as to *why* those properties have the polarity they do at any given time.

Rossian pluralism and character-based moral theories may be particularist in that all-things-considered moral judgments are highly context sensitive. However, principles still play a role in the theories at the other two levels: as we have discussed, for Ross, *pro tanto* duties have a fixed valence: he is an atomist. What is more, there is a *reason* why their valence is fixed: he is a foundationalist. Similarly, while in character-based theories the virtuous person negotiates the various moral features of decisions in a highly context-sensitive way, this is consistent with the idea that the moral valence of the features themselves is fixed (atomism) and that there is a good reason why they point the way they do (foundationalism).

We might also put care ethics in this camp. The fact that we care about someone, for instance, seems to always act as a reason to benefit them (atomism), even if other features of the situation mean that our all-things-considered judgments tells us that we ought not to. Additionally, we can *explain why* the moral features point as they do: they arise from caring relationships (foundationalism).

Daoism and Zen Buddhism are both non-foundationalist moral theories. They see the world as made up of unique particulars that render it irreducibly complex. It is not just that there are *too many* moral properties for us to ever systematize in a useful way; rather, the radical uniqueness of each thing means that there are no generalizations to be had *at all*.

In the Zen case, the enlightened person who realizes the emptiness of all things comes to an understanding of each thing's absolute uniqueness. Each thing can only ever be accurately referred to indexically, as *this* or *that*. This is the concept of *tathātā*, usually translated as "thusness" or "suchness." Essentially, each thing *just is* its specific, particular suchness; it is no more or less than itself. But if so—if each thing has its own absolutely distinct suchness—then nothing shares any *general* property with anything else. And if there are no general properties, then there can be no *general reasons* as to why a thing has a particular moral valence in any specific case. Instead, the enlightened person merely responds to each suchness on its own, wholly unique, terms.

We can find a similar idea in Daoism. Our goal is to have a heart like a mirror; a heart that responds to the world entirely on its own (natural) terms rather than our own (artificial) ones. To have a heart like a mirror, we must cease acting on the basis of *principles*, since principles are inevitably an artificial imposition onto the world, and instead respond *spontaneously* (*ziran* 自然) with non-action (*wuwei* 無為; action without deliberation). But if so, things in the world cannot share general properties: if they did, then we would presumably be able to draw out and apply at least *some* general principles from this fact. On the other hand, if the world is composed of unique particulars, then principles will always fail us, and we can only ever respond to it spontaneously.

Advaita Vedanta, by contrast, is foundationalist. For the non-foundationalist, we can make no general claims about moral properties because of their irreducible complexity; for the Advaita Vedantin, we cannot do so because of their fundamental unity. In other words, for Advaita Vedanta, the issue is not so much that the world is filled with unique particulars, or that moral properties can switch their valence, but rather that ultimately the various properties we imagine grounding moral judgments are unable to be differentiated from each other: the differences between them are illusory. In fact, from the ultimate perspective of the person who has achieved *mokṣa* and realized her—and the universe's—oneness with Brahman, all moral properties themselves are illusory.

Daoism and Zen Buddhism's specific variety of anti-theory, then, leads inevitably to moral particularism and non-foundationalism. But the quite different anti-theoretical stance of Advaita Vedanta leads to a rejection of difference rather than an embrace of it, and so does not entail either particularism or non-foundationalism. Hence, Daoism and Zen are anti-theoretical *and* radically particularist, whereas Advaita Vedanta is merely anti-theoretical.

The Use of Principles

In common between particularists and anti-theorists is the use of skill and perception metaphors: moral practice is a matter of developing the skill of accurately perceiving moral features, rather than relying on generalizations and inferential reasoning. In other words, most of the theories in this section understand morality as a matter of *seeing* the morality in particular cases (McKeever and Ridge 2006, 76). And just as our ability to recognize different cheeses, or appreciate a complex piece of music, is a matter of developing certain capacities and skills, so is moral judgment something that we can get better at through time.

In fact, for particularists and anti-theorists, relying on norms or decision procedures to guide our actions is ultimately harmful to the moral enterprise (Hämäläinen 2009, 541). G. E. M. Anscombe (1958), for instance, criticizes consequentialist and deontological theories for prioritizing rules for guiding our actions at the expense of oversimplifying moral realities and undermining the development of our capacity to discern and evaluate moral situations directly.

However, just because principles *can* be harmful does not mean that we should necessarily abandon them entirely. And in fact, we might deny that principles have any kind of ultimate reality, but nonetheless think that they may still have at least *some* role to play in ethics. We can see this in character-based ethics: character-based theorists might think that moral principles may not *ultimately* explain why an action is right or wrong, but nonetheless hold that they are a useful heuristic—a shortcutting device—for the purposes of moral education. For instance, in Confucian ethics: while a *junzi* understands the meaning of the rites well enough to modify them when needed, for ordinary people following the rites is a path to cultivating an appropriately disposed heart-mind. In reality, the moral landscape cannot be captured by principles, but for the trainee the principles might be provisionally a useful tool, to be later outgrown.

Care ethics, too, does not necessarily think that moral principles are *wholly* useless, but merely that they should be dislodged from their traditionally central place in our moral practices. Principles still have a role to play in regulating relationships between "autonomous" individuals in the public sphere—the realm of "justice." However, since relations of care are more basic—in that they sustain any pretense of "autonomy" in the public sphere in the first place—even the principle-based relations of justice should have care at their heart. Hence, principles do have a role to play, but a secondary one.

The same can be said of radical particularists and anti-theorists. Zen Buddhists think that moral principles are just as empty as anything else. However, they still advocate for rules of thumb as useful guides to action. For instance, the Zen philosopher Dōgen suggests that the aspiring *bodhisattva* (a person one step away from enlightenment who voluntarily delays that final step out of compassion for others) ought to live according to principles of *fuse* (giving 布施); *aigo* (loving speech 愛語); *rigyō* (beneficent action 利行); and *dōji* (identifying with others 同事). However, while these principles are useful guidelines, they are non-absolute and should not be applied in an algorithmic or legalistic way, insensitive to the uniqueness of each situation.

Similarly, while Advaita Vedantins think that, from a transcendental perspective, all is Brahman, most of us have not yet reached this state of being. From our mundane perspective, the world around seems very much real. Whereas someone who has achieved *mokṣa* is in a position to abandon a duty-based (*dharmic*) view of action, the rest of us have no choice but to continue to use it, since we live in the (ultimately illusory) world. Further, achieving *mokṣa* requires developing certain mental capacities and dispositions, and the successful development of these capacities requires that we fulfill our *dharmic* duties to those around us. Hence, the only way to reach a state of mind in which we can truly *perceive* the illusory nature of our duties is to first take these illusory duties seriously.

Yoga Ethics

Our final theory—Yoga ethics—is a unique and *basic* theory of ethics. In other words, it cannot be understood in terms of the four approaches we have considered so far: character-based ethics, consequentialism, deontology, or particularism/anti-theory.

We have considered so far various different ways of understanding the relationship between the right and the good. Character-based approaches hold that the good (in terms of dispositions of character) gives rise to the right. Consequentialist theories identify intrinsically valuable ends, then justify right actions in terms of their ability to bring about those ends. Deontological theories constrain our pursuit of the good with an independently justified right. Most particularist theories do the same, but with a discernment-based account of morality, and while denying that there are ultimate principles that stand behind and explain when and why moral features have the valence they do. Finally, anti-theory thinks that all this moral talk is ultimately groundless in the first place.

Yoga ethics holds to none of these approaches. Instead, for Yoga the good is *produced by* the right. In this sense, Yoga ethics can be partnered with deontology, in that—contrary to teleological theories—the right is *prior to* the good. However, in deontology our pursuit of the good is merely *constrained* by the right; deontology leaves open what goods we might find valuable in the first place. By contrast, in Yoga ethics the good is *created by* it: the good *results from* the right.

In this sense, Yoga is far more procedural than even the most proceduralist deontological theories. There is *no* independence of the good from the right—first we have the right, understood as the three principles of devotion to Sovereignty, unconservatism, and self-governance—and the implementation of these principles in practice *just is* the good. They are not the means to a separate end—a separate good—but rather constitute the good itself. Hence, Yoga ethics can be understood as a distinct kind of theory, though partnered with deontology just as both character-based and consequentialist theories are both considered teleological.

Summary

In this chapter we have considered anti-theory and particularism of various kinds. Anti-theory consists of those approaches that deny the ultimate truth of moral talk, though they may engage in it anyway as a tool for developing a truth-seeker's capacity for discernment. Daoism, Zen Buddhism, and Advaita Vedanta are all anti-theoretical.

Particularism is distinct from anti-theory, in that particularists actively reject moral generalities and hence still engage in metaethical moral talk. However, there are different levels of particularism: some—such as character-based ethics, Rossian pluralism, and care ethics—reject principles at the higher level of all-things-considered judgments, arguing that there is an ineliminable role for the particular in our moral decision-making. However, a more radical kind of particularism—represented here by Daoism and Zen Buddhism—holds that there are no general principles on offer even at the level of *moral inputs*. That is, it is not just that principles cannot help us *decide* what to do, but that there is no principled reason why particular features even have the moral valences they do. For radical particularists, then, we do not need to develop our capacity for moral discernment merely in terms of how different moral features interact at the level of deliberation, but also in seeing the nature of moral features *in the first place*.

Finally, Yoga ethics offers a wholly unique kind of moral theory. Yoga ethics can be paired with deontology, just as character-based and consequentialist approaches are two different varieties of teleological theory. For deontology, the right and the good are independent of one another. The right is prior to the good and constrains how it can be pursued. But for Yoga ethics, the good is not independent of the right; it is *caused by* it. The good is nothing more or less than right practice.

Further Reading

Abe, Masao. 1985. *Zen and Western Thought*. London: MacMillan Press.

Anscombe, G. E. M. 1958. "Modern Moral Philosophy." *Philosophy* 33, no. 124: 1–19.

Crisp, Roger. 2007. "Ethics Without Reasons?" *Journal of Moral Philosophy* 4, no. 1: 40–49. https://doi.org/10.1177/1740468106072782.

Dancy, Jonathan. 1993. *Moral Reasons*. Oxford: Blackwell.

———. 2004. *Ethics without Principles*. Oxford: Clarendon Press.

Fraser, Chris. 2014. "Heart-Fasting, Forgetting, and Using the Heart Like a Mirror: Applied Emptiness in the Zhuangzi." In *Nothingness in Asian Philosophy*, edited by Jeeloo Liu and Douglas L. Berger, 197–212. New York: Routledge.

Hämäläinen, Nora. 2009. "Is Moral Theory Harmful in Practice?—Relocating Anti-theory in Contemporary Ethics." *Ethical Theory and Moral Practice* 12: 539–53. https://doi.org/10.1007/s10677-008-9141-7.

Hemmingsen, Michael. 2022. "Sameness, Difference and Environmental Concern in the Metaphysics and Ethics of Spinoza and Chan Buddhism." *Comparative Philosophy* 13, no. 1: 58–76. https://doi.org/10.31979/2151-6014(2022).130106.

Hooker, Brad. 2008. "Moral Particularism and the Real World." In *Challenging Moral Particularism*, edited by Vojko Strahovnik, Matjaz Potrc, and Mark Norris Lance, 12–30. New York: Routledge.

Kagan, Shelly. 1998. *Normative Ethics*. Boulder, CO: Westview Press.

Lance, Mark, and Margaret Little. 2006. "Particularism and Antitheory." *The Oxford Handbook of Ethical Theory*, edited by David Copp, 567–94. New York: Oxford University Press. https://doi.org/10.1093/01951 47790.003.0021.

Leibowitz, Uri D. 2009. "A Defense of a Particularist Research Program." *Ethical Theory and Moral Practice* 12: 181–99. https://doi.org/10.1007/s10677-008-9135-5.

McKeever, Sean, and Michael Ridge. 2006. *Principled Ethics: Generalism as a Regulative Ideal.* Oxford: Clarendon Press.

McNaughton, David, and Piers Rawling. 2006. "Deontology." In *The Oxford Handbook of Ethical Theory*, edited by David Copp, 424–58. New York: Oxford University Press. https://doi.org/10.1093/oxfordhb/9780195325911.003.0016.

Raz, Joseph. 2000. "The Truth in Particularism." In *Moral Particularism*, edited by Brad Hooker and Margaret Little, 48–78. Oxford: Clarendon Press. https://doi.org/10.1093/0199248001.003.0011.

Smith, Benedict. 2001. *Particularism and the Space of Moral Reasons.* London: Palgrave Macmillan.

14

The Ethics of Daoism

The Dissolving Boundary between Right and Wrong

WAI WAI CHIU

Introduction

In a bookstore, Daoist books are often put under the category of spirituality. To the extent that ethics is about how to live one's life, Daoism is surely a form of ethics. However, it is not immediately clear whether, and if so, how, Daoism conveys any clear ethical argument or theory. Readers of the two classics of philosophical Daoism, the *Laozi* and the *Zhuangzi*, may end up questioning whether it is desirable or even possible to build an ethical theory based on them.

The first feature of these texts that works against ethical theorizing is their writing style, which makes it difficult to identify clear standpoints and arguments. The *Laozi* is full of lofty and cryptic aphorisms, while the *Zhuangzi* is a plethora of parables, jokes, verses, and contradictory statements. Chapter 27 of the *Zhuangzi*[1] lists three kinds of words used to obscure meaning in the text (75/27/1–5): "imputed words" (*yu yan* 寓言), which hide the text's message in metaphors and parables; "weighty words" (*zhong yan* 重言), which hide the message in quotations, real or fictional, of authoritative figures; and "goblet words" (*zhi yan* 卮言), which hide the message in double denial and oxymora.[2] All of these are indirect forms of communication that exploit ambiguity and allow for various textual interpretations.

The second feature of ancient Daoist texts that resists an ethical interpretation concerns their content: the texts often criticize moral frameworks and even the general human tendency to make judgments about right and wrong, good and bad, important and trivial, normal and absurd. Chapter 2 of the *Zhuangzi* laments that "the germs of benevolence and rightness, the paths of right and wrong are inextricably mixed and confused . . . [H]ow could I know how to discriminate between them?" (6/2/70). This statement suggests that Daoists may not be concerned about moral or other normative discriminations.

Twentieth-century scholars who focus on the writing style of ancient Daoist texts tend to characterize Daoism as mystical and anti-rational. A. C. Graham, for example, states that "[l]ike all great anti-rationalists, Chuang-tzû [Zhuangzi] has his reasons for not listening to reason" (Graham 1981, 9). According to Graham, Zhuangzi thus argues that "we should abandon reason for the immediate experience of an undifferentiated world, transforming 'All are one' from a moral into a mystical affirmation" (Graham 1981, 9).

Scholars who emphasize the content of ancient Daoist texts tend to characterize Daoism as skeptical about human conventions and evaluations. Chad Hansen, for example, compares the *Zhuangzi* to Nietzschean perspectivism, stating that both "discover the practical pointlessness of universal or absolute meaning" (Hansen 1992, 285). Graham stresses that the *Zhuangzi* goes beyond the ethical, while Hansen argues that the *Zhuangzi* bypasses the ethical. More recent studies avoid controversial labels such as "mysticism" and "perspectivism," but some still hold the view that Daoism defies morality (Moeller 2009).

Unsurprisingly, the openness of ancient Daoist texts attracts contrary interpretations. While scholars generally agree that Daoism is more detached from rules, conventions, and even ordinary human emotions than its rival Confucianism, some scholars also sense that certain values are more prominent than others in Daoist texts.

For instance, it is generally considered unwise to use brute force to solve a problem or use a single standard to evaluate different people's behavior. Furthermore, the Daoist critique of other schools is often combined with detailed descriptions of ideal personhood and society, as the term "inner sagehood and outer kingship" (*nei sheng wai wang* 內聖外王) in the *Zhuangzi* indicates (91/33/14). This combination encourages readers to conditionally approve and disapprove of certain practices and institutions. Scholars such as Chris Fraser (2014), Huang Yong (2010), and Jung H. Lee (2014) thus argue that we can articulate a Daoist ethics based on the *Zhuangzi*, despite disagreeing about how this should be done.

Against this background, the current chapter explores resources in the *Zhuangzi* that can be articulated as a form of particularist ethics. First, it states how the text diagnoses the problem of human life with the idea of "completed heart-mind." Then it shows how it helps us to navigate a way out by reorienting our attention from rigid rules to the particularities of different entities and contexts. Afterward, there are two sections dealing with disagreement within the *Zhuangzi* and the disagreement between the *Zhuangzi* and Confucianism respectively.

As particularism deemphasizes the status of rules and principles in ethical reasoning, a particularist reading of the *Zhuangzi* can accommodate the text's criticism of universal norms and rigid conventions. Readers should judge for themselves whether this ethical account can be reconciled with the view of the text as defying morality.

The Completed Heart-Mind

In ancient Chinese thought, it is generally agreed that the human faculty responsible for thinking, feeling, and ordering responses is the heart-mind (*xin* 心).[3] The relationship between the heart-mind and other organs resembles that between a ruler and ministers. The ministers are supposed to follow the ruler, just as organs are supposed to follow the heart-mind.[4] The *Zhuangzi*, however, questions the legitimacy of the heart-mind by pointing out that it often assumes its own criterion of right and wrong:

> If people follow the completed heart-mind (*cheng xin* 成
> 心) and regard it as their teacher, who can be without a
> teacher? Why should only people who know how things
> alternate and whose heart-mind self-consciously picks out
> [the preferred side of alternation] have such a teacher?
> Fools have [teachers] as well. But to have right and wrong
> before they are formed in the heart-mind would be to
> "set out for Yue today but arrive there yesterday."[5] This
> would be to regard nothing as something. (4/2/21–22)

In the *Zhuangzi*, every judgment is a distinction, and every distinction involves a criterion. If I judge that there is a table, I must accept that there is a criterion for distinguishing tables from non-tables. Similarly, if I judge that it is good to stay healthy, I must accept that there is a criterion for distinguishing healthy people from unhealthy ones. While other thinkers, such as Confucians and Mohists, propose that we can find the correct criterion for every judgment and practice, at least within the ethical field, the *Zhuangzi* is skeptical about this proposal. It argues that one's heart-mind simply takes a criterion for granted before one judges right and wrong, and any attempt to justify this criterion takes a further criterion for granted. This does not imply that there is ultimately no correct criterion; rather, it suggests that we do not know how to find such a criterion, even if there is one. An act of judgment presupposes a criterion according to which the act makes sense, and the ability to make judgments is inevitably shaped by criteria available in one's upbringing environment. Thus, one's default position in making judgments is shaped by presupposed criteria in the heart-mind, or, as Victor Mair puts it, "prejudice" (1994, 14).

The completed heart-mind creates "the obsession with being right" (Wong 2005, 91), a major cause of human problems. Precisely speaking, it is not the presupposition of criteria that causes problems, because this is a necessary feature of judgments and actions. The problem arises when the completed heart-mind asserts itself and seeks or even demands agreement from others. People then, as the quoted passage above states, "regard [the heart-mind] as their teacher" and insist on the universality of their own criteria to the exclusion of others' criteria. Even if they face clear counter-evidence, they may continue to maintain their own judgments and reject others'. This then leads to the "backfire effect." If I regard my own view as correct, I feel that those who disagree with me have either missed some important evidence or failed to take that evidence seriously. I then exclude them as "others," and such exclusion may lead to what moralists call "immoral attitudes" or "immoral acts," such as distrust, humiliation, and violence. On this basis, it may be said that the existence of the completed heart-mind explains why human life is full of frustration and conflict. This also helps to explain why the promotion of universal rules risks adding fuel to the fire.

It should be noted that the problem caused by the completed heart-mind is not restricted to human affairs. Non-human creatures and things are also affected. The *Zhuangzi* often pokes fun at moralists' anthropocentrism. In a dialogue between two fictional characters, Gaptooth and Wang Ni (6/2/64–73), the latter notes that loaches, apes, and birds have different lifestyles from humans, and it is futile to ask which one knows the "correct" way of life. Wang Ni uses this as a metaphor for his view that "the paths of right and wrong are inextricably mixed and confused." Elsewhere, the *Zhuangzi* tells a story in which a feudal lord feeds a beautiful seabird luxurious human food and entertains it with refined human music, only to cause the creature's death (47/18/33–37). This hints that we cannot rely on a universal path to guide human practices, much less non-human ones. It is just as easy to assume the superi-ority of *my* perspective relative to the perspectives of other people as to assume the superiority of the *human* perspective relative to the perspectives of other creatures.

We can use the term "friction" to summarize the effect of the completed heart-mind on our interaction with other people and things. The *Zhuangzi* comments on this tragic aspect of human lives: "In the strife and friction with other things, people gallop forward on their course as if nothing can stop them. Is this not sad?" (4/2/18–19). Friction is caused by the exclusion of other people and non-human creatures. Rather than attributing the problem to ignorance or disobedience of universal rules, the *Zhuangzi* argues that it is precisely the competition among these rules—including a rule for defining friction—that forces people to gallop without rest and become alienated from the richness and plurality of existence.

Fitting a Context

Refraining from formulating a clear universal rule for distinguishing right from wrong, the *Zhuangzi* reorients readers toward the particularities of the things and contexts we encounter:

> A battering-ram can be used for smashing down a wall but not for plugging a hole, which is to say that tools are different from each other. Hua-liu, the thoroughbred horse, can gallop a thousand miles in a day, but it is not as good at catching rats as a wildcat or a weasel, which is to say that creatures have different skills. Kites and owls can catch a flea or discern the tip of a hair on a dark night, but in the daytime, they blink and can't even see hills and mountains, which is to say that creatures have different natures. Therefore, if someone were to say, "Why don't we make only rightness and order our teacher and eliminate wrongness and disorder?," that person would not yet have understood the patterns of heaven and earth and the perceived characteristics of myriad things. (43/17/35–38)

A horse is inherently neither better nor worse than a cat; it depends on which activity we are talking about. Similarly, racing is neither more nor less valuable than rat-catching; it depends on what kind of lifestyle we are talking about. If we apply this to human society, action-guiding norms lose their meaning when they are taken out of context. The rules of chess are different from those of poker; the rule that you cannot move a piece twice in a turn has no meaning in a poker game. Nevertheless, one may argue that moral norms are inherently more important than other action-guiding norms, such as custom or self-interest, and their rules are imperatives that people cannot reasonably choose to disobey. The *Zhuangzi*'s response would be that what is moral or good still differs from context to context, such that saying that one should always do what is right is an empty statement. The difference between smashing down a wall and plugging a hole suggests that we think differently on the battlefield and in the household. The differences between creatures suggest an even greater heterogeneity of values.

However, the *Zhuangzi* does not claim that we should simply give up normative judgments. In the quoted passage, it is assumed that each thing *is* useful in certain contexts, so we can still make context-specific evaluations of the usefulness of something. It makes little sense to judge in a vacuum whether a soldier or a teacher is better than the other; it makes more sense to compare different teachers teaching the same course. It is the insistence on subjecting all kinds of people to the same standard that results in friction.

Furthermore, the *Zhuangzi*'s particularism is accompanied by an emphasis on change. When it says that different things vary according to their characteristics, it is not saying that a particular thing has a fixed set of characteristics. Rather, the "pattern of heaven and earth" is like a potter's wheel that puts everything into a seamless process of transformation (5/2/39–40). The opening of the *Zhuangzi* introduces a small fish, K'un, that transforms into a giant bird, Peng, with its back extending for thousands of miles (1/1/1–2). Chapter 2 tells the famous story in which Zhuang Zhou[6] dreams that he is a butterfly. The story reaches the following conclusion: "Zhou and the butterfly are necessarily distinct from each other. This is called the transformation of things" (7/2/96). To change is to become something different. For the *Zhuangzi*, whatever exists is also what changes. This implies that whatever exists constantly turns into something different. Therefore, when the text says that different kinds of things should be judged by different criteria, this must be supplemented by two observations. First, differences among things within a kind are not to be ignored. Second, whether something belongs to a kind is an open question. According to the first observation, the *Zhuangzi*'s emphasis on particularity extends to the uniqueness of each individual and even each moment. According to the second observation, there are always ambivalent cases that defy uniformity within one kind. Take humankind as an example: scholars have struggled to define human beings for thousands of years. Different disciplines have different definitions, which in turn influences whether an entity counts as a human being and its ethical status. However, each definition also has particular difficulty accommodating all of and only those people we want to be included under the label "human being." Here, the *Zhuangzi*'s point is that we can learn how best to treat others by fully appreciating their unique positions as well as their relationships with other things, and by being open to all possible moves. If our completed heart-mind is emptied, our understanding will filter out inappropriate moves in a particular context spontaneously. Sometimes we just see the appropriate way through; sometimes we need to pause and think.

Given that one always needs to respond in a context, the thought that one does not predetermine the form of responses leads to the idea of fitting and the realization that we eventually forget this very idea of fitting: "Shoes best fit us when we forget our feet; a belt best fits us when we forget our waist; our hearts best fit us when we know how to forget right and wrong. We fit the situation we encounter when we neither vary inwardly nor yield to external pressure. To fit from the start and never fail to fit is to suit in forgetfulness of what it is that fits" (50/19/62–64). Generally, we do not know whether a pair of shoes will fit us until we actually put them on. If the shoes fit, we will forget them when we walk. Only if they feel uncomfortable will the shoes attract our attention. In response, we may change them because they are worn out or because they are not suited to the ground we walk on or the activities we engage in. Alternatively, we may change our way of walking or simply get used to the discomfort. Using these metaphors, the *Zhuangzi* suggests that we treat judgments of right and wrong issued from the heart in a similar way: they are primarily used to guide our direction in a particular context and are subject to change just like anything else. However, if we become aware of them frequently or stick to them even if we encounter new contexts, our completed heart-mind is taking control of us. In other words, we fit a context best when we do not remind ourselves that we are fitting. Even the idea of fitting itself should be forgotten.

Summarizing the discussion so far, we can say that the *Zhuangzi* invites us to consider the evaluations we make as context-dependent, our perceptions as ever-changing, and the ability to fit a given context as more important than following an absolute principle. This invitation is accompanied by the text's detailed description of "fasting the heart-mind" (*xin zhai* 心齋),[7] a practice that involves dissolving one's completed heart-mind and attuning oneself to the concrete and the particular. In a story about a woodworker who carves wooden bell stands like great works of art (50/19/54–59), the worker says that he always fasts to quiet his heart-mind for seven days before he starts to work. During this process, he becomes less and less concerned about reward, honor, skill improvement, the court that has assigned the job to him, and even his own body. After fasting, he enters the forest and looks at the trees. He is able to perceive the trees' shapes and textures as if they have been already made into bell stands. He can attune his perception to fit his task precisely because he has emptied his heart-mind first. Otherwise, his awareness would be distracted by too many thoughts and he would lose concentration. In particular, that he needs to suspend thoughts about skill improvement shows that he does not even stick to any method he used in the past. It is truly a case of acting in the moment.

Disagreements within the *Zhuangzi*

As the introduction mentions, the *Zhuangzi* employs many indirect forms of communication that exploit ambiguity. The text itself is a demonstration of plurality. Almost every thesis put forward meets its antithesis elsewhere, and the idea of fitting the context is no exception. Besides the debate about whether the text has an ethical vision compatible with its perspectivism, we articulate two themes found in the text that are in tension with what we have discussed so far: the theme of transcendence and the theme of following one's nature (*xing* 性).

Like Confucianism, the *Zhuangzi* has its own conception of ideal personhood. In describing the ideal person, the text often invokes supernatural images. It is said that the daemonic person (*shen ren* 神人) cannot be harmed by fire, water, or natural disasters and is not bothered by anything around them (2/1/32–34). The utmost person (*zhi ren* 至人) has the same immunity and "rides the clouds" to "wander beyond the four seas" (6/2/71–73). It is reasonable to take these descriptions as indicating a general attitude or even the power to transcend worldly affairs. For those who commit to the ideal of transcendence, attachment to worldly affairs is a burden or source of confusion. Daemonic people, therefore, do not pay attention to any particular things or events—they leave them behind altogether. Using the metaphor of shoes, one may argue that daemonic people are those who walk without shoes and think without judgments, if they walk and think at all. This seems incompatible with the suggestion of fitting the context we live in.[8]

Here, one could simply point to the text's pluralistic nature and reiterate that different themes in the text should not be subsumed under a single grand theory. However, one may also wonder whether the particularist perspective offers a way to alleviate the incompatibility. One such suggestion can be found in chapter 17, a few paragraphs after a discussion of the differences between horses, cats, and owls: "Those who have attained utmost virtuosities can neither be burned by fire nor drowned in water, can neither be harmed by cold or heat nor injured by bird or beast. This does not mean that they treat these things lightly, but rather that they are perspicacious about safety and danger . . ." (44/17/48–50). Rather than ascribing miraculous powers to daemonic people, the text here states that these people thoroughly understand a situation when they come across it, so they can walk through it unscathed. If this is combined with the emphasis on changing one's criteria for right and wrong according to context, thorough understanding paradoxically results in both detachment and attachment. This is because one attaches oneself to every context in the sense that one fits it frictionlessly, but this fitting is possible precisely because one does not stick to or insist on any guidance or experience—in other words, one is detached from all guidance. If we view the text's daemonic people in this way, it is arguable that their transcendence is not necessarily the antithesis of particularism.

The theme of following one's nature mainly appears in the *Zhuangzi*'s Outer Chapters, which offer a fierce critique of economic, social, moral, and political norms. There is a story about Bo Le, the legendary horse tamer, who trains wild horses by trimming their hooves and fettering them with martingales and cruppers, contrary to the horses' inborn dispositions, which results in their death (22/9/2–4). Using this metaphor, the text claims that sages who establish and enforce norms of civilization actually build their achievements through suppressing and distorting people's inborn dispositions, which only include living a simple life without the influence of a commodity economy, formal organization, and political ideology. In a suppressive society, it is wrong to propose that people should fit the context they are living in. Even if one disagrees with the content of human nature here, one can still argue that fitting the context and forgetting right and wrong do not help one to challenge the status quo.

In response, it could be argued that if norms and institutions create too much friction, then there is no reason to make people fit into them. After all, it is advisable to change a pair of poorly fitting shoes. In the sociopolitical realm, ideal rulers are said to "follow the self-so of each thing and leave no room for partiality" (20/7/11), indicating that they refrain from interfering in things so that everything can act from itself (*ziran* 自然). If there is any norm that results in broad interference, then there is a reason to change or abolish it. It does not follow, however, that any norm that is not in accordance with human inborn nature should be rejected. It depends on how far one takes the theme of transformation to be. If people and things never cease changing, then insisting on taking humans' inborn dispositions as absolute guidance for society is yet another form of the completed heart-mind.

Responding to Confucian Criticism

As a text compiled in ancient China's "hundred schools" period, the *Zhuangzi* is a good reflection of the contemporaneous intellectual climate.[9] Other texts respond to the *Zhuangzi*'s ideas just as the *Zhuangzi* responds to theirs. Their dialogue and mutual criticism are carried forward throughout Chinese intellectual history. This section discusses some areas of disagreement between the *Zhuangzi* and Confucianism regarding the role of humankind and the source of morality.

Confucianism had already evolved into various versions by the time of the writing of the *Zhuangzi*. Mencius, for example, claims that humans are naturally inclined to act morally. Mencius does not formulate clear moral rules but proposes that one should make one's heart-mind the commander of one's person instead of following sensory pleasure or orders from the upper class.

The heart-mind contains sprouts (*duan* 端) that can spontaneously develop into four virtues: benevolence, rightness, observance of propriety, and wisdom. If this development is not thwarted or hastened, one will be capable of making reasonable judgments and actions in every context. This development is also essential to qualify as a mature human being. For Mencius, it is acceptable to say that how one should act in a particular context is not fixed by rules. Nevertheless, one must cultivate the development of sprouts in all contexts, because this is a distinctive human task and the only way to secure human happiness. Thus, the *Zhuangzi*'s view of fitting the context prescribes too little, as it does not emphasize the superiority of moral values over non-moral ones. Although one cannot judge whether a soldier is better than a teacher, or vice versa, one should be able to judge that a benevolent person is better than a non-benevolent one, despite any differences in the non-moral values they realize. Mencius thinks that the hierarchy of ethical status among things is not subject to change: those who can develop their sprouts to the fullest extent are always better than those who cannot, and those who can develop their sprouts to at least a certain extent should occupy a higher status than non-human creatures. For this reason, Mencius would say that the *Zhuangzi* overemphasizes the transformation of things.

Without further delving into these differences in the metaphysics of change, the *Zhuangzi* can respond to Mencius in two ways. The first is covered in its diagnosis of the completed heart-mind. Humans tend to think that there is something superior about human beings, but this belief can only be justified if we stick to the human perspective in the first place. Detachment from human civilization may even contribute to our happiness, if only by alleviating distinctive problems that human activities bring into the world.

The *Zhuangzi*'s second reply is that even if sprouts of virtue exist, it is unclear whether they can all be realized to the same extent simultaneously or whether they exist in the forms prescribed by Mencius's list in the first place. A comparison of philosophical traditions reveals significant differences in stipulating what attributes count as virtue and how one comes to possess virtue. Furthermore, developing non-moral traits such as equanimity may be more important than developing moral traits in some contexts, such as when one is too stressed to demand anything more from oneself or others. The disagreement mentioned in the previous section also gives reason to doubt that we should always take human nature as the measure of all things.

Another Confucian, Xunzi, disagrees with both Mencius and the *Zhuangzi*. He proposes that people should follow the guidance of propriety, which is not developed from human nature but designed by human deliberation and convention. The details of propriety may vary, but it is subject to certain constraints. These constraints are derived partly from environmental resources and partly from human biological, emotional, and social needs. These needs are more or less constant as long as we are born in human form. We need basic things such as food, safety, self-expression, and company, so we design rules to produce and distribute these things. In adapting to these rules, we form our own culture, which gradually becomes another good and constitutes another layer of constraint on our moral thoughts. Changes to moral rules, if needed, can only be achieved in our own cultural context. Therefore, for Xunzi, the *Zhuangzi*'s view of fitting the context ignores the fact that our needs and affinity with culture are relatively stable. We do not enter a fresh context every day. In this sense, Xunzi would also criticize the *Zhuangzi* for overemphasizing the transformation of things.

Again, the *Zhuangzi* has two lines of response. The first is also covered in its diagnosis of the completed heart-mind: culture both enhances and limits our abilities. Even if we assume that we cannot live meaningfully without culture and our culture inevitably shapes our moral reasoning, when we get more and more used to one culture, we risk losing the ability to appreciate other cultures. When we meet people from other cultures, our completed heart-mind leads us to urge them to conform to our moral norms, resulting in conflict or suppression. A better approach is to make requests based on norms that are accepted by others. In other words, when we want others to do x, we should show not only that x is justified but also that x is justified according to their own perspective. This means that sometimes we need to detach ourselves from our own culture and adopt others' perspectives to see why an action is advisable. The *Zhuangzi* can justify this detachment based not on its own proposal but on that of its opponents: avoiding conflict is a basic good that informs the formation of culture, according to Xunzi. If this detachment can help us to avoid conflict, there is at least a prima facie reason for a culture to incorporate it.

Another response involves questioning Xunzi's account of basic goods. For the sake of argument, we can regard Xunzi as allowing that the priority among those goods before human design and convention is indeterminate. For the *Zhuangzi*, however, whether something is a basic good is also indeterminate. The *Zhuangzi* often uses life as an example: "How do I know that delighting in life is not a delusion? How do I know that hating death is not like being one who lost their way in youth and no longer knows the way home?" (6/2/78–79). From an impartial perspective, without considering any particular species or entity, it is difficult to justify the claim that life is always good and death always bad, much less the claim that human life is always good. Many activities can be carried out only if there are living humans, but one needs to show that those activities are also valuable for non-human entities. That we cannot hear first-person testimonies about whether death is bad also renders one-sided the judgment that life is good. In real life, problems and disasters can become so great that one starts to doubt whether wishing for death or feeling happy for dead people is irrational. It is also possible to accept death calmly and suspend judgment about death's disvalue. Combining these points, the *Zhuangzi* would avoid universalizing even the value of life. The judgment that life is good is justified only in some contexts or from certain perspectives; thus we need a case-by-case analysis. This also applies to other basic goods.

Summary

As David Wong says, the pluralistic nature of the *Zhuangzi* and its self-interrogation should caution commentators against extrapolating a stable thesis from it (2005, 105). Accordingly, the current chapter presents the text as offering a bottom-up approach to ethics. Rather than setting up rules and virtues as guidance, the text orients readers toward the particularity and heterogeneity of contexts and one's spontaneous responses to them after the dissolution of prejudice. While this is not a definite, comprehensive interpretation, the chapter shows that the *Zhuangzi*'s reluctance to universalize judgments of right and wrong is intertwined with its emphasis on flexibility and transformation.

The disagreement between Daoism and Confucianism is complex, especially as neither side is a unified school with a single set of principles and methods. However, a key theme characterized this disagreement during the period when classical Daoist and Confucian texts were compiled, namely the role of human beings in the universe. Confucians believe that there is something distinctive about human lives, both at the individual level and at the social level, and that morality reflects the superiority of humans in one way or another. Daoists, however, remain skeptical about these two beliefs and blur the distinctions between moral and non-moral, human and non-human, and life and death, and eventually all distinctions. Rather than fixating on attachment or detachment, the ideal way of life sees no end to the interplay of attachment and detachment.

Notes

1. In this chapter, all translations of the *Zhuangzi* are my own, although I draw on the following commentaries and translations: Graham (1981), Mair (1994), Chen (2001), and Ziporyn (2020). The arrangement of chapters follows that of Chen (2001). All references to the Chinese *Zhuangzi* text are to Hong (1986), which can be accessed via the Chinese Text Project website (https://ctext.org/zhuangzi).

2. For a detailed discussion of the *Zhuangzi*'s linguistic style and its impact on Zen Buddhism, see Wang (2014).

3. The Zhuangzi and many other ancient Chinese texts do not draw a sharp distinction between emotion, judgment, and rational thought. This is one reason why it is not easy to separate "heart" and "mind" when translating *xin*.

4. This relationship becomes even more obvious when one notices that the Chinese character 官 can refer to both "organs" and "officials."

5. "Yue" refers to a southern state in ancient China.

6. The putative author of the *Zhuangzi*. There is no consensus on which, if any, stories about him are factual.

7. The Chinese character 齋 originally referred to abstinence from eating meat in preparation for important rituals. It is used in the *Zhuangzi* as a metaphor for "clearing away" preconceptions. See the fictional dia-

logue between Confucius and his most talented disciple, Yan Hui, at the beginning of chapter 4 of the *Zhuangzi* (8/4/1–9/4/34).

8. Readers who are interested in Chinese religion may argue that the description of ideal personhood reflects the religious rather than ethical nature of the text's vision.

9. For an overview of this period from a philosophical perspective, see Graham (1989).

Further Reading

Primary Sources

Chen, Guying. 2001. *Contemporary Annotations and Translations of the Zhuangzi*. Hong Kong: Chung Hwa Book Co. [In Chinese]

Graham, A. C. 1981. *Chuang-Tzu: The Seven Inner Chapters and Other Writings from the Book Chuang-tzu*. London: George Allen and Unwin Publishers.

Hong, Y., ed. 1986. *A Concordance to the* Zhuangzi. Shanghai: Shanghai Classics Publishing. [In Chinese]

Mair, Victor H. 1994. *Wandering on the Way: Early Taoist Tales and Parables of Chuang Tzu*. New York: Bantam Books.

Ziporyn, Brook. 2020. *Zhuangzi: The Complete Writings*. Indianapolis: Hackett Publishing Company.

Secondary Sources

Chong, Kim-chong. 2016. *Zhuangzi's Critique of the Confucians: Blinded by the Human*. Albany: State University of New York Press.

Fraser, Chris. 2008. "Psychological Emptiness in the Zhuāngzǐ." *Asian Philosophy* 18, no. 2: 123–47. https://doi.org/10.1080/09552360802218025.

———. 2009. "Skepticism and Value in the Zhuāngzǐ." *International Philosophical Quarterly* 49, no. 4: 439–57. https://doi.org/10.5840/ipq200949462.

———. 2014. "Wandering the Way: A Eudaimonistic Approach to the Zhuāngzǐ." *Dao: A Journal of Comparative Philosophy* 13, no. 4: 541–65. https://doi.org/10.1007/s11712-014-9402-1.

Graham, A. C. 1989. *Disputers of the Tao*. La Salle: Open Court.

Hansen, Chad. 1992. *A Daoist Theory of Chinese Thought: A Philosophical Interpretation*. New York: Oxford University Press.

Huang, Yong. 2010. "The Ethics of Difference in the *Zhuangzi*." *Journal of the American Academy of Religion* 78, no. 1: 65–99. https://doi.org/10.1093/jaarel/lfp082.

Lee, Jung H. 2014. *The Ethical Foundations of Early Daoism: Zhuangzi's Unique Moral Vision*. New York: Palgrave Macmillan.

Moeller, Hans-Georg. 2009. *The Moral Fool: A Case for Amorality*. New York: Columbia University Press.

Wang, Youru. 2014. *Linguistic Strategies in Daoist Zhuangzi and Chan Buddhism*. New York: Routledge.

Wong, David. 2005. "Zhuangzi and the Obsession with Being Right." *History of Philosophy Quarterly* 22, no. 2: 91–107. https://www.jstor.org/stable/27745016.

Yearley, Lee. 2010. "The Perfected Person in the Radical Zhuangzi." In *Experimental Essays on Zhuangzi*, edited by Victor H. Mair, 122–36. Dunedin: Three Pines Press.

15

Zen Buddhist Ethics
and the *Bodhisattva* Vow

RIKA DUNLAP

However innumerable sentient beings are,
I vow to save them;
However inexhaustible the passions are,
I vow to extinguish them;
However limitless Dharma-teachings are,
I vow to master them;
However supreme the Buddha-way is,
I vow to perfect it

—*The Four Bodhisattva Vows* (Kim 2004, 204)

Introduction

When I gave a talk on Zen Buddhism a few years ago, someone in the audience raised a hand and told me a story about Zen Buddhists monks who were collecting money to help the victims of the devastating earthquake that had hit northern Japan in 2011. While the story itself was nothing out of the ordinary, what struck me was her comment about this particular act of kindness—that she did not expect it from Zen Buddhist monks. Ever since then, I have been thinking about this comment and why charity was thought uncharacteristic of Zen Buddhist practices. Of course, we could easily shrug off this comment by attributing it to her ignorance. Yet I also think that it touches on misconceptions surrounding Zen Buddhism, and in particular Zen Buddhist ethics. Although many of these misconceptions do not merit any serious consideration, examining some of them may be a good starting point to investigate the charge that Zen Buddhism is an amoral or immoral religious tradition as a consequence of its teachings of emptiness, no-self, and its elusive *kōans*—the striking dialogues between Zen masters and their students that facilitate enlightenment for practitioners by helping them see the emptiness of all things.

My aim in this chapter is to explain why this charge of amorality or immorality is misguided by referring to the Zen Buddhist writings of Dōgen, a thirteenth-century Buddhist monk and the founder of Sōtō Zen in Japan. I argue that Zen Buddhism, despite its emphasis on emptiness, has its own ethics based in compassion: saving all sentient beings from suffering. Before establishing this point, however, I analyze how this charge may have emerged in the first place by explaining the emptiness of good and evil in Zen Buddhism. Thus, this chapter proceeds in the following order: I first illustrate the emptiness of good and evil in Zen Buddhism by analyzing some of the common misconceptions about Zen Buddhism. Once I dispel these misconceptions, I show that Zen Buddhism is not an amoral or immoral religious tradition by focusing on compassion and the *bodhisattva* ideal in Dōgen's philosophy.

For the sake of simplicity, I refer to Zen Buddhism as if it were one unified tradition in this chapter, although it is worth noting that this is far from the truth. So even though I refer to Dōgen's writings as representative of Zen Buddhism, we should keep in mind that Zen Buddhism refers to an umbrella of living traditions with different sects, each with its own history, culture, practice, and community of followers.

The Emptiness of Good and Evil and the Sources of Misunderstanding

Zen belongs to Mahāyāna Buddhism, a school of Buddhism that focuses on saving all sentient beings from suffering. Mahāyāna

Buddhists call their tradition "the great-vehicle school" (*mahāyāna*) because their teachings intend to carry all sentient beings to enlightenment with practices that release them from suffering. In Buddhism, the enlightened ones are called Buddhas (Siddhārtha Gautama—"*the*" Buddha—in fact *became* a Buddha only when he achieved enlightenment). Buddhas are distinguished from *bodhisattvas*, beings who delay their own enlightenment to save all sentient beings from suffering first.[1] The *bodhisattva* path is characterized by compassion; caring for all without discrimination between self and others. From this short description of the *bodhisattva* vow, I think it is clear that Mahāyāna Buddhism has its own ethics with a focus on compassion, which should explain why Zen Buddhists were dedicated to charity to help the victims of the earthquake.

Nevertheless, while compassion is an important pillar of Mahāyāna ethics, Hajime Nakamura, a Japanese scholar of Buddhism from the twentieth century, asserts that the texts of Chan Buddhism[2] do not have many references to compassion compared with other sects of Chinese Buddhism (Nakamura 2010, 93). Nakajima cautiously states that a further study is necessary to establish the historical and theoretical background for this absence, but he thinks that it may be attributed to the Daoist influence on Chan, and in particular their suspicion of conventional norms and traditional moral values.[3]

In addition to the lack of references to compassion, there are some *kōans* that seem to positively suggest that Zen Buddhism may be amoral or even immoral. One example is the famous *kōan* of "Nansen Cutting the Cat in Half":

> Nansen Oshō [Chin: Nan-chuan] saw monks of the Eastern and Western halls quarreling over a cat. He held up the cat and said, "If you can give an answer, you will save the cat. If not, I will kill it." No one could answer, and Nansen cut the cat in two.
>   That evening Jōshū [Chin: Chao-chou] returned, and Nansen told him of the incident. Jōshū took off his sandal, placed it on his head, and walked out. "If you had been there, you would have saved the cat," Nansen remarked. (Sekida 2014, *Mumonkan* 14)

The lack of reference to compassion in Zen may be considered *a*moral (the absence of morality altogether), but this *kōan* sounds *im*moral (against morality) and contrary to the *bodhisattva* vow. Even though a cat is not human, it is a sentient being that is capable of feeling pain. If Buddhists are devoted to ending suffering for all, why did Nansen kill it?

There are multiple ways of answering to this question. But let me first start with the role of *kōans* in Zen Buddhism. It is important to keep in mind that *kōans* are not to be read literally or as the instructions on how to respond in a given situation. The main aim of *kōans* is therapeutic rather than instructive: to make you see the problems and dissolve them by challenging the problematic assumptions therein. They are to be read metaphorically as an expedient means to bringing people to enlightenment by awakening them from misguided conceptions that impede enlightenment. Therefore, even though this *kōan* talks about a cat, we should not think of the cat literally as a cat. Instead, we should reflect and think about what the cat symbolizes. This particular *kōan* is therefore not suggesting that what Nansen did was absolutely necessary for enlightenment, but instead it challenges us to consider what each of us might have done to respond to the master's challenge.

Second, and more importantly, we must keep in mind the Buddhist teachings of no-self, emptiness, and dependent origination when reading the *kōans*, for the conversations therein convey these teachings in various forms. Emptiness is a central theme in the Mādhyamika school of Mahāyāna Buddhism and is essential to understanding the teachings of no-self and dependent origination. According to the Mādhyamika school, emptiness is the middle way (literally "*mādhyamika*") that transcends the duality of being and non-being (Sanskrit: *bhāva* and *svabhāva*, respectively) because no-self (Sanskrit: *anātman*) means that self is empty of an enduring self-nature or an essence.

But lacking an essence does not mean that self does not exist or that the self is unreal. According to Thich Nhat Hanh, a contemporary Vietnamese Zen Buddhist monk, no-self is equivalent to what he calls "interbeing," the idea that "[n]othing has a separate existence or a separate self" (Hanh 1998, 133). No-self therefore does not mean unreality, but that the self is impermanent and depends on everything else to be in the world (dependent origination). The teaching of no-self is that self is empty of an essence, inasmuch as it is becoming what it is in each moment in the flux of the transient world. Think of the self as a river that never stops flowing. Without the flowing water, the river stops being a river, so the river is always going through change. In addition, the flowing water is always shaping and being shaped by the surrounding environment.

A lack of understanding that the self is impermanent and dependent on everything else to become what it is in each moment is a significant source of suffering. Accordingly, many of the *kōans* are therapeutic in the sense that they aim to deconstruct our conception of self as something permanent with an unchanging essence.

In this specific *kōan*, there are some salient points that we need to highlight to understand its significance. For example, according to Katsuki Sekida, we should focus not on what the monks were quarreling about (a cat), but rather *that* they were quarreling:

> What they were quarreling about is not known and is unimportant. The point is that they were quarreling, and in this instance the object of the quarrel is personified by a cat. At the bottom of all disputes, egocentric thinking is invariably present. Even though there seems to be no egotism, and one may suppose oneself to be acting objectively, differences of temperament, ideals, understanding, and background inevitably bring about subjective—that is, self-centered—thinking. How is the dispute to be settled? Kill the cat. But what is the cat? (Sekida 2014, *Mumonkan 14*)

This interpretation by Sekida emphasizes the therapeutic dissolution of the problem in this *kōan*: that we need to act without the egoism that gives rise to a dispute in the first place, regardless of what this dispute may be ostensibly about. In other words, we should understand this *kōan* as Nansen's attempt to stop the disagreement that divides the assembly.

We can also look at Dōgen's comment on this *kōan* in Book 1.6 of the *Shōbōgenzō Zuimonki*:

> If I had been Nan Ch'uan, I would have said, "Even if you can speak, I will kill it; and if you can't speak I will also kill it. Who quarrels over the cat? Who saves the cat?" In behalf of the community, I would say, "We

> cannot speak; go ahead and kill the cat, teacher!" Or
> I would say in behalf of the community, "The teacher
> only knows about one stroke cutting into two pieces; he
> does not know about one stroke cutting into one piece."
> (Ejō 1980, 1.6)

Given that egotism emerges from the problematic discrimination between self and others, Dōgen thinks that it is necessary to dissolve this dichotomy (the division into opposing parts). Interestingly, in his comment on this *kōan*, Dōgen problematizes the dichotomies that are present in the master's remarks too, such as that of speaking and not speaking, that of killing and not killing, and the dichotomous act of cutting in half. So even if the master is trying to stop the quarrel that divides the assembly, his remarks too are full of dichotomies, and Dōgen makes it clear that the best response would be to point that out. Hence, Dōgen says that he would kill it regardless of speaking or not speaking, which indicates that these two choices that the master gave actually create another false dichotomy. Dōgen also adds, "When the assembly did not reply, if I were Nan Ch'uan I would say the assembly had already spoken and would have released the cat" (Ejō 1980, 1.6). This comment also blurs the dichotomy of speaking and not speaking by stating that silence is a form of speech. When Dōgen says as a response to the assembly that the teacher should cut in one piece, Dōgen suggests yet again that the act of cutting in half is a dichotomy, so we need to cut (dissolve) this divide into one. In short, Dōgen sees that the main point of the *kōan* is to recognize the problem of dichotomous thinking, especially the dichotomy of self and other that splits the assembly. Whatever words help to overcome this misguided thinking are acceptable.

In summary, the Buddhist teachings of no-self, emptiness, and dependent origination are important in understanding Zen Buddhist ethics, and the *kōans* are not to be read literally but rather metaphorically and therapeutically, as a way to dissolve the dichotomous thinking that causes us to suffer.

With this in mind, we can now examine the teaching of the emptiness of good and evil. This teaching is that which is most susceptible to misunderstanding in Zen Buddhist ethics. To analyze this issue, let me introduce Dōgen's own interpretation of

"*Shoakumakusa*," a fascicle of the *Shōbōgenzō* that focuses on the Buddhist precepts, which state:

> Refraining from committing various evils 諸悪莫作 *Shoakumakusa*

> Carrying out all sorts of good actions 衆善奉行 *Shuzenbugyō*

> Personally clarifying this mind 自浄其意 *Jijyōgoi*

> This is the essential teaching of all the Buddhas. 是諸仏教 *Zeshobukkyō* (Dōgen 2004, 220)

Traditionally speaking, the first line of "*Shoakumakusa*" is to be read as a prescription, that one must refrain from committing various evils. However, Dōgen alters this reading to elucidate his understanding of Buddhist ethics based on the emptiness of all. From the perspective of emptiness, one must see good and evil as dependent on each other and thus empty of an enduring essence. To illustrate this point, Dōgen develops his own interpretation of the first Buddhist precept and changes the meaning of "*makusa*," from "Do no evil" to "Non-production of evil." This is a radical reinterpretation that changes the meaning of the precept from the prescription of what one ought not to do to the description of how things are. "*Makusa*" in Japanese consists of two characters "莫作." The first character means "not to" or "refrain from," and the second character "making" or "doing." While the original meaning of the precept is a prescription—it tells one what one ought to do—Dōgen thinks that from the perspective of emptiness there is no essence of evil or good. Evil arises contextually and emerges with the good; hence the Zen Buddhist cannot be prescribing that we do no evil. Therefore, Dōgen changes the meaning of *makusa* such that it alters this teaching from "Do no evil" to "Non-production of evil."[4]

This non-production of evil from the perspective of emptiness is often misunderstood as a licensing of evil action due to good and evil ultimately lacking any absolute ground. In other words, some mistakenly think that because evil lacks any essential self-nature, nothing one does can be evil. However, this is a grave misunderstanding of the emptiness of evil. Buddhism teaches no-self, but it does not mean that self does not exist or that self is unreal. Instead, it means that self lacks an essence or a permanent self-nature; that self emerges with everything else. If someone were to therefore say, "There is no evil, thus I am incapable of committing evil," this is a misunderstanding of emptiness. Here, the emptiness of evil is equated with the absence of evil altogether. But this is a nihilistic error that treats emptiness itself as if it had an essence: that of non-being.

Instead, to appreciate the nature of evil for Zen, we must remember that emptiness is the middle way: it transcends the duality of being and non-being. It is therefore wrong to essentialize emptiness as non-being or to reify it as ultimate reality. Furthermore, think of what the absence of good and evil might entail: if anything is acceptable without any distinction between good and evil, then what is the point of Buddhism anyway? Do Buddhist practices not assume that there is a superior form of life, namely the Buddhist way of life with the vow to end suffering for all? Does it not assume that some forms of life are *better* than others?

To put it another way, even though dichotomous thinking can be problematic, it does not mean that we can get rid of these distinctions completely, especially when it comes to an important distinction between a crude form of life that is full of delusion and a superior form of life according to the Buddha way. Hence, the Buddhist teaching of emptiness is not to be essentialized, most especially when it comes to the emptiness of good and evil. Emptiness is the middle way that transcends being and non-being because it is empty of any enduring essence, including the essence of non-being or nothing. Hence, the emptiness of evil should not be taken to mean that there is no evil at all. Instead, we should understand the emptiness of evil as saying that evil emerges contextually with good. We therefore need to see evil as dependently arising in the network of the ever-complex and fleeting conditions of our lives.

Compassion and the Bodhisattva Ideal

So far, I have shown that the emptiness of good and evil in Zen Buddhism does not mean that it is an amoral or immoral philosophy. What guides these meanings of good and evil is the *bodhisattva* vow to save all sentient beings from suffering. To better understand Zen Buddhist ethics in light of the *bodhisattva* vow, let us examine Dōgen's writings on *bodhisattvas* and Buddhist practices of compassion.

Hee-Jin Kim, a renowned scholar of Dōgen's Buddhism, explains that Dōgen was against the popular interpretation of Buddhist ethics as "beyond good and evil," the interpretation that I just explained as the misunderstanding of emptiness (Kim 2004, 221). For Dōgen, enlightenment is always bound by the *bodhisattva* vow to help to cease suffering, and anything one does has to be governed by this vow. Thus, Kim explains Dōgen's view of the emptiness of good and evil in the following way: "The moral values of good, evil, and neutral did not exist in themselves or for themselves with any independent metaphysical status, because they were nothing more than the temporary configurations resulting from infinitely complex interactions of conditions. In brief, good and evil did not have the self-same metaphysical ground or source; they were without self-nature (*mujishō*) and were the unattainable (*fukatoku*), to use customary Buddhist phraseology" (2004, 224–25). Despite lacking a metaphysical grounding of morality, Dōgen is adamant about following the Buddhist precepts. Kim thinks this is because "moral precepts, norms, and values were the concrete expressions of the way of *bodhisattva*-hood governed by wisdom and compassion" (2004, 223). Dōgen is perfectly clear that "these norms were not fixed values to which we legalistically conform, but living expressions of the bodhisattva's free and pure activities in accordance with circumstances and occasions" (2004, 223). Hence, Kim explains that one of the central concerns for Dōgen was "how to live out relativity without falling into the trap of relativism, or how to realize spiritual freedom and purity amid radical relationality" (2004, 224). In other words, the greatest challenge for Zen Buddhists is to figure out the most appropriate response in light of the *bodhisattva* ideal of compassion while also heeding the fleeting conditions of our lives and distinguishing the salient features in the particularity of our own personal struggles.

Zen Buddhist ethics of compassion, therefore, becomes much more like what Aristotle says about virtues: we can only give the general rules of thumb, for much depends on the context. Thus, there are some epistemological questions that arise with the ambiguity of living out relativity without relativism; it is hard to know how to apply Buddhist ethics to our everyday life, given that it requires our creative response to the fleeting conditions while also being true to the *bodhisattva* ideal. For now, let me address the question of how to apply Zen Buddhist ethics in our everyday life with the general rules of thumb, with which we can aim to enact a good response in a given situation.

What are these rules of thumb for Zen Buddhist ethics? For Dōgen, compassion finds its concrete expression in anything that conforms to the non-discrimination of self and other. Specifically, Dōgen refers to the four virtues of the *bodhisattva* in the *Shōbōgenzō*: 1. giving (*fuse* 布施), 2. loving speech/kind speech (*aigo* 愛語), 3. service for the welfare of all being/beneficial action (*rigyō* 利行), and 4. identity with others/identity action (*dōji* 同事) (Kim 2004, 208).

Let me explain these briefly. *Fuse* is usually defined as alms-giving and is required of a *bodhisattva* in Buddhism more generally. But according to Dōgen, "giving" is the same as any action without greed. So *fuse* is not just about charity in the traditional sense. Dōgen says that any action can be a form of giving if done without any greed. According to Dōgen, "To launch a boat or build a bridge is an act of giving. If you study giving closely, you see that to accept a body and to give up the body are both giving. Making a living and producing things can be nothing other than giving. To leave flowers to the wind, to leave birds to the seasons, are also acts of giving" (Dōgen 2012, 474). According to Dōgen, then, everything we do should be a form of almsgiving. This attitude is especially crucial for anyone who pursues the *bodhisattva* ideal of compassion.

Second, "loving speech" or "kind speech" means anything that you say with the heart of compassion: "kind speech arises from kind heart, and kind heart from the seed of compassionate heart" (Dōgen 2012, 475). According to Dōgen:

> When you see sentient beings, you arouse the heart of compassion and offer words of loving care. It is contrary to cruel or violent speech.
>
> Praise those with virtue; pity those without it. If kind speech is offered, little kind speech expands. Thus, even kind speech that is not ordinarily known or seen comes into being. Be willing to practice it for this entire present life; do not give up, world after world, life after life. Kind speech is the basis for reconciling rulers and subduing enemies. Those who hear kind speech from you

have a delighted expression and a joyful mind. Those who hear of your kind speech will be deeply touched; they will always remember it. (2012, 475)

The third and fourth virtues are closely related to the nonduality of self and other. "Beneficial action" is any action that benefits all sentient beings. To benefit others is to benefit self or vice versa precisely because self and others are nondually connected to each other. This point is evident when Dōgen says, "Foolish people think that if they help others first, their own benefit will be lost, but this is not so. Beneficial action is an act of oneness, benefiting self and others together" (2012, 475). What is significant here is that Dōgen extends this benefit to not only sentient beings, but also insentient beings, such as grass, trees, wind, and water. After all, sentient beings dependently arise with insentient beings in the world. Therefore, many of Dōgen's writings have references to mountains, waters, and stones as preaching the Buddhist teaching. From this, some argue that there are some ecological implications in Zen Buddhism that are not necessarily emphasized in other forms of Buddhism.[5]

"Identity action" is to see the "nondifference" of self and others. Thus, it is closely linked with the third virtue of beneficial action. We can see that these virtues function as the general rules of thumb for those who are on the path to enlightenment in addition to the Buddhist precepts of what one ought to do or ought not to do. All of this guidance aims at the *bodhisattva* ideal of compassion based on the non-discrimination of self and others as an overcoming of an egocentric view. Therefore, the emptiness of self and other is what motivates Zen Buddhist ethics in a nutshell.

Summary

Dōgen explains, "Arousing the aspiration for enlightenment is making a vow to bring all sentient beings [to the shore of enlightenment] before you bring yourself, and actualizing the vow. Even a humble person who arouses this aspiration is already a guiding teacher of all sentient beings" (2012, 655). From these references to compassion and the *bodhisattva* vow and virtues, I think it is abundantly clear that Zen Buddhism is not amoral or immoral.

Even if it is hard to determine conclusively what one ought to do in any given situation, it does not mean that one need not try to seek out the best response in these fleeting conditions and the uncertainty of life using the guiding light of compassion. Even though there is much diversity within Zen Buddhism with their various communities of practitioners and followers around the world, the *bodhisattva* vow to end suffering is and should be the moral compass for all Zen Buddhists regardless of their distinct and wide-ranging practices.

Notes

1. This distinction between Buddhas and *bodhisattvas* is sometimes blurred.
2. "Chan" is the Chinese transliteration of 禅, while Zen is the Japanese transliteration of the same character.
3. Chan originated in China during the Tang dynasty as a Sinicized Buddhist tradition. There are some obvious overlaps of ideas between Daoism and Chan Buddhism. For instance, the Madhyamaka teaching of emptiness was equated with the Daoist teaching of *wu*: nothingness (無). However, Nakajima emphasizes that the absence of references to compassion does not necessarily imply that Chan Buddhists did not practice it. Furthermore, Japanese Zen Buddhist texts, especially those written by Eisai, who introduced Rinzai Zen in the twelfth century, explicitly refer to compassion more frequently as the important pillar of Zen: that compassion is to act on the nonduality of self and other, to think of the benefit of others as my own.
4. Dōgen changes the meaning of words in many of his writings. This radical reinterpretation or an intentional misreading of a text is supposed to indicate that the meanings of words need to be understood contextually.
5. See "Mountains and Waters Sutra" or "Valley Sounds, Mountain Colors" in the *Shōbōgenzō*.

Further Reading

PRIMARY SOURCES

Dōgen, The *Shōbōgenzō*. Vol. 1. Edited by Fumio Masutani. Tokyo: Kōdansha Gakujyutsubunko, 2004.

————. *The Treasury of the True Dharma Eye: Zen Master Dōgen's Shōbōgenzō*. Edited by Kazuaki Tanahashi. Boulder: Shambhala, 2012.

Ejō. *Record of Things Heard from the Treasury of the Eye of the True Teaching*. Translated by Thomas Cleary. Boulder: Prajñā Press, 1980.

Sekida, Katsuki. *Two Zen Classics: The Gateless Gate and the Blue Cliff Records*. Boston: Shambhala, 2014.

SECONDARY SOURCES

Kim, Hee-Jin. 2004. *Eihei Dōgen: Mystical Realist*. Somerville, MA: Wisdom Publications.

Mikkelson, Douglas. 1997. "Who Is Arguing about the Cat? Moral Action and Enlightenment According to Dōgen." *Philosophy East and West* 47, no. 3 (July): 383–97.

Nakajima, Hajime. 2010. *Jihi* (慈悲). Tokyo: Kōdansha Gakujyutsubunko.

Nhat Hanh, Thich. 1998. *The Heart of the Buddha's Teaching*. New York: Harmony.

Uchiyama, Kōshō. 2018. *Deepest Practice, Deepest Wisdom*. Translated by Daitsū Tom Wright and Shōhaku Okumura. Somerville: Wisdom Publications.

16

Ethical Dimensions of Advaita Vedānta

SANDHYA PRUTHI

Introduction

This chapter examines the ethical aspect of the Indian philosophical system, Advaita Vedānta. Vedānta is one of the six orthodox systems of Indian philosophy: Sāṅkhya, Yoga, Nyāya, Vaiśeṣika, Pūrva-mīmāṁsā (popularly known as Mīmāṁsā), and Uttara-mīmāṁsā (popularly known as Vedānta). These six systems are called orthodox because they believe in the authority of the Vedas. Vedānta itself has various sub-schools: the Advaita Vedānta of Śaṅkara, Śivādvaita of Kashmira, Śuddhādvaita of Vallabha, Bhedābheda of Nimbārka, Viśiṣṭādvaita of Rāmānuja, Dvaita of Madhva, and Acintyabhedābheda of Caitanyamahāprabhu.

Here we focus mainly on Vedānta philosophy as elaborated by Śaṅkara. Śaṅkara enjoyed great fame as a saint and reformer of the Hindu ethos. According to general agreement, he was active between 788 and 820 AD. He developed the philosophy of Vedāntic non-dualism ("Advaita" literally means "non-dual") into a full-fledged philosophical system.

Śaṅkara's Advaita Vedānta conceives the non-dual consciousness as the ultimate reality. It emphasizes the realization of non-dual consciousness in this (embodied) life in which, most of the time, consciousness—or self—remains entangled with the mind-body complex, which generates the false view about the world or about oneself. Advaita Vedānta holds that we therefore ought to consider the "self" under two main aspects: the self from the perspective of primal nescience or ignorance (that is, the non-dual self as it exists as identified with the mind-body complex) and the non-dual nature of the self (consciousness) from the point of view of supreme reality (Brahman). The most important feature of the non-dualistic Vedānta ethics is this metaphysical foundation. Śaṅkara's ethics is inseparably connected with his metaphysics and cannot be adequately understood without a sufficient understanding of it.

The central goal of Advaita Vedānta is liberation (*mokṣa*) through self-realization, understood as the realization of the identification of the self with the absolute (Brahman). The Muṇḍaka Upaniṣad 3.2.9 clearly states that the "knower of Brahman becomes Brahman himself." This means that the goal of Advaita Vedānta is not merely knowledge, but also a concrete state of existence in which the knower and the known, the subject and the object, the cognizer and the cognition, the good person and the goodness, merge into one complete whole: the absolute truth, knowledge, and infinity. Hence, for Śaṅkara, self-realization is a spiritual experience (*Brahmānubhava*); it is not merely a theoretical/philosophical knowledge of the Absolute.

Vedānta's basic doctrine, that the supreme reality—the non-dual self—is not only truth, but also absolute bliss (*ānanda*), makes the Vedāntic thought an ethico-metaphysical theory; a synthesis of theory and practice, of intellectual understanding and self-realization. The highest goal of Advaitic ethics—*mokṣa*—signifies perfection not only in the theoretical sphere but also in the practical sense of rising above all the contradictions of pleasure and pain, praise and blame, loss and gain, and even right and wrong and good and evil. Advaitic ethics points out that the spiritual aspect of human nature is its divinity. This divinity as infinite consciousness is eternal, perfect, and blissful. Hence, Advaita regarded morality to be the necessary antecedent of knowledge of Brahman.

Advaita Vedānta Metaphysics

According to Advaita Vedānta, the spiritual aspect of human nature is (non-dual) consciousness. It is this consciousness as an independent principle that is thought to be divine. Realization of the absolute in non-dualistic philosophy is attainable by human beings through spiritual discipline. When realization of the absolute has been attained, the relative nature of morality is transcended. In other words, morality is a lower stage that is ultimately transcended by the seeker of truth.

According to Śaṅkara, the day-to-day phenomenal world is real from the empirical (or *vyāvahārika*) point of view and unreal from the transcendental (or *pāramārthika*) point of view. In like manner, from the empirical point of view, Brahman is not only immanent cause, source of all, but also man's highest spiritual value. All things spring from Brahman, thrive on Brahman, and ultimately merge into Brahman (Chāndogya Upaniṣad 3.14.1). In this sense, Brahman is the all-pervasive, omniscient, omnipresent, and omnipotent basis and background of the entire visible universe. It is both the material cause as well as the efficient cause of the cosmic creation. In other words, everything *is* Brahman (material cause), and everything is also created *by* Brahman (efficient cause).

From the transcendental point of view, Brahman is truth, knowledge, and infinity without any attributes; that is, Brahman is not limited by any qualities whatsoever (Taittirīya Upaniṣad 2.1.1). To characterize Brahman in any way ("Brahman is *x*"; "Brahman is not *y*") is to put limits on it; Brahman is absolute, and so unlimited. The same can be said about individual selves (*jīva*). A self is a being that experiences change, becoming, and plurality at the empirical (*vyāvahārika*) level; but at the transcendental level, that same individual self is identical with the spiritual, infinite, universal Brahman.

Śaṅkara is emphatic that knowledge of Brahman, which amounts to self-realization, is the sole gateway to *mokṣa*. Sarvepalli Radhakrishnan, Advaitic philosopher and former president of India, describes *mokṣa* as follows: "To realize Brahman is the end of all activities, or the realization of the identity with the infinite reality, is the final end of life. Until it is reached, the finite soul is at unrest with itself. The only object that can give us permanent satisfaction is the experience of Brahman (*Brahmānubhava*). It is the supreme state of joy and peace and the perfection of individual development" (Radhakrishnan 1958,613). The word *Brahmānubhava*, which means the experience of Brahman, is worth noting carefully. Śaṅkara uses this term frequently, indicating thereby that Brahman-experience is not merely a concept or an ideal beyond the empirical pale, but is rather and more exactly an actual experience that the individual undergoes. This fact also explains the acceptance of *jīvanmukti* (those who become enlightened while existing in this body) by Śaṅkara. *Mokṣa* is therefore ethico-spiritual and so is neither merely ethical nor merely spiritual.

Śaṅkara's view of metaphysics and ethics is that human beings are truly the highest reality. The essential characteristic of human beings is that they can and should behave in accordance with the empirical, pluralistic nature of the world, but also that they can and should realize (see) the underlying spiritual unity (i.e., unity of all beings and all differences, including the lack of distinction between one *jīva* and another) of the visible pluralistic universe.

The divorce between the empirical and the transcendental is the sole cause of the partial and imbalanced development of human personality. Because of this dual nature, Śaṅkara gives equal weight to ethical duties—which are necessary for the material progress (*abhyudaya*) of the individual and of society—and to the spiritual duty necessary for the attainment of *mokṣa* (liberation). Hence, though *jīvanmukti* is the final or the ultimate stage of enlightenment, Śaṅkara does not wish away the stages prior to the final one. These stages can be thought of as a ladder on which one climbs to the height at which the highest good becomes attainable. Hence, the discipline of these earlier stages is essential for the seeker of Brahman.

Śaṅkara is at pains to stress that it is only at the highest stage that the distinctions of the knower and the known and the doer and the act vanish, and that not recognizing these dualities at the practical, everyday level would amount to foolishness. This explains why Śaṅkara time and again refers to the utility of morality and meditation (*karma and upāsanā*) for the aspirant. Since the approach to the spiritual state of eternal life is by way of the intellect, moral life—which he considers the only means of the intellectual development of the individual—cannot and should not be given up altogether. A synthesis of knowledge and action is required (Brahmasūtra 3.1.7). Liberation involves an all-around realization involving a complete transformation of the whole consciousness. To secure this firm attitude of the soul, it is necessary to go through not only intellectual training, but moral discipline as well.

Ethics as *Mokṣasādhana*

The most basic criterion for moral judgment recommended by Advaita is that those acts, desires, and thoughts that lead the moral agent to the highest good, namely, self-realization, are "good," and that those that lead him toward the fulfillment of egoistic desire, so far as they prevent self-realization, are "bad." All activities of the *jīva* who has not realized his true Self—whether they be mental (*mānasika*), verbal (*vācika*), or physical (*kāyika*), and no matter how noble or altruistic they may appear to be—suffer, according to Advaita, from the fact that they are rooted in a pleasure-seeking desire; consequently, unless transformed and redirected, they prevent one from attaining self-realization. According to the Kaṭha Upaniṣad (I.2.1), for instance, "the good (*śreyaḥ*) is one thing, the pleasant (*preyaḥ*) is another, and he who chooses the pleasant, falls from his true goal." The good is spiritual wisdom and self-knowledge; the pleasant is sensuous satisfaction or ego gratification: the good is the Real; the pleasant is the phenomenal.

Those activities of the self, then, that are so grounded in egoistic desire are bad, and those transformed and redirected activities that lead one to the good are good. Stated baldly, as long as an act, desire, or thought leads one along the path of realization, it is morally justified, according to Advaita Vedānta. The end does justify the means, provided that the end is the highest value, the *summum bonum*, self-realization. Apart from its general adherence to the traditional code of conduct, as it is limited or confined to the social order within the phenomenal world, this is the sole moral criterion proffered by the Upaniṣads as set forth in systematic Advaita.

A list of qualifications is drawn up by Vedānta for an aspirant to attain moral purification for achieving absolute knowledge. These are:

a) *nityānityavastuviveka*, i.e., knowledge of what is eternal/permanent and what is transient/ephemeral.

The word permanence here denotes truth. The systematic practice of discrimination between the eternal and the transient, and the unfailing choice of the permanent, leads to the evaluation of the whole world of empirical experience as incapable of satisfying the seeker's hunger for the eternal. This has been beautifully explained by a discourse in Bṛhadāraṇyaka Upaniṣad 2.4.2–5, where Maitreyī, wife of the sage Yājñavalkya, asks him, "Sir, if this whole earth filled with wealth were mine, would I be immortal through that? [and is answered], no, of immortality there is no hope through wealth" (Radhakrishnan 2015,195).

> b) *ihāmutrārthaphalabhogavirāga*, i.e., shrinking from all the rewards of this world and the world to come.

This consists in a renunciation of the enjoyments of this life and of the heavenly life after death. It is well-known that we are drawn toward external objects through our senses and derive pleasure from them. But we are not able to have stable or abiding satisfaction from them. Objects are transient, and so are the pleasures derived from them. A human being must feel the profoundly unsatisfactory character of all worldly enjoyments before he can profit by the teachings of the Vedānta. *Ihāmutrārthaphalabhogavirāga* is therefore a desire to renounce all personal longings to attain a pure, lofty, unprejudiced view of the ultimate reality.

> c) The third requirement is the cultivation of the six virtues: restraint of mind / mental tranquility (*śama*); restraint of body / self-control (*dama*); fortitude / renunciation / dispassion (*uparati*); endurance / resignation (*titikṣā*); concentration / intentness of mind (*samādhi*); and faith / belief in the scriptural texts (*śradhhā*).

Śama, that is, tranquility, signifies victory over mind won through dispassion. *Dama* refers to control over the sense organs. *Uparati* is the formal renunciation of the acts enjoined by the Vedas, including the obligatory and occasional ones. *Titikṣā* is the stoic endurance of dualities like heat and cold. *Samādhi* is intellectual alertness acquired by the avoidance of sleepiness, indolence, and carelessness. Finally, *śraddhā* is receptiveness regarding knowledge from the scriptures and teachers. These six virtues are the fruits of intense moral training. They are based on the Upaniṣadic dictum "therefore, having become calm, subdued, quiet, patiently enduring and collected one sees the Self in his own self, sees all in the Self" (Bṛhadāraṇyaka Upaniṣad 4.4.23 and Brahmasūtra 3.4.27).

> d) Last, we have *mumukṣatva*, i.e., a keen sense of the vanity and suffering-riddled nature of the world and eagerness to be free from it.

Mumukṣatva presupposes the three preceding qualifications. But it is an additional insight to realize one's essential nature and to feel one is dissatisfied with one's life as it is at present. As Isherwood puts it, "Most people feel content the way they are, but great ones doubt and question this complacency of the herd-mind" (1949, 3). In addition to the intolerable sense of the limitations of the present, *mumukṣatva* is also the foundation of the hope of liberation.

What matters most when it comes to the above qualifications is an eagerness for self-knowledge. Just as only the knower of the self can cross over sorrow, and only a clean mirror can faithfully reflect objects, a pure and disciplined mind alone can apprehend the absolute.

The practice of these principles and their perfection excludes the possibility of any egoistic or antisocial conduct. As Govind Chandra Pande describes it:

> The liberated person transcends *dharma* as prescription or prohibition but illustrates the ideal virtues of egolessness and universal compassion, detachment and desirelessness, peace and harmony as illustrated by the description of the *sthitaprajña* in whom the moral will is transmuted into the spontaneity of the holy will. Such a person must regard others as the same as himself and cannot make any invidious distinctions. Although he has no personal ends to serve, he must inevitably help any genuine seeker of truth. This is the characteristic kind of service which belongs to the *jñānin*. (1994, 241)

Through this training, "impurities are removed by dutiful actions, while knowledge is the supreme movement. When actions have burnt up impurities, knowledge emerges" (Brahmasūtra Śaṅkara commentary 3.4.26). The significance of the moral life consists in the constant endeavor to make this principle more and more explicit. Vedāntic ethics consists in training an individual to rise to a state of monistic realization, universal kinship, and unity of spirit. The practical ideal of Vedāntic ethics is the divine solidarity of the world-life as a fact of one's immediate consciousness (Bhagavadgītā 3.20).[1]

We might note here how Śaṅkara in his commentary to the Īśa Upaniṣad (5 and 6) links two Vedic verses. First, he highlights the verse "the self that is within all" (Bṛhadāraṇyaka Upaniṣad 3.4.1) and then associates it with the verse "when a man sees all beings in this self and the self in all beings, he feels no hatred" (Īśa Upaniṣad 6). In this commentary he claims that such a sense of identification extends even to inanimate objects. In addition to presenting us with the potential for an Advaitin environmental ethics, two important teachings follow from this: (a) Just as one who is fully satisfied can have no selfish desire, so he who is one with the self can feel no evil impulses; and (b) from the ultimate perspective of self-knowledge, the other is non-different from oneself. This gives an interesting twist to the notion that a motivational model of altruism, which focuses on the person's intentions and conscience, must allow for a combination of self-in-others and others-in-self (Śaṅkara's commentary on Bhagavadgītā 5.7).

We can therefore see that Śaṅkara does not deride or disparage action or morality in comparison with the knowledge of Brahman. The very fact that qualities like discrimination, self-devotion, self-control, and desire to attain *mokṣa*—which are all clearly ethical in nature—are accepted as qualifications for the students of the Vedānta goes to show how necessary a virtuous life is for a seeker of the ultimate truth.

Ritual Duties

The acceptance of the duties meant for different stages (*āśramas*) of life further shows how much importance Śaṅkara attaches to the embrace of ethical life as the means for the attainment of liberation. Brahmasūtra 3.4.19 says, "the duties laid down for the various *āśrama*s have to be performed as declared in Chāndogya Upaniṣad 2.23.1."

The term *āśrama-dharma* means the duties of the several classes of society and of the different stages of life. There is a two-fold classification of them: (i) those described as "general" (*sādhāraṇa-dharma*), which comprise acts involving virtues like kindness and truth speaking and are equally obligatory on all; and (ii) those termed "special" (*varṇāśrama-dharma*s), which are relative to one's social class (*varṇa*) and to the particular stage (*āśrama*) one has reached in life's discipline. These duties include the performance of rites and sacrifices. On the strength of the Upaniṣadic sanction of sacrifices and so forth, all religious activities assist in *cittaśuddhi* (clearness of mind), which is the prerequisite of attaining knowledge.

Hence, knowledge supervenes from actions only after ritual actions have purified uncleanliness. A person desirous of final release must be equipped with calmness and control over his sense organs because they are said to be the means by which knowledge can emerge. According to Bṛhadāraṇyaka Upaniṣad 4.4.23, "therefore, one who knows it to be so, sees the self, in the self itself, by becoming calm, subdued, satisfied, patient and collected" and also because what is so enjoined by the scriptures necessarily has to be followed. Hence, performance of *āśramakarma*s (duties related to a person's stage of life) and *nityakarma*s (obligatory Vedic duties) helps to obtain clearness of mind and further leads to knowledge of Brahman.

A Conflict Between Morality and Liberation

It is evident from the discussion so far that morality is accepted by Śaṅkara as the necessary means of attaining true knowledge of the self/Brahman. The cultivation of ethical virtues (*śama, dama,* etc.) constitute a prerequisite for knowing Brahman. At the same time, however, non-dualistic axiology (the study of value/ethics) does admit in principle the possibility of a conflict between morality and liberation. In other words, there can be a conflict between leading an impeccable moral life and a life devoted to the attainment of liberation. With Advaita Vedānta, this problem is allied to the implications of a strict interpretation of the doctrine of *māyā* and the contention that the ultimate reality is without qualities. (*Māyā* is the mysterious power that, through indefinable association with the Absolute, turns the non-qualitative Brahman into the qualitative, so that the unmanifested becomes manifested. It is the principle of individuation and the fullest explanation we can give of the visible universe in all the variety of its name and forms and the opportunities it presents for the existence and responsible activities of mankind.)

Śaṅkara warns us against attributing objective qualities to the subject, that is, we should not attempt to view the self as if it were merely an ordinary object, particularly conceived. The application of predicates to consciousness is illegitimate; even describing a consciousness with the predicate "exists" is inaccurate. Ascribing duality to consciousness—the idea that it (a subject) is separate from the things it knows (objects)—is a misrepresentation. In this sense, the world is *māyā* (illusion), and the lower knowledge (*apara-vidyā*) we have of this world is false. Our aim is to overcome this ignorance and realize our oneness with Brahman.

However, no matter how earnest the ethical aspirant may be and how successfully she might eliminate selfishness and be devoted to the interests of others, it is not obviously possible to get rid of the ego when it comes to ethical endeavor. After all, ethics is predicated on the difference between self and other. Ethical endeavor, even of the highest kind, is impossible except in conjunction with the assertion of individuality and personality. Yet without deliverance from even the limited egoism of the selfless person, the final state does not appear to be attainable. Hence, an aspirant's ethical development is not carried forward into the ultimate state, and the final state of *mokṣa* does not depend on the performance of any act (since acts presume the dualism of subject/object). We must conclude, then, that because the ego cannot be eliminated in moral progress, and yet the assertion of the ego renders impossible the attainment of the highest state, then if we seek *mokṣa*, ethics must be left behind. Ethics must be transcended if the end of ethics, that is, perfection, is to be attained.

Śaṅkara himself seems to support such a view. For him, activity, whether intellectual or practical, does not belong to the essence of the soul and is alien to the sphere in which higher knowledge (knowledge of Brahman) moves. Action has to do with what has not yet come into existence, whereas knowledge, and especially the knowledge of Brahman, has to do with something already existent.

It is concerned not with that which is to be, but with that which already *is*. Sureśvara[2] makes this idea clear while commenting on the Naiṣkarmyasiddhi 1.53: "self is neither *āpya* (to be attained) nor *utpādya* (to be generated or originated) nor *vikārya* (to be modified) nor *saṁskārya* (to be refined or purified), it is ever-existent, and is not something to be produced by action."

In the practical sphere, even if we confine our attention to action of the highest moral character, we cannot say, according to Śaṅkara, that liberating knowledge results from this. The self that even the most elevated action serves to purify is only the empirical self, whereas the self we wish to attain in the consummation of salvation is the unchangeable self, which can only be realized and cannot be improved or changed by the addition of good qualities or the removal of defects. Moral predicates are out of place with respect to any ultimate and ever-existent entity since the concept of morality is meaningless except in connection with activity.

A critic of Advaita Vedānta may therefore wonder whether it can assign any ultimate validity or value to morality that seems to be required when aiming for moral perfection, either individually or socially. Are the goals of morality and the highest condition of the soul inevitably different from—and in conflict with—each other?

For Śaṅkara, not only *may* we apply ethical predicates to the ultimate, but we *must* do so, if our ethical struggle is not to be meaningless and futile. The problem of ethics is to deal with the evil and sorrow of the world, and these cannot be dealt with adequately simply by relegating them to the sphere of unreality. As George Galloway puts it, "Spiritual selves claim to be real; and our consciousness of freedom and our sense of moral evil decline to be relegated to the category of illusions" (1922, 216). Evil cannot be overcome by denying its reality, especially when this is accompanied by a denial of the reality of the good as well. Evil cannot be overcome by negation, but only by a positive reality. Selfishness, for instance, can be overcome not merely by thinking about its dissipation but by an assertion or at least a consciousness of objective unselfishness. All great virtues are the result of faith in a positive impact of goodness.

Additionally, it is important to remember that the Vedānta does not maintain that the universe as it presents itself to the ordinary mind is simply illusion. It is true that the phenomenal world is the outcome of *avidyā*, but it has a certain relative reality. It is real for him who has not attained the knowledge of Brahman. Thus, Śaṅkara says, "the entire complex of phenomenal existence is considered as true so long as the knowledge of Brahman and the self of all has not arisen, just as the phantoms of a dream are considered to be true until the sleeper wakes" (Muller 1899, 202). The stage of lower knowledge (*aparā-vidyā*) provides a religious philosophy, relatively true, for those who have not attained the higher knowledge, even if from the view of higher knowledge (*para-vidyā*) all is false.

Śaṅkara's split-level ontology of ultimate and relative truth (*pāramārthika* and *vyāvahārika*) therefore proposes a non-egalitarian, two-level standard of ethics. Advaita recognizes a lower standpoint where all differences are real. At the empirical level we do feel the difference between one person and another even as we are alive to the difference between ourselves and God, and at this level there is full scope for all the obligations of moral life.

Summary

We can conclude, then, that (a) the ethical system described in part 3 has its place for those who have not yet realized Brahman as Self; (b) The four prerequisites discussed above support such provisional ethics; and (c) This system cannot be violated by any individual unless that particular individual has realized that he has no ultimate individuality and can further be judged that such an individual would be eventually behaving ethically. This is the gist of Śaṅkara's insistence on provisional ethics. In the commentary on the Bṛhadāraṇyaka Upaniṣad 3.5.1, he writes, "nor do we deny the validity, for the ignorant of actions with their factors and results while the relative world of name and form exists." Again in his commentary on Brahmasūtra 2.2.31, "for worldly behaviour, conforming as it does to all right means of valid knowledge can only be denied when a different eternal order of reality is attained, such an exception aside, tradition should prevail." Ethics ought to be seen as a soteriological device. But through the self-discipline that such a soteriological device involves, one can thrust out the false and misleading and proceed toward what is truly real: Brahman.

This training purifies the mind from sin and cultivates devotion toward duties that in turn prepare the base for possessing virtuous qualities and an edifice of self-realization.

Notes

1. Hence, the command to work for the welfare of the world, *"lokasaṅgraha"* (Bradley 1940, 267).

2. Sureśvara was a direct disciple of Śaṅkara and is believed to have been popular between the eighth and ninth centuries. He is known in the tradition as the *Vārttikakāra* (an author of the critical treatment of a commentary), and the tradition associated with him is called the *Vārttikakāra-prasthāna*. He is known for his three major works, *Naiṣkarmyasiddhi*, *Bṛhadāraṇyaka-bhāṣya-Vārttika*, and *Taittirīya-bhāṣya-Vārttika* (Potter 2015, vol. 3, 420).

A *vārttika* has been defined as a work that explains what is said (*ukta*), what is left unsaid (*anukta*), and what is imperfectly said (*durukta*) (Apte 1959, 1417).

Further Reading

PRIMARY SOURCES

Balasubramanian, R. 1988. *The Naiṣkarmyasiddhi of Sureśvara*. Madras: University of Madras.

Gambhirananda, Swami. 1995. *Bhagavadgītā*. 3rd ed. Calcutta: Advaita Ashram.

———. 2013. *Brahmasūtra Śaṅkarabhāṣya*. Kolkata: Advaita Ashrama.

Karmarkar, Raghunath Damodar. 1973. *The Māṇḍūkya Upaniṣad with Gauḍapāda's Kārikā and Śaṅkara Commentary*. Poona: Bhandarkar Oriental Research Institute.

Shastri. J. L. 2010. *Manusmṛti*. Delhi: Motilal Banarsidass.

SECONDARY SOURCES

Apte, Vaman Shivram. 1959. *The Practical Sanskrit-English Dictionary*. Poona: Prasad Prakashan.

Bradley, Andrew. 1940. *Ideals of Religion Gifford Lectures Delivered in the University of Glasgow in 1907*. London: Macmillan.

Galloway, George. 1922. *Religion and Modern Thought*. Edinburgh: Morrison and Gibb.

Isherwood, Christopher. 1949. *Vedānta for the Western World*. London: Allen and Unwin.

Muller, Max. 1899. *The Six Systems of Indian Philosophy*. London: Longsman, Green and Co.

Pande, Govind Chandra. 1994. *Life and Thought of Śaṅkarācārya*. Delhi: Motilal Banarsidass.

Potter, Karl H. 2015. *Encyclopedia of Indian Philosophies* Vol. 3. Delhi: Motilal Banarsidass Publishers.

Radhakrishnan, S. 1958. *Indian Philosophy*. Vol. II. London: George Allen and Unwin.

———. 2015. *The Principal Upaniṣads*. 25th ed. London: George Allen and Unwin.

17

Care Ethics

Love, Care, and Connection

ALLAUREN SAMANTHA FORBES

Introduction

Care ethics is best known as a paradigmatically feminist moral theory. And yet it is seldom treated with the same moral gravity as some of the other moral theories popular in Northern, Western, and liberal traditions.

Imagine that you find yourself in the Trolley Problem: a trolley is headed for five people tied to the track. In front of you is a lever that, if pulled, would divert the trolley to another track—one that has only one person tied to it. Anyone hit by the trolley will certainly die, and you are the only person with access to the lever. There is no way to reach the would-be victims, nor can the trolley divert without your help. What do you do?

This thought experiment has become a staple in moral theorizing in part because how we answer the question of what to do is thought to indicate the results of our moral intuitions as well as the moral values we endorse upon reflection. A common intuition is that it is morally worse for five people to die than only one—which would suggest that one ought to pull the lever—but it is also quite common for people to be uncomfortable with this option upon reflection because it means that they would, in effect, be killing someone rather than letting five people die. One of the most common questions that arises in the context of the Trolley Problem is this: do we know who the people on the tracks are? If, for example, the single person tied to the track is your child, would you still pull the lever? For many people, the answer is no: intuitively, there are special moral obligations in virtue of one's relationships to others. Care ethics does not require that we abstract away from these personal relations and their intuitive moral valences. As a view of what has moral value, it explains our intuition that we have a special obligation not to harm our loved ones.

CARE ETHICS

Moral theories purport to provide guidance on what matters and what one ought to do, morally speaking. In care ethics, care is the primary moral consideration. According to care ethicist Virginia Held, care is best understood as both a practice and a value by which we evaluate those practices (Held 2006, 10). To put this another way, caring is something we do, like parenting a child, but it is also a way of engaging in other tasks, such as adopting a caring attitude in one's teaching practices.

There are three core dimensions of care ethics as a moral theory: metaphysical, epistemological, and political. Metaphysically, care ethics views individuals as inherently relational beings (Held 2006, 14). Who we are is at least partly constituted by our relationships of care: parents or caregivers and their children; romantic partners and friends; teachers and students. This is because care ethics proceeds from the basis that humans begin as completely dependent beings, and while we do become more self-sufficient over time, most of us are interdependent—we need each other and are needed in turn (Held 2006, 10). So, for care ethics, the relationships of care between people have moral weight because they shape and sustain us. This, care ethicists argue, calls for a system of morality that is sensitive to the importance of noticing and meeting the needs of the people for whom we care.

With respect to the epistemic domain, care ethics values emotions as a means of knowing what is morally appropriate. As

Held points out, because it is the ethics of care, bare feelings are insufficient as moral guidance, but neither should they be ignored altogether: feelings can be valuable insights into salient moral features (such as the well-being of a loved one) in moral situations (Held 2006, 11). Moreover, moral theories that abstract away from the emotions altogether are rightly criticized for being so impartial as to be overly demanding or unrealistic. Most people do not approach moral decisions with complete dispassion or distance, especially when those decisions would bear on one's loved ones.

Finally, care ethics—as a feminist view—has a crucial political element in that it both rejects the firm border between the public and the private and it problematizes systems and practices antithetical to mutual interdependence and care (Held 2006, 13). In some moral theories, moral obligations are limited to contractual agreements or universal principles, but much of our moral lives takes place in our more casual interpersonal relationships. Furthermore, in prioritizing relations of care, care ethics seems to disincentivize relations that are exploitative or alienating, such as those informed by class, race, gender, sex, and ability-based hierarchies, or capital relations of exchange.

ORIGINS AND CENTRAL FIGURES

Care ethics is often credited as beginning with Carol Gilligan's book *In Another Voice*. Gilligan, a psychologist, began her research into moral reasoning and moral development in part as a response to psychologist Lawrence Kohlberg's theory of moral development (Gilligan 1982). Because Kohlberg's research participants were limited to young and adolescent boys, his data suggested that moral reasoning generally proceeded as it did in these boys (Kohlberg 1958). His analysis suggested that moral reasoning began with self-interested justifications (e.g., obedience, self-interest), moved through concern for rules or norms (e.g., law and order), and finished with concern for universalizable moral principles (e.g., human rights) (Kohlberg 1973; 1976). On Kohlberg's view, human moral reasoning develops cross-culturally toward a concern for justice in a Kantian, Rawlsian sense (Kohlberg 1973, 630ff.). Young and adolescent girls, working through the same research scenarios, seemed not to reach the same heights of moral reasoning at similar ages—some girls failed to "progress" to the final, impersonal stages of moral reasoning. Gilligan argued that it was not that these girls were less morally mature, but that they were using a different system of moral reasoning—one that prioritized care for others over adherence to abstract principles (Gilligan 1982).

Subsequent feminist theorists seized on this insight. As Held and other feminist philosophers such as Annette Baier, Diemut Bubeck, Eva Feder Kittay, Sara Ruddick, and Joan Tronto pointed out, caring for others—in both the sense of care as a practice and as a value—was largely absent from the major philosophical theories of morality (Baier 1994; Bubeck 1995; Kittay 1999; Ruddick 1989; Tronto 1993, 2006). Care work was not seen as labor, and when it was discussed, it was seen as a uniquely feminine disposition, not as something of general moral concern or of public interest. While these philosophers do not foreground the same elements of care ethics—for example, Baier focuses on trust, Bubeck on meeting needs, and Kittay on dependence—all agree that care is of central moral significance (Baier 1994, Bubeck 1995, Kittay 1999).

LORDE, HOOKS, AND LOVE

Though Audre Lorde and bell hooks are not generally considered to be care ethicists, and though love is not identical to care, both feminists highlight the transformative and critical power of care ethics. As Lorde and hooks show, care is a means of change, resistance, and revolution.

Near the end of her life, Lorde wrote, "Caring for myself is not self-indulgence, it is self-preservation, and that is an act of political warfare" (Lorde 1988, 124). Care can be directed inward. The sort of self-care Lorde means here is not vanity, but resistance to a system that does not value you, your labor, and your well-being. As a Black woman in America, Lorde was dealing with medical racism as well as a social and political environment steeped in racism, sexism, and classism. There is something revolutionary in insisting on one's worth and taking steps to preserve oneself, to respect that worth, even and especially when the world fails to care. If relations of care fail to materialize in the institutions in which we participate, we must develop those relations for ourselves.

Indeed, we must resist the incentivizing of these systems to care only about ourselves, or about ourselves insofar as we can approximate those in power. Elsewhere, Lorde writes, "For women, the need and desire to nurture each other is not pathological but redemptive, and it is within that knowledge that our real power is rediscovered. It is this real connection which is so feared by a patriarchal world . . . For the master's tools will never dismantle the master's house. They may allow us temporarily to beat him at his own game, but they will never enable us to bring about genuine change" (Lorde 2017, 90–91). In this essay, Lorde was critiquing white feminists who chose to ally with white, heteropatriarchal principles. But in this passage specifically, Lorde is pointing to how mutual interdependence and care—that is, care as a rejection of racist, sexist, and homophobic subordination—is a political, transformational act. We ought not imitate the dominant group's ways of thinking, acting, and relating to one another: we will only further entrench the systems that oppress us. Harming any set of women—Black, queer, or trans—harms the global project of feminism as gender equality. We are interconnected and interdependent. We must recognize this and care for one another, for we are all we have.

In a similar vein, hooks argues for an ethic of love as a means of moderating how members of a society relate to one another. Genuine love, on hooks's view, is partially constituted by care (hooks 2000, 5). For hooks, care is the foundation of love; we learn what care looks like, and what love looks like, through our childhood relations of care with our parents/guardians (hooks 2000, 5–6). Because love requires care—and affection, respect, trust, and a host of other elements present in various iterations of care ethics—it is uniquely positioned to resist systems and practices of subordination and domination. We do not willfully mistreat those we love. For example, hooks suggests that an ethic of love is at odds with capitalism; capitalism requires exploitation of and alienated labor from its workers. But if we recognize ourselves as standing in relations of love and care, we will no longer be content to let such relations continue (hooks 87ff.). So, for hooks, an ethic of love and care can reshape and improve social and political relations. Caring is transformative because it is at odds with mistreatment.

Care Ethics: A Comparison

Care ethics is notoriously tricky to assimilate to common categories of moral theory. This is in part because of its provenance; that is, because care ethics emerged as a moral system that is a feminist critique of traditional Northern, Western, liberal conceptions of morality, it can be difficult to slot into categories informed by these commitments. While it engages with other Northern, Western moral theories, it is not reducible to any of them.

CARE ETHICS AS PARTICULARIST

Care ethics is best categorized as a particularist moral theory. Just as utilitarianism proceeds from determining the utilities of possible actions or outcomes, care ethics proceeds from the *particular* care relations in which an agent stands. For example, if Dominique is trying to sort out the morally best way to spend her lottery winnings, a utilitarian perspective would say to do what will produce the most pleasure or greatest good—perhaps spend it on fun experiences or donate it to charity. A Kantian deontological perspective would say to do what she could will into universal law—perhaps donate it all to a charity, or perhaps a direct transfer of cash to impoverished folks. A care ethics perspective would say that her relations of care come first in determining how to distribute funds: perhaps she has children or siblings for whom she is responsible and wants to create a trust, or perhaps Dominique's close friend has just lost her scholarship and will have to leave university without immediate assistance. There is something deeply intuitive about the care ethics approach; it does not create the most happiness to help one's siblings, nor could we universalize a law that says financial windfalls ought to go to one's friends, and yet there is clearly something morally good here. Moreover, if someone else—for example, Javier—found himself in the same situation, he could end up with a parallel albeit different response (for example, sending money to his abuela and to his partner)—one with similar logic though different care relations and thus different results.

Care ethics is best categorized as a particularist theory because it is sensitive to contextually relevant moral features. Some moral theories, like utilitarianism or Kantian deontology, require a burdensome and impractical scope for moral reasoning. This abstracts away from where we make moral decisions—in our real lives. Care ethics is practically useful and intelligible across agents without requiring objective, universally endorsable moral principles.

RELATION TO OTHER ETHICAL THEORIES

Part of why care ethics is difficult to categorize and understand is not only because it is particularist, but also because it is similar to virtue ethics and also bears some similarities to other common Northern, Western moral theories.

Some philosophers, like Michael Slote, have argued that care ethics is best understood as a kind of virtue theory (Slote 2006). There is significant appeal to this approach. Strategically, virtue ethics has a long and respected history and is not specifically feminist, so if care ethics were a form of virtue ethics, it would no longer be subject to criticisms of its relative youth, nor would anti-feminists immediately reject it.

Perhaps more persuasively, care ethics and virtue ethics have much in common in their philosophical commitments. Care is almost certainly a virtue, if not on the Aristotelian account, then certainly on other accounts of virtue ethics (e.g., Christianity). And, insofar as virtue ethics is concerned with how an agent acts—that is, agent- and context-specifically—care ethics is structurally akin to virtue ethics. Most persuasively, care ethics and virtue ethics seem to emerge from similar motivations. A virtuous agent *just is* the kind of person who acts virtuously; it is a reflection of who she is and how she values. A care ethicist *just is* the kind of person who takes care relations as morally significant determinants of her action; she just values them.

However, there is a significant difference between virtue and care ethics. Some care ethicists have suggested that it is unlike virtue because it is an other-directed action rather than an agent-dependent disposition. Bubeck, for example, defines care as successfully meeting the needs of others, as one does with other forms of work (Bubeck 1995, 9). Held disagrees with both Slote and Bubeck: care ethics is neither a virtue theory nor merely concerned with activity, but something in-between. Per Held,

> If virtue ethics is interpreted, as with Slote, as primarily a matter of motives, it may neglect unduly the labor and objective results of caring, as Bubeck's emphasis on actually meeting needs highlights. Caring is not only a question of motive or attitude or virtue. On the other

hand, Bubeck's account is unduly close to a utilitarian interpretation of meeting needs, neglecting that care also has an aspect of motive and virtue. If virtue ethics is interpreted as less restricted to motives, and if it takes adequate account of the results of the virtuous person's activities for the persons cared for, it may better include the concerns of the ethics of care. It would still, however, focus on the dispositions of individuals, whereas the ethics of care focuses on social relations and the social practices and values that sustain them. (Held 2006, 20)

Held reminds us that care is not just a value, but a practice. Virtue ethics is about the character of the moral agent, but care ethics is about not just how the agent values or what motivates her action, *but the action itself.* Caring is labor, work, effort. Moreover, it is not about the carer, or the cared-for, but the relation between them. This distinction is not captured by virtue ethics. Care ethics is, at least partly, what we do and not just how we do it.

And yet, as Held also points out, there are similarities to other moral theories. Bubeck's conception of care ethics emphasizes results: it is not enough to intend or try to meet the needs of the cared-for—one must succeed. This is closer to utilitarianism than to virtue ethics. Indeed, how can we distinguish between prioritizing care relations and what produces the most pleasure or good? Further, caring and being cared for can be its own kind of pleasure; are these kinds of pleasures motivational in care ethics? It is possible that prioritizing care relations and maximizing utility may overlap. In this case, intentions or motivations will likely make the difference, but intentions are notoriously opaque to others and even sometimes to ourselves; how can we know that the pleasure of caring is not what is motivating someone who seems to be a care ethicist?

The distinction between care ethics and deontology can get murky. One might think that one's relations of care impose moral burdens because of duties we already endorse. Few would disagree that a parent has a duty to care for their child, even if there is disagreement on the particulars of what that care entails. We might also think we have a duty to care for someone otherwise incapable of caring for themselves. It is less obvious why this duty might obtain in this case, but perhaps it is due to compassion or respect for human dignity. In these cases, why not think that care ethics is just a special iteration of a deontological approach?

Much as in the virtue ethics case, care ethics is not a kind of utilitarianism or deontology, not because their content or moral outputs are inconsistent, but because the structures are incompatible. Utilitarianism and other consequentialist theories are ultimately concerned with quantifiable outputs, whereas care ethics is concerned with relations. Relations may be informed by those outputs, but outputs do not determine the standing of those relations. Similarly, deontology is concerned with duties, but specifically with the *motivations* for those duties—human dignity, universal principles, or rights—while care ethics is concerned with the action *and* its motivation.

So care ethics is tricky: it incorporates elements—motivations, results, duties—that are thought to be paradigmatic representatives of other kinds of moral theory, and yet it stands apart. Perhaps this is because care ethics gets at something—care—that is more fundamentally human than the ideological bedrock of other moral theories (Held 2006, 17).

Using Care Ethics

Despite being so fundamentally human, as a particularist theory, it lacks the concrete action-guiding rules of, for example, a utilitarian pleasure calculus or a deontological universal law. "It is all well and good," a skeptic might say, "to claim that care is a fundamental principle of moral value which is instantiated by the activity of caring, but *how* do I implement that in my own life?" This is a fair question: a moral theory that cannot offer practical guidance has limited use. Fortunately for care ethics, it can offer such guidance, even if the specifics will vary. From a practical standpoint, care ethics asks us to engage in moral reasoning across three main steps: assess, attend, and act. This section offers a brief, broad-strokes account of care ethics in practice.

We must first assess the circumstances in which we find ourselves. Care ethics reminds us that not only individuals, but also relationships, have moral value. How many relations are in play, and of what kind? Perhaps some are closer and more important to us than others, such as between longtime friends or spouses versus neighbors or fellow citizens. What kinds of duties might come along with these relationships—for example, might a person have different kinds of duties to their spouse relative to their child, or to their neighbor relative to their friend?

Once we have a sense of our circumstances and potentially competing morally valuable relations, we should attend to the nuances of those relations. A person might owe something to several parties, but what is owed will depend on which relation that person considers, for some relationships are more intimate, more loving, and thus more morally demanding than others. As a parallel, consider a gift-giving holiday. If we need to give a gift to our spouse, friend, and neighbor, the right gift depends on us, the needs and interests of the recipient, and the history and intimacy that we share with them. It would be inappropriate to give them all the same thing: a spouse, a friend, and a neighbor are not equally intimate and significant relationships in our lives. Similarly, we must attend to the person's needs and interests: an expensive bottle of wine might be a good gift for a friend, but not for a friend who does not drink wine or one who prefers experiences rather than physical gifts. Care ethics operates in a similar way: care is owed and instantiated in different ways, depending on the specifics of the relationships we assess to be important.

Finally, care ethics is about action. As Held and other care ethicists remind us, care ethics is not merely theoretical: we make decisions every day, and we ought to do so in ways that instantiate care for the relationships in which we are enmeshed. Just as well-intentioned but ill-suited gifts miss the mark, so too is merely *trying* to care for others insufficient—we must attend to others and their needs in order to act in the right way for this *specific* person and our relationship with them. To do so requires successfully attending to the particulars of that relationship and recognizing the relationship as important. Perhaps Alex notices that Jennifer has been down lately and wants to cheer her up. A surprise birthday party is a way to gather loved ones to celebrate Jennifer and could be a wonderful gesture . . . but not if Jennifer hates surprise parties. To care for Jennifer and their friendship, Alex ought to act in a way that is informed by knowledge of her friend.

To bring this together, consider the Trolley Problem again. The most obvious challenge of the Trolley Problem is that we cannot save everyone. Even though this case is particularly extreme, one might think that there are often competing choices and limited resources in daily life. So how can a person determine which care relations to prioritize? In part, this will depend on the agent and their determination of which relationships are in play and are most meaningful or most in need of tending. But so too is it limited by what we owe to ourselves: as Lorde notes, caring for ourselves is crucial. We may have to make difficult choices, but care ethics provides a broad model for us to do so, and moreover, in a way that is tailored to our specific circumstances, communities, and self-understanding.

CARE ETHICS AS FEMINIST

A final element of care ethics relative to other moral theories and perspectives is that it is historically and paradigmatically feminist. While feminism is better understood as feminisms, as there are many ways of thinking about and practicing feminism, what links all these approaches is a concern for the equality and well-being of women and other subordinated genders. Care ethics is historically feminist in that it emerged as a challenge to a patriarchal theory of moral development. It is also tied to the long-standing devaluing of care and care labor that was descriptively part of common norms of femininity and maternity. There are many ways for feminists to respond to the systematic devaluation of labor relegated to women and girls. The response at the heart of care ethics is the rejection of this unjust division and valuation failure. A care ethics perspective insists that what was thought to make women and girls lesser—invisible labor, close ties, and care—is instead a recognition of their moral agency. Moreover, care ethicists point out that while women may be more likely to display this kind of moral reasoning, given gendered socialization practices, care ethics is open and useful to folks of all genders.

Care ethics is also feminist in the sense of being consistent with various other political and social commitments in various iterations of feminism. Lorde and hooks's care ethics as a means of social and political transformation is consistent with and an iteration of Black feminism and Marxist feminism, for example. So too is care ethics consonant with perspectives like ecofeminism and decolonial feminism. If care relations are the locus of moral value, then why limit those relations of care to humans and not extend them to other species, biomes, and ecosystems? Decolonial feminism rejects the narrow scope of Northern, Western experiences as the "true" definitions, arbiters, or markers of womanhood and feminist concern; if Lorde is right and caring is transformative and anti-patriarchal, then surely this extends cross-culturally.

Critiques of Care Ethics

As with other moral theories, care ethics is not without its challenges. This section explores two of the most trenchant: the justice challenge and the feminist status concern.

THE JUSTICE CHALLENGE

Many moral theories—and many folks' moral intuitions—suggest that justice is something with which we ought to be fundamentally concerned. While theories of justice vary, a persuasive account shaping present liberal theorizing comes from John Rawls's account of justice as fairness. On views like Rawls's, justice is determined by impartial, universal principles. This is in part because Rawls was influenced by Kantian deontology. For Kant, Rawls, and many others, individuals are biased and flawed beings; we cannot help but be swayed by personal considerations. Determining what is morally best via impartial instruments ensures equality of opportunity and genuine fairness irrespective of personal connections. This view motivates the presumed impartiality of the law: at least theoretically, a law binds all citizens equally.

An important part of views of justice like this one, and which are common in Northern, Western, liberal societies like those in North America, is that the primary units of concern for justice are first, persons in the liberal sense—that is, rational, reasonable, autonomous individuals—and second, social, political, and economic institutions like a government or education system.

Care ethics seems fundamentally at odds with this liberal conception of justice in two ways: First, care ethics rejects impartiality and universal fairness (cf. Held 2006). It proceeds from particular care relationships; from attending to, and actually meeting, the needs of those with whom one is in care relations. A person does not prioritize the well-being of their spouse because that is what we all ought to do; they prioritize the well-being of their spouse because *they are their spouse*. That care relation is of central moral concern to them. Second, care ethics does not conceive of individuals as autonomous atomistic individuals, nor is it primarily concerned with institutions (cf. Held 2006). Rather, care ethics acknowledges that what it is to be a particular person is to stand in many social, political, and care relations with many others. We may be autonomous, but the sense in which that obtains is because of rather than despite our connections to others.

Does this mean that a care ethicist is fundamentally unjust? If justice is important, and if care ethics and justice are incompatible, then this seems a reason for worry. Held suggests that this seeming tension is in fact a kind of category error:

> At the level of morality, we need to decide which "models" are appropriate for which contexts. Many of the arguments of recent decades about the priority of justice were developed against a background of utilitarian ascendancy. Rawls's theory of justice and its many offshoots are good examples . . . From the perspective of the ethics of care, however, this debate can be interpreted as being largely internal to the legal-political context. Rawls has explicitly confined his theory to the domain of the political and has argued that it should not be interpreted as a full-fledged moral theory. (Held 2006, 103–4)

What works best on a grand scale—sociopolitical institutions, public policy, the judicial system—is not necessarily going to track what works best for regular, day-to-day human interaction. We ought not prioritize utilitarian calculi or universal principles in every situation. A spouse who is cared for out of duty rather than genuine interest may find that care inadequate for reasons difficult to articulate; a child whose well-being is sought because it maximizes family utility may well sense that *they* are not truly what is being valued. Held and other care ethicists argue that care is a fundamental moral consideration prior to justice. After all, "There can be care without justice: There has historically been little justice in the family, but care and life have gone on without it. There can be no justice without care, however, for without care no child would survive and there would be no persons to respect" (Held 2006, 17).

One might be tempted to think that this discussion implies that we ought to adopt a care ethics perspective in our private/ personal lives and a justice perspective in our public/political lives. Care ethicists reject this because, as feminists, they reject the distinction between the private and public domains. Domestic concerns have always been of political value. But moreover, as Held notes, the distinction between justice and care is artificial. Care is the universal domain in which we, as persons with interpersonal connections, exist; the question of justice is intelligible *only within* the domain of care. Indeed, we already make accommodations on account of relations of care. For example, a *fair* distribution of tax breaks takes into account a citizen's number of dependents. Fairness is not sameness; part of what differentiates us are the care relations in which we stand. Held and others remind us that what is just *depends on* relations of care.

THE FEMINIST STATUS CONCERN

Another major criticism of care ethics questions whether care ethics is in fact a feminist moral theory. This kind of critique has several manifestations, but the main thrust of it is that there are elements of care ethics as it has traditionally been understood that seem to commit the kinds of wrongs that a consistent, useful feminism ought to reject.

One iteration of the feminist status concern is based in the seeming essentialism at the core of care ethics. Specifically, it seems like care ethics is concerned with the plight of women and girls as carers, and as femininity as being conceived of as partly constituted by caring. While it is true that women and girls do the vast majority of care labor across the globe and that this labor tends not to be taken seriously, critics like Michelle Moody-Adams point out that this does not indicate that there is some kind of essence of women or femininity related to caring or that women *as a class* actually engage in care ethics–style moral reasoning. At best, there is a descriptive claim about how care labor has been distributed and how women have been conditioned to think about morality (Moody-Adams 1991). This kind of concern with essentialism also would likely be exclusionary of trans women and nonbinary/genderqueer folks. Feminism should respect and celebrate the differences among women and other subordinated genders even as it acknowledges that there are certain commonly shared experiences—it is neither biology nor common experience that makes someone a woman.

The essentialism version of the feminist status concern need not be a devastating problem. While care ethics did, descriptively speaking, emerge from research based on gender differences (and where gender was conceived of as a binary), nothing about care ethics requires that women share the experience of undervalued care labor, related socialization of what femininity is, or even that care ethicists be women at all. Rather, care ethics is itself a kind of critique and rebuke of moral systems that overlook the kind of labor and valuing that was historically relegated to the private domain and to "women's work": gender is an accidental rather than essential feature of care ethics. What matters is that care work and some relations are not valued on other systems, not *necessarily* who is doing care work.

A second iteration of the feminist status concern comes from philosophers such as Barbara Houston, who suggest that care ethics enables the exploitation of care workers and can develop into a morality that internalizes and valorizes gendered subordination (Houston 1990). If care ethics casts care relations and care work as of great moral value, and others in the society do not share this morality, then perhaps women (and other care laborers) will be willing to accept no wages or extremely low wages to do this kind of work. This will have serious effects on care laborers, most of whom are women: at minimum, they will not receive respect and recognition for the important work they do, nor will they have the same access to financial independence as men/non-care workers.

This is a significant concern that is borne out in the American childcare system. Wages for daycare workers—the majority of whom are women—are seriously depressed relative to other forms of work that require similar or lower levels of training and effort (Miller 2021; Long 2021). A worker could, in many states, make more money per hour in retail or at a restaurant than in a day care (Miller 2021; Long 2021). Since America does not have federally mandated parental leave, day care is a necessity for many households.

Care ethicists tend to take on these concerns across two different strategies. First, they—as do many other progressives in American society—argue for parental leave, childcare benefits, subsidies for care homes, and other material changes that would alleviate some of the economic burdens on carers. Second, care ethicists like Bubeck argue that there is a category error in conceiving of care ethics as a morality that celebrates one's own subordination: there is a crucial difference between looking after someone who *requires* support—children, some disabled folks, some elderly folks—and looking after someone who *merely enjoys* support, such as someone who employs a house cleaner to preserve their free time or a spouse who chooses not to learn how to cook (Bubeck 1995). For Bubeck, the former qualifies as care, while the latter is service. Care ethics does not valorize service to those who choose not to be self-sufficient.

Summary

Care ethics has intuitive appeal as well as practical value for assisting us in making everyday moral decisions. While it may not be the appropriate theory for public policy or the judicial system, in part because it is particularist and thus somewhat narrow in scope, it does seem to be motivating some of the background assumptions of those domains. Moreover, a care perspective can be used as a kind of check on how justice is functioning in practice. But perhaps most importantly, care ethics foregrounds the way in which we are all interconnected and interdependent: none of us would be where (and how) we are now if not for the care—both practice and value—of others. Keeping this in mind, we may find new ways to use care to aid those we love, as in traditional care ethics, and perhaps also discover means to use care to transform the social and political relations and institutions in which we participate, as

Lorde and hooks imply. In political and economic systems that set us in competition, care ethics reminds us that our relations to others and ourselves matter, morally speaking.

Further Reading

PRIMARY SOURCES

Gilligan, Carol. 1982. *In A Different Voice*. Cambridge, MA: Harvard University Press.
Held, Virginia. 2006. *The Ethics of Care*. New York: Oxford University Press.

SECONDARY SOURCES

Baier, Annette. 1985. "What Do Women Want in a Moral Theory?" *Nous* 19 no. 5: 53–63. https://doi.org/2215117.
———. 1994. *Moral Prejudices: Essays on Ethics*. Cambridge, MA: Harvard University Press.
Bubeck, Diemut. 1995. *Care, Gender and Justice*. Oxford: Clarendon Press.
hooks, bell. 1984. *Feminist Theory: From Margin to Center*. New York: Routledge.
———. 2000. *All About Love*. New York, NY: Harper Collins.
Houston, Barbara. 1990. "Review: Caring and Exploitation." *Hypatia* 5, no. 1: 115–19. https://doi.org/ 10.1111/j.1527-2001.1990.tb00395.x.
Kittay, Eva Feder. 1999. *Love's Labor: Essays on Women, Equality, and Dependency*. New York: Routledge.
Kohlberg, Lawrence. 1958. "The Development of Modes of Thinking and Choices in Years 10 to 16." PhD diss., University of Chicago.
———. 1973. "The Claim to Moral Adequacy of a Highest Stage of Moral Development." *The Journal of Philosophy* 70, no. 18: 630–46.
———. 1976. "Moral Stages and Moralization: The Cognitive-Developmental Approach." In *Moral Development and Behavior: Theory, Research, and Social Issues*, edited by Thomas Lickona. Holt, NY: Rinehart and Winston.
Long, Heather. 2021. "'The Pay Is Absolute Crap': Child-Care Workers Are Quitting Rapidly, a Red Flag for the Economy." *The Washington Post*. https://www.washingtonpost.com/business/2021/09/19/childcare-workers-quit/.
Lorde, Audre. 1984. "Age, Race, Class, and Sex: Women Redefining Difference." In *Sister Outsider: Essays and Speeches*. Berkeley: Crossing Press.

———. 1988. *A Burst of Light: Essays by Audre Lorde*. New York: Firebrand.

———. 2017. "The Master's Tools Will Never Dismantle The Master's House." In *Your Silence Will Not Protect You*. London: Silver Press.

Miller, Claire Cain. 2021. "'Can't Compete': Why Hiring for Child Care Is a Huge Struggle." *New York Times*. https://www.nytimes.com/2021/09/21/upshot/child-care.html

Moody-Adams, Michele M. 1991. "Gender and the Complexity of Moral Voices." In *Feminist Ethics*, edited by Claudia Card, 195–212. Lawrence: University of Kansas Press.

Noddings, Nel. 1984. *Caring: A Feminine Approach to Ethics and Moral Education*. Berkeley: University of California Press.

Slote, Michael. 2007. *The Ethics of Care and Empathy*. New York: Routledge.

Ruddick, Sara. 1989. *Maternal Thinking: Toward a Politics of Peace*. New York: Ballentine Books.

Tronto, Joan C. 1993. *Moral Boundaries: A Political Argument for an Ethic of Care*. New York: Routledge.

———. 2006. "Women and Caring: What Can Feminists Learn about Morality from Caring?" In *Justice and Care: Essential Readings in Feminist Ethics*, edited by Virginia Held, 101–15. Boulder, CO: Westview Press.

18

Yoga

Procedural Devotion to the Right

SHYAM RANGANATHAN

Introduction

It is common for people the world over to become aware of Yoga
(the philosophical system) via postural exercises (*āsana*), also called
"yoga." It is hence common for people to understand, learn, and
practice yoga in terms of these exercises. And insofar as people
are motivated to engage in these exercises called "yoga" (whatever
they may be) for further ends (such as mental or physical health,
liberation from trouble, enlightenment, etc.), it seems that yoga
is a consequentialist project, where the practice of yoga is itself
motivated and justified by further ends.

Another reason that Yoga is interpreted as being a version of
consequentialism is that it is typical for people to interpret East
Asian and South Asian moral theory in terms of available and
familiar options in the Western tradition (cf. Sreekumar 2012; cf.
Theodor 2010). However, the reason that these exercises are called
"yoga" is that they are a way to practice the distinct moral philosophy: Yoga. This metaethical and normative theory is systematically
elaborated in Patañjali's *Yoga Sūtra*, but also in the *Bhagavad Gītā*

(and the wider epic it is a part of, the *Mahābhārata*) (both 200 CE), and much earlier in the *Upaniṣads* (1000–500 BCE).[1]

While Yoga (also called Bhakti, "devotion") is a comprehensive philosophy, it is importantly an ancient and *basic* ethical theory, unique to South Asia (what is commonly called the Indian tradition). It is not a variant of virtue ethics, consequentialism, and deontology, but is an additional *kind* of moral theory. And in its literary articulation, in dialogue and story (such as the *Mahābhārata* and the *Upaniṣads*), it has a long history of criticizing teleological ethical theories, including—and especially—consequentialism. It is a radically procedural ethical theory, does not require the good to elucidate the right, and provides a critical response to all three alternatives.

The main obstacle to understanding Yoga is methodological. It pertains to how we can understand philosophical options that we do not necessarily agree with, and which are novel relative to our background assumptions and beliefs. Without methodological clarity, we will be doomed to understand alternatives in terms of familiar options. Yoga itself provides direction on how to engage in the project of philosophical understanding, thereby grounding itself not only as a normative ethical theory, but as the philosophy (and the metaethics) we need to understand all possible philosophical and theoretical options.

Grounding Philosophical Understanding

Before I began my contributions to the study of South Asian moral philosophy, the ordinary way that authors wrote on Indian philosophy, and anything connected to South Asia, was to proceed by assuming their own worldview—including a range of options for ethical theory—which would then be used as the stock of explanatory resources for making sense of South Asian philosophical discourse. In the literature, this mode of explanation is called *interpretation*. If South Asians had a word that they used to discuss ethical issues—and they did: *"dharma"*—each such use would be interpreted in light of the beliefs of the interpreter. The result is that *"dharma"* could only be acknowledged as meaning "ethics" or "morality" when the use of *"dharma"* in South Asian literature coincided with what the interpreter would be willing to call "ethics" or "morality."

Narcissism in the ordinary sense involves an inflated sense of the importance of one's own opinions. Interpretation as an explanation by way of one's own opinions is methodological narcissism. With the interpretive method, South Asian moral philosophy disappears. The result of this methodological narcissism is the widespread erroneous conclusion that *"dharma"* is a term with many irreconcilable meanings.[2]

Interpretation itself has many defenders in contemporary Western philosophy.[3] It is a most Western mode of explanation, just as, and especially because, reliance on belief (an attitude that a thought, *p*, is true) as an explanatory resource is a very basic feature of the Western tradition. To the extent that belief plays a role in South Asian philosophy, it is identified as the key factor in erroneous cognition and the fabrication of an ersatz mental reality.[4]

From what I can tell, the motivation for this approach to understanding as dependent on belief (as though the conflation of thought and belief is unavoidable) is a historical and ancient theory of thought and language in the Western tradition that we might call the Linguistic Account of Thought (LAT).[5] Accordingly, thought is the meaning of what we say—a theory that has roots in the ancient Greek idea of *logos* (thought, speech, reason). If thought is the meaning of what I say, then the line between what I say and what I think is blurred. But as what I would say is typically what I believe, then the line between belief (the propositional attitude of endorsing a thought *p*) and a thought (*p*) is blurred: all explanation seems like an interpretive exercise.

Given this methodology, a deep commitment to the LAT in the Western tradition, and the preeminence of virtue ethics, consequentialism, and deontology in the Western tradition, Western interpreters would only be able to account for South Asian ethical theory insofar as it was an example of familiar theories. But since South Asian ethical theories differ from Western counterparts, even when we are considering examples of virtue ethics, consequentialism, and deontology, South Asian examples cannot be identified by interpretation. Worse, Yoga/Bhakti—a theory unique to South Asia—would be completely uninterpretable. Instead, as the philosophical tradition with roots in ancient Greek thought expands (a tradition I call the *West*), it tries to interpret everything on the basis of its intellectual history, and the residuum gets called "religion"—with South Asian religious identity explicitly manufactured in contexts of British colonialism (Ranganathan 2018b, 2022b). The acknowledgment of South Asian moral theorizing and South Asian religion are hence inversely correlated.

One problem with interpretation is that it relies on our beliefs to deliver explanation. Our beliefs in turn depend on the contingencies of our experiences, as well as various sociological and natural factors. Whatever result we arrive at in an interpretation tells us more about our history than what is being interpreted. These beliefs will be determined (in part) by empirical influences outside our control. In Yoga, these external empirical considerations comprise nature, or *prakṛti*. But these considerations are also narcissistic, as they consist in the inflation of the importance of one's own opinion. Yoga identifies this fault of narcissism as egotism (*asmitā*): the fault of conflating oneself with one's outlook (YS II.6). While we might feel that our interpretations protect our independence, as they rely on our beliefs, belief undermines our independence, as it depends on external influence.

In contrast to interpretation, I favor what I call *explication*. Explication is the application of logical validity to the task of understanding a philosophical theory. An argument is logically valid if the premises are true, the conclusion has to be true. Valid arguments can be composed of false propositions, and an argument composed of what we believe, or is true, can be invalid. If we were to explicate talk about *dharma* in South Asian philosophy, we would look to every perspective's propositions to derive, via logical validity, a theory that entails, via validity, its claims about *dharma*. We would further deduce (via validity) that the topic or concept of DHARMA is what everyone is disagreeing about with competing theories of *dharma*. If we were to engage in explication, we would observe that the topic of disagreement where *dharma* is concerned is THE RIGHT (PROCEDURE) or THE GOOD (OUTCOME). We could apply this same method to discussions of morality or ethics in the European tradition, or the *dao* in the Chinese tradition, and we would find the same topic of dissent. Moreover, we would see that there are four basic theories that differ on the relationship between THE RIGHT or THE GOOD. One of these basic four normative theories includes an option not heard of in the Western tradition: Yoga.

While this distinction between explication (explanation by the logical ordering of propositions in perspectives that entails their claims and furthermore the topic of conversation) and interpretation (explanation by way of propositional attitudes, especially belief, that are not the objects of logic) is a modern way of talking about two mutually incompatible methodologies, they are themselves modern retellings of a basic distinction between Yoga and anti-yoga, which we learn about at the start of the *Yoga Sūtra*. But—and here's the catch—we will only be able to understand this if we are explicating. For if we choose to interpret, as has been common in the "study" of South Asian philosophy, we would only ever appreciate what we already believe, which is narcissistic. However, if we explicate, we see that the *Yoga Sūtra* begins with an important distinction: First, we learn that Yoga is the normative constraint of mental content that results in the autonomy of the agent from what they contemplate (YS I.2–3). Second, failure to engage in this activity results in the identification with what one contemplates via propositional attitudes (*vṛtti-sārūpyam*) (YS I.4).

What is centrally important about this distinction is that it presents us with a *choice* between two mutually exclusive approaches to relating to mental content. As they are mutually exclusive, they cannot both be endorsed without contradiction. Which methodology we endorse is up to us, but there are distinct consequences to either option. And the choice is methodological, not a matter of what the facts are. Yet the anti-yoga interpretive option treats the facts (especially as one sees it) as dispositive. The anti-yoga option is thereby out of step with what is required to appreciate the methodological choice before us. Hence, we must endorse Yoga, which is the methodology of distinguishing between options. We can spell this out, in standard form, in a disjunctive syllogism implicit in the opening aphorisms of the *Yoga Sūtra*:

1. Either we should organize mental content to understand the options and preserve our autonomy (Yoga), or we simply identify with the facts as we see it (anti-yoga).

2. As we understand that (1) is a disjunction of two mutually exclusive methodologies, and not a fact, in understanding (1) it is not the case that we can simply identify with the facts as we see it (anti-yoga).

- Therefore, we must organize mental content to understand the options and preserve our autonomy (Yoga).

Adopting Yoga does allow us to appreciate the choice before us, but what we have to give up is our self-identification with a perspective, or interpretation. This is described as an ethical cleansing (*dharmameghasamādhi*) that results in our autonomy (*kaivalya*) (YS IV 29–34). Put another way, even understanding that there are choices and options requires getting over a moral impediment, namely the egotism/narcissism of interpretation. This metaethical disjunction is also a disjunction of the possibilities of moral responsibility. If we explicate, we can appreciate that there are options, which is required for responsible choosing. If we interpret, we undermine our appreciation of options by endorsing an outlook as our explanation of everything, and then we cannot engage in responsible choosing of options.

This disjunctive syllogism, implicit in the dense opening aphorisms of the *Yoga Sūtra*, captures the metaethics—or metaphilosophical procedure—of Yoga. It entails the methodology of Yoga, which in general terms allows us to make sense of the options. Explication is an example of this Yogic methodology, and in the next section I explicate four basic ethical theories, of which Yoga is one. Yoga functions both as a metaethics and as a normative ethics insofar as one can endorse the practice of Yoga (the metaethics) as one's personal practice (normative ethics). Then it is recast not merely as a methodology, but as the practice of devotion to the ideal of the right, the ideal of personhood, and the ideal of Sovereignty: Īśvara. Īśvara in turn is comprised of two procedural aspects (YS I.24) that we are further committed to by way of this devotion: unconservatism (*tapas*) and self-governance (*svādhyāya*) (YS II.1). When we explicate, for instance, we engage in both of these subsidiary procedures. To explicate requires that we get over prejudices and narcissism that get in the way of understanding other perspectives (unconservativism), and we also give ourselves the freedom to choose our own values, not as a matter of casual propositional attitudes of what comes before our attention, but as a matter of deliberate, determinative choice (self-governance).

Normative Theory

To employ explication in understanding the options is to deductively derive from a perspective its theory that entails its controversial claims about its topic. We can then understand the central concept of the topic in terms of what competing theories are disagreeing about. In the case of DHARMA or ETHICS, this is THE RIGHT or THE GOOD. The first three options are familiar:

> *Virtue Theory*: the *good* (state) conditions / causes the *right* (actions).

> *Consequentialism*: the *good* (ends) justifies the *right* (actions).

These two theories are teleological. What is distinctive about virtue ethics is that it is a theory of moral production, of the requirements of making the right kinds of decisions and doing the right kind of thing (Hursthouse 1996, 2013). Consequentialism in contrast is a theory of moral justification: it helps us determine what we should do given certain ends. Both can be run together in a teleological ethical theory. For sure, philosophers and authors writing on virtue ethics or consequentialism may have fuzzier or more expansive theories in mind. This may be because their project is fundamentally interpretive, concerned with elaborating the implications of what they believe is virtue ethics or consequentialism. For our explicatory purposes, we reconstruct these options in terms of a basic disagreement. And this sheds light on two *procedural* options. The first is well-known:

> *Deontology*: the *right* (choice, reasoning, considerations) justifies the *good* (actions, rights, outcomes . . .).

Deontology is the mirror image of consequentialism. It occupies the same kind of philosophical space, as it too is concerned with providing moral justification. But in this case, what is being justified are outcomes (whether actions or freedoms) that already have something going for them (they are good in some measure). These outcomes become duties or rights insofar as they can be justified by the relevant procedural considerations (cf. Alexander and Moore Winter 2012).

The first three options can be found in the South Asian tradition (Ranganathan 2017a). But what is certainly unique to this tradition is a fourth basic ethical theory, which is the mirror opposite of virtue ethics:

> *Bhakti/Yoga*: The *right* (procedure) conditions or produces the *good* (outcome).

Whereas virtue ethics gives priority to the goodness of the virtuous agent in its account of moral activity, Yoga is the opposite: it gives priority to right procedure as *producing* good outcomes. Here is one reason that Yoga is incorrectly interpreted as a version of consequentialism. Like consequentialism, it identifies good ends as something that should be valued. However, unlike in consequentialism, these ends do not justify our moral activity. Rather, in Yoga, right activity consists in devotion to the procedural ideal of the right, called Īśvara, which we could translate as "Sovereignty" or "the Lord." If anything counts as a justification for our doing, it is this procedural devotion to the right, not the good (and hence Yoga is not a form of consequentialism).

Īśvara is often confused for a theistic God, but they are opposites. The theist's God (a virtue theoretic model agent) is defined by Its goodness. Īśvara, in contrast, is defined by Its rightness. It is hence an ideal of choosing and doing that plays a role in our own personal transformation when we decide to be devoted to it. Whereas the good God might tell us the right thing to do, we have to figure that out via our devotion to Īśvara.

Īśvara is composed of two essential traits: it is unconservative and it is also self-determining or self-governing. Hence to fully practice this devotion to Īśvara (*Īśvara praṇidhānāna*), the Yogi practices these two traits of Sovereignty: self-challenge by getting over old habits (*tapas*), while also owning choices and values as a matter of self-governance (*svādhyāya*). These three practices—devotion to Sovereignty, unconservatism, and self-governance—constitute the three basic practices of Yoga as a normative theory (YS II.1). The good is nothing more than the perfection of this practice. It is not an independent outcome that can justify practice, and hence practice cannot be treated as a means to an end. Instead, good outcome is rather what we bring about via our devotion to the practice. Therefore, goodness can play no role in the Yoga account of right action. In this respect, Yoga is even more procedural than deontology.

A basis of the Yoga criticism of both consequentialism and virtue ethics is the observation that while good outcomes correlate with ethical practice, it is a mistake to treat these outcomes as conditions or causes of proper ethical practice. True, good outcomes and character are important. But these are best thought of as outcomes of moral practice, not as the conditions of moral practice or moral justification. For instance, the expected utility of unusual and wonderful accomplishment (including an improved character) is usually very low, statistically. Even while working to achieve these accomplishments, they remain distant and unlikely outcomes. If we measured the meaningfulness of our effort in terms of that unlikely outcome, our effort will seem like time wasted. Many other common, unspectacular ends will have a higher expected utility, as we have a higher likelihood of success in pursuing them. But if we give up measuring the meaningfulness of our activity in terms of the outcomes, we can commit procedurally to the Ideal of being a procedure-based individual. And in due time, with repeated practice, the unusual outcome will be produced as a by-product of our devotion. This is not because that end justified the practice, but because we got rid of ends as justifications for practice. This is a theme of Kṛṣṇa's famous argument for Yoga in the *Bhagavad Gītā*.

The *Bhagavad Gītā* is part of the epic the *Mahābhārata*, which is a sustained dialectical investigation into the problems of the familiar three ethical theories. These theories are united in defining the right by way of the good. This commonality gives rise to *conventional morality*: the morality of good character (virtue ethics), good ends (consequentialism), and good rules (deontology). The story reveals the problem with this approach to ethics: it leads to morally good people (in the story, the Pāṇḍavas, including Arjuna) constraining their activity by way of the possibilities of the good, which are undermined by moral parasites (in the story, the Kauravas).

While the conventionally moral constrain themselves by conventional morality, moral parasites downgrade the prospects of the conventional moralist's utility by (a) acting outside the bounds of conventional morality to usurp the conventional moralists' utility, and by (b) relying on the self-imposed moral restraint of the conventionally moral that prevents them from retaliating. Conventional morality is hence turned into a weapon by moral parasites against the conventionally moral. This is already a state of war. Arjuna, the protagonist of the *Gītā*, provides virtue theoretic, consequentialist, and deontological arguments against fighting the moral parasites, while Kṛṣṇa (in the dialogue, Īśvara) spends the entire dialogue motivating Yoga on its own terms, and as a means of resetting the moral order. By switching to Yoga, the formerly conventionally moral are no longer bound by conventional constraints, and this deflates the advantage of moral parasites. And whereas the moral parasites have no common cause with all other people, Yoga consists in devotion to the common interest of people (Ranganathan 2019). The just (Yoga) warrior hence acts outside the bounds of conventional moral expectation, but in a manner that is consistent with everyone's interests, thereby resetting the moral order and ridding the world of moral parasites.

Ideal and Non-Ideal Ethical Theory

In the *Yoga Sūtra*, as with the *Bhagavad Gītā*, we see a similar recognition of the importance and requirement to destroy moral convention as a foundation for Yogic practice. This is formalized in the Eight Limbs of Yoga, which Patañjali describes as a remedial measure (*upāya*) to correct difficulties faced in the practice of Yoga (II.26). In modern terms, the basic practice of Yoga as devotion to Īśvara, with the concomitant practice of the traits of Sovereignty (unconservativism and self-governance), constitutes ideal theory—an account of how we ought to proceed in contexts lacking obstacles. The Eight Limbs of Yoga corresponds to Yoga's non-ideal theory, and it is what we engage when there are impediments.

The first limb, called *yama* (YS II. 30–36), is a universal obligation to disrupt systemic harm (*ahiṃsā*), which reveals the fact (*satya*) of people not deprived of their requirements (*asteya*), their personal boundaries respected (*bramhacaraya*), and no one appropriating (*aparigrahaya*). This activism has the effect of getting opponents to renounce their hostility (YS II.36). It not only exemplifies a devotion to Sovereignty, but also has the effect of attenuating social impediments to the ideal practice.

Having engaged in this activism, one can then proceed on to the *niyama* (the second limb), where the practitioner commits to the three basic ideal practices of Yoga while working on being content and pure in this commitment (YS II.32).

The third limb is *āsana*, which is literally described as the comfortable steady state of continuous yogic practice (YS II.46–48). In contemporary yoga talk, "*āsana*" is the word for postural exercise. This exercise bears a resemblance to what is discussed in the *Yoga Sūtra* to the extent that postures are ways to practice the three basic procedural commitments of Yoga. This, and all further yogic practice, happens within the context of the original activism: *yama*. Contemporary practices called "yoga" are often ethical deviations insofar as they do not occur within the context of this activism. The philosophical importance of *āsana* is more than physical posture. It is described as initiating the twin procedural accomplishments of continuous effort and endless relaxation. This is the practice of occupying the space created by the first two limbs (YS II.47).

The fourth Limb is *prāṇāyāma*, which superficially relates to practices of breath, but is also described as the process of deconstructing natural barriers between oneself and the external world (*YS* II.51). The fifth limb of *pratyāhāra* is the withdrawal of the senses from objects, but the correlative abstraction of objects from beliefs. This puts the senses under the control of the person (*YS* II.54–55).

The first five limbs form the core of the social aspects of Yoga's non-ideal theory. While it may seem as though many of the limbs are goal oriented, they are called *limbs* of yoga, as they are means of implementing Yoga, the ultra-procedural ethical theory, both metaethically and ethically. Each limb involves the metaethical challenge of appreciating alternatives, and each exemplifies devotion to Sovereignty and the two component practices of unconservatism and self-governance.

The last three limbs are bundled together as what one practices "with-*yama*" (*saṃyama*). They constitute three procedures essential for research and problem-solving: *dhāraṇā* (concentration, focus), *dhyāna* (following implications), and *samādhi* (involvement with findings). Together they allow the practitioner to overcome problems and gain unusual powers. Patañjali notes that these very same powers can pose obstacles for achieving liberating outcomes, as striving for them is a consequentialist endeavor (YS III.38, 52). The way out of being stuck in non-ideal ethical practice, by avoiding this regression to consequentialism, is overcoming methodological narcissism (interpretation) in every context via an ethical cleanse: *dharma-megha-samādhi*. This refocuses activity to methodological and procedural considerations free of teleology and delivers the practitioner into an ideal state of autonomy (*kaivalya*) (IV.29–34).

Influence of Yoga

Martin Luther King's influence on subsequent, progressive protest movements is general knowledge. And it is also well-known that King cites M. K. Gandhi as his source for, and for demonstrating the effectiveness of, nonviolent direct action (King September 1, 1958 [accessed 2021]). What is not widely appreciated is that Gandhi derived his political philosophy from the *Yoga Sūtra* (cf. Puri 2015, who shows Gandhi extensively crediting Patañjali for his politics in his collected works). Yoga has had a global influence on progressive politics, and it (a) understands persons not in terms of superficial natural attributes (whether race, sex, gender, orientation, or species) but in terms of a person's interest in their own self-mastery as the crucial ingredient in thriving; and (b) acknowledges the necessity of discarding conventional ideas of the good to make room for people of diverse natural constitutions. Indeed, whereas the LAT that we find dominating the Western tradition encourages anthropocentric and communitarian models of personhood (as language as studied by linguistics is anthropocentric and communitarian), the lack of such a commitment in the Yogic tradition and the emphasis on the procedural requirements of thriving allows for an expansive approach to moral standing.

Not all living things are persons (for instance, plants), but those that *are* persons (most animals, and the Earth) require their own unconservativism and self-governance as a condition of their thriving. On the Yoga account, legitimate activism is devotion to an abstract ideal of Sovereignty, and this makes room for a diversity of sovereign individuals with a diversity of perspectives. Yogic activism is indistinguishable from the ordinary life activity of the yogi, except that it meets with conventional moral resistance. It is a public exercise of explication. This activism continues even after conventional moral resistance ends. By contrast, illegitimate protest is conservative and revolves round the egoism of individuals, which is their identification with their perspective (which they may share with others by way of national or ethnic identity or by way of voluntary affiliation). Conservative activism in this case is purely strategic, centered around some idea of the good, and ceases when ends are met, or the cost associated with the activity downgrades the expected utility of the activity. It is a public exercise of interpretation.

Summary

All ethical theories are practical insofar as they illuminate THE RIGHT or THE GOOD as the foundation of choosing. The concrete applicability of Yoga begins with its metaethics, which makes clear that there are two incompatible methods we could adopt to understand the options. Interpretation reifies our experiences and prejudices as the criterion of explanation. Explication, by contrast, allows us to understand options that we may not agree with, and this essential practice of Yoga's metaethics has concrete epistemic outcomes for choosers and deliberators: it helps make the diversity of options clear.

Next, the normative ethics of Yoga, which consists in devotion to Sovereignty and the practice of the essential traits of Sovereignty—unconservatism and self-governance—is the DIY (Do It Yourself) normative ethical practice. Here, each practitioner—via their own devotion to Sovereignty—has to come to terms with their own past as something that they will not allow to constrain them (unconservatism). But they must also be transparent to themselves about the values they choose to live by (self-governance). While this in the abstract is the same for all people, how it plays out in people's lives will depend in part on the past that they must come to terms with and the values they choose to abide by.

However, this normative practice entails a certain *normative* account of persons as the types of things that thrive given their own unconservatism and self-governance. This normative practice hence entails a solidarity with other people who similarly have an interest in the same practice. This requires political activism, as flushed out by the non-ideal ethical theory. As the normative practice of Yoga teaches us that the interests of persons are identical, it entails a requirement for a shared, safe, public space for individuals. It was historically the ground of social justice movements the world over and continues to provide the *deep structure* rationale for activity that disrupts systemic harm. Yoga brings to light the ways in which people are often willing to put up with systemic injustice because it seems to maximize utility, measured in some way. But what this measure ignores are persons who are united in sharing an interest in unconservatism and self-governance. The activism of Yoga is an outcome of the normative practice, which is decolonial: it emphasizes ensuring that people are not deprived of what is theirs, that their personal boundaries are respected, and that at the end, there is no appropriation or hoarding.

The philosophy of Yoga is unique in specifying the procedure that we require to understand alternative options. Any such option has to be understood not in terms of our propositional attitudes, but rather its theoretical implications, and Yoga the metaethical practice specifies what this looks like. It involves organizing and controlling mental content to permit our own autonomy as evaluators. But it also entails a normative practice of devotion to Sovereignty, which has been historically influential beyond its cultural origin, but has been occluded by colonialism, which operates according to the interpretive considerations Yoga criticizes. Learning from this ancient practice can help us correct the course of the academic study of philosophy and bring clarity to the challenges of normative practice.

Notes

1. All translations from the Sanskrit are mine. For my translation of the *Yoga Sūtra*, see Patañjali 2008; see Ranganathan 2017b for a review of the text and its ethical theory; see Ranganathan 2021a for a similar deep dive into the Bhagavad Gītā and its moral dialectic.

2. For a review of the secondary literature, see Ranganathan 2017c, 52–77.

3. For a review of the literature, and for the alternative, see Ranganathan 2022a.

4. For a historical review of South Asian diagnosis of propositional attitudes like belief as the source of error, see Ranganathan 2021b.

5. For an account of how this theory influences dominant approaches to thought, translation, and understanding in the Western tradition, see Ranganathan 2018a.

Further Reading

Primary Sources

Patañjali. 2008. *Patañjali's Yoga Sūtra: Translation, Commentary and Introduction by Shyam Ranganathan*. Black Classics. Delhi: Penguin Black Classics.

Secondary Sources

Alexander, Larry, and Michael Moore. 2012. "Deontological Ethics." In *The Stanford Encyclopedia of Philosophy*, edited by Edward N. Zalta. http://plato.stanford.edu/archives/win2012/entries/ethics-deontological/.

Hursthouse, Rosalind. 1996. "Normative Virtue Ethics." In *How Should One Live?*, edited by Roger Crisp, 19–33. Oxford: Oxford University Press.

———. 2013. *Virtue Ethics*. Edited by Edward N. Zalta. The Stanford Encyclopedia of Philosophy. http://plato.stanford.edu/archives/fall2013/entries/ethics-virtue/.

King, Martin Luther, Jr. September 1, 1958. "My Pilgrimage to Nonviolence." In *The Martin Luther King, Jr. Research and Education Institute*. https://kinginstitute.stanford.edu/king-papers/documents/my-pilgrimage-nonviolence.

Maas, Philipp A. 2013. "A Concise Historiography of Classical Yoga Philosophy." In *Historiography and Periodization of Indian Philosophy*, edited by Eli Franco, 53–90. Vienna De Nobili Series.

Puri, Bindu. 2015. *Tagore-Gandhi Debate on Matters of Truth and Untruth*. New Delhi: Springer.

Ranganathan, Shyam. 2016. "Review of David Gordon White's *The Yoga Sutra of Patanjali: A Biography*." *Philosophy East and West* 66, no. 3: 1043–48.

———. 2017a. *The Bloomsbury Research Handbook of Indian Ethics*. Edited by Chakravarthi Ram-Prasad and Sor-hoon Tan. Research Handbooks in Asian Philosophy. London: Bloomsbury Academic.

———. 2017b. "Patañjali's Yoga: Universal Ethics as the Formal Cause of Autonomy." In *The Bloomsbury Research Handbook of Indian Ethics*, edited by Shyam Ranganathan, 177–202. London: Bloomsbury Academic.

———. 2017c. "Western Imperialism, Indology and Ethics." In *The Blooms-bury Research Handbook of Indian Ethics*, edited by Shyam Ranganathan, 1–122. London: Bloomsbury Academic.

———. 2018a. "Context and Pragmatics." In *The Routledge Handbook of Translation and Philosophy*, edited by Philip Wilson and J. Piers Rawling, 195–208. New York: Routledge.

———. 2018b. *Hinduism: A Contemporary Philosophical Investigation*. Investigating Philosophy of Religion. New York: Routledge.

———. 2019. "Just War and the Indian Tradition: Arguments from the Battlefield." In *Comparative Just War Theory: An Introduction to International Perspectives*, edited by Luis Cordeiro-Rodrigues and Danny Singh, 173–90. Lanham, MD: Rowman & Littlefield.

———. 2021a. Bhagavad Gītā. In *Internet Encyclopedia of Philosophy*, edited by James Feiser and Brad Dowden. https://iep.utm.edu/bha-gita/.

———. 2021b. "Idealism and Indian Philosophy." In *The Routledge Handbook of Idealism and Immaterialism*, edited by Joshua Farris and Benedikt Paul Göcke. Oxfordshire: Routledge.

———. 2022a. "Modes of Interpretation." In *Encyclopedia of Religious Ethics*, edited by William Schweiker, David A. Clairmont, and Elizabeth Bucar. Hoboken, NJ: Wiley Blackwell.

———. 2022b. "Hinduism, Belief and the Colonial Invention of Religion: A Before and After Comparison." *Religions* 13, no. 10: 891.

Sreekumar, Sandeep. 2012. "An Analysis of Consequentialism and Deontology in the Normative Ethics of the Bhagavadgītā." *Journal of Indian Philosophy* 40, no. 3: 277–315.

Theodor, Ithamar. 2010. *Exploring the Bhagavad Gita: Philosophy, Structure, and Meaning*. Farnham: Ashgate.

Contributors

Martin Odei Ajei is an associate professor of philosophy in the Department of Philosophy and Classics at the University of Ghana. He obtained a DLitt et Phil in philosophy from the University of South Africa, an MPhil from University of Ghana, and a BA (Hons) from the University of Stockholm, Sweden. His research interests include African philosophy, applied ethics, political philosophy, and philosophies of liberation. He is the author of more than thirty peer-reviewed journal articles and book chapters and of two books: *The Paranormal: An Inquiry into Akan Metaphysics and Epistemology* and *Africa's Development: The Imperatives on Indigenous Knowledge and Values*. He is also the editor of an anthology of philosophical commentary on Kwame Nkrumah's philosophy: *Disentangling Consciencism: Essays on Kwame Nkrumah's Philosophy*. He has held several fellowships, the latest of which was fellow of the German Reference Center for Ethics in the Life Sciences, University of Bonn. He is currently working on his third book: *Empathetic Humanism: A Legon Tradition of African Philosophy*. Martin is a fellow of the Ghana Academy of Arts and Sciences.

Dirk Baltzly is a professor emeritus of philosophy at the University of Tasmania and a specialist in the history of ancient Greek philosophy. He has contributed to the translation of texts from late antiquity, including Proclus's *Commentary on Plato's Timaeus* (vols. 3–6, Cambridge University Press) and Hermias's *Commentary on Plato's Phaedrus* (2 vols., Bloomsbury). He is among the editors of the *Brill Companion to the Reception of Plato in Antiquity*. Dirk is a fellow of the Australian Academy of Humanities. He has previously taught philosophy to students at Ohio State University, the

University of Texas at Austin, King's College London, and Monash University, Melbourne.

Wing-Cheuk Chan is an emeritus professor at Brock University, Canada. His major fields of research include phenomenology, Chinese philosophy, and Buddhism. He was DAAD Scholar, Alexander von Humboldt Foundation Fellow, and Indo-Canadian Shastri Foundation Fellow. Important publications include *Heidegger and Chinese Philosophy* (1986), *A Study of Yoshifumi Ueda's Yogācāra Thought: A Phenomenological Approach* (in Chinese) (2022), and *Connection and Extension: Confucianism in Dialogues* (forthcoming). Currently he is preparing a volume titled *Phenomenology of Thinking*.

Wai Wai Chiu is an associate professor at Lingnan University. His main research interests are pre-Qin and Wei-Jin Daoist philosophy, especially epistemology and ethics. He has published articles on Zhuangzi's conception of knowledge, language, and efficacious action; as well as Mozi's conception of benefit. He is a co-editor of *Skill and Mastery: Philosophical Stories from the Zhuangzi* (with Karyn Lai).

Gordon F. Davis is an associate professor of philosophy at Carleton University in Ottawa, Canada. His work in comparative philosophy includes "Moral Realism and Anti-Realism outside the West: A Meta-Ethical Turn in Buddhist Ethics" (*Comparative Philosophy* 4: 2, 2013), "The *Atipada* Problem in Buddhist Meta-Ethics" (*Journal of Buddhist Ethics* 2018), and the volume *Ethics without Self, Dharma without Atman: Western and Buddhist Philosophical Traditions in Dialogue* as editor and contributor (Springer 2018).

Nicholas Drake is a PhD student in philosophy at the Australian National University, and was a Global Priorities Fellow at the Forethought Foundation, Oxford. He has published articles on metaethics, applied ethics, and the history of ethics. His current research is on what theory of well-being governments should use when measuring well-being and developing well-being policy.

Rika Dunlap is an assistant professor of philosophy at Mount St. Mary's University. Her primary areas of research are East Asian philosophy, ethics, and aesthetics. She is the author of "Practice as a Work of Art: A Study of "*Gabyō*" in Dōgen's Buddhist Philosophy" in *Philosophy East and West* (forthcoming); "The Ethical Implications of Enlightenment in Dōgen's Philosophy of Compassion" in *Tetsugaku Companion to Feeling in Japanese Philosophy* (Springer, forthcoming); and "A Buddhist Conception of Hope" in *Moral Psychology of Hope* (Rowman and Littlefield International, 2019).

Allauren Samantha Forbes is an assistant professor in the Department of Philosophy at McMaster University. She is also a faculty member in McMaster's Gender and Social Justice program. Her research focuses on the history of feminist philosophy, especially in Europe in the sixteenth to eighteenth centuries.

Pradeep P. Gokhale retired as a professor of philosophy from Savitribai Phule Pune University, Pune (India), after thirty-one years of postgraduate teaching experience and subsequently worked as a research professor in the Central Institute of Higher Tibetan Studies, Sarnath (Varanasi). Presently he is an "honorary adjunct professor" in the Department of Pali and Buddhist Studies in Savitribai Phule Pune University. His research areas include Classical Indian Philosophy, moral and social philosophy, and modern Buddhism. He is the author of *Inference and Fallacies Discussed in Ancient Indian Logic* (Satguru Publications, 1992), *Lokāyata/Cārvāka: A Philosophical Inquiry* (Oxford University Press, 2015), and *Yogasūtra of Patañjali: A New Introduction to the Buddhist Roots of the Yoga System* (Routledge, 2020). Recently he has edited *Classical Buddhism, Neo-Buddhism and the Question of Caste* (Routledge, 2021).

Michael Hemmingsen is an associate professor in the International College of Tunghai University, Taiwan. His research focuses on social and political philosophy—often with a comparative dimension—and the philosophy of sport and games.

Yong Huang, PhD (Fudan) and ThD (Harvard), is currently a professor and the chairperson of the Philosophy Department at The Chinese University of Hong Kong. He served as the president of the Association of Chinese Philosophers in America, co-chair of University Seminar on Neo-Confucian Studies at Columbia University, and co-chair of the Confucian Tradition Group of American Academy of Religion. He is the founding editor of *Dao: A Journal of Comparative Philosophy* and *Dao Companions to Chinese Philosophy* (a book series), both by Springer. His research interests include ethics, political philosophy, and Chinese and comparative philosophy. Author of *Religious Goodness and Political Rightness: Beyond the Liberal and Communitarian Debate*, *Confucius: A Guide for the Perplexed*, and *Why Be Moral: Learning from the Neo-Confucian Cheng Brothers*, as well as four volumes of essays in Chinese, Huang also has published more than 100 journal articles and book chapters each in English and Chinese.

Damien Keown is an emeritus professor of Buddhist Ethics at Goldsmiths College, University of London. His main research interests are theoretical and applied aspects of Buddhist ethics, with particular reference to contemporary issues. He is the author of many books and articles including *The Nature of Buddhist Ethics* (Palgrave, 2001), *Buddhism and Bioethics* (Palgrave, 2001), *Buddhism: A Very Short Introduction* (Oxford University Press, 2000), *Buddhist Ethics: A Very Short Introduction* (Oxford University Press, 2006), and the *Oxford Dictionary of Buddhism* (Oxford University Press, 2003). In 1994 he founded *The Journal of Buddhist Ethics* with Charles S. Prebish.

Yat-hung Leung, PhD (CUHK), is a researcher at Si-Mian Institute for Advanced Studies in Humanities, East China Normal University. He works mainly on comparative philosophy, focusing on Confucianism and ethics. His articles can be found in *Philosophy East and West*, *Sophia*, and *Journal of Value Inquiry*. He has also contributed to the *Dao Companion to Zhu Xi's Philosophy* and other volumes on Chinese philosophy.

Sandhya Pruthi received an MBA in human resources and BA and MA degrees in Sanskrit at the Department of Sanskrit, University of Delhi, where she received a PhD in 2018 with a thesis on the Advaita Vedānta text, the Brahmasūtras. Since 2017, she has served as an assistant professor on a guest basis at various colleges at the University of Delhi and Indira Gandhi National Open University. At present she is a guest faculty member at NCWEB University of Delhi. Her research interests include metaphysics and theory of knowledge in various Indian philosophical systems, and cultural studies.

Shyam Ranganathan, editor of the *Bloomsbury Research Handbook of Indian Ethics* (2017) and translator of *Patañjali's Yoga Sūtra* (Penguin 2008), founder of yogaphilosophy.com, is a member of the Department of Philosophy and York Center for Asian Research, York University, Toronto. His research covers ethics and political philosophy, philosophy of language, philosophy of thought, Asian philosophy (especially South Asian philosophy), and the decolonization of philosophical research.

Philip Stratton-Lake (1959–2022) was a professor of philosophy at the University of Reading. He is the author of *Kant, Duty, and Moral Worth* (Routledge, 2000) and editor of *Ethical Intuitionism: Re-evaluations* (Oxford University Press, 2002) and *On What We Owe to Each Other* (Blackwell, 2004). He was also editor of the new edition of Ross's *The Right and the Good* (Oxford University Press, 2002). Furthermore, he has written numerous articles on Kant, intuitionism, metaethics, and moral epistemology.

Jussi Suikkanen is a reader in philosophy at the University of Birmingham. His research focuses on metaethics on core questions concerning moral language, thought, and properties; and in normative ethics on traditional ethical theories such as contractualism and consequentialism. He has published widely in these areas and is also the author of two textbooks, *Contractualism* (Cambridge University Press) and *This Is Ethics—An Introduction* (Wiley-Blackwell).

Lucas Thorpe is an associate professor of philosophy and deputy chair of the cognitive science program at Boğaziçi University in Istanbul, Turkey; and associate professor at Thapar Institute of Engineering and Technology in Patiala, India. Prior to this he taught at St. Andrews University and Bilkent University. His main areas of research are Kant, Thomas Reid, ethics, political philosophy, and the philosophy of cognitive science. He is author of the *Kant Dictionary* (Bloomsbury, 2014) and numerous articles.

Index